T0202715

Communications
in Computer and Information Science   **2018**

Rationale

The CCIS series is devoted to the publication of proceedings of computer science conferences. Its aim is to efficiently disseminate original research results in informatics in printed and electronic form. While the focus is on publication of peer-reviewed full papers presenting mature work, inclusion of reviewed short papers reporting on work in progress is welcome, too. Besides globally relevant meetings with internationally representative program committees guaranteeing a strict peer-reviewing and paper selection process, conferences run by societies or of high regional or national relevance are also considered for publication.

Topics

The topical scope of CCIS spans the entire spectrum of informatics ranging from foundational topics in the theory of computing to information and communications science and technology and a broad variety of interdisciplinary application fields.

Information for Volume Editors and Authors

Publication in CCIS is free of charge. No royalties are paid, however, we offer registered conference participants temporary free access to the online version of the conference proceedings on SpringerLink (http://link.springer.com) by means of an http referrer from the conference website and/or a number of complimentary printed copies, as specified in the official acceptance email of the event.

CCIS proceedings can be published in time for distribution at conferences or as post-proceedings, and delivered in the form of printed books and/or electronically as USBs and/or e-content licenses for accessing proceedings at SpringerLink. Furthermore, CCIS proceedings are included in the CCIS electronic book series hosted in the SpringerLink digital library at http://link.springer.com/bookseries/7899. Conferences publishing in CCIS are allowed to use Online Conference Service (OCS) for managing the whole proceedings lifecycle (from submission and reviewing to preparing for publication) free of charge.

Publication process

The language of publication is exclusively English. Authors publishing in CCIS have to sign the Springer CCIS copyright transfer form, however, they are free to use their material published in CCIS for substantially changed, more elaborate subsequent publications elsewhere. For the preparation of the camera-ready papers/files, authors have to strictly adhere to the Springer CCIS Authors' Instructions and are strongly encouraged to use the CCIS LaTeX style files or templates.

Abstracting/Indexing

CCIS is abstracted/indexed in DBLP, Google Scholar, EI-Compendex, Mathematical Reviews, SCImago, Scopus. CCIS volumes are also submitted for the inclusion in ISI Proceedings.

How to start

To start the evaluation of your proposal for inclusion in the CCIS series, please send an e-mail to ccis@springer.com.

Ying Tan · Yuhui Shi
Editors

Data Mining and Big Data

8th International Conference, DMBD 2023
Sanya, China, December 9–12, 2023
Proceedings, Part II

 Springer

Editors
Ying Tan 🆔
Peking University
Beijing, China

Yuhui Shi
Southern University of Science and Techn
Shenzhen, China

ISSN 1865-0929   ISSN 1865-0937 (electronic)
Communications in Computer and Information Science
ISBN 978-981-97-0843-7   ISBN 978-981-97-0844-4 (eBook)
https://doi.org/10.1007/978-981-97-0844-4

This Springer imprint is published by the registered company Springer Nature Singapore Pte Ltd.
The registered company address is: 152 Beach Road, #21-01/04 Gateway East, Singapore 189721, Singapore

Paper in this product is recyclable.

Preface

The Eighth International Conference on Data Mining and Big Data (DMBD 2023) was held on December 9–12, 2023 in Sanya, China. DMBD 2023 served as an international forum for researchers to exchange the latest advances in theories, models, and applications of data mining and big data as well as artificial intelligence techniques. DMBD 2023 was the eighth event after the successful first event (DMBD 2016) at Bali Island of Indonesia, second event (DMBD 2017) at Fukuoka City of Japan, third event (DMBD 2018) at Shanghai of China, fourth event (DMBD 2019) at Chiang Mai of Thailand, fifth event (DMBD 2020) at Belgrade of Serbia, sixth event (DMBD 2021) at Guangzhou of China and seventh event (DMBD 2022) at Beijing of China virtually.

These two volumes (CCIS vol. 2017 and vol. 2018) contain papers presented at DMBD 2023. The contents of those papers cover some major topics of data mining and big data. The conference received 79 submissions, at least three reviewers per submission in a double-blind review. The committee accepted 38 regular papers to be included in the conference program with an acceptance rate of 48.1%. The proceedings contain revised versions of the accepted papers. While revisions are expected to take the referee's comments into account, this was not enforced and the authors bear full responsibility for the content of their papers.

DMBD 2023 was organized by the International Association of Swarm and Evolutionary Intelligence (IASEI), and co-organized by Peking University and Southern University of Science and Technology, Computational Intelligence Laboratory of Peking University (CIL@PKU), Advanced Institute of Big Data, Beijing, Key Lab of Information System Requirement, Science and Technology on Information Systems Engineering Laboratory, and technically co-sponsored by City Brain Technical Committee, Chinese Institute of Command and Control (CICC), International Neural Network Society, and also supported by Nanjing Kangbo Intelligent Health Academy, Springer-Nature, and Beijing Xinghui High-Tech Co. The conference would not have been such a success without the support of these organizations, and we sincerely thank them for their continued assistance and support.

We would also like to thank the authors who submitted their papers to DMBD 2023, and the conference attendees for their interest and support. We thank the Organizing Committee for their time and effort dedicated to arranging the conference. This allowed us to focus on the paper selection and deal with the scientific program. We thank the Program Committee members and the external reviewers for their hard work in reviewing the submissions; the conference would not have been possible without their expert reviews. Furthermore, this work is partially supported by the National Natural Science Foundation of China (Grant No. 62250037, 62276008, and 62076010), and also partially supported by the National Key R&D Program of China (Grant No. 2022YFF0800601).

Finally, we thank the EasyChair system and its operators for making the entire process of managing the conference convenient.

December 2023   Ying Tan
                                                                  Yuhui Shi

Organization

General Chair

Ying Tan   Peking University, China

Programme Committee Chairs

Yuhui Shi	Southern University of Science and Technology, China
Wenbin Zhang	Michigan Technological University, USA

Advisory Committee Chairs

Xingui He	Peking University, China
Gary G. Yen	Oklahoma State University, USA

Technical Committee Co-chairs

Benjamin W. Wah	Chinese University of Hong Kong, China
Guoying Wang	Chongqing University of Posts and Telecommunications, China
Enhong Chen	University of Science and Technology of China, China
Fernando Buarque	Universidade of Pernambuco, Brazil
Haibo He	University of Rhode Island Kingston, USA
Jihong Zhu	Tsinghua University, China
Jin Li	Guangzhou University, China
Kay Chen Tan	Hong Kong Polytechnic University, China
Nikola Kasabov	Auckland University of Technology, New Zealand
Qirong Tang	Tongji University, China
Yew-Soon Ong	Nanyang Technological University, Singapore
Yi Zhang	Sichuan University, China

Invited Speakers Session Co-chairs

Andres Iglesias   University of Cantabria, Spain
Shaoqiu Zheng   28th Research Institute of China Electronics
                                              Technology Group Corporation, China

Special Session Co-chairs

Ben Niu   Shenzhen University, China
Kun Liu   Advanced Institute of Big Data, China

Publications Co-chairs

Radu-Emil Precup   Politehnica University of Timisoara, Romania
Weiwei Hu   Tencent Corporation, China

Publicity Co-chairs

Eugene Semenkin   Siberian Aerospace University, Russia
Junqi Zhang   Tongji University, China

Finance and Registration Chairs

Andreas Janecek   University of Vienna, Austria
Suicheng Gu   Google Corporation, USA

Conference Secretariat

Wenbo Yan   Peking University, China

Program Committee

Muhammad Abulaish   South Asian University, India
Abdelmalek Amine   Tahar Moulay University of Saida, Algeria
Sabri Arik   Istanbul University, Turkey
Nebojsa Bacanin   Singidunum University, Serbia
Carmelo J. A. Bastos Filho   University of Pernambuco, Brazil

Chenyang Bu	Hefei University of Technology, China
Bin Cao	Tsinghua University, China
Junfeng Chen	Hohai University, China
Walter Chen	National Taipei University of Technology, Taiwan, China
Shi Cheng	Shaanxi Normal University, China
Prithviraj Dasgupta	U. S. Naval Research Laboratory, USA
Khaldoon Dhou	Texas A&M University Central Texas, USA
Hongyuan Gao	Harbin Engineering University, China
Weifeng Gao	Xidian University, China
Ke Gu	Changsha University of Science and Technology, China
Roshni Iyer	UCLA, USA
Ziyu Jia	Beijing Jiaotong University, China
Mingyan Jiang	Shandong University, China
Colin Johnson	University of Nottingham, UK
Liangjun Ke	Xi'an Jiaotong University, China
Lov Kumar	National Institute of Technology, Kurukshetra, India
Germano Lambert-Torres	PS Solutions, Brazil
Tai Le Quy	Leibniz University Hannover, Germany
Ju Liu	Shandong University, China
Jun Liu	Carnegie Mellon University, USA
Kun Liu	Advanced Institute of Big Data, China
Qunfeng Liu	Dongguan University of Technology, China
Yi Liu	Advanced Institute of Big Data, China
Hui Lu	Beihang University, China
Wenjian Luo	Harbin Institute of Technology (Shenzhen), China
Haoyang Ma	National University of Defense Technology, China
Jinwen Ma	Peking University, China
Chengying Mao	Jiangxi University of Finance and Economics, China
Mengjun Ming	National University of Defense Technology, China
Seyedfakhredin Musavishavazi	BAuA, Federal Institute for Occupational Safety and Health, Germany
Sreeja N. K.	PSG College of Technology, USA
Qingjian Ni	Southeast University, China
Neelamadhab Padhy	GIET University, India
Mario Pavone	University of Catania, Spain
Yan Pei	University of Aizu, Japan
Xin Peng	Hainan University, China

Mukesh Prasad	University of Technology, Sydney, Australia
Radu-Emil Precup	Politehnica University of Timisoara, Romania
Aniket Shahade	SSGMCE, India
Min Shi	Hunan University of Science and Technology, China
Zhongzhi Shi	Institute of Computing Technology, Chinese Academy of Sciences, China
Jiten Sidhpura	Sardar Patel Institute of Technology, India
Adam Slowik	Koszalin University of Technology, Porland
Ying Tan	Peking University, China
Eva Tuba	University of Belgrade, Serbia
Mladen Veinović	Singidunum University, Serbia
Guoyin Wang	Chongqing University of Posts and Telecommunications, China
Hong Wang	Shenzhen University, China
Hui Wang	Nanchang Institute of Technology, China
Yuping Wang	Xidian University, China
Ka-Chun Wong	City University of Hong Kong, China
Shuyin Xia	Chongqing University of Posts and Telecommunications, China
Jianhua Xu	Nanjing Normal University, China
Rui Xu	Hohai University, China
Yu Xue	Nanjing University of Information Science and Technology, China
Yingjie Yang	De Montfort University, UK
Peng-Yeng Yin	National Chi Nan University, China
Ling Yu	Jinan University, China
Hui Zhang	Southwest University of Science and Technology, China
Jie Zhang	Newcastle University, UK
Jiwei Zhang	Beijing University of Posts and Telecommunications, China
Xiaosong Zhang	Tangshan University, China
Yong Zhang	China University of Mining and Technology, China
Yuchen Zhang	Northwest A&F University, USA
Xinchao Zhao	Beijing University of Posts and Telecommunications, China
Shaoqiu Zheng	28th Research Institute of China Electronics Technology Group Corporation, China
Jiang Zhou	Texas Tech University, USA

Additional Reviewers

Cai, Long
Dhou, Khaldoon
Hu, Zhongyuan
Jin, Feihu
Lei, Jiaqi
Lian, Xiaoyu

Weinan, Tong
Wenbo, Yan
Zhang, Yixia
Zhang, Yixuan
Zhang, Zhenman

Contents – Part II

Contents – Part I

Information Security Approaches

A Local Interpretability Model-Based Approach for Black-Box Adversarial Attack

Yuanjie Duan[1,2], Xingquan Zuo[1,2(✉)], Hai Huang[1,2], Binglin Wu[1,2], and Xinchao Zhao[3]

[1] School of Computer Science, Beijing University of Posts and Telecommunications, Beijing, China
zuoxq@bupt.edu.cn
[2] Key Laboratory of Trustworthy Distributed Computing and Service, Ministry of Education, Beijing, China
[3] School of Science, Beijing University of Posts and Telecommunications, Beijing, China

Abstract. Deep learning models are vulnerable to adversarial examples due to their fragility. Current black-box attack methods typically add perturbations to the whole example, and added perturbations may be large and easily detected by human eyes. This study proposes a Local Interpretable Model-agnostic Explanations (LIME)-based approach for black-box adversarial Attack (LIME-Attack). The approach can reduce the size of perturbations via adding perturbations in discriminative regions of an example. First, LIME is used to interpret a black-box model to obtain discriminative regions of an example. Then, the gradient information of the example is estimated by a derivative-free optimization method (Nature Evolution Strategy). Utilizing the gradient information, two white-box attack methods are adapted to generate perturbations, which are added in discriminative regions of the example to form an adversarial example. LIME-Attack is applied to several typical neural network models. Experiments show that it can achieve a high attack success rate with perturbation size 10%–30% lower than that of comparative methods.

Keywords: Black-box Attack · Adversarial Attack · Adversarial Example · Local Interpretability Model

1 Introduction

Deep Learning Models (DLMs) has been widely applied in fields of image recognition, speech recognition, and computer vision [1]. DLMs are easily attacked by adversarial examples due to their fragility, which leads DLMs to make wrong decisions [2].

Adversarial attacks can be divided into white-box attacks and black-box ones [3, 4]. For white-box attacks, all information of a target model is known, while for black-box attacks, the structure and parameters of a target model are unknown. As it is hard to obtain a target model' information, studying black-box attack methods is more significance and practical.

© The Author(s), under exclusive license to Springer Nature Singapore Pte Ltd. 2024
Y. Tan and Y. Shi (Eds.): DMBD 2023, CCIS 2018, pp. 3–15, 2024.
https://doi.org/10.1007/978-981-97-0844-4_1

There exist many black-box attack methods, such as ZOO [5], AutoZOOM [6] and Curls&Whey [7]. Most of them add perturbations to the whole image to generate an adversarial example. Some studies [8, 9] have shown that DLMs pay more attention to regions with rich semantic information in an image, and those regions are called *discriminative regions*. When removing discriminative regions from an image, classification accuracy of the target model would drop sharply. As non-discriminative regions are not important for the classification, adding perturbations in those regions does not play an important role in generating an adversarial example.

Some literature studied generating adversarial examples via adding perturbations in discriminative regions. For example, Class Activation Mapping (CAM) [11], Grad-CAM [10] and saliency map methods [12] were used to find discriminative regions of an example and then perturbations are added in those regions to attack a target model. Those methods need the target model's structure information to identify discriminative regions of an example, such that for black-box attacks, they must first build a reference model of a target model to find discriminative regions, and then add perturbations in those regions to create an adversarial example [10]. The difference between the reference model and the target model may reduce the attack success rate.

In this paper, we propose a Local Interpretable Model-agnostic Explanations (LIME)-based approach for black-box adversarial Attack (LIME-Attack). First, LIME [13] is used to obtain discriminative regions of an example. Then, Natural Evolution Strategy (NES) [14] is introduced to estimate the gradient of the example. Using the gradient information, two white-box attack approaches are adapted to add perturbations in discriminative regions of an example to generate an adversarial example.

This paper tends to make the following contributions:

1) A black-box attack approach based on a local interpretability model is proposed to generate adversarial examples. In this approach, LIME is used to extract discriminative regions of an image example, and then perturbations are added to those regions to attack the target model.
2) Current black-box attack approaches based on local perturbations need a reference model of the black-box model, while LIME-Attack does not need such reference model and can obtain discriminative regions of an example via interpreting the black-box model.
3) LIME-Attack is applied to four neural network models and compared with other attack approaches. Experiments show that compared to the approaches adding perturbations to the whole example, LIME-Attack can generate adversarial examples with much smaller perturbations while maintaining a high attack success rate.

2   Related Work

2.1   Adversarial Attack Approaches

For white-box attacks, all information of a target model is known, including model parameters, network structure and data distribution. Therefore, the backpropagation algorithm can be used to obtain the gradient direction of an example, and then an adversarial example is generated by changing the original example in its gradient direction. Goodfellow et al. [15] proposed Fast Gradient Sign Method (FGSM) to add perturbations to an original image along the gradient ascent direction, to increase the loss function to generate an adversarial example. Madry et al. [16] further developed Projected Gradient Descent (PGD) method to adjust the gradient direction according to the updated example in each iteration, and an adversarial example were generated through multiple iterations.

Different from white-box attacks, black-box attacks do not know the structure and parameters of a target model, and sometimes need to consider the constraints of the number of queries. Black-box attack methods are mainly divided into gradient estimation-based attack, transfer-based attack and local search-based attack [17]. Tu et al. [6] developed a black-box attack method, AutoZOOM, to reduce the number of queries. Shi et al. [7] used a heuristic algorithm to search for extreme points in the direction of gradient ascent and gradient descent simultaneously, and then selected the gradient direction of adding perturbations to generate an adversarial example. Andriushchenko et al. [18] proposed a score-based black-box attack method that can be used in both untargeted and targeted attacks.

2.2 Interpretability-Based Adversarial Attack Approaches

Explainable artificial intelligence (XAI) aims to present decision-making results of an artificial intelligence model to decision-makers in an interpretable way, thereby helping them to understand the model's working mechanism. The model's interpretability can be divided into global and local interpretability. The global interpretability is to make users understand the complex logic and working mechanism of a model [19], while the local interpretability is to help users understand the decision-making process for a specific example [20].

Local interpretability technologies can obtain discriminative regions on which a model making decisions is based, and adding perturbations in those regions can construct an adversarial example with smaller perturbations. Some studies introduced local interpretability technologies into adversarial attacks. For white-box attacks, Duan et al. [11] used a prominent object detection method to obtain discriminative regions of an example and then transformed those regions into a binary mask form. After using backpropagation to calculate the example's gradient, a mask method was used to add perturbations in discriminative regions only. For black-box attacks, Xiang et al. [10] established a reference model for a target model and used the Grad-CAM method to select local regions of an example, and then added perturbations in those regions to form an adversarial example.

Above methods either added local perturbations to generate an adversarial example for white-box attack [11], or established a reference model of the black-box model and then generate local perturbations based on the reference model to produce an adversarial example [10]. The difference between the reference model and the target model may be large, which reduces the attack success rate. LIME [13] is a local interpretability technology to find discriminative regions of an example without accessing the model structure. In this paper, a LIME-based black-box attack approach is proposed, which does not need the reference model.

3   Local Interpretability Model-Based Attack Approach

The adversarial attack problem can be considered as a constrained optimization problem. Assume that an original image is represented by a vector x. Each dimension of x represents one pixel. The x can be classified by a target model f. The perturbation vector has the same dimension as x and is denoted as δ, whose norm is not greater than K. The optimization objective is to find the minimum perturbation δ'.

$$\delta\prime = \underset{\delta}{\mathrm{argmin}}\{f(x+\delta) \neq f(x)\}$$

$$s.t.\ \|\delta\| \leq K \qquad (1)$$

LIME-Attack serves to find minimum perturbations added to the original image x to make the target model f misclassify the image. The framework of LIME-Attack is shown in Fig. 1, and are described as follows.

Step 1: For a target model, LIME is used to find discriminative regions of an original example and those regions are represented as a binary matrix (see Sect. 3.1).
Step 2: Natural Evolution Strategy (NES) [14] is used to obtain the gradient matrix of the original example by estimating the probability changes of labels output by the target model. Then, using the gradient information, FGSM [15] or PGD [16] is used to identify a perturbation matrix via adding perturbations along the gradient direction of the original example (see Sect. 3.2).
Step 3: A local perturbation matrix is obtained by combining the binary matrix in Step 1 and the perturbation matrix in Step 2.
Step 4: Perturbations represented by the local perturbation matrix are added to the original image to create an adversarial example.

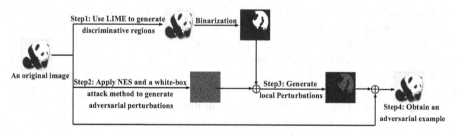

Fig. 1. Framework of LIME-Attack.

3.1   Identify Discriminative Regions by LIME

LIME is a locally interpretable method for black-box models. It uses a linear model to locally approximate a target model. For a target model and an example x to be interpreted, perturbations are produced around x to generate some samples. Those samples are input into the target model, and the model's outputs are regarded as the labels of those samples. Those samples with their labels are used to train a linear model around x to interpret

(a) Original image.   (b) Segmented image.   (c) Discriminative regions.

Fig. 2. Identify discriminative regions of an image example via LIME.

the example x. The features corresponding to non-zero weights in the linear model are important features for the classification of x.

The procedure of identifying discriminative regions of an image example by LIME is described below. Each super-pixel is a small region including a number of adjacent pixels with similar color, brightness and texture. For example, Fig. 2(a) is the original image example x. A linear iterative clustering method in [21] is used to segment the original image x into k super-pixels, as shown in Fig. 2(b), such that x can be expressed by its interpretable representation $x' = [1, 1, 1, \ldots, 1]_k$. Each dimention of x' corresponds to a super-pixel, and its value 1 (0) indicates that the super-pixel is (not) included in x'.

Algorithm 1. Identify discriminative regions of an image via LIME

Input: Image x, interpretable version x' of x, classifier f, and number of samples M.
Output: Binary matrix of the image example x, B_{mask}.
  1: Set of samples $Z \leftarrow \{\}$;
  2: Set of labels $H \leftarrow \{\}$;
  3: **for** $i \in \{1,2,\ldots,M\}$ **do**
  4:    $z_i' \leftarrow sample\_noise(x')$;
  5:    $Z \leftarrow Z \cup \{z_i'\}$;
  6:    $H \leftarrow H \cup \{f(z_i)\}$;
  7: **end for**
  8: $w \leftarrow$ Linear regression (Z, H) with z_i' as a sample and $f(z_i)$ as its label;
  9: w is used to determine a weight vector of discriminative regions, F_{mask};
 10: F_{mask} is mapped to a binary matrix B_{mask}.

Algorithm 1 presents the process of identifying discriminative regions by LIME. In line 4, b randomly selected super-pixels of x' are kept and other super-pixels are removed to obtain a perturbation example z'. By this means, M samples of x' are created. Those M samples with their labels are exploited to fit a linear model with a weight vector w. The weight values in w are sorted in descending order, and only the super-pixels corresponding to the top b weight values are kept to form a binary vector $F_{mask} = [1, 1, 0, 1, 0, \ldots, 1]_k$. F_{mask} is mapped to a binary matrix B_{mask}, whose dimensions are the same as x and each dimension represents a pixel. In B_{mask}, all pixels in the super-pixel with "1" in F_{mask} are set as "1", and other pixels are set as "0".

3.2 Black-Box Attack Approaches Based on Discriminative Regions

As parameters of a black-box model are unknown, we cannot use the loss function to calculate the gradient of an example. In this study, NES [14] is used to estimate the gradient. Based on the gradient, two white-box attack approaches, FGSM and PGD, are adapted to add perturbations in discriminative regions of an image example to obtain an adversarial example, respectively.

LIME-Attack (FGSM). FGSM is a one-step attack method that generates an adversarial example via adding perturbations to an original example along its gradient ascent direction [15].

Taking the intersection of the gradient matrix g obtained by NES and B_{mask}, the gradient of discriminative regions of the original example can be obtained. Then, FGSM is used to generate an adversarial example by

$$x_{adv} = x - \alpha \times sign(g \wedge B_{mask}) \tag{2}$$

where α is perturbation size, and $sign(\cdot)$ is the sign function.

It is hard to set an appropriate α for Eq. (2). A small α would lead to a failure attack, while a large α would make the adversarial example easy to be detected. Therefore, in LIME-Attack (FGSM), α is creased from a small value to a large one until it reaches a threshold α_{max}. If an adversarial example x_{adv} is produced before α reaches α_{max}, the attack is successful. In this case, an adversarial example with least perturbation size is created. If an adversarial example cannot be generated if α reaches α_{max}, the attack fails. Pseudocode of LIME-Attack (FGSM) is given in Algorithm 2.

Algorithm 2. LIME-Attack (FGSM)

Input: An original example x, classifier f.
Output: An adversarial example, x_{adv}.
Parameters: Perturbation size α, threshold α_{max}, image dimensionality N.
  1: Compute the binary matrix B_{mask} using Algorithm 1;
  2: Estimate gradient matrix g of the example x using NES;
  3: $g \leftarrow g \cap B_{mask}$; $\alpha = 0.1$;
  4: **While** $\alpha < \alpha_{max}$ **do**
  5:    $x' = x - \alpha \times sign(g)$;
  6:    if $f(x') \neq f(x)$ **do**
  7:      $x_{adv} \leftarrow x'$;
  8:      **break**
  9:    **end if**
10:    $\alpha \leftarrow \alpha + 0.02$;
11: **end while**
12: Output the adversarial example, x_{adv}.

LIME-Attack (PGD). PGD is an iterative attack method, which can adjust the gradient direction when adding perturbations to an example in each iteration [16]. In each iteration t, the gradient of discriminative regions of the example can be obtained by combining

B_{mask} and the gradient matrix g_t generated by NES. The example is perturbed at the $(t + 1)$th iteration by

$$x_{t+1} = clip_{x_0,\epsilon}\left(x_t - \eta \times sign\left(g_t \wedge B_{mask}\right)\right) \tag{3}$$

where x_t is the example generated at the t-th iteration; η is the perturbation step; g_t is the gradient matrix generated by NES at the t-th iteration; and $clip(\cdot)$ constrains the range of each pixel of x_{t+1} to be within the ϵ neighborhood of the l_∞ norm of x_0.

Algorithm 3 is the pseudocode of LIME-Attack (PGD). Different from LIME-Attack (FGSM), LIME-Attack (PGD) recalculates the gradient for the updated example in each iteration, such that it tends to generate an adversarial example with a higher attack success rate.

Algorithm 3. LIME-Attack (PGD)
___
Input: An original example x_0, classifier f.
Output: An adversarial example, x_{adv}.
Parameters: Perturbation step η, maximum number of iterations m, hyper-parameter ϵ.
1: Compute binary matrix B_{mask} using Algorithm 1;
2: **for** $t \in \{0,1,...,m\}$ **do**
3:    Estimate g_t of the example x_t using NES;
4:    $x_{t+1} \leftarrow clip_{x_0,\epsilon}(x_t - \eta \times sign(g_t \wedge B_{mask}))$;
5:    **if** $f(x_{t+1}) \neq f(x_0)$ **do**
6:        $x_{adv} \leftarrow x_{t+1}$;
7:        **break**
8:    **end if**
9:    $x_t \leftarrow x_{t+1}$;
10: **end for**
11: Output the adversarial example, x_{adv}
___

4   Experimental Results

4.1   Target Models and Datasets

Inception_V3 [22], ResNet50 [23], VGG16 [24] and Xception [25] are selected as target models to be attacked. Since above models are all pre-trained models, training those models is not needed. Datasets used in experiments are as follows:

1) Caltech 101: A dataset with 101 categories of images. To make the samples cover each category, we randomly select 5–10 images from each category, and such 487 images are selected.
2) Caltech 256: A dataset with 256 categories. We randomly select 459 images in 80 categories of the dataset.
3) ILSVRC2012: A dataset commonly used in image classification and target recognition. We randomly select 545 images from 74 categories.

4.2 Comparison Methods

LIME-Attack is compared with Bandit [26], a black-box attack method based on gradient estimation. The code of Bandit is available at https://github.com/brianw-0/ECE260Fin alProject. LIME-Attack is compared with FGSM and PGD to verify the effect of the local interpretability model (LIME). To make a fair comparison, FGSM and PGD also adopt the iterative method in LIME-Attack. As the target model is regarded as a black-box model, both FGSM and PGD require the gradient information calculated by NES. In other words, the FGSM (PGD) is constructed by removing LIME from LIME-Attack.

To further verify the effect of LIME to identify discriminative regions, LIME in LIME-Attack is replaced by Class Activation Mapping (CAM) [27] to form two attack approaches, CAM-FGSM and CAM-PGD. As CAM needs the models' information to obtain an example's discriminative regions, it must use a reference model of the target model. In this paper, ResNet101 is used as the reference model of all target models.

4.3 Experimental Results

In FGSM, the threshold α_{max} is set to 0.5. In PGD, the number of iterations m, the perturbation step size η, and hyper-parameter ϵ are set to 50, 0.05 and 0.3, respectively. Parameters of CAM-FGSM (CAM-PGD) are the same as those of FGSM (PGD). The number of samples of LIME in LIME-Attack, M, is given by 1000, and the number of super-pixels, b, is set to be 12. Other parameters of LIME-Attack are the same as those of FGSM and PGD.

Four commonly used metrics are used to evaluate attack approaches:

1) Attack Success Rate (SR): the ratio of the successful attack examples to all examples.
2) Average robustness (AR): evaluate the perturbation size of an adversarial example in l_2 norm. A small AR value indicates a small perturbation size.
3) Peak signal-to-noise ratio (PSNR) [28]: measure the difference of two images in terms of pixel-to-pixel error. A large PSNR value means that the difference of two images is small.
4) Structural similarity (SSIM) [28]: use brightness, contrast and structure between two images to measure their similarity. A large SSIM value means that two images are more similar.

All algorithms are run on a PC with Intel i7–6700 CPU, 32G memory and operating system Linux (Ubuntu 18.04.5). LIME-Attack is coded in python and its code is available at https://github.com/BUPTAIOC/Trustworthy_AI. Table 1 presents experimental results of LIME-Attack and other approaches. LIME-Attack and other approaches have similar SR values. Compared with FGSM, LIME-Attack (FGSM) can reduce AR values of the four target models by 32.52% on average, and increase PSNR values by 16.29% and SSIM values by 101.85% on average, respectively. Compared with PGD, LIME-Attack (PGD) reduces AR values by 26.92% on average, and increase PSNR values by 14.77% and SSIM values by 91.69% on average, respectively. It means that LIME-Attack can generate adversarial examples with smaller perturbations than the methods adding perturbations to the whole example and meanwhile maintain a high SR values.

Although SR values of LIME-Attack is similar to those of CAM-FGSM (CAM-PGD), the former adds less perturbations to an example than the latter. Compared with CAM-FGSM (CAM-PGD), LIME-Attack (FGSM) (LIME-Attack (PGD)) improves AR, PSNR and SSIM values by 15.71% (8.36%), 5.18% (6.97%), and 16.66% (28.79%) on average, respectively. The reason of adding greater perturbations by CAM-FGSM (CAM-PGD) may be that there is difference between the reference model and the target model, which makes CAM unable to accurately extract discriminative regions of an example.

Table 1. Comparison of LIME-Attack and other approaches.

Methods	Dataset: Caltech 101, Network: Inception_V3				Dataset: Caltech 101, Network: ResNet50			
	SR (%)	AR	PSNR	SSIM	SR (%)	AR	PSNR	SSIM
FGSM	97.53	0.29	18.81	0.38	97.12	0.25	20.34	0.51
PGD	**99.59**	0.26	20.62	0.40	**99.38**	0.27	19.68	0.54
CAM-FGSM	96.49	0.26	19.19	0.62	97.74	0.19	22.61	0.71
CAM-PGD	98.66	0.22	20.53	0.48	97.92	0.19	21.31	0.77
Bandit	93.31	0.41	15.89	0.39	94.23	0.33	14.61	0.43
LIME-Attack (FGSM)	97.53	**0.17**	21.60	0.80	97.33	0.18	22.75	0.76
LIME-Attack (PGD)	99.39	0.22	**21.91**	**0.85**	99.18	**0.17**	**23.67**	**0.83**
Methods	Dataset: Caltech 256, Network: VGG16				Dataset: ILSVRC2012, Network: Xception			
	SR (%)	AR	PSNR	SSIM	SR (%)	AR	PSNR	SSIM
FGSM	92.37	0.20	20.64	0.41	73.94	0.35	17.57	0.32
PGD	**96.73**	0.19	20.86	0.45	81.47	0.28	18.25	0.36
CAM-FGSM	92.68	0.18	**22.33**	0.75	72.33	0.23	21.25	0.65
CAM-PGD	94.99	0.19	20.47	0.61	80.32	0.17	22.39	0.78
Bandit	95.48	0.23	15.84	0.34	**85.49**	0.34	16.25	0.35
LIME-Attack (FGSM)	92.81	**0.17**	21.98	**0.76**	73.21	0.19	23.19	0.84
LIME-Attack (PGD)	96.30	0.18	20.99	0.74	82.06	**0.14**	**24.08**	**0.85**

LIME-Attack (PGD) has higher SR values than LIME-Attack (FGSM) for all the four models. Both of them add similar perturbation size to an example. SR values of LIME-Attack (PGD) are higher than those of Bandit for three models, and LIME-Attack (FGSM) and LIME-Attack (PGD) achieve much less perturbations than Bandit.

4.4 Sensitivity Analysis of Parameters

To analyze the impact of parameters on algorithm performance, the number of discriminative super-pixels b and perturbation size are analyzed. Caltech 256 and VGG16 are

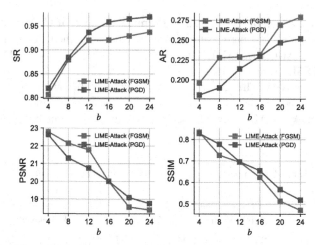

Fig. 3. Effect of the number of super-pixels b on performance of LIME-Attack.

used as the dataset and target model, respectively. The larger the value of b, the larger the number of discriminative regions. For LIME-Attack (FGSM), perturbation size is expressed by α_{max}, and for LIME-Attack (PGD), perturbation size is controlled by the number of iterations, m.

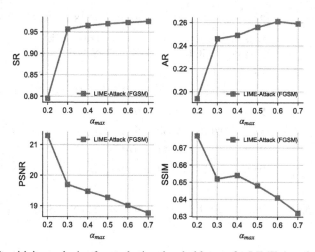

Fig. 4. Sensitivity analysis of perturbation threshold α_{max} for LIME-Attack (FGSM).

The value of b is changed from 4 to 24, and other parameters in Sect. 4.3 remain unchanged. Figure 3 shows the change of four metrics along with the increase of b value. The change of SR value is relatively steep when b value is small, i.e., a small change of the number of super-pixels causes a large change in SR values. The reason may be that the semantic information of an image requires a certain number of pixels. With the number of discriminative regions increasing, it is easier to generate an adversarial

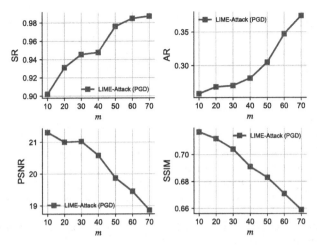

Fig. 5. Sensitivity analysis of iteration number m for LIME-Attack (PGD).

example via adding perturbations in those regions with rich semantic information. When b reaches 16, increasing b value will not improve SR values greatly.

The value of α_{max} is creased from 0.2 to 0.7, and other parameters remain unchanged. The target model (VGG16) is attacked by LIME-Attack (FGSM) with each α_{max} value, and experimental results are shown in Fig. 4. Increase of α_{max} will improve SR values greatly when α_{max} is smaller than 0.3. For α_{max} greater than 0.3, increasing α_{max} value cannot significantly improve SR values.

Keeping other parameters of LIME-Attack (PGD) unchanged, and the number of iterations m changes from 10 to 70. The experiments are shown in Fig. 5. Increase of m value will improve SR value continuously. After m reaches 60, SR value tends to be stable and is more than 98%. Correspondingly, increasing α_{max} and m will lead to the increase of AR and the decrease of PSNR and SSIM for LIME-Attack.

5 Conclusions

In this paper, a local interpretable model-based black-box attack approach (LIME-Attack) is proposed, which combines a local interpretable model-agnostic explanation (LIME) and two popular attack methods FGSM and PGD. First, LIME is used to extract discriminative regions of an example. Then, nature evolution strategy is used to estimate the gradient of the example for the target model. Finally, FGSM and PGD use the gradient information to add perturbations in those discriminative regions in the example to generate an adversarial example.

LIME-Attack is applied to the attack of several neural network models and compared with other attack methods. Experiments show that LIME-Attack achieves much smaller perturbations than comparative methods. As the perturbations added to the original example by LIME-Attack is very small, the produced adversarial example is not easily detected by human eyes.

Future research directions include: 1) study more effective local interpretability models to reduce the number of queries; and 2) explore attack approaches combining local interpretability models and black-box attack methods.

References

1. Dong, S., Wang, P., Abbas, K.: A survey on deep learning and its applications. Comput. Sci. Rev. **40**, 100379 (2021)
2. Szegedy, C., Zaremba, W., Sutskever, I., et al.: Intriguing properties of neural networks. In: 2nd International Conference on Learning Representations (2014)
3. Huang, X., Kroening, D., Ruan, W., et al.: A survey of safety and trustworthiness of deep neural networks: verification, testing, adversarial attack and defence, and interpretability. Comput. Sci. Rev. **37**, 100270 (2021)
4. Qiu, S., Liu, Q., Zhou, S., Wu, C.: Review of artificial intelligence adversarial attack and defense technologies. Appl. Sci. **9**(5), 909 (2019)
5. Chen, P., Zhang, H., Sharma, Y., et al.: ZOO: zeroth order optimization based black-box attacks to deep neural networks without training substitute models. In: Proceedings of the 10th ACM Workshop on Artificial Intelligence and Security, pp. 15–26 (2017)
6. Tu, C., Ting, P., Chen, P., et al.: Autozoom: Autoencoder-based zeroth order optimization method for attacking black-box neural networks. In: Proceedings of the AAAI Conference on Artificial Intelligence, vol. 33, pp. 742–749 (2019)
7. Shi, Y., Wang, S., Han, Y.: Curls & Whey: boosting black-box adversarial attacks. In: Proceedings of the IEEE/CVF Conference on Computer Vision and Pattern Recognition, pp. 6519–6527 (2019)
8. Zeiler, M.D., Fergus, R.: Visualizing and understanding convolutional networks. In: Fleet, D., Pajdla, T., Schiele, B., Tuytelaars, T. (eds.) ECCV 2014. LNCS, vol. 8689, pp. 818–833. Springer, Cham (2014). https://doi.org/10.1007/978-3-319-10590-1_53
9. Selvaraju, R., Cogswell, M., Das, A., et al.: Grad-CAM: visual explanations from deep networks via gradient-based localization. In: Proceedings of the IEEE International Conference on Computer Vision, pp. 618–626 (2017)
10. Xiang, T., Liu, H., Guo, S., Zhang, T., Liao, X.: Local black-box adversarial attacks: a query efficient approach. arXiv preprint arXiv:2101.01032 (2021)
11. Duan, Y., Zhou, X., Zou, J., Qiu, J., Zhang, J., Pan, Z.: Mask-guided noise restriction adversarial attacks for image classification. Comput. Secur. **100**, 102111 (2021)
12. Papernot, N., McDaniel, P., Jha, S., et al.: The limitations of deep learning in adversarial settings. In: IEEE European Symposium on Security and Privacy, pp. 372–387 (2016)
13. Ribeiro, M., Singh, S., Guestrin, C.: "Why should i trust you?" Explaining the predictions of any classifier. In: Proceedings of the 22nd ACM SIGKDD International Conference on Knowledge Discovery and Data Mining, pp. 1135–1144 (2016)
14. Wierstra, D., Schaul, T., Glasmachers, T., et al.: Natural evolution strategies. J. Mach. Learn. Res. **15**(1), 949–980 (2014)
15. Goodfellow, I., Shlens, J., Szegedy, C.: Explaining and harnessing adversarial examples. In: International Conference on Learning Representations (2015)
16. Madry, A., Makelov, A., Schmidt, L., et al.: Towards deep learning models resistant to adversarial attacks. In: International Conference on Learning Representations (2018)
17. Bhambri, S., Muku, S., Tulasi, A., et al.: A survey of black-box adversarial attacks on computer vision models. arXiv preprint arXiv:1912.01667 (2019)

18. Andriushchenko, M., Croce, F., Flammarion, N., Hein, M.: Square attack: a query-efficient black-box adversarial attack via random search. In: Vedaldi, A., Bischof, H., Brox, T., Frahm, J.-M. (eds.) ECCV 2020. LNCS, vol. 12368, pp. 484–501. Springer, Cham (2020). https:// doi.org/10.1007/978-3-030-58592-1_29
19. Guidotti, R., Monreale, A., Ruggieri, S., et al.: A survey of methods for explaining black box models. ACM Comput. Surv. **51**(5), 1–42 (2018)
20. Baehrens, D., Schroeter, T., Harmeling, S., et al.: How to explain individual classification decisions. J. Mach. Learn. Res. **11**, 1803–1831 (2010)
21. Achanta, R., Shaji, A., Smith, K., Lucchi, A., Fua, P., Süsstrunk, S.: SLIC superpixels compared to state-of-the-art superpixel methods. IEEE Trans. Pattern Anal. Mach. Intell. **34**(11), 2274–2282 (2012)
22. Szegedy, C., Vanhoucke, V., Ioffe, S., et al.: Rethinking the inception architecture for computer vision. In: Proceedings of the IEEE Conference on Computer Vision and Pattern Recognition, pp. 2818–2826 (2016)
23. He, K., Zhang, X., Ren, S., et al.: Deep residual learning for image recognition. In: Proceedings of the IEEE Conference on Computer Vision and Pattern Recognition, pp. 770–778 (2016)
24. Simonyan, K., Zisserman, A.: Very deep convolutional networks for large-scale image recognition. In: 3rd International Conference on Learning Representations, pp. 7–9 (2015)
25. Chollet, F.: Xception: Deep learning with depthwise separable convolutions. In: Proceedings of the IEEE Conference on Computer Vision and Pattern Recognition, pp. 1251–1258 (2017)
26. Ilyas, A., Engstrom, L., Madry, A.: Prior convictions: black-box adversarial attacks with bandits and priors. In: International Conference on Learning Representations (2019)
27. Zhou, B., Khosla, A., Lapedriza, A., Oliva, A., and Torralba, A.: Learning deep features for discriminative localization. In: Proceedings of the IEEE Conference on Computer Vision and Pattern Recognition, pp. 2921–2929 (2016)
28. Hore, A., Ziou, D.: Image quality metrics: PSNR vs. SSIM. In: 20th International Conference on Pattern Recognition, pp. 2366–2369 (2010)

FirewaLLM: A Portable Data Protection and Recovery Framework for LLM Services

Bin Huang⬤, Shiyu Yu⬤, Jin Li⬤, Yuyang Chen⬤, Shaozheng Huang⬤,
Sufen Zeng⬤, and Shaowei Wang$^{(\boxtimes)}$⬤

Guangzhou University, Guangzhou 510006, China
wangsw@gzhu.edu.cn

Abstract. In the era characterized by the swift proliferation of large language models such as ChatGPT and GPT-4, there is a mounting escalation of apprehension regarding user privacy. These large language models possess the potential to inadvertently expose sensitive information, encompassing personal identities, health particulars, and financial data. The inadvertent exposure and misuse of such information can lead to significant privacy breaches, thereby exposing model owners to potential legal ramifications. This emphasizes the imperative necessity to amplify efforts in enhancing and evaluating data privacy and security protocols within the domain of large language models. Remarkably, a comprehensive framework for safeguarding user security and privacy is presently absent, leaving a discernible void in established standards for evaluating the privacy and security aspects of Big Predictive Models. To address this gap, we have proposed FirewaLLM, a portable framework that aims to protect user data security within the realm of Large Language Model services. This framework is specifically designed to encompass data protection and recovery measures, mitigating potential vulnerabilities and enhancing overall privacy safeguards. Within this framework, users employ a smaller model to locally desensitize sensitive aspects of text before submitting it to the large language model. By adopting this approach, privacy concerns are addressed proactively, as potentially identifying information is obfuscated prior to interacting with the large language model. Subsequently, the responses obtained from the large language model are matched with the original local text, facilitating the restoration of private information. This process ensures that the desired output is generated while preserving the confidentiality of sensitive data. Furthermore, we have introduced a bespoke benchmark specifically designed to evaluate the security and accuracy of large language models. This benchmark provides a comprehensive assessment of Large Language Models from two key perspectives: security and accuracy. Leveraging this benchmark, we have conducted a detailed evaluation and analysis of the security attributes of our local text desensitization tool in

Supported by National Natural Science Foundation of China (No. 62102108, No. 62372120), Natural Science Foundation of Guangdong Province of China (No. 2022A1515010061).

Y. Tan and Y. Shi (Eds.): DMBD 2023, CCIS 2018, pp. 16–30, 2024.
https://doi.org/10.1007/978-981-97-0844-4_2

conjunction with ChatGPT-3.5. In conclusion, our research endeavors to tackle the pressing privacy concerns associated with large language models, providing a robust safeguard for user data and presenting a practical approach to evaluating the performance of these models, by employing a relatively smaller model for local desensitization. We believe that this study holds significant practical implications for upholding user privacy and data security within the context of LLM services. FirewaLLM is publicly released at https://github.com/ysy1216/FirewaLLM .

Keywords: FirewaLLM · Data Privacy · Model Interaction

1   Introduction

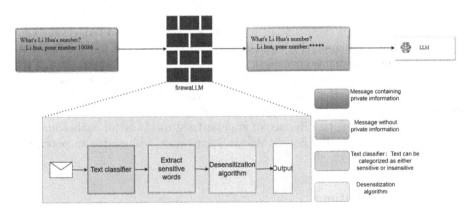

Fig. 1. Overview of our method. We propose FirewaLLM, which enables the user to desensitize the text information locally, then send the text to the Big Language Model, which returns the result, and FirewaLLM completes the recovery of the sensitive information of the result locally.

In recent years, the rapid proliferation of large language models has ushered in a new era in natural language processing and artificial intelligence [1,3]. Models like ChatGPT [10] and GPT-4 have demonstrated exceptional capabilities, enabling various applications across industries, from enhancing customer support services to automating content creation and providing seamless language translation [12]. However, this technological advancement has brought to the forefront a pressing concern—user data privacy and security. This concern primarily revolves around the inadvertent disclosure of sensitive information by this models [8,17]. While these language models are designed to generate coherent and contextually relevant responses, instances of unintentional revelation of personal, confidential, and sensitive data have arisen. Such data may encompass personally identifiable information (PII), health records, financial details, or other private information that users entrust to these models. The inadvertent exposure of such information poses substantial threats to user privacy, potentially resulting in identity theft, the disclosure of sensitive medical conditions, and financial fraud. In light of these challenges [36], it becomes imperative to develop robust privacy protection mechanisms that safeguard user data across diverse fields (Fig. 1).

Recent years have seen remarkable advancements in the field of data privacy and security. Privacy-preserving techniques, such as differential privacy and federated learning [32], have revolutionized how we approach data protection. These techniques find application in a wide array of domains, including healthcare [15], finance, and the legal sector [16], allowing us to strike a balance between leveraging data for valuable insights and ensuring individual privacy.

In healthcare, for example, de-identification methods and secure data-sharing protocols have enabled groundbreaking medical research while safeguarding patient confidentiality [34]. In finance, the application of cryptographic techniques has become standard practice to protect sensitive financial data during transactions. Legal professionals regularly employ advanced redaction tools driven by Natural Language Processing [31] to ensure that sensitive information in legal documents remains concealed.

The existing landscape, unfortunately, falls short of addressing these pressing concerns. Despite the wide adoption of large language models, there is a noticeable absence of a generalized framework for safeguarding user security and privacy. Moreover, the absence of standardized methods for evaluating the privacy security of Big Predictive Models leaves users vulnerable to potential breaches.

1.1 Our Contributions

In the context of this paper, we endeavor to bridge vital gaps by presenting a comprehensive approach dedicated to safeguarding user data security within Large Language Model services. We introduce a localized text desensitization framework, granting users the capability to locally redact sensitive text segments before forwarding them to the LLMs. This framework establishes a robust layer of privacy and confidentiality specifically tailored for LLM services.

Furthermore, to gauge the effectiveness and reliability of our framework, we introduce a benchmark meticulously designed to assess the security and accuracy of large language models. By scrutinizing the performance of ChatGPT-3.5 in conjunction with our desensitization tool, our goal is to provide a clear and standardized method for evaluating the capabilities of these models in terms of both privacy and accuracy within LLMs services.

In summary, our research squarely addresses the mounting privacy concerns arising from the widespread adoption of large language models in LLMs services. We present a practical solution aimed at enhancing data privacy and security in this specialized context, with the ultimate objective of contributing to a more secure and responsible use of these potent AI tools within a data-driven world.

The remainder of this paper is structured as follows. In Sect. 2, we review related work. In Sect. 3, We introduce an implementation of the FirewaLLM framework. In Sect. 4, We introduce benchmarks for evaluating the security and accuracy of large language models.

2   Related Work

This section may not just focus on the relevant techniques of this work.

We can divide this section into two parts. The first one is what the privacy concerns about large language models may be faced with (especially in our Interactive context) and how other works address those problems. This may be the motivation and the reason why we should do this work. The second one is the following techniques.

Before describing the FirewaLLM frame, we briefly review some of the concepts and background that are necessary to understand our algorithm. We introduce the relevant background on Large Language Models [22], LSTM [27], BERT [18], TF-IDF [14], Cosine similarity matching [33] and AI model evaluation [6].

2.1   Large Language Models

Large Language Models are language models that contain hundreds of billions of parameters trained on large amounts of textual data [3], such as GPT-3, PaLM, Galactica, and LLaMA. These models are built on top of the Transformer [11] architecture and have demonstrated strong capabilities on various natural language processing tasks through techniques such as pre-training and fine-tuning [18]. Large language models have some emergent capabilities that small language models do not have, such as context learning, instruction following, and step-wise reasoning [12]. These capabilities allow large language models to generate desired outputs based on a given task description or example right at the testing stage without additional training or gradient updating [22].

However, the widespread use of big language models is accompanied by some potential risks and challenges [8]. On the one hand, since big language models are trained on massive textual data [26], these data may contain a variety of sensitive information, such as personal identities, health conditions, financial accounts, and so on. If this information is leaked or misused, it may bring serious privacy damages and legal risks to users [8]. On the other hand, The output results of large models may also expose user's private information, such as generative large models can generate relevant content based on the input text [30]. If the input text contains the user's privacy information, then the output content may also contain or imply this information [17].

In response to these problems, there are already some technologies and methods that are being explored and applied, such as multi-party secure computing, homomorphic encryption, differential privacy, etc. [5]. They can perform computation and analysis without exposing the original data, or increasing the randomness and untraceability of data while ensuring data availability, thereby improving the security and privacy of data and models [32].

2.2   LLM Privacy Protection

LLM privacy protection can be roughly divided into centralized and local approaches Many existing works focus on a centralized privacy setting, where a central entity is responsible for protecting the data from being exposed. There are various methods to train a large language model that preserves the privacy of the data [13,23], but they are not relevant to this work. Some works use differentially private fine-tuning to prevent the leakage of private data that is used to fine-tune a public language model [7]. Some works use lightweight fine-tuning methods such as adapters and prefix-tuning to protect the privacy of the data during the fine-tuning stage [37]. Some people propose differential privacy as a way to protect the privacy of the training data while preserving the utility of the pre-trained language models. Differential privacy is a mathematical framework that quantifies the privacy loss of a data analysis algorithm by adding random noise to the output [28]. Some people apply differential privacy to the fine-tuning or distillation of pre-trained language models, such as BERT and GPT-2, and evaluate the trade-off between privacy and performance [25]. Some people use federated learning to train NLP models on different data sources, such as mobile devices, hospitals, or social media platforms, and investigate the issues of communication efficiency, data heterogeneity, and model personalization [20]. Our setting is different from all these works. We aim to protect the private data of the users when they use large language model services, and we do not assume that there is a central entity that can protect the data.

Local approaches provide a stronger level of privacy protection, but they also reduce the utility of the model. Some people propose a differentially private neural representation method to preserve the utility of the model under local privacy protection, but they only consider privacy protection during the inference stage, not the fine-tuning stage [13]. Some people propose a privacy-constrained fine-tuning (PCF) method that protects privacy during both fine-tuning and inference stages, but their method requires fine-tuning the whole model on privatized data, which is expensive for large language models [24]. Our approach does not use fine-tuning, we propose a completely new paradigm where we implement a framework that masks sensitive words locally and can restore textual information locally.

2.3   LSTM

LSTM [27] is a variant of the recurrent neural network [31], which stands for Long Short-Term Memory. The principle of LSTM is to use a special cell structure to store and update past information, thus solving the vanishing and exploding gradient problems of conventional RNNs when dealing with long sequences1. The cell structure of LSTM consists of a cell state and three gates, namely input gate, forget gate, and output gate1 [29]. The cell state is the core of LSTM, which can pass information between time steps, and also add or reduce information through the control of gates1. The input gate determines the influence of the current input and the previous output on the cell state [22], the forget gate determines the influence of the previous cell state on the current cell state, and the output gate determines the influence of the current cell state on the current output [2].

We add an LSTM after the BERT. The word embeddings generated by the BERT are fed into the LSTM. Add a classification layer, usually a fully connected neural network layer, after the LSTM. This layer will learn how to map the output of LSTM to different sensitive word classification labels.

2.4   TF-IDF

TF-IDF is a statistical method, which stands for Term Frequency-Inverse Document Frequency [21]. The principle of TF-IDF is to measure the importance of a word in a document or a collection of documents, based on its frequency and rarity [14]. The frequency of a word is the number of times it appears in a document, which reflects its relevance to the document. The rarity of a word is the inverse of the number of documents that contain it, which reflects its discrimination power among different documents1 [29]. The product of frequency and rarity is the TF-IDF score, which represents the weight of a word in a document or a collection of documents

TF-IDF is used in sensitive word recognition to determine which words in the text are more critical in recognizing sensitive information. By calculating the TF-IDF values, we filter the potentially sensitive words from the text and further classify the sensitive words into classes.

2.5   BERT

BERT is a large language model [17], which stands for Bidirectional Encoder Representations from Transformers. The principle of BERT is to use the Transformer architecture to pre-train deep bidirectional representations from unlabeled text, thus learning the semantic and structural information of the text [18]. The Transformer is a neural network module based on a self-attention mechanism, which can capture the relationship between any two positions in the text. Bidirectional pre-training means that both left and right contexts are considered simultaneously during the training process, thus better understanding the meaning of the text. The application scenarios of BERT are various natural languages processing tasks, such as question answering, language inference, and sentiment analysis [17], etc. BERT can adapt to these tasks by simple fine-tuning, without a lot of task-specific architectural modifications. Fine-tuning is to add an extra output layer on the pre-trained BERT model and train it for a small amount of time according to the objective function of different tasks [11]. This way, the general language knowledge learned by the BERT model can be used to improve the performance of each task [11].

For sensitive word classification, we fine-tuned BERT by adding a classification layer to the top of BERT and then trained BERT using the dataset so that it learns to classify sensitive and non-sensitive text. The results show that BERT classifies well, and BERT becomes an essential part of our experiments and an important piece of the FirewaLLM.

2.6   AI Model Evaluation

Our FirewaLLM employs cosine similarity to serve as an important metric for recovering sensitive utterances. Cosine similarity matching is a method to measure the similarity between two vectors, based on the cosine of the angle between them [33]. The principle of cosine similarity matching is to calculate the dot product of two vectors and divide it by the product of their magnitudes, which gives the cosine value of the angle between them [9]. The cosine value ranges from -1 to 1, where -1 means the vectors are opposite, 0 means they are orthogonal, and 1 means they are identical. The higher the cosine value, the smaller the angle, and the more similar the vectors are [38]. The application scenarios of cosine similarity matching are various tasks involving vector representation of data, such as text analysis, image retrieval, recommender systems [33], etc. Cosine similarity matching can be used to compare the similarity between two texts, by representing each text as a vector of word frequencies or word embeddings and calculating the cosine value between them. Cosine similarity matching can also be used to find the most similar images to a query image, by representing each image as a vector of pixel values or feature descriptors and ranking them by their cosine values with the query image [38]. Cosine similarity matching can also be used to recommend items to users, by representing each user and item as a vector of preferences or ratings and predicting the user's interest in an item based on their cosine value.

Evaluating AI models is a crucial step in gauging their performance. Several standard protocols for model evaluation exist, such as k-fold cross-validation, holdout validation, leave-one-out cross-validation, bootstrap, and reduced set [4]. For instance, k-fold cross-validation [19] divides the dataset into k parts, using one as a test set and the rest as training sets, which minimizes data loss and provides a relatively accurate model performance assessment. Holdout validation, on the other hand, splits the dataset into training and test sets, requiring fewer calculations but potentially introducing more bias [6]. LOOCV is a unique variant of k-fold cross-validation [19] where only one data point serves as the test set. Lastly, a reduced set trains the model with one dataset and tests it with the remaining data, which is computationally simple but has limited applicability [35].

The choice of the appropriate evaluation method should be based on the specific problem and data characteristics to ensure more dependable performance metrics.

3   FirewaLLM Framework

In this paper, we propose a novel local text desensitization framework named FirewaLLM. The local text desensitization framework is a technique devised to protect user privacy and data security, which enables the Large Model to process user-entered text without accessing or disclosing any sensitive information, such as names, phone numbers, ID numbers, and the like. The primary objective of this framework is the enhancement of users' confidence and satisfaction in utilizing the Big Model, mitigating any reservations stemming from privacy concerns.

By employing the local text desensitization framework, users can engage with the Big Model while maintaining their privacy intact.

FirewaLLM is implemented by desensitizing the text before the user inputs it to the big model, replacing the sensitive information in it with special symbols or random characters, and then passing the processed text to the big model. In this way, the big model can't obtain or generate any sensitive information, and can only perform corresponding tasks based on the processed text, such as QandA, chatting, generating, and so on. After the big model outputs the results, it then restores the results and restores the replaced sensitive information before displaying it to the user. In this way, users can see the complete and safe results without feeling any discomfort or unnaturalness (Fig. 2).

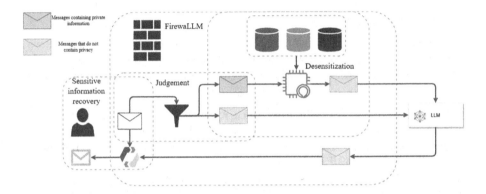

Fig. 2. Implementation framework for FirewaLLM

The implementation of the desensitization framework comprises three distinct components: the sensitive text discrimination algorithm, the desensitization algorithm, and the text recovery algorithm. These components work collaboratively to ensure the effective operation of the framework.

3.1 Sensitive Text Discrimination Algorithm

In this section, we present the algorithm responsible for identifying and distinguishing sensitive information within the input text. Our approach involves multiple stages and the combined use of various techniques. We'll begin by discussing each stage and its respective functions.

The sensitive text discrimination algorithm is responsible for identifying and distinguishing sensitive information within the input text. In the initial stage of text classification, both BERT and BERT + LSTM models are employed to perform preliminary classification tasks. Following the preliminary classification, traditional TF-IDF analysis is utilized to further identify and determine sensitive information. The sensitive words identified through the TF-IDF analysis are then returned as the output.

Data Preparation. The initial step in the process involves data preparation. The data set $D = d_1, d_2, \ldots, d_N$, N represents the number of text samples. Preprocessing text data: The preprocessed text set D_{cleaned} is obtained by text cleaning, word segmentation, stop word removal, and other operations.

Model Training. The next stage involves training a text classification model: BERT and BERT+LSTM: The model M_{BERT} and $M_{\text{BERT+LSTM}}$ is trained to classify the text sample d_i into two categories: sensitive(S) or insensitive(NS). We train the model MBERT with the label data (d_i, label_i), where label_i represents the real label(sensitive or insensitive) of the text d_i.

Text Classification. After training our models, we employ them to predict the classification of each text sample.For each text sample d_i, the trained models M_{BERT} and $M_{\text{BERT+LSTM}}$ are used to predict the classification results : $P(\text{S}|d_i)$ represents the probability that d_i is classified as sensitive(S).

Sensitive Sentence Segmentation. For text samples classified as sensitive, we further process them through word segmentation. For the sensitive text sample d_i, the word segmentation operation is performed and it is divided into words or phrases. This can be expressed as $W_{\text{tokenized}}(d_i)$.

TF-IDF Similarity Calculation. Once we have text samples identified as sensitive, we proceed to represent them using the TF-IDF algorithm. For the text sample d_i that is classified as sensitive, the TF-IDF algorithm is used to represent it as the TF-IDF vector $TFIDF(d_i)$. The similarity between the sensitive text sample d_i and other samples in the entire text data set can be calculated, and measures such as cosine similarity can be used. The similarity is expressed as $S(d_i, d_j)$, where d_j represents other text samples in the dataset.

Return Sensitive Words. According to the results of similarity calculation, the most similar text fragment d_j to the sensitive text sample d_i is determined. Extract sensitive words or phrases from the text fragment d_j, these words constitute the final set of sensitive words S_{words}.

3.2 Desensitization Algorithm

The desensitization algorithm, employs a randomization technique to obfuscate sensitive words, thereby safeguarding the privacy of the associated information. This randomization process enhances the security of sensitive information by introducing variability, making it challenging for potential attackers to deduce or exploit the concealed words.

In the algorithm, each sensitive word undergoes a transformation based on its length and a specified sensitivity level. For words shorter than 8 characters, a lower sensitivity level (0) is applied, while longer words utilize the provided sensitivity level. The algorithm then proceeds to replace characters in each sensitive word randomly with asterisks (*) according to a randomly generated pattern.

This desensitization process is applied iteratively to all sensitive words in the input text. The result is a text where sensitive information is partially or completely replaced with asterisks, contributing to privacy protection. The sensitivity level, a user-defined parameter with low, medium, and high options, allows customization of the desensitization intensity.

In the context of text data processing, desensitization algorithms are instrumental in preserving the privacy and security of sensitive information. These algorithms strategically mask potentially sensitive content by introducing controlled randomness, effectively mitigating risks while preserving the overall readability of the text. The incorporation of a random character replacement strategy further bolsters the confidentiality of sensitive information, ensuring a robust safeguarding of privacy and security.

3.3   Text Recovery Algorithm

Prepare Alternative Answers. Let $A_1, A_2, \ldots, A_n$ denote the set of alternative answers, where each A_i is also a text vector and is represented as a representation of the answer.

Calculate Similarity. using cosine similarity to calculate the similarity between the original question Q and each alternative answer A_i. Cosine similarity $\text{cosine}(Q, A_i)$ is usually used to measure the similarity between texts, and its calculation formula is as follows:

$$\text{cosine}(Q, A_i) = \frac{Q \cdot A_i}{\|Q\| \cdot \|A_i\|} \tag{1}$$

where $Q \cdot A_i$ denotes the dot product of the original question Q and the alternative answer A_i, and $|Q|$ and $|A_i|$ denote the Euclidean norm of the original question and the alternative answer, respectively.

Select the Highest Similarity Answer. Choose from the calculated similarity scores the alternative answer with the highest score A_j, i.e. :

$$j = \arg \max_i \text{cosine}(Q, A_i) \tag{2}$$

where j is the index of the selected alternative answer, corresponding to the highest similarity score.

Return to the Best Answer. Return the selected alternative answer A_j with the highest similarity score as the final answer. This algorithm mathematically calculates the similarity between the original question and the alternative answer, and then selects the alternative answer with the highest similarity score to determine the best answer.

4   Model Effect Evaluation

The evaluation of the desensitization effect refers to the process of analyzing and evaluating the results after data desensitization. The main purpose is to test whether the data desensitization has achieved the expected goal, that is, while protecting data privacy, it does not affect the availability and value of data. In this paper, the method of automatic inspection is used to realize the model evaluation.

4.1 Measure Index

This paper defines sensitive information exposure and question-answering accuracy, which are used to evaluate the performance and safety of large language models in processing sensitive information and output answers.

Exposure Rate of Sensitive Information is an indicator used to evaluate the security of the model. It reflects the extent to which sensitive information is exposed or leaked during the input problem to the large language model. Let E denote the exposure rate of sensitive information, N denote the total number of answers generated, and I denote the number of answers containing sensitive information. Sensitive information exposure can be expressed as:

$$E = \frac{I}{N} \times 100\% \tag{3}$$

The value of this indicator is usually between 0 and 100. The closer to 100 indicates the higher the exposure of sensitive information, and the closer to 0 indicates that the model better protects sensitive information.

Accuracy is an indicator used to evaluate the correctness of the model's output answers. Here, it is used to evaluate whether the answers generated by the large language model match the real answers to the questions. Let A denote the accuracy, T denote the number of times the answer generated by the model matches the real answer, and Q denote the total number of questions. The accuracy can be expressed as:

$$A = \frac{T}{Q} \times 100\% \tag{4}$$

The value of accuracy is usually between 0 and 100. The closer to 100 indicates that the answer generated by the model is more accurate, and closer to 0 indicates that the accuracy of the model is lower.

4.2 Test Datasets

This paper utilizes a bilingual Chinese-English dataset to thoroughly assess the model's performance, with a particular emphasis on its ability to identify and categorize sensitive information. The dataset is effectively bifurcated into two principal segments: non-sensitive sentences (denoted as "N") and sensitive sentences (labeled as "Y"). Each of these segments comprises 5,000 samples in English and 5,000 samples in Chinese, amounting to a total of 20,000 diverse instances. The sensitive sentence category is further stratified into 10 distinct classes, with each class containing 500 samples, encompassing a wide spectrum of sensitive information types. These encompass mobile phone numbers, bank card details, identity card information, company names, corporate addresses, health-related data, religious affiliations, political affiliations, annual income details, and credit assessments. Datasets are publicly released at https://github.com/ysy1216/privacy_gpt_sys/tree/main/DataSet.

4.3   Result

Table 1. performance and safety of mode

measure index	ChatGPT 3.5	FirewaLLM
Exposure rate of sensitive information	78.17%	4.28%
Accuracy	96.98%	92.81%

The above data showed that FirewaLLM showed excellent ability in desensitization, and its E value was 78.17 %, which was much higher than that of ChatGPT 3.5 (4.28%). This means that FirewaLLM can protect sensitive information more effectively, making it difficult to restore or leak (Table 1).

In addition, the A value of FirewaLLM is 92.81%, which is close to 96.98% of ChatGPT 3.5. This shows that FirewaLLM is comparable to ChatGPT 3.5 in terms of answer accuracy. This is very impressive because FirewaLLM can still maintain excellent desensitization while maintaining high accuracy.

In summary, these data show that FirewaLLM has made significant progress in protecting sensitive information, while also performing well in providing accurate answers. This comprehensive effect makes it a very promising model that can be used in applications that require a high degree of privacy and security.

4.4   Conclusion

In this study, we propose a native text desensitization framework, FirewaLLM, which aims to address the privacy preservation problem in online large language model services. FirewaLLM can effectively protect users' private data while guaranteeing the performance and functionality of large language models through the key steps of identifying sensitive information, assigning sensitive weights, and recovering text. Experimental and evaluation results show that FirewaLLM has efficient effects and performance in desensitizing and recovering sensitive information, providing users with more secure and reliable large-scale modeling services. However, we should also recognize that FirewaLLM has some potential limitations, such as the need to be customized and optimized for different domains or scenarios, the reliance on a high-quality and sufficient amount of training data, and the need to consider the balance between computational resources and performance in practical applications. In conclusion, FirewaLLM provides an innovative solution to the privacy preservation problem in online large-scale modeling services and offers users a more secure and trustworthy language processing tool. This study provides new ideas and methods for privacy preservation in the field of large-scale language modeling and makes a useful contribution to this important issue.

References

1. Abdelali, A., et al.: Benchmarking Arabic AI with large language models (2023). https://doi.org/10.48550/arXiv.2305.14982
2. Aliyu, E.O., Kotzé, E.: Stacked language models for an optimized next word generation. In: 2022 IST-Africa Conference (IST-Africa), pp. 1–12 (2022). https://doi.org/10.23919/IST-Africa56635.2022.9845545
3. Arora, D., Singh, H.G., Mausam: have LLMs advanced enough? A challenging problem solving benchmark for large language models (2023). https://doi.org/10.48550/arXiv.2305.15074
4. Bubeck, S., et al.: Sparks of artificial general intelligence: early experiments with GPT-4 (2023)
5. Byrd, D., Polychroniadou, A.: Differentially private secure multi-party computation for federated learning in financial applications (2020)
6. Chang, Y., et al.: A survey on evaluation of large language models (2023). https://arxiv.org/abs/2307.03109v7
7. Chatzikokolakis, K., Andrés, M.E., Bordenabe, N.E., Palamidessi, C.: Broadening the scope of differential privacy using metrics. In: De Cristofaro, E., Wright, M. (eds.) PETS 2013. LNCS, vol. 7981, pp. 82–102. Springer, Heidelberg (2013). https://doi.org/10.1007/978-3-642-39077-7_5
8. Chen, Y., Arunasalam, A., Celik, Z.B.: Can large language models provide security & privacy advice? Measuring the ability of LLMs to refute misconceptions (2023). https://doi.org/10.48550/arXiv.2310.02431
9. de Vos, I.M.A., van den Boogerd, G.L., Fennema, M.D., Correia, A.D.: Comparing in context: improving cosine similarity measures with a metric tensor (2022). https://doi.org/10.48550/arXiv.2203.14996
10. Deshpande, A., Murahari, V., Rajpurohit, T., Kalyan, A., Narasimhan, K.: Toxicity in ChatGPT: analyzing Persona-assigned Language Models (2023). https://doi.org/10.48550/arXiv.2304.05335
11. Devlin, J., Chang, M.W., Lee, K., Toutanova, K.: BERT: pre-training of deep bidirectional transformers for language understanding (2019). https://doi.org/10.48550/arXiv.1810.04805
12. Fan, L., Li, L., Ma, Z., Lee, S., Yu, H., Hemphill, L.: A bibliometric review of large language models research from 2017 to 2023 (2023). https://doi.org/10.48550/arXiv.2304.02020
13. Hoory, S., et al.: Learning and evaluating a differentially private pre-trained language model. In: Moens, M.F., Huang, X., Specia, L., Yih, S.W.T. (eds.) Findings of the Association for Computational Linguistics: EMNLP 2021, pp. 1178–1189. Association for Computational Linguistics, Punta Cana (2021). https://doi.org/10.18653/v1/2021.findings-emnlp.102, https://aclanthology.org/2021.findings-emnlp.102
14. Jalilifard, A., Caridá, V.F., Mansano, A.F., Cristo, R.S., da Fonseca, F.P.C.: Semantic sensitive TF-IDF to determine word relevance in documents. In: Thampi, S.M., Gelenbe, E., Atiquzzaman, M., Chaudhary, V., Li, K.-C. (eds.) Advances in Computing and Network Communications. LNEE, vol. 736, pp. 327–337. Springer, Singapore (2021). https://doi.org/10.1007/978-981-33-6987-0_27
15. Jin, H., Luo, Y., Li, P., Mathew, J.: A review of secure and privacy-preserving medical data sharing. IEEE Access **7**, 61656–61669 (2019). https://doi.org/10.1109/ACCESS.2019.2916503

16. Katz, D.M., Hartung, D., Gerlach, L., Jana, A., Bommarito II, M.J.: Natural language processing in the legal domain (2023)
17. Kshetri, N.: Cybercrime and privacy threats of large language models. IT Prof. **25**(3), 9–13 (2023). https://doi.org/10.1109/MITP.2023.3275489
18. Lewis, M., et al.: BART: denoising sequence-to-sequence pre-training for natural language generation, translation, and comprehension. In: Proceedings of the 58th Annual Meeting of the Association for Computational Linguistics, pp. 7871–7880. Association for Computational Linguistics (2020). https://doi.org/10.18653/v1/2020.acl-main.703
19. Liu, H., Wei, Z., Li, F., Lin, Y., Qu, H., Wu, H., Feng, Z.: ISAC signal processing over unlicensed spectrum bands (2023)
20. Liu, M., Ho, S., Wang, M., Gao, L., Jin, Y., Zhang, H.: Federated learning meets natural language processing: a survey (2021)
21. Liu, Q., Wang, J., Zhang, D., Yang, Y., Wang, N.: Text features extraction based on TF-IDF associating semantic. In: 2018 IEEE 4th International Conference on Computer and Communications (ICCC), pp. 2338–2343 (2018). https://doi.org/10.1109/CompComm.2018.8780663
22. Liu, X., Liu, Z.: LLMs can understand encrypted prompt: towards privacy-computing friendly transformers (2023). https://doi.org/10.48550/arXiv.2305.18396
23. Lyu, L., He, X., Li, Y.: Differentially private representation for NLP: formal guarantee and an empirical study on privacy and fairness (2020)
24. Lyu, L., He, X., Li, Y.: Differentially private representation for NLP: formal guarantee and an empirical study on privacy and fairness. In: Cohn, T., He, Y., Liu, Y. (eds.) Findings of the Association for Computational Linguistics: EMNLP 2020, pp. 2355–2365. Association for Computational Linguistics, Online (2020). https://doi.org/10.18653/v1/2020.findings-emnlp.213, https://aclanthology.org/2020.findings-emnlp.213
25. Mahendran, D., Luo, C., Mcinnes, B.T.: Review: privacy-preservation in the context of natural language processing. IEEE Access **9**, 147600–147612 (2021). https://doi.org/10.1109/ACCESS.2021.3124163
26. Naveed, H., et al.: A comprehensive overview of large language models (2023). https://doi.org/10.48550/arXiv.2307.06435
27. Sak, H., Senior, A., Beaufays, F.: Long short-term memory based recurrent neural network architectures for large vocabulary speech recognition (2014). https://doi.org/10.48550/arXiv.1402.1128
28. Sousa, S., Kern, R.: How to keep text private? A systematic review of deep learning methods for privacy-preserving natural language processing (2022)
29. Staudemeyer, R.C., Morris, E.R.: Understanding LSTM - a tutorial into long short-term memory recurrent neural networks (2019)
30. Sun, H., Zhang, Z., Deng, J., Cheng, J., Huang, M.: Safety assessment of Chinese large language models (2023). https://doi.org/10.48550/arXiv.2304.10436
31. Sutskever, I., Vinyals, O., Le, Q.V.: Sequence to sequence learning with neural networks (2014). https://doi.org/10.48550/arXiv.1409.3215
32. Wang, S.: Privacy amplification via shuffling: unified, simplified, and tightened (2023). https://doi.org/10.48550/arXiv.2304.05007
33. Wannasuphoprasit, S., Zhou, Y., Bollegala, D.: Solving cosine similarity underestimation between high frequency words by L2 norm discounting (2023). https://arxiv.org/abs/2305.10610v1

34. Wirth, F.N., Meurers, T., Johns, M., Prasser, F.: Privacy-preserving data sharing infrastructures for medical research: systematization and comparison. BMC Med. Inform. Decis. Mak. **21**(1), 242 (2021). https://doi.org/10.1186/s12911-021-01602-x

35. Wong, T.T.: Performance evaluation of classification algorithms by k-fold and leave-one-out cross validation. Pattern Recogn. **48**(9), 2839–2846 (2015). https://doi.org/10.1016/j.patcog.2015.03.009

36. Xu, R., Baracaldo, N., Joshi, J.: Privacy-preserving machine learning: methods, challenges and directions (2021). https://doi.org/10.48550/arXiv.2108.04417

37. Yu, D., et al.: Differentially private fine-tuning of language models (2022)

38. Zhou, K., Ethayarajh, K., Card, D., Jurafsky, D.: Problems with cosine as a measure of embedding similarity for high frequency words (2022). https://doi.org/10.48550/arXiv.2205.05092

Data Query and Image Clustering

AL-SQUARES: SQL Synthesis System with the Addition of Reducer

Huimin Liu[1]([✉])(iD), Quansheng Dou[1](iD), and Huixian Wang[2](iD)

[1] School of Computer Science and Technology, Shandong Technology and Business University, Yantai 264005, Shangdong, China
{2021410075,douqsh}@sdtbu.edu.cn
[2] School of Information and Electronic Engineering, Shandong Technology and Business University, P191 Binhai Middle Road, Yantai 264005, Shandong, China

Abstract. During the early stages of artificial intelligence development, researchers began exploring methods for computer-aided program synthesis. Among these methods, SQL reverse synthesis emerged as a crucial branch in the field of data analysis and became a research hot spot for applying artificial intelligence in the database domain. Program synthesis can be categorized into different types based on various requirements. This paper primarily focuses on input-output-based program synthesis, which involves generating programs based on given examples. SQUARES, an SQL reverse synthesizer proposed by scholars from the University of Lisbon, serves as the foundation of our work. We extend SQUARES by incorporating a reducer module based on attention-based RNN to guide program synthesis. With the integration of this module, the system is capable of removing less-relevant production rules, reducing the generation of irrelevant program statements, and effectively shrinking the program search space. Our model achieves an accuracy of 91.6% on the test set, while the baseline model only achieves 80.9%. This represents a significant improvement in success rate, with an increase of 10.7%.

Keywords: Program synthesis · SQL reverse synthesis · Machine learning

1 Introduction

Artificial intelligence is an important research topic within computer science and technology. Its goal is to simulate human intelligence capabilities through machine learning, eventually bringing convenience and progress to society and presenting a wide range of application prospects. Program synthesis, a minor branch within this field, can be traced back to the intersection of AI, computer science, and formal methods. It integrates logic reasoning, formal methods, machine learning, and optimization techniques to automatically generate program codes that meet user-defined specifications, constraints, or needs. In addition, scholars have also developed numerous new methods, for example:

CodeRL [1], DEEPCODER [2], AutoGrader [3], dAMP [4], DA4CLR [5], FAIR [6], CODEGEN [7], NPI [8], PCcoder [9], TYGAR [10], NPL [11].

Example-based program synthesis is a research direction in computer science, aiming to automatically generate program codes that meet the given input and output requirements. It integrates program synthesis, AI, and machine learning techniques to address the complexity and tediousness of programming. Today, numerous scholars have made significant contributions to the method of program synthesis based on input-output. For example, Menon et al. [12] used features derived from input-output examples to learn parameterized probability context grammars to accelerate synthesis. FlashFill [13] is a highly successful technique in inductive program synthesis used for automating data filling in electronic spreadsheets. It has been integrated into Microsoft Excel 2013, demonstrating its practical implementation. Example-based program synthesis has vast potential in various application domains, providing developers with a rapid and precise coding assistance tool. It enables automatic generation of code snippets, API call sequences, and data transformation logic, among other valuable functionalities. Several new research studies and methods have emerged, such as TALOS [14, 15], QFE [16], SQLSynthesizer [17], SCYTHE [18,19], REGAL [20], REGAL+ [21], UNMASQUE [22], RELIC [23], DExPlorer [24], and many others. These approaches continue to advance and contribute to the field.

This paper proposes the addition of a reducer to SQUARES [25], aiming to reduce the space complexity during the synthesis process. The reducer consists of sequential RNNs with an added attention mechanism. Its primary function is to predict the relevance of productions, thereby reducing the synthesis of irrelevant statements. Experimental evaluations were conducted under the same conditions, and the results showed a 10.7% improvement in the synthesis performance of the new synthesizer.

2   Relates Work

2.1   Domain Specific Language and Attributes

Language is the key to generating legitimate programs. Given the complexity of constructing SQL [26] syntax, direct synthesis tasks are difficult, leading to the use of DSL language as a replacement. The use of a more concise DSL language means developers do not need to expend significant energy mastering the complexities and syntax of general database programming languages, allowing for the swift development of high-quality code.

Five different types of Domain Specific Language (DSL) have been inspired in this way, including table, tableSelect, op, distinct, and empty, as shown in Fig. 1.

A typical program, p, in QRE tasks accepts a table as input and returns a tableSelect as output. Program p is typically constructed by production rules defined by DSL. The functions on the right side of Fig. 1 are predefined, while the left side can be considered the return type of these functions. The semantics of productions (1–10) are related to SQL statements.

table	→	input	(0)
		left_join(table , table)	(1)
		inner_join(table , table , joinCondition)	(2)
		cross_join(table , table , crossJoinCondition)	(3)
		filter(table , filterCondition)	(4)
		summarise(table , summariseCondition ,cols)	(5)
		mutate(table , summariseCondition)	(6)
		anti_join(table , table , cols)	(7)
		semi_join(table , table)	(8)
		union(table , table)	(9)
		intersect(table , table , col)	(10)

tableSelect   →   select(table , selectCols , distinct)

Fig. 1. The types of DSL used in this article.

2.2 SQUARES

SQUARES is a SQL synthesizer using Query Reverse Engineering, a PEB system based on enumeration developed on the state-of-the-art synthesis framework, Trinity. The goal of SQUARES is to synthesize SQL query statements from input-output example tables. The input of SQUARES includes a set of input-output example table pairs, DSL, and an interpreter. Its operation involves an enumerator generating candidate programs that are then passed to a verifier for analysis. If a statement capable of solving the problem is obtained, it is considered successful. Otherwise, the verifier returns the reason for failure to the enumerator, and this process is repeated until a program satisfying the conditions is found. The following diagram depicts the general structure of SQUARES (see Fig. 2).

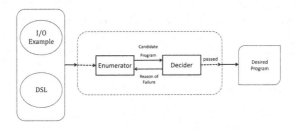

Fig. 2. The structure of SQUARES.

3 Program Synthesis Model Architecture

3.1 Problem Formulation

Assuming the instructor wishes to identify students in the class with credits greater than 5 after the final exams. A simplified description is presented in Fig. 3, where the input tables are Student and SC, and the resulting output table is Output, which represents all students with credits greater than or equal to 5. To derive the desired output table, the target SQL statement can be synthesized by our SQL synthesis system based on the DSL production rules. The target program P can be represented as follows: select(inner_join(Students, filter($SC, Ccredit \geq 5$)), Sno, Sname, Ccredit, true).

Students				SC		
Sno	**Sname**	**Sage**		**Sno**	**Cno**	**Ccredit**
01	Anna	21		01	59341	5
02	Jane	20		01	59342	4
03	Jack	21		01	59343	3
04	Tom	21		02	59341	4
05	Mary	19		02	59342	6
06	Hans	20				
07	Rose	21		Output		
08	Ben	20		**Sno**	**Cno**	**Ccredit**
09	Joly	21		01	59341	5
10	Danica	18		02	59342	6

Fig. 3. Example of QRE task.

In the previous section, a synthesis demonstration of a single simple example was presented. However, in general cases, when given a set of input-output table pairs, and input table sequences without matching, Our goal is to generate corresponding output table sequences, For each input-output table pair, we assume that there is at least one program P capable of correctly completing the synthesis task. Intuitively, we aim to design a system where multiple input-output table pairs are used for training, and users can manually create input tables. Subsequently, the system automatically generates the target output tables.

3.2 Model Architecture

SQUARES, the system aims to acquire candidate programs, which requires multiple rounds of enumeration, resulting in a huge search space.

To address this issue, this paper proposes a method to reduce the program space. This method builds upon the initial SQUARES model by incorporating a reducer, allowing the enumerator to skip enumerating all programs. Instead, it first eliminates irrelevant production rules and then feeds the remaining rules into the enumerator, reducing the generation of irrelevant programs and improving the efficiency of the synthesis task.

Subsequent paragraphs, however, are indentedFor the addition of the reducer module, a series of Recursive Neural Networks (RNNs) were employed to encode the correlation between the observed I/O example tables and DSL production rules. It should be noted that multiple sets of input-output table pairs and DSL production rules were provided as input. Each production rule was associated with a relevance indicator vector, denoted as $S^z = (S_1^z, S_i^z, ..., S_n^z)$, and z represents the input, $S_i^z \in [0, 1]$, and n = 10 represents 10 DSL production rules. Two models incorporating different structured reducers were explored for experimental evaluation. The overall structure after the addition of the reducer is depicted as follows (see Fig. 4):

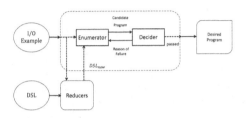

Fig. 4. The system structure with the addition of the reducer.

3.3 Neural Network Architecture of the Reducer

The proposed SQL reverse synthesis system based on program space reducer is presented in this paper. During synthesis, the reducer eliminates production rules unrelated to the input-output table pairs, reducing the generation of irrelevant programs and reducing the size of the program space, thus improving the efficiency of QRE tasks.

We explored two models with the addition of a reducer, Fig. 5 depicts the network architectures of the two reducers: L-SQUARES: Each table is encoded using a non-attention LSTM, and the final hidden state is used as the initial hidden state for the next LSTM. AL-SQUARES: Attention mechanism is introduced into the LSTM.

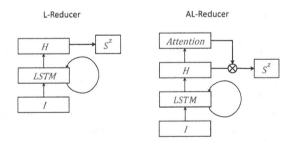

Fig. 5. Network structure of the reducer.

3.4 LSTM

The general RNN networks are prone to information loss. Therefore, we employ a variant of RNN called LSTM (Long Short-Term Memory) network, which modifies the processing layers within the recurrent neural network module by introducing the concept of gates. LSTM is composed of a series of LSTM units. Each LSTM unit consists of three main components: the forget gate, the input gate (update gate), and the output gate. And calculate the state according to the following formula:

$$f_t = sig\left(W_f \cdot [h_{t-1}, x_t] + b_f\right) \tag{1}$$

$$i_t = sig\left(W_i \cdot [h_{t-1}, x_t] + b_i\right) \tag{2}$$

$$\tilde{C}_t = tan\left(W_C \cdot [h_{t-1}, x_t] + b_C\right) \tag{3}$$

$$C_t = f_t \cdot C_{t-1} + i_t \cdot \tilde{C}_{t-1} \tag{4}$$

$$o_t = sig\left(W_o \cdot [h_{t-1}, x_t] + b_o\right) \tag{5}$$

$$h_t = o_t \cdot tan\left(C_t\right) v \tag{6}$$

where C_t represents the long-term state value of the cell, f_t is forget gate, responsible for controlling the information to discard or retain, i_t is input gate, responsible for controlling the flow of input information, o_t is output gate, responsible for determining whether the feature information in the long-term state should be outputted; after the cell state is updated, $\tilde{C}_t$ becomes the current input unit state, each hidden layer is influenced by the previous layer h_{t-1} and the current input x_t; W_f, W_i, W_C, W_o, denotes the weight matrices for the forget gate, input gate, current input unit state, and output gate; b_f, b_i, b_C, b_o, represents the bias terms for the forget gate, input gate, current input unit, and output gate.

3.5 Attention

The attention mechanism is a computational model inspired by the human visual attention mechanism in neuroscience. Its essence lies in shifting focus from the entire input to the relevant parts. Given a specific target, the attention mechanism generates weight coefficients to weigh and sum the inputs, identifying which features are important and which are irrelevant to the target, thereby enhancing the expressive power of the model.

Another approach we explored for the simplification module is the incorporation of attention mechanism into LSTM to enhance the output. The attention layer transforms the LSTM output into attention scores through linear transformation. Based on the significance of each hidden state, the attention mechanism utilizes the softmax function to convert the attention scores into attention weights. The formula commonly used with the softmax function to compute a normalized probability distribution for output is as follows:

$$softmax\left(x_i\right) = \frac{e^{x_i}}{\sum_{j=1}^{n} e^{x_j}} \tag{7}$$

where is the i-th element of the input vector, n is the length of the vector. The function Softmax converts each element of the vector into a probability value, distributed between 0 and 1, such that the sum of these elements is equal to 1.

4 Experiments

4.1 Preparation

To enhance the persuasiveness of our testing, we collected multiple test sets, including 36 instances extracted from database textbooks, 55 instances used in SQUARES, 108 instances collected from various websites and online forums, and 3690 instances generated from Spider. In total, we curated approximately 4000 instances, denoted as "Textbook", "Website", "55-Tests", and "Spider". Since these datasets were obtained through our collection process, we consider them to be more representative, leading to more accurate experimental results. To improve efficiency, we set a time limit of 10 min for each experiment, considering synthesis failure if the time exceeds 3600 s. Each experiment was repeated multiple times, and only the best result was retained.

4.2 The Parameter N

In the system, we acknowledge that the deletion of N production rules has a significant impact on system performance. This raises some questions regarding the value of N: How many production rules should be deleted to achieve optimal synthesis results? If a small number of production rules are removed, it may not yield significant improvements over the baseline system and fail to achieve optimal synthesis. On the other hand, removing an excessive number of production rules can lead to more severe consequences, such as the deletion of critical production rules, resulting in the inability to synthesize programs that could be synthesized by the baseline model. This would contradict the original intention of our research. Therefore, we conducted experiments on the removal of N production rules separately for the L-SQUARES system, which incorporates a basic LSTM module, and the AL-SQUARES system, which incorporates an LSTM module with attention, We denote them as L-SQUARES-N and AL-SQUARES-N, respectively. The figures below shows the final experimental comparison results in the 55-tests test set.

From Figs. 6(a–b) and 7(a–b), it can be observed that when N takes values from the set 1, 2, 3, 4, the deletion of a certain number of production rules has an impact on the synthesis results. The synthesis results of L-SQUARES and AL-SQUARES exhibit minor differences in the experiments. However, as the number of deleted production rules increasesm, the success rate of synthesis gradually improves. From Fig. 6(c–d) and Fig. 7(c–d), both models compare the synthesis results for N = 4, 5, and 6. We can observe that the synthesis results for N = 4 are significantly better than those for N = 5 and 6. This indicates that beyond a certain critical point, increasing the value of N has a diminishing impact on

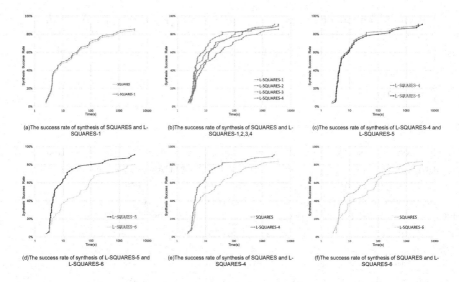

Fig. 6. Comparison graph of synthesis results for L-SQUARES-N with different values of N.

the synthesis results. The critical parameter value, in this case, is determined to be 4. At the same time we can find, it is evident that when N is set to 6, both curves lie below the curve of SQUARES. This indicates that excessive deletion of production rules does not improve search efficiency but rather significantly reduces the success rate of synthesis results. However, it is apparent from the figures that when N falls within a suitable range, both models show significant improvements over the baseline model.

Furthermore, the comparison in Figs. 6(f) and 7(f) reveals the negative impact of excessive rule deletion, as the experimental results fall behind the baseline model. This highlights the adverse effects of excessive deletion, including the removal of crucial production rules, which render the system unable to synthesize meaningful program statements from the remaining rules, ultimately leading to synthesis failure. Finally, in Figs. 6(e) and 7(e), we compare the models after deleting four production rules with the baseline model. Both the L-SQUARES and AL-SQUARES models show respective improvements of 8% and 11%.

We attribute the improvement in accuracy to several reasons. Firstly, we effectively incorporate the powerful attention mechanism into the model, leading to significant performance enhancements. Secondly, the use of a domain-specific language (DSL) proves to be more expressive in this context. DSL offers a natural, concise, and easy-to-understand approach when addressing tasks within a specific domain.

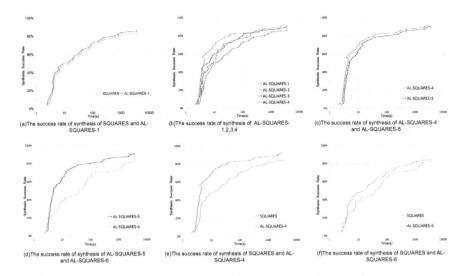

Fig. 7. Comparison graph of synthesis results for AL-SQUARES-N with different values of N.

4.3 Speedup Results

In Table 1, five different test sets are presented, along with the results obtained from experiments conducted at two different observation times, considering varying numbers of input-output examples.

Table 1. Ablation study results for 10 s and 10 min grouped by benchmark.

Data Set	Textbook	55-Tests	Website	Spiser	All
10 s					
SQUARES	27.8%	34.5%	4.6%	24.7%	23.6%
L-SQUARES	51.3%	65.5%	40.7%	71.5%	69.8%
AL-SQUARES	53%	69.1%	41.4%	73.0%	72.3%
10 min					
SQUARES	38.9%	80.9%	15.6%	31.0%	32.2%
L-SQUARES	73.4%	90.1%	56.8%	87.6%	87.9%
AL-SQUARES	76.2%	91.6%	70.7%	89.6%	88.7%

Table 1 illustrates the percentage of instances that each synthesizer can solve within two different time ranges. Regardless of the 10-s and 10-min intervals and across all five test sets, it is evident that AL-SQUARES outperforms the other synthesizers in terms of the number of instances resolved. Within the 10-s time limit, AL-SQUARES exhibits varying degrees of improvement compared to the baseline system and L-SQUARES. Notably, the increase is more substantial compared to SQUARES, with an average improvement ranging from approximately 25% to 39%. In contrast, the improvement over L-SQUARES is only around 2% to 3.5%. Examining the results within the ten-minute time limit, it is apparent from the table that all three models collectively resolve a greater number of instances compared to the 10-s time limit. This can be attributed, in part, to the time required for language interpretation and execution environment initialization.

The following figure depicts a time comparison between AL-SQUARES and SQUARES for a sample of 90 extracted instances:

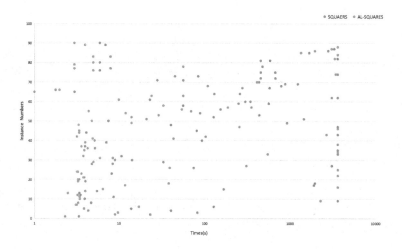

Fig. 8. The synthesis results for L-SQUARES-N and AL-SQUARES-N systems with N = 1, 2, ..., 6.

In Fig. 8, the y-axis represents the sample number, while the x-axis represents time. Simultaneously, we observe that the data points representing AL-SQUARES are more concentrated on the left side, indicating shorter synthesis times. This implies that AL-SQUARES requires less time to solve instances compared to SQUARES, where some instances take up to 1 min. Therefore, AL-SQUARES is significantly more efficient than SQUARES.

5 Discussion

In this paper, a reducer is proposed to decrease the space complexity during program synthesis. By incorporating the reducer into SQUARES, the optimal success rate for instance programming tasks reached 91.6%. This represents a performance improvement of 10.7% compared to the original SQUARES system. In this paper, we provide a detailed explanation of the added reducer structure and the training process. The trained neural network is capable of predicting the production rules for synthesizing target program statements, employing a strategy that eliminates the least N significant bits during prediction. The final AL-SQUARES system determines that optimal performance is achieved by removing four specific production rules. By eliminating low-relevance synthesis productions, the system reduces the space complexity during queries, decreases the generation and verification of irrelevant programs, and improves synthesis efficiency.

References

1. Le, H., Wang, Y., Gotmare, A.D., Savarese, S., Hoi, S.C.H.: CodeRL: mastering code generation through pretrained models and deep reinforcement learning. In: Advances in Neural Information Processing Systems, vol. 35, pp. 21314–21328 (2022)
2. Balog, M., Gaunt, A.L., Brockschmidt, M., Nowozin, S., Tarlow, D.: DeepCoder: learning to write programs. In: 5th International Conference on Learning Representations, ICLR 2017, Toulon, France, 24–26 April 2017, Conference Track Proceedings. OpenReview.net (2017)
3. Zhou, F.S., Wang, L.Z., Li, X.D.: Automatic defect repair and validation approach for C/C++ programs. J. Softw. **30**(5), 1243–1255 (2019)
4. Zhou, P., Wu, Y.J., Zhao, C.: Hybrid programming system of differentiable abstract machines. J. Softw. **30**(5), 1224–1242 (2019)
5. Tao, C.Q., Bao, P.P., Huang, Z.Q., Zhou, Y., Zhang, Z.Y.: Code line recommendation based on deep context-awareness of onsite programming. J. Softw. **32**(11), 3351–3371 (2020)
6. Xu, H.R., Wang, Y.J., Huang, Z.J., Xie, P.D., Fan, S.H.: Compiler fuzzing test case generation with feed-forward neural network. J. Softw. **33**(6), 1996–2011 (2022)
7. Gu, B., Yu, B., Dong, X.G., Li, X.F., Zhong, R.M., Yang, M.F.: Intelligent program synthesis techniques: literature review. J. Softw. **32**(5), 1373–1384 (2020)
8. Reed, S., De Freitas, N.: Neural programmer-interpreters. arXiv preprint arXiv:1511.06279 (2015)
9. Shrivastava, D., Larochelle, H., Tarlow, D.: Learning to combine per-example solutions for neural program synthesis. In: Advances in Neural Information Processing Systems, vol. 34, pp. 6102–6114 (2021)
10. Guo, Z., et al.: Program synthesis by type-guided abstraction refinement. In: Proceedings of the ACM on Programming Languages, vol. 4, no. POPL, pp. 1–28 (2019)
11. Gulwani, S., Marron, M.: NLyze: interactive programming by natural language for spreadsheet data analysis and manipulation. In: Proceedings of the 2014 ACM SIGMOD International Conference on Management of Data, pp. 803–814 (2014)
12. Menon, A.K., Tamuz, O., Gulwani, S., Lampson, B.W., Kalai, A.: A machine learning framework for programming by example. In: Proceedings of the 30th International Conference on Machine Learning, ICML 2013, Atlanta, GA, USA, 16–21 June 2013, volume 28 of JMLR Workshop and Conference Proceedings, pp. 187–195. JMLR.org (2013)
13. Cambronero, J., et al.: FlashFill++: scaling programming by example by cutting to the chase. In: Proceedings of the ACM on Programming Languages, vol. 7, no. POPL, pp. 952–981 (2023)
14. Tran, Q.T., Chan, C.-Y., Parthasarathy, S.: Query by output. In: Proceedings of the 2009 ACM SIGMOD International Conference on Management of Data, pp. 535–548 (2009)

15. Tran, Q.T., Chan, C.-Y., Parthasarathy, S.: Query reverse engineering. VLDB J. **23**(5), 721–746 (2014)
16. Li, H., Chan, C.-Y., Maier, D.: Query from examples: an iterative, data-driven approach to query construction. Proc. VLDB Endow. **8**(13), 2158–2169 (2015)
17. Zhang, S., Sun, Y.: Automatically synthesizing SQL queries from input-output examples. In: 2013 28th IEEE/ACM International Conference on Automated Software Engineering (ASE), pp. 224–234. IEEE (2013)
18. Wang, C., Cheung, A., Bodik, R.: Interactive query synthesis from input-output examples. In: Proceedings of the 2017 ACM International Conference on Management of Data, pp. 1631–1634 (2017)
19. Wang, C., Cheung, A., Bodik, R.: Synthesizing highly expressive SQL queries from input-output examples. In: Proceedings of the 38th ACM SIGPLAN Conference on Programming Language Design and Implementation, pp. 452–466 (2017)
20. Tan, W.C., Zhang, M., Elmeleegy, H., Srivastava, D.: Reverse engineering aggregation queries. Proc. VLDB Endow. **10**(11), 1394–1405 (2017)
21. Tan, W.C., Zhang, M., Elmeleegy, H., Srivastava, D.: REGAL+ reverse engineering SPJA queries. Proc. VLDB Endow. **11**(12), 1982–1985 (2018)
22. Khurana, K., Haritsa, J.R.: UNMASQUE: a hidden SQL query extractor. Proc. VLDB Endow. **13**(12), 2809–2812 (2020)
23. Rehman, M.S., Huang, S., Elmore, A.J.: A demonstration of relic: a system for retrospective lineage inference of data workflows. Proc. VLDB Endow. **14**(12), 2795–2798 (2021)
24. Qin, X., et al.: Interactively discovering and ranking desired tuples by data exploration. VLDB J. **31**(4), 753–777 (2022)
25. Martins, R., Chen, J., Chen, Y., Feng, Y., Dillig, I.: Trinity: an extensible synthesis framework for data science. Proc. VLDB Endow. **12**(12), 1914–1917 (2019)
26. Feng, Y., Martins, R., Van Geffen, J., Dillig, I., Chaudhuri, S.: Component-based synthesis of table consolidation and transformation tasks from examples. In: Cohen, A., Vechev, M.T. (eds.) Proceedings of the 38th ACM SIGPLAN Conference on Programming Language Design and Implementation, PLDI 2017, Barcelona, Spain, 18–23 June 2017, pp. 422–436. ACM (2017)

Query Reverse Engineering of Pre-deleted Uncorrelated Operators

Quansheng Dou[1,3](✉)(ID), Huixian Wang[2](ID), Huanling Tang[3](ID), Hao Pan[2](ID), and Shun Zhang[3](ID)

[1] School of Computer Science and Technology, Kashi University, 29 Xueyuan Road, Kashi 844006, Xinjiang, China
douqsh@sdtbu.edu.cn
[2] School of Information and Electronic Engineering, Shandong Technology and Business University, P191 Binhai Middle Road, Yantai 264005, Shandong, China
[3] College of Computer Science and Technology, Shandong Technology and Business University, P191 Binhai Middle Road, Yantai 264005, Shandong, China

Abstract. Recent years have seen an increasing reliance on data processing to accomplish work tasks. However, many users do not have the programming background to write complex programs, especially query statements. Query Reverse Engineering solves the problem of deriving query statements from the database and the desired output table in reverse. SQUARES, which is based on Domain-Specific Languages (DSL), is one of the most advanced models in this field. However, the existence of uncorrelated DSL operators constrains the synthesis efficiency. This paper proposes PdQRE based on SQUARES, which improves efficiency by predicting whether DSL operators are correlated with the query statement and pre-deleting uncorrelated operators. On the *test-55* dataset, the synthesis rate of PdQRE improved from 80.0% to 89.1%, and the average synthesis time was reduced from 251 s to 127 s compared to SQUARES. Comparison with Scythe et al. in the *Recent posts* dataset shows that PdQRE outperforms other models in *Query Synthesis*.

Keywords: Query Reverse Engineering · Query Synthesis · Programming By Example · Machine Learning · Program Synthesis

1 Introduction

In the era of big data, research has turned to *Query Synthesis* to address the lack of database query statement writing skills among data analysts. Two approaches that have been widely studied in *Query Synthesis* include input-output example-based [1,2,6,8–10,12,13,15,16,19] and natural language description-based [5,14,17]. *Query Synthesis* based on input-output examples is also known as *Query Reverse Engineering* (QRE).

In recent years, a number of models have been proposed in the field of QRE. TALOS [12] treats *Query Synthesis* as a dataset partitioning task, dividing the input dataset based on the values of data attributes. It forms a decision tree, mapping the root node of the tree to the database and the leaf nodes to the desired output table. By traversing the path from the root node to the leaf nodes, the corresponding query conditions can be obtained to generate query statements that meet expectations. In 2014, the team improved TALOS [13] by dividing the examples into positive and negative tuples. By reducing the number of positive tuples, it overcomes the excessive constraints in dividing the dataset and improves the efficiency of *Query Synthesis*.

Scythe [15,16] developed an abstract query language in which abstract queries are syntactically similar to SQL queries, except that filter predicates are replaced with holes that can be instantiated with any valid predicate. Since operators in abstract queries are no longer parameterized by predicates, the search space for abstract queries is significantly reduced.

Cubes [1] enhances the efficiency of *Query Synthesis* through the utilization of a parallel architecture and a divide-and-conquer approach. By introducing new pruning techniques and an interactive disambiguation process, Cubes can generate queries that are not only more accurate but also more diverse.

Neo [3] proposes a new conflict-driven program synthesis technique capable of learning from past mistakes. Trinity [7] has enhanced Neo in several ways. Firstly, it provides users with finer control by allowing preference predicates for guided searches. Secondly, Trinity's search engine incorporates a MaxSMT solver for optimal user preference satisfaction. Lastly, building new synthesizers on Trinity is much easier than on Neo.

Trinity uses a tree-based encoding to search for programs. As the number of operators in a program increases, the number of nodes used by Trinity's encoding grows exponentially. This situation leads to an explosive growth of the search space. To address this problem, SQUARE proposes a line-based encoding derived from Trinity. Compared to tree-based encoding, line-based encoding is more efficient in searching for query statements.

However, due to the large program space, the synthesis efficiency of SQUARES in existing test problems is still low, and there is still room for improvement. The PdQRE proposed in this paper incorporates a machine learning-based predictor into SQUARES. The predictor predicts whether each DSL operator is correlated with the query statement and improves synthesis efficiency by pre-deleting uncorrelated DSL operators.

The contributions of this paper are summarized as follows:

- An encoding method for the QRE task is proposed, enabling the prediction of which DSL operators are correlated with the query statement.
- Introduces a new Query Reverse Engineering model that enhances *Query Synthesis* performance by predicting the correlation between DSL operators and the query statement, and pre-deleting uncorrelated operators.
- We experimentally evaluate the effectiveness of PdQRE. Specifically, we compare PdQRE with other models to demonstrate its performance in *Query Synthesis*.

2   Background Knowledge

2.1   Query Reverse Engineering

Query Reverse Engineering refers to the process of inferring an unknown query statement (referred to as Q) from a given pair $<D, Q(D)>$. Here, D represents a database comprising multiple tables, and $Q(D)$ represents the desired output table obtained by executing Q on the database D.

An instance of a QRE task is illustrated as follow.

Table 1. Students

Sno	Sname	Ssex
01	John	Male
02	Tom	Male
03	Elaine	Male
04	Rose	Male
05	Fay	Female

Table 2. SC

Sno	Cno	Grade
01	001	5
01	002	4
02	001	3
02	002	3
04	001	2

Table 3. Desired output

Sno	Sname	Grade
01	John	5
01	John	4

There are two data tables in the database: Students and SC, as depicted in Table 1 and 2 respectively. Table 3 displays the desired output table. The QRE task, utilizing the provided database and the desired output table as input, will produce the query statement as shown in Fig. 1.

```
SELECT 'Sno', 'Sname', 'Grade'
FROM 'input0' AS 'TBL_LEFT'
INNER JOIN (
      SELECT *
      FROM 'input1'
      WHERE 'Grade' > 3.0
) AS 'TBL_RIGHT' ON
'TBL_LEFT'.'Sno' = 'TBL_RIGHT'.'Sno';
```

Fig. 1. Query statement

SQUARES uses not only the primary parameters D and $Q(D)$ but also offers the flexibility for users to optionally furnish Additional information ($Add-Info$). This supplementary information may encompass constants, aggregate functions, attributes, and enumeration rounds necessary for the query. The inclusion of $Add-Info$ serves to diminish the enumeration space and enhance the efficiency of synthesis.

Due to the intricate syntax rules of query statements, many QRE models employ predefined Domain-Specific Languages (DSL) to transform *Query Synthesis* problems into program synthesis problems.

2.2   Domain-Specific Languages

Domain-Specific Languages are defined as binary groups represented by the tuple (G, Ops), where G is a context-independent grammar, and Ops refers to the semantics of DSL operators.

table$\rightarrow$ $input^0$|inner_join($table,table$)[1]|inner_join3($table,table,table$) [2]|inner_join4($table,table,table,table$) [3]
    |left_join($table,table$) [4] |anti_join($table,table$) [5] |bind_rows($table,table$) [6]
    |filter($table,filterCondition$) [7]|filters($table,filterCondition,filterCondition,op$) [8]
    |summariseGrouped($table,summmariseCondition,Cols$) [9]|intersect($table,selectCols,distinct$) [10]
tableselect$\rightarrow$select($table,selectCols,distinct$) [11]
op$\rightarrow$ Or|And
distinct$\rightarrow$rue|false
empty$\rightarrow$empty

Fig. 2. Grammar defined by Domain-Specific Language

The DSL used by SQUARES is shown in Fig. 2. The number in the upper right corner of the DSL operators indicates its identifier index. These operators include join operators ($inner\_join$, $inner\_join3$, and $inner\_join4$), which merge tables based on shared columns. Additionally, there is an anti-join operator, $anti\_join$, which retrieve rows from the first table that have no matching rows in the second table. The row-bind operator $bind\_rows$ is used to combine two tables with the same column structure by appending rows. The operator $intersect$ is employed to obtain a new table that contains common rows from two tables. $filter$ and $filters$ are utilized to exclude rows that do not meet specific conditions. $summariseGrouped$ is applied to group tables by grouped columns and apply summary conditions to each group. The select operator $select$ retrieves the corresponding column from the data table, with an optional parameter $distinct$ to eliminate duplicates. The $table$ can be generated as a composite result of multiple operators. The terminal symbols of the grammar, such as $filterCondition$, $selectCols$, $Cols$, and $summariseCondition$, are dynamically computed based on the input and output examples provided by the user. DSL programs can be indirectly translated into query statements. For example, a DSL program might look like this:

$select(summariseGrouped(input,meanage=mean(age),level),level,meanage)$

The corresponding query statement is as follows:

SELECT $level$, AVG(age) AS $meanage$ FROM $input$ GROUP BY $level$

Enumeration-Based Program Synthesis is one of the various methods used in program synthesis, and SQUARES falls under this category. Here, we present an introduction to it.

2.3   Enumeration-Based Program Synthesis

Enumeration-Based Program Synthesis is a method of program synthesis in which an enumerative search is performed over the space of programs that satisfy the specification. It involves generating and checking all possible programs within a defined search space, using a set of library components or Domain-Specific Languages. The process consists of an Enumerator that generates programs and a Verifier that checks if they meet the specification, often specified through input-output examples. Recent approaches combine enumerative search with derivation to prune infeasible programs early [4] or to learn from failed candidates and prune inconsistent equivalents [3].

The program space and the number of constraints of SQUARES are related to the number of DSL operators. Use $Prod(D)$ and $Term(D)$ to denote the sets of operators and terminal symbols in the DSL, respectively. Let IN denote the set of symbols provided by the user as input, n denote the number of enumeration rounds, k denote the maximum number of operator parameters, and $|\cdot|$ denote the number of elements in a set. In the worst case, the number of constraints used by SQUARES [9] increases quadratically with the number of operators, as follows:

$$O(n \times k \times |Prod(D)| \times (|Term(D)| + n) + |IN|) \tag{1}$$

The size of the program space is:

$$O(|Prod|^n) \tag{2}$$

For a given instance of QRE, it is notable that not all operators (1–10) exhibit correlation with the query statement. The deductions drawn from Eq. 1 and 2 establish that the inclusion of uncorrelated operators results in an augmented set of constraints and an expanded program space, consequently impeding the efficiency of query synthesis. This arises from the enhanced intricacy introduced by the additional constraints and expanded program space, contributing to a less efficient synthesis process.

3   PdQRE

In order to mitigate the challenge posed by the presence of uncorrelated operators, which diminishes the efficiency of synthesis, we introduce PdQRE, a model founded on SQUARES. PdQRE employs a collection of GBDT-LR (Gradient Boosted Decision Tree-Logistic Regression) classifiers to ascertain the correlation between each operator and the query statement, facilitating the pre-deletion of uncorrelated operators. This procedural step serves to diminish the program space, thereby enhancing the efficiency of the synthesis process. Compared to neural network-based prediction models, GBDT-LR requires relatively little data and is relatively fast to train.

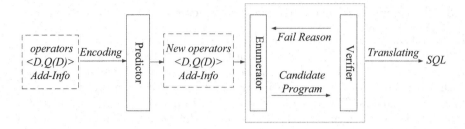

Fig. 3. The structure plot of PdQRE, the model consists of three parts: Predictor, Enumerator and Verifier.

3.1 Structure of PdQRE

The structure of PdQRE is shown in Fig. 3. PdQRE consists of three parts: Predictor, Enumerator, and Verifier.

The input to the Predictor is encoded from the database, desired output table, and Additional information. The Predictor's output indicates whether each operator is correlated with the query statement, and uncorrelated operators are pre-deleted.

The Enumerator is used to enumerate candidate programs based on constraints and operators with the help of an SMT solver.

The Verifier checks that each enumerated candidate DSL program satisfies $<D, Q(D)>$. As long as the program satisfies the example, the synthesis process can be terminated, and the DSL program will be indirectly translated into a query statement.

3.2 Encoding of Data

Encoding Rules. To predict the correlation operators, $<D, Q(D)>$ and $Add-Info$ are encoded as a vector X_{iv} of length 50, with each element of X_{iv} being of numeric type. X_{iv} consists of three main parts: table structure information, table contents information, and Additional information, encoded as follows:

Table structure information (14 items): Number of input tables in D, Number of columns in the input tables, Number of distinct columns in the input tables, Number of columns in the output table that are in the input tables, etc.

Table contents information (20 items): Number of input tables in which the output data appears, Number of columns in which duplicate data exists in the output table, Number of columns in which duplicate data does not exist in the output table, Whether there are columns in the output table whose output order is different from that of the input table (True is 1, False is 0), etc.

Additional information (16 items): Number of constants, Number of attributes, Number of aggregate functions, etc. Since Additional information is optionally provided by the user, relevant items that are not provided by the user will be encoded as -1.

Table 4. Class

C_name	F_key
class1	f1
class2	f2
class3	f3
class4	f4
class5	f4

Table 5. Enroll

S_key	S_name	level
S1	stu1	JR
S2	stu2	SR
S3	stu3	JR
S4	stu4	SR
S5	stu5	JR
S6	stu6	SR
S7	stu7	JR
S8	stu8	SR

Table 6. Faculty

F_key	F_name
f1	faculty1
f2	faculty2
f3	faculty3
f4	faculty4

Table 7. Student

Sno	S_name
S1	class1
S2	class1
S3	class2
S3	class5
S4	class2
S4	class4
S5	class3
S6	class3
S6	class2
S7	class5
S8	class4

Table 8. $Add-Info$

const:	"faculty1", "JR"
aggrs:	
attrs:	"F_name", "level"
bools:	"=="
loc:	2

Table 9. Desired output

S_name
stu1
stu2

Table 4, 5, 6, 7, 8 and 9 shows a QRE instance that will be encoded as X_{iv}, X_{iv} = [4, 9, 6, 2, 0, 0, 0, 1, 0, 1, 9, 0, 1, 0, 2, 4, 5, 8, 11, 2, 2, 3, 2, 1, 0, 0, 0, 1, 0, 1, 0, 0, 0, 0, 2, 2, 2, 0, 0, 0, 0, 0, 1, 1, 0, 0, 0, 0, 0, 1].

Since the length of X_{iv} is 50, only some items are selected for illustration here. In the instance shown above, the database contains four tables, so $X_{iv}[0] = 4$. The input tables of the database contain a total of nine columns, thus $X_{iv}[1] = 9$. The data for the output table comes from a single input table, therefore, $X_{iv}[27] = 1$. Additionally, the Additional information shows that the query uses two constants, so $X_{iv}[34] = 2$.

Correlation of X_{iv} and Operators. There is some connection between X_{iv} and operators that are correlated with the query statement. For example:

If the number of tables in D is less than 3, and the output table has no columns calculated by the aggregation function, then it can be initially determined that the operators $inner\_join3$ and $inner\_join4$ have a low probability of being correlated with the query. Second, if a column in the output table exists in multiple input tables, and the data for that column comes from a single input

table, the operator *anti_join* may be correlated with the query. Finally, if the *Add−Info* contains an aggregation function, it can be inferred that the operator *summariseGrouped* is correlated with the query statement.

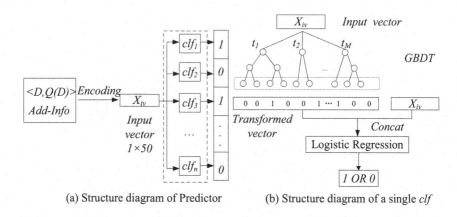

(a) Structure diagram of Predictor   (b) Structure diagram of a single *clf*

Fig. 4. Structure diagram of Predictor and *clf*.

3.3   Structure of Predictor

Figure 4(a) illustrates the structure of the predictor. It consists of n independent and identically structured binary classifiers $\{clf_1, clf_2, \ldots, clf_n\}$, where n is the number of DSL operators. Each clf_i takes X_{iv} as input and outputs 0 or 1, indicating whether the i-th operator is correlated with the query statement.

A single classifier, denoted as clf, is structured as shown in Fig. 4(b). The clf combines Gradient Boosting Decision Trees (GBDT) and Logistic Regression (LR). GBDT is employed as a feature preprocessing step to understand how features are represented and combined. This is achieved by training M decision tree models. Specifically, GBDT takes X_{iv} as input and undergoes multiple rounds of training. In each round, it learns a new decision tree model by fitting the prediction residuals of the previous models.

GBDT generates individual trees from the root node to the leaf nodes, where each tree corresponds to a specific combination of features present in the sample data. The leaf nodes of each tree can be interpreted as dimensions, and their positions after processing the sample data are recorded and one-hot coded, resulting in a transformed vector.

To create a new vector for training the LR model, concatenate the transformed vector with the original X_{iv}. The LR model then predicts whether each operator is correlated with the query statement.

3.4   Generation of Dataset

The training set consists of: $<D, Q(D)>$, $Add−Info$, and corresponding ground truth vectors $Y[y_1, y_2, \ldots, y_n]$. D is selected randomly from the literature [6,11,18], based on the associated schema subgraphs. We generate a random query statement Q using the DSL operators and execute the query on D to obtain a diverse output table $Q(D)$. Additional information such as the aggregation function used by the query is known for the construction of $Add-Info$. We randomly supplement Additional information and employ the [UNS] keyword to indicate the presence of additional items not provided. Each Q has a corresponding label vector $Y[y_1, y_2, ..., y_n]$, which represents the correlation with each DSL operator. The value of y_i is 1 if the query statement is correlated with the i operator and 0 otherwise. y_i will be used for training clf_i.

To avoid data leakage, instances with the same query statements as those in the test set are excluded from the training set. The entire process is repeated, resulting in a total of 30,000 samples in the training set.

3.5   Training of Predictor

Each clf consists of two parts, GBDT and LR, and the training process of both is described here.

Training of GBDT. For a given dataset $T = \{(x_1, y_1), (x_2, y_2), \ldots, (x_N, y_N)\}$ where $x_i \in X$ and $y_i \in Y$, the loss function is $L(y, f(x))$.

Initialization of the classifier:

$$f_0(x) = \arg\min_c \sum_{i=1}^{N} L(y_i, c) \tag{3}$$

Iteratively train $m = 1, 2, \ldots, M$ decision trees:

(a) For each instance $i = 1, 2, \ldots, N$, calculate the negative gradient, i.e., the residual:

$$r_{mi} = - \left[\frac{\partial L(y_i, f(x_i))}{\partial f(x_i)} \right]_{f(x) = f_{i-1}(x)} \tag{4}$$

(b) Train a decision tree to fit to r_{mi}, obtaining the leaf node region $R_{mj}, j = 1, 2, \ldots, J$ of the mth tree.

(c) For $j = 1, 2, \ldots, J$, compute

$$c_{mj} = \arg\min_c \sum_{x_i \in R_{mj}} L(y_i, f_{m-1}(x_i) + c) \tag{5}$$

(d) Update strong classifiers:

$$f_m(x) = f_{m-1}(x) + \rho \sum_{j=1}^{J} c_{mj} I(x \in R_{mj}) \tag{6}$$

ρ is a regularization term to prevent overfitting, with $0 < \rho < 1$. When $x \in R_{mj}$, $I = 1$. When $x \notin R_{mj}$, $I = 0$.

Get the final strong classifier:

$$\hat{f}(x) = f_0(x) + \sum_{m=1}^{M} \rho \sum_{j=1}^{J} c_{mj} I(x \in R_{mj}) \tag{7}$$

Training of LR. $\theta_1, \theta_2, \ldots, \theta_n$ are the parameters of the LR model, which need to be learned through training; $f_1, f_2, \ldots, f_n$ are the features of the instance.

The Logistic Regression layer is:

$$\hat{y} = sigmoid(\theta_0 + \theta_1 f_1 + \theta_2 f_2 + \ldots + \theta_n f_n) \tag{8}$$

N represents the number of instances in the training set, where y_i denotes the ground truth of the i-th instance. The loss function is defined as:

$$J(\theta) = -\sum_{i=1}^{N}(y_i \log(\hat{y}_i) + (1 - y_i) \log(1 - \hat{y}_i)) \tag{9}$$

Adjust parameters θ by minimizing the loss function using the gradient descent method to better fit the training data.

4 Experiments and Comparisons

4.1 Selection of Hyperparameter λ

Not pre-deleting enough operators before synthesis does not maximize speed. On the other hand, pre-deleting too many operators can result in the removal of correlated operators, potentially leading to synthesis failure or an increase in the number of enumeration rounds, consequently reducing synthesis efficiency.

To balance synthesis efficiency and synthesis rate, the threshold (λ) of LR classifiers is utilized as a hyperparameter to pre-delete operators with a predictive probability lower than λ, denoted as PdQRE-λ. The determination of the hyperparameter λ was conducted using the *test-55* dataset.

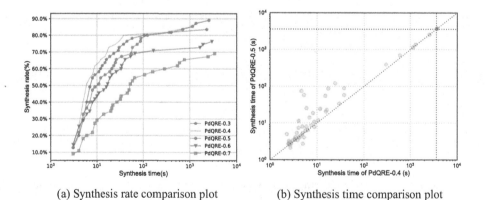

(a) Synthesis rate comparison plot   (b) Synthesis time comparison plot

Fig. 5. (a) Comparison of the synthesis rate between PdQRE-λ for different values of λ, with the x-axis representing the synthesis time and the y-axis representing the synthesis rate. (b) Comparison of synthesis time for PdQRE-0.4 and PdQRE-0.5.

Figure 5(a) shows the variation curves of the synthesis rate for each model over 3600 s at different λ values. When λ is set to 0.3, the synthesis rate is higher than 80% of the baseline. When λ is set to 0.4 and 0.5, the synthesis rate is further increased and reaches the highest value. This suggests that pre-deleting operators with less correlation can greatly improve the synthesis rate. However, when λ is further increased to 0.6 and 0.7, the synthesis rate starts to decrease. Specific example analysis shows that when λ is set to 0.6 and 0.7, some of the operators correlated with the query are pre-deleted, resulting in a lower synthesis rate.

Figure 5(b) shows the scatterplot of the synthesis time of PdQRE-0.4 and PdQRE-0.5. The x-axis represents the synthesis time of PdQRE-0.4, the y-axis represents the synthesis time of PdQRE-0.5, and most of the data points are located above the diagonal, which indicates that the synthesis efficiency of PdQRE-0.4 is better than that of PdQRE-0.5.

The results of Fig. 5 can be summarized as follows: the synthesis performance of PdQRE-λ is best when the hyperparameter λ is set to 0.4, and all the PdQRE mentioned below are PdQRE-0.4.

4.2   Comparison of PdQRE and SQUARES

The PdQRE and SQUARES were evaluated using the $test - 55$ dataset with a time limit of 3600 s to compare their synthesis rate and synthesis efficiency.

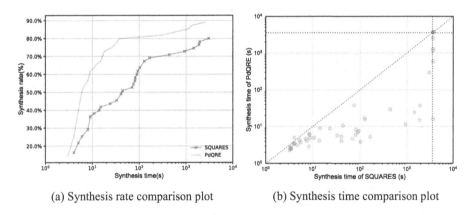

(a) Synthesis rate comparison plot   (b) Synthesis time comparison plot

Fig. 6. (a) Comparison of synthesis rates between PdQRE and SQUARES. The x-axis shows synthesis time, and the y-axis shows synthesis rate. (b) Comparison of synthesis times between PdQRE and SQUARES.

Figure 6(a) shows the variation curves of synthesis rates for PdQRE and SQUARES over 3600 s. As seen from the plot, PdQRE has a higher program synthesis rate compared to SQUARES. Figure 6(b) shows a comparison of the synthesis time between PdQRE and SQUARES, where each point represents an instance. The x-axis represents the synthesis time of SQUARES, and the y-axis represents the synthesis time of PdQRE. Most points fall below the diagonal line, indicating that for most instances, the synthesis time of SQUARES is longer. This shows that the synthesis efficiency of PdQRE is better than that of SQUARES.

Under the same experimental conditions, PdQRE increased the synthesis rate of the *test-55* dataset from 80.0% to 89.1% and reduced the average synthesis time from 251 s to 127 s. These results show that pre-deleting uncorrelated operators improves program synthesis performance.

4.3 Comparison of PdQRE with Other Models

We conducted an empirical examination to assess the performance of PdQRE relative to other models using the *Recent Posts* dataset, focusing on synthesis rate and average synthesis time.

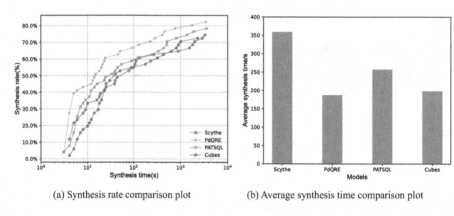

(a) Synthesis rate comparison plot   (b) Average synthesis time comparison plot

Fig. 7. (a) Comparison of synthesis rate between PdQRE with other models, x-axis shows synthesis time, y-axis shows synthesis rate. (b) Comparison of average synthesis time between PdQRE with other models.

Figure 7(a) shows the variation curve of the synthesis rate of PdQRE versus other models over 3600 s, where the x-axis represents the synthesis time and the y-axis the corresponding synthesis rate. It is observed that the curve representing PdQRE is always at the top, which indicates that the synthesis rate of PdQRE is always higher than the other models.

In Fig. 7(b) shows a histogram of the average synthesis time for PdQRE versus the other models. x-axis represents the different models and y-axis represents the respective average synthesis time. As can be seen from the plot, Scythe has the longest average synthesis time, followed by PATSQL, and PdQRE has the shortest average synthesis time.

Table 10. Results of experiments on the *Recent Posts* dataset.

Models	Synthesis rate	Average synthesis time
Scythe	74.5%	359 s
PATSQL	78.4%	257 s
Cubes	72.5%	198 s
PdQRE	82.4%	187 s

The specific experimental data are shown in Table 10. The synthesis rate of PdQRE was the highest, and although the synthesis rate of PATSQL was similar to that of PdQRE, the average synthesis time of PATSQL was much higher than that of PdQRE. Similarly, although the average synthesis time of Cubes was similar to that of PdQRE, the synthesis rate was much lower than that of PdQRE.

Compared with Scythe, PATSQL and Cubes, the synthesis rate of PdQRE is improved by 7.9%, 4.0% and 9.9% respectively, and the average synthesis time is reduced by 172 s, 70 s and 11 s respectively, which also fully proves the effectiveness of PdQRE.

5   Conclusions

Query Reverse Engineering is of great significance in the field of database research. SQUARES is one of the most advanced models in this field, PdQRE predicts correlated DSL operators on the basis of SQUARES and pre-deletes uncorrelated operators according to the prediction results, thus reducing the search space and improve the efficiency of program synthesis. Experimental results on the $test - 55$ dataset show that this approach significantly improves synthesis performance compared to the baseline. Furthermore, experiments on the *Recent Posts* dataset show that the synthesis performance of PdQRE exceeds that of models such as Scythe.

References

1. Brancas, R., Terra-Neves, M., Ventura, M., Manquinho, V., Martins, R.: CUBES: a parallel synthesizer for SQL using examples. arXiv preprint arXiv:2203.04995 (2022)
2. Catalfamo, W., Censuales, S.: Schema query reverse engineering
3. Feng, Y., Martins, R., Bastani, O., Dillig, I.: Program synthesis using conflict-driven learning. ACM SIGPLAN Not. **53**(4), 420–435 (2018)
4. Feng, Y., Martins, R., Van Geffen, J., Dillig, I., Chaudhuri, S.: Component-based synthesis of table consolidation and transformation tasks from examples. ACM SIGPLAN Not. **52**(6), 422–436 (2017)
5. Huang, P.S., Wang, C., Singh, R., Yih, W.T., He, X.: Natural language to structured query generation via meta-learning. arXiv preprint arXiv:1803.02400 (2018)

6. Li, H., Chan, C.Y., Maier, D.: Query from examples: an iterative, data-driven approach to query construction. Proc. VLDB Endow. **8**(13), 2158–2169 (2015)
7. Martins, R., Chen, J., Chen, Y., Feng, Y., Dillig, I.: Trinity: an extensible synthesis framework for data science. Proc. VLDB Endow. **12**(12), 1914–1917 (2019)
8. Meiying, L.: Techniques for efficient query reverse engineering. Ph.D. thesis, National University of Singapore (Singapore) (2022)
9. Orvalho, P., Terra-Neves, M., Ventura, M., Martins, R., Manquinho, V.: SQUARES: a SQL synthesizer using query reverse engineering. Proc. VLDB Endow. **13**(12), 2853–2856 (2020)
10. Takenouchi, K., Ishio, T., Okada, J., Sakata, Y.: PATSQL: efficient synthesis of SQL queries from example tables with quick inference of projected columns. arXiv preprint arXiv:2010.05807 (2020)
11. Tan, W.C., Zhang, M., Elmeleegy, H., Srivastava, D.: Reverse engineering aggregation queries. Proc. VLDB Endow. **10**(11), 1394–1405 (2017)
12. Tran, Q.T., Chan, C.Y., Parthasarathy, S.: Query by output. In: Proceedings of the 2009 ACM SIGMOD International Conference on Management of Data, pp. 535–548 (2009)
13. Tran, Q.T., Chan, C.Y., Parthasarathy, S.: Query reverse engineering. VLDB J. **23**(5), 721–746 (2014)
14. Wang, B., Shin, R., Liu, X., Polozov, O., Richardson, M.: RAT-SQL: relation-aware schema encoding and linking for text-to-SQL parsers. arXiv preprint arXiv:1911.04942 (2019)
15. Wang, C., Cheung, A., Bodik, R.: Interactive query synthesis from input-output examples. In: Proceedings of the 2017 ACM International Conference on Management of Data, pp. 1631–1634 (2017)
16. Wang, C., Cheung, A., Bodik, R.: Synthesizing highly expressive SQL queries from input-output examples. In: Proceedings of the 38th ACM SIGPLAN Conference on Programming Language Design and Implementation, pp. 452–466 (2017)
17. Yu, T., et al.: SyntaxSQLNet: syntax tree networks for complex and cross-domaintext-to-SQL task. arXiv preprint arXiv:1810.05237 (2018)
18. Zhang, S., Sun, Y.: Automatically synthesizing SQL queries from input-output examples. In: 2013 28th IEEE/ACM International Conference on Automated Software Engineering (ASE), pp. 224–234. IEEE (2013)
19. Zloof, M.M.: Query-by-example: the invocation and definition of tables and forms. In: Proceedings of the 1st International Conference on Very Large Data Bases, pp. 1–24 (1975)

No-Reference Quality Assessment for HDR Images Based on Multi-scale Retinex Decomposition

Donghui Wan[1,2] , Yehui Liu[3(✉)], Xiuhua Jiang[1], Hongtao Yang[1,3] , Ling Lei[1], and Jiaxing Liu[4]

[1] Communication University of China, Beijing 100024, China
[2] Huzhou College, Huzhou 313000, China
[3] Beijing Polytechnic College, Beijing 100042, China
lyh@bgy.edu.cn
[4] Beijing Electronic Science and Technology Institute, Beijing 100070, China

Abstract. High dynamic range (HDR) content is increasingly entering our life for super realistic representation of real-word scenes. Compared to low dynamic (LDR) images, HDR images contain significantly higher peak luminance and contrast, making traditional LDR image quality assessment (IQA) metrics inefficient for HDR image applications. Towards developing HDR IQA, we propose a new no-reference metric based on Retinex decomposition. First, multi-scale Retinex decomposition is used to generate luminance and reflectance maps through gaussian filtering. Then, we calculate gradient similarities and natural scene statistics (NSS) from the reflectance and luminance maps, respectively. Finally, all features are fused by support vector regression (SVR) for score prediction. Experimental results on two databases demonstrate the superiority of the proposed method over the other state-of-the-arts for HDR IQA.

Keywords: High Dynamic Range · Image Quality Assessment · No Reference · Retinex Decomposition

1 Introduction

High dynamic range (HDR) images can potently represent real-world scene radiance, ranging from faint starlight to bright sunlight. As a mean to generate more realistic image content, HDR imaging is now widely welcomed by the industry and consumer society with the development of image technology and hardware support. Just like low dynamic range (LDR) images, distortion may occur on HDR content during the processes of image acquisition, compression, and transmission, coming from camera artifacts, coding compression, channel errors and noise, etc. [1–3]. Therefore, an efficient image

This work was supported in part by the Innovation Fund for Chinese Universities-Beichuang Teaching Assistant Project (Phase II) under Grant No. 2021BCE0101; and in part by the Key Program of Beijing Polytechnic College under Grant No. BGY2023KY-16Z.

quality assessment (IQA) metric is critical for either evaluating the viewing experience or optimizing processing algorithms. However, compared with the LDR counterpart, the substantially higher peak luminance and contrast within the HDR image may have different visual impact and pose new challenges for IQA.

The subjective evaluation is recognized as the most accurate approach for IQA by recruiting raters and setting up standard environment. Due to the huge consumption of human resource and time, subjective methods are unpractical to be embedded into real-time applications [4]. Thus, developing objective metrics is an urgent necessity. Objective methods can be classified as three categories i.e., full-reference (FR), reduced-reference (RR), and no-reference (NR). FR methods need access full content of reference images, NR methods make prediction just from test images without any access of reference information, and RR methods need limited access to reference images. Among the three types of objective methods, the task of NR is apparently most challenging.

Rich achievements of technologies on LDR image quality assessment have been obtained in recent decades [5–9]. However, these technologies aim for evaluating gamma-coded LDR images, different from HDR images where pixel values are linear to radiance. Thus, those quality metrics for LDR should not be straightforwardly employed for HDR content. Aydin et al. [10] introduced a perceptually uniform (PU) encoding to convert the linear HDR values into perceptually uniform ones, which can effectively extend two classical LDR quality metrics, such as PSNR and SSIM, to HDR applications. Following such idea, a variety of coding algorithms were proposed to perceptually linearize HDR image values [11]. In addition, HDR visual difference predictor (HDR-VDP) [12, 13] and HDR video quality measure (HDR-VQM) [14] were designed for HDR images and videos, respectively, based on modeling visual processing. Specifically, they model intra-ocular scattering, luminance masking, and photoreceptor response and calculate visual difference between the reference and test images for quality evaluation. Zhang et al. [15] found that subjective scores were not affected by display luminance, and proposed a FR metric by computing gradient similarity.

While these FR metrics can reach desirable results, the large-data reference HDR content is normally inaccessible. For instance, the transmission of reference HDR images needs substantially extra bandwidth and is not economical. Furthermore, nowadays, HDR content can universally be created from the SDR images and there are actually no corresponding reference HDR images available. Hence, developing NR methods for HDR images is a more practical and competitive way. Guan et al. [16] built a NR quality predicting model for HDR based on tensor space. From tensor decomposition, they first generated three feature maps and extracted structure and contrast features from these maps to get prediction through learning a support vector regression (SVR). Besides, little research work on NR methods for HDR images has been found. Therefore, it is of high demand to profoundly explore the characteristics of distorted HDR images and further advance the NR evaluation technology. To objectively predict scores of HDR images correlated well with subjective ratings, we propose a new NR method based on Retinex decomposition [17, 18]. Retinex can decompose an image into two components i.e., luminance and reflectance. The basic idea of the Retinex theory is that the luminance intensity determines the dynamic range of all pixels, while the intrinsic properties of the original image are determined by the reflection values. Accordingly, it is feasible to make HDR image evaluation in these two decomposing domains. We first decompose HDR images into two components by Retinex decomposition with different scales, and then extract multiple quality-related features in the two domains for quality prediction by learning an SVR.

The rest of the paper is organized as follows. How the method is proposed is described in Sect. 2. And, Sect. 3 gives experimental comparisons. Conclusions are finally drawn in Sect. 4.

2 Proposed Method

Figure 1 shows the flowchart of our proposed metric. At first, the RGB-represented test image is transformed into L * a * b color space and its lightness map is decomposed by Retinex with four different scales, from low to high. The left column of maps from Retinex decompositions of different scales are luminance components, and the right ones are reflectance maps. After the decompositions, quality related features are extracted. Specifically, we extract natural scene statistics (NSS) from luminance maps, and extract gradient similarities from reflectance maps. Finally, all features are fed into an SVR for score prediction.

2.1 Retinex Decomposition

Retinex is blended from the words of retinal and cortex, implying that Retinex decomposition involves eye and brain processing, which was first proposed for explaining color constancy under varying illumination environments [17]. The Retinex theory states that an image can be divided as the product of reflectance component and illumination component, which can be given by

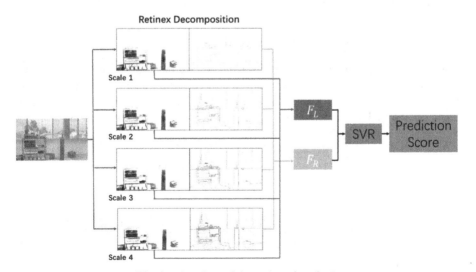

Fig. 1. Flowchart of the proposed method.

$$I^{ch}(x, y) = \mathcal{L}^{ch}(x, y).\mathbb{R}^{ch}(x, y) \tag{1}$$

where x, y are spatial indices, ch indicates color channel, and I, $\mathcal{L}$ and $\mathcal{R}$ denote image, luminance and reflectance, respectively. Among them, the luminance component generally changes slowly, which is recognized as low-frequency component and determining the dynamic range of the pixel. The reflectance component, which is manifested as a high-frequency component, depends on the inherent properties of the image object. Commonly, the Formula (1) is calculated in logarithm domain, given as

$$log\left(I^{ch}(x, y)\right) = log(\mathcal{L}^{ch}((x, y)) + log(\mathbb{R}^{ch}(x, y)) \tag{2}$$

The logarithm transformation simplifies the multiplication operation into the add operation, and the logarithmic value can well demonstrate HVS perception uniformity.

AS HVS is most sensitive to the brightness, we first transform the color image into L * a * b space, and obtain the lightness map for Retinex decomposition. The Retinex decomposition process is shown in Fig. 2. Here, we employ gaussian filter to low pass the L channel map to obtain luminance component. Gaussian filter is defined as

$$G(x, y, \sigma) = \frac{1}{2\pi\sigma^2}\exp\left(-\frac{x^2 + y^2}{2\sigma^2}\right) \tag{3}$$

where σ is the standard deviation of gaussian distribution. we adopt four different scales of gaussian filters as listed in Table 1. The Scale 1 gaussian function has the smallest size and standard deviation, which means the pixels are smoothed by the nearest neighbor pixels, while other scales will weight bigger areas of pixels according to the set parameters. Perceptually, the four scales of gaussian filtering can be recognized as four receptive fields of HVS with different sensitivities.

2.2 Feature Extraction from Reflectance Maps

As mentioned above, the reflectance map indicates the intrinsic property of an image object. Different gaussian filters will create different reflectance maps. With the increase in scale, we calculate the gradient similarity [19, 20] between current and scale 1 reflectance maps. The gradient map of a reflectance map can be calculated as.

$$G_{\mathbb{R},S}(x, y) = \sqrt{\left(I_{\mathbb{R},S}(x, y) * \varkappa_h(x, y)\right)^2 + \left(I_{\mathbb{R},S}(x, y) * \varkappa_v(x, y)\right)^2} \tag{4}$$

with

$$\varkappa_h(x, y) = \begin{bmatrix} -1 & 0 & +1 \\ -2 & 0 & +2 \\ -1 & 0 & +1 \end{bmatrix} \varkappa_v(x, y) = \begin{bmatrix} +1 & +2 & +1 \\ 0 & 0 & 0 \\ -1 & -2 & -1 \end{bmatrix} \tag{5}$$

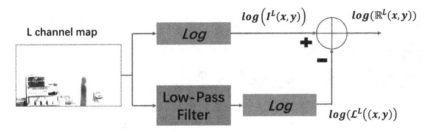

Fig. 2. Retinex decomposition of L channel map in L * a * b color space.

Table 1. Parameters of gaussian filters.

Scale	Standard deviation	Size
1	0.5	3×3
2	1	5×5
3	1.5	7×7
4	2	9×9

where S denotes the scale number, and $x_h(x, y)$ and $x_v(x, y)$ are respectively the horizontal and vertical filter kernels of Sobel filter. Then, the gradient similarity between the scale 1 and scale s ($s \in \{2, 3, 4\}$) can be computed by

$$\wp_G(x, y) = \frac{2G_{\mathbb{R},1}(x, y).G_{\mathbb{R},S}(x, y) + \mathbb{C}}{G_{\mathbb{R},1}{}^2(x, y) + G_{\mathbb{R},S}{}^2(x, y) + \mathbb{C}} \tag{6}$$

where $\mathbb{C}$ is a small constant to eliminate instability of equation.

There are three HDR images shown in Fig. 3, all from the database built by Narwaria [24]. The MOS values of Fig. 3(a), (b) and c are 1, 2.9, and 4.7 respectively, where 4.7 means the best score and 1 stands for the worst quality. Figure 4 displays the trend lines of gradient similarities for Fig. 3. It can be seen that Fig. 3(a) has the biggest values and flattest line, yet the highest scoring Fig. 3(c) has the smallest similarity values. The reason for the phenomena may come from that Fig. 3(a) lacks detail information and different gaussian filtering will make not much difference. Similarly, the smallest values of Fig. 3(c) can be explained as well. Hence, these gradient similarities correlate well with the HDR image quality scores, and we calculate three gradient similarity values as quality-related features categorized as F_R.

| (a) | (b) | (c) |

Fig. 3. Comparison of three HDR images of same content. (a) is severely blurred with banding artifacts, (b) barely show details in the dark area, and (c) can perfectly exhibit all the scene.

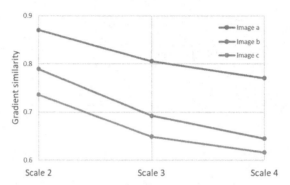

Fig. 4. Gradient similarities of Fig. 3, and image a, b and c correspond to Fig. 3(a), (b) and (c), respectively.

2.3 Feature Extraction from Luminance Component

There are also four luminance maps generated from the Retinex decomposition. The luminance map is low-frequency component of the image, and we calculate its NSS for feature extraction [21, 22]. First, each luminance map is computed by the mean subtraction and divisive normalization (MSCN) defined below

$$\widehat{\mathcal{L}}(x, y) = \frac{\mathcal{L}(x, y) - \mu_{\mathcal{L}}(x, y)}{\sigma_{\mathcal{L}}(x, y) + 1} \tag{7}$$

with

$$\mu_{\mathcal{L}}(x, y) = \sum_{m=-M}^{m=M} \sum_{n=-N}^{n=N} w_{m,n} \mathcal{L}(x + m, y + n) \tag{8}$$

$$\sigma_{\mathcal{L}}(x, y) = \sqrt{\sum_{m=-M}^{m=M} \sum_{n=-N}^{n=N} w_{m,n} \big[\mathcal{L}(x + m, y + n) - \mu_{\mathcal{L}}(x, y) \big]^2} \tag{9}$$

where $\mu_{\mathcal{L}}(x, y)$ and $\sigma_{\mathcal{L}}(x, y)$ are the local mean and the local standard deviation respectively, and $w_{m,n}$ is the values of a circularly symmetric 2D 15×15 Gaussian kernel. Figure 5 gives MSCN distributions of luminance maps of Fig. 3. We can find that the

MSCN distributions of Fig. 3(a) are most centralized and similar among all the scales. On the other hand, the distributions of Fig. 3(b) are most dispersed and has biggest dissimilarities among all scales compared to the other two HDR images. We use the shape and scale parameters of the generalized Gaussian distribution (GGD) to represent the distributions and as the quality-related features, which can be calculated by

$$f\left(x, \alpha, \Upsilon^2\right) = \frac{\alpha}{2\beta\Gamma(1/\alpha)} \exp\left[-\left(\frac{|x|}{\beta}\right)^{\alpha}\right] \tag{10}$$

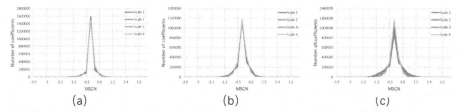

Fig. 5. Luminance MSCN distributions of Fig. 3. Image (a), (b), and (c) correspond to Fig. 3(a), (b) and (c), respectively.

with

$$\beta = \Upsilon\sqrt{\frac{\Gamma(1/\alpha)}{\Gamma(3/\alpha)}} \tag{11}$$

$$\Gamma(\alpha) = \int_0^\infty t^{(\alpha-1)}e^{-t}dt, \alpha > 0 \tag{12}$$

where α and β are the shape and scale values. Hence, we create 8 features here grouped as F_L.

The visibility of image details may depend on the viewing distance and display resolution. To model such viewing situation, we downsample the original image to generate two low resolution images by factors of 2×2 and 4×4, respectively. Same features are likewise extracted from the two sampled images. Totally, there are 33 features derived.

2.4 Learning Metric

We utilize SVR [23, 24] to fuse the extracted features into the final score. The SVR algorithm is given by

$$\min_{w,b,\kappa,\kappa'} \frac{1}{2}||w||_2^2 + \lambda \sum_{i=1}^{\Omega}(\kappa_i + \kappa_i')$$

$$s.t. \, w^t\phi(X_i) + b - y_i \leq \eta + \kappa_i$$

$$y_i - w^t \phi(X_i) - b \leq \eta + \kappa'_i$$

$$K(X_i, X_j) = \phi(X_i)^T \phi(X_j)$$

$$K(X_i, X_j) = \exp\left(-P||X_i - X_j||^2\right)$$

$$\kappa_i, \kappa'_i \geq 0, i = 1, 2, \cdots, \Omega \tag{13}$$

where X_i and y_i are the input vector value and output score, respectively. K is a radial basis function kernel (RBF).

3 Experimental Results

3.1 Databases

The proposed algorithm is evaluated on two public databases i.e., Narwaria's database [25] and Korshunov's database [26].

Narwaria's Database: The database was developed based on ten reference HDR images, including both indoor and natural scenes. The reference image was first tone mapped to LDR by the iCAM06 operator, then the tone-mapped image was JPEG compressed and expanded to create the distorted HDR image by inverse tone mapping. There are 14 different distorted HDR images generated for each pristine content by setting up JPEG and iCAM06. The database provides MOS values ranging from 1 to 5, where higher value means better quality.

Korshunov's Database: The database has twenty pristine HDR images, containing scenes with architecture, landscapes, and portraits. The distorted images were created by JPEG-XT standard. And, there are total 240 compressed images generated through allocating different profiles and quality levels of JPEG-XT. Each image is offered an impairment scale value ranging from 1 to 5, where higher value indicates lower impairment.

3.2 Assessment Criteria

The database is first randomly split into two parts with different contents: 80% for training set, and 20% for testing set. To avoid bias, such train-test procedure is executed 500 times and median results are adopted.

Three common criteria i.e., Pearson Linear Correlation Coefficient (PLCC) and Spearman Rank Order Correlation Coefficient (SRCC), Root Mean Squared Error (RMSE), are utilized for performance evaluation [27].

Before computing PLCC and RMSE, prediction scores are fitted by a logistic regression, which is given by

$$\mathcal{M} = \rho_1 \left[\frac{1}{2} - \frac{1}{1 + e^{\rho_2(\aleph - \rho_3)}} \right] + \rho_4 \aleph + \rho_5 \tag{14}$$

where $\aleph$ is the prediction score, $\mathcal{M}$ is the MOS value, and ρ_1, ρ_2, ρ_3, ρ_4 and ρ_5 are the parameters to be fitted.

3.3 Performance Comparison

We compare our method with a variety of quality metrics: a) FR LDR quality metrics adapted to HDR images using PU-transform, such as PU-PSNR, PU-SSIM [5] and PU-VIF [9]; B) NR LDR quality metrics, including PU-BRISUE [7] and PU-NIQE [8]; c) metrics for HDR content, containing NR Guan's method [16], FR HDR-VDP-2.2 [13] and Zhang's methods [15].

Table 2. Performance comparison on Narwaria's and Korshunov's databases. The best results are bolded.

Meteics	Types	Narwaria			Korshunov		
		PLCC	SRCC	RMSE	PLCC	SRCC	RMSE
PU-PSNR	FR	0.523	0.479	1.091	0.861	0.861	0.892
PU-SSIM	FR	0.866	0.855	0.643	0.950	0.919	0.584
PU-VIF	FR	0.785	0.763	0.798	0.877	0.931	0.557
PU-BRISUE	NR	0.331	0.340	0.462	0.344	0.373	0.245
PU-NIQE	NR	0.328	0.336	0.481	0.341	0.369	0.272
HDR-VDP-2.2	FR	0.733	0.705	0.649	0.950	0.942	**0.374**
HDR-VQM	FR	0.895	0.887	0.574	0.961	0.957	0.433
Guan	NR	**0.927**	0.915	0.367	0.902	0.874	0.502
Zhang	FR	0.899	0.893	–	**0.963**	**0.958**	–
Proposed	NR	0.921	**0.916**	**0.365**	0.960	0.957	0.417

Table 2 represents the comparison results on two public databases, and the best indices are bolded. From the table, we can find: a) the LDR metrics have worse results compared to HDR-specific metrics. In addition, the NR metrics of PU-NIQE and PU-BRISQUE perform worst; b) Our method obtains best results on Narwaria's database, even better than the FR HDR quality metrics (HDR-VDP-2.2 and HDR-VQM); c) albeit no data ranked first best on the Korshunov's database, two indices of our method can be ranked second best; d) our method have close results between two databases, showing the great robustness of the algorithm. In general, compared to the other competing methods, the proposed method can make prediction more consistent with subjective evaluation.

3.4 Computational Complexity

Our method decomposes images through the simple gaussian filtering and only needs to extract 33 quality-related features for quality prediction by SVR. Empirically, such a relatively uncomplicated approach is practical for small datasets with little tendency to overfit. The proposed algorithm is implemented in a laptop with a 2.5 GHz i5 CPU and 8 GB RAM. And, the operating system is win 10 and working software is MATLAB 2016B. It takes an average of 1.27 s for predicting a score on Narwaria's database.

Considering the independent feature extraction from four scales of gaussian filtering, introducing parallel computing may be a reasonable way of significantly reducing the run time for real-time applications.

4 Conclusion

In this paper, we propose a NR HDR IQA algorithm based on multi-scale Retinex decomposition. At first, the test image is decomposed by Retinex to get the luminance and reflectance components. Considering the different characteristics of two components, we extract quality-related features from two components respectively. Specifically, we calculate gradient similarities from luminance maps generated by gaussian filtering at four scales. And, NSS features are computed on reflectance components of four scales. Finally, all the features are fed into SVR for quality prediction. The experimental results show the proposed method outperforms the other competing methods. However, some parameters, such as gaussian filter sizes and scales, are Empirically determined and may not be optimal. In the future work, we will focus on optimizing parameters and feature extraction to develop more efficient assessment methods for HDR content.

References

1. Wong, C.-W., Su, G.-M., Wu, M.: Impact analysis of baseband quantizer on coding efficiency for HDR video. IEEE Signal Process. Lett. **23**(10), 1354–1358 (2016)
2. Niu, Y., Wu, J., Liu, W., Guo, W., Lau, R.-W.: HDR-GAN: HDR image reconstruction from multi-exposed LDR images with large motions. IEEE Trans. Image Process. **30**, 3885–3896 (2021)
3. Panetta, K., Kezebou, L., Oludare, V., Agaian, S., Xia, Z.: TMO-net: a parameter-free tone mapping operator using generative adversarial network, and performance benchmarking on large scale HDR dataset. IEEE Access **9**, 39500–39517 (2021)
4. Chang, H.-W., Bi, X.-D., Kai, C.: Blind image quality assessment by visual neuron matrix. IEEE Signal Process. Lett. **28**, 1803–1807 (2021)
5. Wang, Z., Bovik, A.-C., Sheikh, H.-R., Simoncelli, E.P.: Image quality assessment: from error visibility to structural similarity. IEEE Trans. Image Process. **13**(4), 600–612 (2004)
6. Zhang, L., Zhang, L., Mou, X., Zhang, D.: FSIM: a feature similarity index for image quality assessment. IEEE Trans. Image Process. **20**(8), 2378–2386 (2011)
7. Mittal, A., Moorthy, A.-K., Bovik, A.-C.: No-reference image quality assessment in the spatial domain. IEEE Trans. Image Process. **21**(12), 4695–4708 (2012)
8. Jiang, Q., Shao, F., Gao, W., Chen, Z., Jiang, G., Ho, Y.-S.: Unified no-reference quality assessment of singly and multiply distorted stereoscopic images. IEEE Trans. Image Process. **28**(4), 1866–1881 (2019)
9. Sheikh, H.-R., Bovik, A.-C.: Image information and visual quality. IEEE Trans. Image Process. **15**(2), 430–444 (2006)
10. Aydin, T.-O., Mantiuk, R., Seidel, H.-P.: Extending quality metrics to full luminance range images. In: Human Vision and Electronic Imaging XIII, vol. 6806, p. 68060B (2008)
11. Mantiuk, R.-K., Azimi, M.: PU21: a novel perceptually uniform encoding for adapting existing quality metrics for HDR. In: 2021 Picture Coding Symposium (PCS), pp. 1–5. IEEE Press, Bristol (2021)

12. Mantiuk, R.-K., Kim, K.-J., Rempel, A.-G., Heidrich, W.: HDR-VDP-2: a calibrated visual metric for visibility and quality predictions in all luminance conditions. ACM Trans. Graph. **30**(4), 1–14 (2011)
13. Narwaria, M., Mantiuk, R.-K., Silva, M.-P.-D., Callet, P.-L.: HDR-VDP-2.2: a calibrated method for objective quality prediction of high-dynamic range and standard images. J. Electron. Imaging **24**(1), 010501 (2015)
14. Narwaria, M., Silva, M.- P.-D., Callet, P.-L.: HDR-VQM: an objective quality measure for high dynamic range video. Signal Process.: Image Commun. **35**(1), 46–60 (2015)
15. Zhang, K., Fang, Y., Chen, W., Xu, Y., Zhao, T.: A display-Independent Quality Assessment for HDR Images. IEEE Signal Process. Lett. **29**, 464–468 (2022)
16. Guan, F., Jiang, G., Song, Y., Yu, M., Peng, Z., Chen, F.: No-reference HDR image quality assessment method based on tensor space. In: ICASSP 2018, pp. 1218–1222. IEEE Press, Calgary (2018)
17. Jobson, D.-J., Rahman, Z., Woodell, G.-A.: Properties and performance of a center/surround Retinex. IEEE Trans. Image Process. **6**(3), 451–462 (1997)
18. Land, E.-H: An alternative technique for the computation of the designator in the Retinex theory of color vision. Proc. Natl. Acad. Sci. U.S.A. **83**(10), 3078–3079 (1986)
19. Gu, K., Zhai, G., Yang, X., Zhang, W.: An efficient color image quality metric with local-tuned-global model. In: Proceedings of the IEEE International Conference on Image Processing, pp. 506–510. IEEE Press, Paris (2014),
20. Liu, A., Lin, W., Narwaria, M.: Image quality assessment based on gradient similarity. IEEE Trans. Image Process. **21**(4), 1500–1512 (2012)
21. Geisler, W.-S.: Visual perception and the statistical properties of natural scenes. Annu. Rev. Psychol. **59**, 167–192 (2008)
22. Ruderman, D.-L.: The statistics of natural images. Netw.: Comput. Neural Syst. **5**(4), 517–548 (1994)
23. Scholkopf, B., Smola, A.-J.: Learning With Kernels: Support Vector Machines, Regularization, Optimization, and Beyond. MIT Press, Cambridge (2002)
24. Chang, C.-C., Lin, C.-J.: LIBSVM: a library for support vector machines. ACM Trans. Intell. Syst. Technol. **2**(27), 1–27 (2011)
25. Narwaria, M., Silva, M.-P.-D., Callet, P.-L., Pepion, R.: Tone mapping-based high-dynamic-range image compression: Study of optimization criterion and perceptual quality. Opt. Eng. **52**(10), 102008-1–102008-15 (2013)
26. Korshunov, P.: Subjective quality assessment database of HDR images compressed with JPEG XT. In: Proceedings of the 7th International Workshop Quality of Multimedia Experience (QoMEX), pp. 1–6. IEEE Press, Pilos (2015)
27. VQEG, Final report from the video quality experts group on the validation of objective models of video quality assessment (2003). http://www.vqeg.org/

Node Importance-Based Semi-supervised Nonnegative Matrix Factorization for Image Clustering

Jintao Wu and Youlong Yang[(✉)]

School of Mathematics and Statistic, Xidian University, Xian, China
jtwu@stu.xidian.edu.cn, ylyang@mail.xidian.edu.cn

Abstract. As a typical dimensionality reduction method, non-negative matrix factorization (NMF) is widely used in image clustering tasks. However, the traditional NMF is unsupervised and cannot fully utilize the label information. In this research, we propose a joint feature representation and node importance propagation framework called semi-supervised nonnegative matrix factorization based on node importance (NISNMF). Firstly, by considering the overlap degree of the shared neighbors of the labeled node, a new importance index is proposed based on local structure to increase the influence of important node. Secondly, NISNMF integrates semi-supervised non-negative matrix factorization and node importance propagation into a unified feature representation and information propagation framework to improve the discriminative ability of the model. Finally, an efficient alternating iteration method is designed and its convergence is proved. Experimental results in a large number of image clustering tasks verify the superiority of the algorithm. In addition, the accuracy, parameters and sensitivity of the algorithm are also experimentally investigated.

Keywords: Nonnegative Matrix Factorization · Label Information · Node Importance · Image Clustering

1 Introduction

With the rapid development of visual representation [1], Web document [2], and gene cell analysis [3], the dimensionality of data can usually reach hundreds or thousands of dimensions, and the increase of dimensionality leads to the challenge of "curse of dimensionality". Therefore, extracting valuable feature information from complex high-dimensional data has been a hot issue in recent years [4]. Recently, data representation plays an important role in the field of visual pattern recognition in order to discover important underlying structures and useful information in high-dimensional data. Among the existing methods,

Supported by Natural Science Basic Research Program of Shaanxi (No. 2021JM-133).

nonnegative matrix factorization (NMF) [5] is the most typical matrix factorization dimensionality reduction approach, which guarantees dimensionality reduction without losing too much information and maintains model performance.

Since manifold learning method guarantees the spatial structure of high-dimensional data, many variants of NMF have been proposed. Cai et al. [6] proposed Graph-regularized Nonnegative Matrix Factorization (GNMF), which explicitly takes into account the geometrical structure of high-dimensional data by adding additional regularization terms. Considering the elimination effect of $L_{2,1}$-norm on outliers, Kong et al. [7] proposed Robust Nonnegative Matrix Factorization with $L_{2,1}$-norm (RNMF), which can better handle more practical and complex application tasks.

As a popular unsupervised learning technique, the aforementioned NMF cannot fully utilize the limited available information. Semi-supervised learning (SSL) is a popular research area because it can use the information from labeled nodes to expand the recognition ability of the model [8]. Numerous semi-supervised matrix factorization algorithms have been proposed, which have been successfully applied to image clustering, text processing, face recognition. Lee et al. [9] proposed Semi-supervised Nonnegative Matrix Factorization (SNMF) by considering a joint factorization of partial label matrix and data matrix. Liu et al. [10] presented a Constrained Nonnegative Matrix Factorization (CNMF) which projects the same labeled node to the same coordinate to better improve clustering performance. To maintain the block diagonal structure in the subspace perspective, Li et al. [11] proposed a Robust Structural Nonnegative Matrix Factorization (RSNMF) which embeds the potential representations of different classes into different subspaces. Jia et al. [12] found that the current SNMF tends to focus on labeled data and neglect the intrinsic connections of the unlabeled sample. In order to make full use of unlabeled node to obtain broader prior knowledge to improve the accuracy of the model, they proposed a Semi-supervised Nonnegative Matrix Factorization with Dissimilarity and Similarity Regularization (SNMFDSR) by two complementary regularizers, namely, dissimilarity and similarity regularizers, which are incorporated into the traditional NMF to direct the decomposition.

Due to there are not enough labeled samples available, semi-supervised algorithms can utilize supervisory information from partially labeled samples to enhance the discriminative ability. However, they usually treat label information as a rigid limitation and do not fully exploit the prior knowledge. Label propagation (LP) is an effective semi-supervised iterative algorithm that assumes that nearby samples from the same global cluster should share similar labels [13]. LP assigns labels to unlabeled points through propagation, is useful when there are few labeled datas.

In this paper, we introduce a node importance-based label propagation model into NMF and propose a new semi-supervised method called semi-supervised nonnegative matrix factorization based on node importance (NISNMF). Firstly, by considering the overlap degree of shared neighbors of labeled data, we propose a importance metric based on local information, which solves the problem of equal influence of labels and improves the role of important nodes. Then, we introduce node importance into label propagation and propose a label propagation model based on node importance. Finally, our model implements NMF and node importance propagation into a joint framework that enhances the differences of representations in the feature space. In this model, we use the predictive membership matrix as a soft constraint increase the interpretability of the model.

The rest of the paper is organized as follows. In Sect. 2, we briefly describe the algorithm of NMF. Section 3 describes NISNMF algorithm in detail. In Sect. 4, some comparative experiments are conducted to verify the effectiveness of the proposed algorithm. Conclusions are given in the last section.

2   Related Works

In this section, we will briefly review NMF and existing relevant variants. Throughout this paper, matrix is stand for in capital letters A. The Frobenius norm of A is denoted by $\|A\|_F = \sqrt{(\sum_i \sum_j A_{ij}^2)}$. A^T means the transpose of A. The trace of A is $\mathrm{Tr}(A)$. The symbol $\odot$ indicates the elementwise multiplication operator.

2.1   Unsupervised NMF and Its Variants

Suppose that a nonnegative data matrix $X = [x_1, \cdots, x_n] \in \mathbb{R}^{m \times n}$, where x_i is a m-dimensional sample. NMF [5] is a dimensionality reduction method that a matrix X could be approximately transformed into two matrix factors $U \in \mathbb{R}^{m \times d}$ and $V \in \mathbb{R}^{n \times d}$, satisfying the following optimization problems:

$$\min_{U,V} \|X - UV^T\|_F^2,$$
$$\text{s.t. } U \geqslant 0, V \geqslant 0, \tag{1}$$

where the rank parameter $d \ll min(m,n)$. The nonnegative restrictions on matrices ensure that only additive combinations are allowed during the decomposition process. The iterative multiplicative update rules of Eq. (1) is as mentioned:

$$U_{ij} \leftarrow U_{ij} \frac{[XV]_{ij}}{[UV^TV]_{ij}}, \tag{2}$$

$$V_{ij} \leftarrow V_{ij} \frac{[X^TU]_{ij}}{[VU^TU]_{ij}}. \tag{3}$$

The above NMF fails in discovering the intrinsic geometric and discriminatory structure of the original data, which is crucial for complex high-dimensional data representation. For purpose of preserving these properties, Cai et al. [6] presented the GNMF approach. The model optimization function of GNMF is:

$$\min_{U,V} \|X - UV^T\|_F^2 + \alpha \, \mathrm{Tr}(V^T LV),$$
$$\text{s.t. } U \geqslant 0, V \geqslant 0, \tag{4}$$

where $\alpha > 0$ is the regularization parameter, which adjusts the smoothness of the manifold. $L = D - W$ is called graph Laplacian and W is a weight matrix. D is a diagonal matrix whose element is $D_{ii} = \sum_{j=1}^{n} W_{ij}$. GNMF optimization problem is addressed by the following updating rules:

$$U_{ij} \leftarrow U_{ij} \frac{[XV]_{ij}}{[UV^TV]_{ij}}, \tag{5}$$

$$V_{ij} \leftarrow V_{ij} \frac{[X^TU + \alpha WV]_{ij}}{[VU^TU + \alpha DV]_{ij}}. \tag{6}$$

For purpose of enhancing the ability of NMF, other variants of NMF are proposed. By taking into account that sparsity can produce a better representation of the data, NMF with sparseness constraint is derived in [14]. By capturing the global information and the local manifold, Zhang et al. [15] integrated adaptive graph regularization and NMF to obtain better clustering results.

2.2 Semi-supervised NMF

NMF and its variants in Sect. 2.1 are approaches that do not use the prior information. Numerous studies [16] have proven that the prior information can substantially improve learning accuracy, so the NMF method is widely used in the field of SSL. For example, Lee et al. [9] proposed the SNMF that decomposes both data and class label matrices into a common coefficient matrix with different basis matrices. The optimization problem of SNMF can be expressed:

$$\min_{U,B,V} \left\| H \odot (X - UV^T) \right\|_F^2 + \alpha \left\| E \odot (Y - BV^T) \right\|_F^2, \tag{7}$$
$$\text{s.t. } U \geqslant 0, B \geqslant 0, V \geqslant 0,$$

where $Y = [y_1, \cdots, y_n] \in \mathbb{R}^{k \times n}$ is a binary label matrix of X, k is the class number. Explicitly, y_i stands for the label vector of the i-th data, where $y_{ij} = 1$ if x_i belongs to class j and $y_{ij} = 0$ otherwise. H is a binary weight matrix. E is a weight matrix to handle missing labels. α is a trade-off parameter that determines the weight of the supervision term. The update rules of SNMF are:

$$U_{ij} \leftarrow U_{ij} \frac{[(H \odot X)V]_{ij}}{[(H \odot (UV^T))V]_{ij}}, \tag{8}$$

$$B_{ij} \leftarrow B_{ij} \frac{[(E \odot Y)V]_{ij}}{[(E \odot (BV^T))V]_{ij}}, \tag{9}$$

$$V_{ij} \leftarrow V_{ij} \frac{[U^T(H \odot X) + \alpha B^T(E \odot Y)]_{ij}}{[U^T(H \odot (UV^T)) + \alpha B^T(E \odot (BV^T))]_{ij}}. \tag{10}$$

In order to improve recognition ability and facilitate supervisory information, Liu et al. [10] proposed the parameter-free CNMF that merge the label constraint information. It assumes that when high-dimensional data is mapped to a low-dimensional feature space, datas belonging to the same label will have the same coordinates. Specifically, the formulation is stated as:

$$\min_{U,Z} \left\| X - U(CZ)^T \right\|_F^2,$$
$$\text{s.t. } U \geqslant 0, Z \geqslant 0,$$

(11)

where $C \in n \times (n - l + k)$ is a label constraint matrix, $Z \in (n - l + k) \times d$ is called an auxiliary matrix, l represents the amount of labeled datas. Utilizing the following update rule, the minimal value for the Eq. (11) can be solved:

$$U_{ij} \leftarrow U_{ij} \frac{[XCZ]_{ij}}{[UZ^T C^T CZ]_{ij}},$$

(12)

$$Z_{ij} \leftarrow Z_{ij} \frac{[C^T X^T U]_{ij}}{[C^T CZU^T U]_{ij}}.$$

(13)

In order to exploit useful label information, Xing et al. [17] proposed discriminative SNMF for data clustering, which ensures that label datas in a new low-dimensional space can be classified into the same group. By utilizing graph regularization term and prior information as constraints, Xing et al. [18] subsequently proposed a new graph regularized NMF model with label discrimination, which effectively characterizes the intrinsic manifold shape of the data.

3   The Proposed NISNMF Algorithm

We present the NISNMF algorithm in this section. In first section, a new index is proposed to evaluate node importance and the objective function of NISNMF is presented in a joint framework by combining the new index with SNMF. In Sect. 3.2, we design an optimization algorithm based on iterative multiplicative update rule for solving the problem of NISNMF. In Sect. 3.3, we give a proof of convergence for iteration rules.

3.1   Construction of NISNMF Model

Assume that $X = [x_1, x_2, \cdots, x_l, x_{l+1}, \cdots, x_n] \in \mathbb{R}^{m \times n}$ is divided into two subsets, namely, $X = [X_l, X_u]$, where $X_l \in \mathbb{R}^{m \times l}$ are l samples of labeled data and $X_u \in \mathbb{R}^{m \times u}$ contains remaining unlabeled datas. $F = [f_1, f_2, \cdots, f_n] \in \mathbb{R}^{k \times n}$ denotes the predicted label matrix. The SNMF algorithm aims to seek a nonnegative decomposition of X based on label information. Therefore, how to fully exploit the information of the labeled datas plays a crucial role in SNMF.

The first objective of the NISNMF is to evaluate the importance of the node. If the more important a node is, the more influence it has on other nodes, then this label is more possibly to propagate. Here, we introduce the node importance from the local structure [19] (Fig. 1).

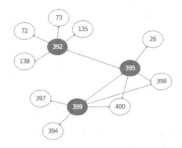

Fig. 1. Node importance example of ORL. (Solid and hollow represent labeled and unlabeled data, respectively. One-way arrow indicates that the arrow node is a neighbor of the tail node, and two-way arrow indicate that they are neighbor of each other).

Definition 1. *Let O be a set and the elements in the set may appear more than once, then O is called a multiset. The cardinality of a multiset O is recorded as $|O|$.*

Definition 2. *In a directed p-NN graph, when x_j is one of the p nearest neighbors of x_i, an edge is linked from x_i to x_j, and if x_i is neighbors of x_j and x_m, x_i is referred to as the shared neighbor of x_j and x_m. If both x_i and x_j are neighbors of each other, which is denoted as $x_i \leftrightarrow x_j$.*

Definition 3. *Let $P_i \cap P_j$ be a set of shared neighbors between x_i and x_j, defined as:*

$$P_i \cap P_j = \begin{cases} P_i \cap P_j \cup \left\{ x_{ij}^* \right\}, & x_i \leftrightarrow x_j, \\ P_i \cap P_j, & otherwise. \end{cases} \tag{14}$$

where P_i represents the set of the i-th label node and its p nearest neighbors. x_{ij}^* is a virtual data point that represents both x_i and x_j are neighbors of each other. (Note that the cardinality of the virtual data point is 2).

Based on Definitions 1, 2 and 3, we introduce a new index, i.e., Node Importance (NI). Assuming that $G = (O, E)$ denotes an unweighted and directed network graph, where O is the multiset of label nodes from the same class and its p nearest neighbors, and E represents a union of the shared neighbors of labeled data, e.g., $E = \bigcup_{i \neq j} P_i \cap P_j$.

Definition 4. *The importance of label node i is defined as follows:*

$$NI(i) = \frac{vd(P_i, C_O(P_i))}{|E|} \times l, \tag{15}$$

where $C_O(P_i)$ represents the complement of P_i with respect to O, l represents the number of the labeled data. $vd(P_i, C_O(P_i))$ is the overlap degree which is elements of P_i occurs in $C_O(P_i)$.

The second objective of the NISNMF is that classify numerous unlabeled datas with few labeled datas. Here, the weight matrix W is expressed as follows:

$$W_{ij} = \begin{cases} \exp\left(-\|x_i - x_j\|^2/2\sigma^2\right), & \text{if } x_i \in P_j \text{ or } x_j \in P_i, \\ 0, & otherwise, \end{cases} \quad (16)$$

where $\sigma > 0$ is a spread parameter [20].

Combining the new metric and the LP algorithm, the optimization problem of node importance propagation is presented as:

$$\min \sum_i^n \sum_j^n \|f_i - f_j\|^2 W_{ij} + \sum_i^n \beta_i \|f_i - y_i\|^2 M_{ii}^*, \quad (17)$$

where β_i is the NI of the labeled node, which is obtained from Eq. (15), and the unlabeled data is 0. M^* is a diagonal matrix, if $x_i \in X_l$, $M_{ii}^* = 1$, otherwise 0. The first term is penalized in case of significant differences in the predicted labels of nearby samples. The second item aims to ensure that the predicted label probabilities are close to the known labels.

By simple matrix expansion, Eq. (17) can be rewritten,

$$\min_F \text{Tr}\left(FLF^T\right) + \text{Tr}\left((F - Y)M(F - Y)^T\right), \quad (18)$$

where $L = D - W$ is called graph Laplacian. Considering there is very little labeled data in the LP, we first define a new diagonal matrix M,

$$M_{ii} = \begin{cases} \beta_i, & LI(i) \geqslant 1, \\ 1, & LI(i) < 1, \\ 0, & \text{otherwise.} \end{cases} \quad (19)$$

The third objective of NISNMF is to joint the node importance propagation and the matrix factorization into a unified framework. Each m-dimensional data x_i is mapped to the d-dimensional space using NMF. To fully utilize the label information, NISNMF maps low-dimensional coordinates to the label space, and unlike CNMF, the model introduces a predictive membership matrix F as a soft constraint. Thus, V in NISNMF is denoted as

$$V = F^T Z, \quad (20)$$

where $F \in \mathbb{R}^{k \times n}$ and $Z \in \mathbb{R}^{k \times d}$. The SSL framework of NMF can be developed by integrating the label information, i.e.,

$$\min_{U,Z,F} \left\|X - U(F^T Z)^T\right\|_F^2, \\ \text{s.t. } U \geqslant 0, Z \geqslant 0, F \geqslant 0. \quad (21)$$

Through combining Eq. (18) to Eq. (21), the optimization problem of NIS-NMF algorithm is as follows:

$$\mathcal{O}_{NISNMF} = \min_{U,Z,F} \left\|X - U(F^T Z)^T\right\|_F^2 + \alpha \, \text{Tr}\left(FLF^T\right) \\ + \lambda \, \text{Tr}\left((F - Y)M(F - Y)^T\right), \quad (22) \\ \text{s.t.} U \geqslant 0, Z \geqslant 0, F \geqslant 0.$$

The first constraint in NISNMF is a dimensionality reduction process for the initial data, the second is a label propagation regularization term, and the third constraint allows the model to increase the effect of important node based on NI.

3.2 Optimization

In this subsection, we design a solution for optimizing our algorithm. Although the optimization problem of NISNMF is non-convex for U, Z and F, it is convex for them respectively. Thus we provide an alternating iterative solution to avoid this issue.

By algebraic formulas, Eq. (22) can be transformed into the following form:

$$
\begin{aligned}
\mathcal{O}_{NISNMF} &= \mathrm{Tr}\left(\left(X - U(F^T Z)^T\right)\left(X - U(F^T Z)^T\right)^T\right) \\
&\quad + \alpha\,\mathrm{Tr}(FLF^T) + \lambda\,\mathrm{Tr}\left((F-Y)M(F-Y)^T\right) \\
&= \mathrm{Tr}\left(XX^T\right) - 2\,\mathrm{Tr}\left(X(F^T Z)U^T\right) + \lambda\,\mathrm{Tr}\left(YMY^T\right) \\
&\quad + \mathrm{Tr}\left(U(F^T Z)^T(F^T Z)U^T\right) + \alpha\,\mathrm{Tr}\left(F(D-W)F^T\right) \\
&\quad + \lambda\,\mathrm{Tr}\left(FMF^T\right) - 2\lambda\,\mathrm{Tr}\left(FMY^T\right),
\end{aligned} \tag{23}
$$

s.t. $U \geqslant 0, Z \geqslant 0, F \geqslant 0$.

Let $\Psi = [\Psi_{ij}]$, $\Phi = [\Phi_{ij}]$ and $\Omega = [\Omega_{ij}]$ be the Lagrangian multipliers that constrain $U_{ij} \geqslant 0$, $Z_{ij} \geqslant 0$ and $F_{ij} \geqslant 0$, the Lagrange function of Eq. (23) is as follows:

$$
\begin{aligned}
\mathcal{L}_{NISNMF} &= \mathrm{Tr}\left(XX^T\right) - 2\,\mathrm{Tr}\left(X(F^T Z)U^T\right) + \lambda\,\mathrm{Tr}\left(YMY^T\right) \\
&\quad + \mathrm{Tr}\left(U(F^T Z)^T(F^T Z)U^T\right) - 2\lambda\,\mathrm{Tr}\left(FMY^T\right) \\
&\quad + \alpha\,\mathrm{Tr}\left(F(D-W)F^T\right) + \lambda\,\mathrm{Tr}\left(FMF^T\right) \\
&\quad + \mathrm{Tr}(\Psi U) + \mathrm{Tr}(\Phi Z) + \mathrm{Tr}(\Omega F).
\end{aligned} \tag{24}
$$

To obtain the iterative formulas for the variables in the objective function of $\mathcal{L}_{NISNMF}$, the partial derivative operations are first done for U, Z, and F, as follows:

$$
\frac{\partial \mathcal{L}}{\partial U} = 2UZ^T FF^T Z - 2XF^T Z + \Psi,
$$

$$
\frac{\partial \mathcal{L}}{\partial Z} = 2FF^T ZU^T U - 2FX^T U + \Phi, \tag{25}
$$

$$
\frac{\partial \mathcal{L}}{\partial F} = 2(ZU^T UZ^T F - ZU^T X + \alpha F(D-W) + \lambda FM - \lambda YM^T) + \Omega.
$$

Taking into account the KKT conditions $\Psi_{ij}U_{ij} = 0$, $\phi_{ij}Z_{ij} = 0$ and $\Omega_{ij}F_{ij} = 0$, respectively, we get

$$
[UZ^T FF^T Z - XF^T Z]_{ij}U_{ij} = 0,
$$

$$
[FF^T ZU^T U - FX^T U]_{ij}Z_{ij} = 0, \tag{26}
$$

$$
[(ZU^T UZ^T F - ZU^T X + \alpha F(D-W) + \lambda FM - \lambda YM^T)]_{ij}F_{ij} = 0.
$$

From the Eq. (32), the formulas of updating U, Z and F are as mentioned below:

$$U_{ij} \leftarrow U_{ij} \frac{[XF^T Z]_{ij}}{[UZ^T FF^T Z]_{ij}}, \tag{27}$$

$$Z_{ij} \leftarrow Z_{ij} \frac{[FX^T U]_{ij}}{[FF^T ZU^T U]_{ij}}, \tag{28}$$

$$F_{ij} \leftarrow F_{ij} \frac{[ZU^T X + \alpha FW + \lambda YM^T]_{ij}}{[ZU^T UZ^T F + \alpha FD + \lambda FM]_{ij}}. \tag{29}$$

When convergence is reached, the solutions of U, Z and F in Eq. (22) can be attained by using the above update rules. Based on the above process of NI calculation, weight matrix construction and update rules, Algorithm 1 summarizes the optimization process of NISNMF.

Algorithm 1. NISNMF Algorithm

Input: The dataset $X \in \mathbb{R}_+^{m \times n}$, label matrix $Y \in \{0,1\}_+^{k \times n}$, parameters α and λ.
Output: The basis matrices $U \in \mathbb{R}_+^{m \times d}$, the auxiliary matrix $Z \in \mathbb{R}_+^{k \times d}$ and the
    predicted label matrix $F \in \mathbb{R}_+^{k \times n}$.
1: **Initialize:** $U \in \mathbb{R}_+^{m \times d}$, $Z \in \mathbb{R}_+^{k \times d}$, $F \in \mathbb{R}_+^{k \times n}$ as arbitrary nonnegative matrices, t
    = 0.
2: Compute the importance of the labeled data $NI(i)$ by Eq. (15).
3: Construct weight matrix W by Eq. (16) and diagonal matrix M by Eq. (19);
4: **Repeat**
5:     Fixed Z_t and F_t, update U_{t+1} by Eq. (27);
6:     Fixed U_t and F_t, update Z_{t+1} by Eq. (28);
7:     Fixed U_t and Z_t, update F_{t+1} by Eq. (29);
8: $t = t + 1$;
9: **until** Converges.

3.3 Convergence

In this section, we prove the convergence of the proposed iterative rule in Eq. (27) to Eq. (29).

Theorem 1. *When $U \geqslant 0$, $Z \geqslant 0$, $F \geqslant 0$, the objective function is nonincreasing under the iteration rules of Eq. (27)–Eq. (29).*

To prove the Theorem 1, we first introduce the concept of auxiliary function and give Lemma 1:

Definition 5. *If $\mathcal{R}(w, \hat{w})$ satisfies $\mathcal{R}(w, \hat{w}) \geq \mathcal{O}(w)$ and $\mathcal{R}(w, w) = \mathcal{O}(w)$, $\mathcal{R}(w, \hat{w})$ is called an auxiliary function of $\mathcal{O}$.*

Lemma 1. *If $\mathcal{R}$ is an auxiliary function of $\mathcal{O}$, then $\mathcal{O}$ is nonincreasing under the update*

$$w^{t+1} = \arg \min_w \mathcal{R}(w, w^t). \tag{30}$$

Proof: $\mathcal{O}\left(w^{t+1}\right) \leqslant \mathcal{R}\left(w^{t+1}, w^t\right) \leqslant \mathcal{R}\left(w^t, w^t\right) = \mathcal{O}\left(w^t\right).$

Next, when we fix F and Z, we get the iterative formula by using the auxiliary function of U. With the Taylor expansion, we define $\mathcal{G}$ to represent only the part of $\mathcal{O}_{NISNMF}$ involving U.

$$\begin{aligned}\mathcal{G}(U) &= -2\operatorname{Tr}\left(X(F^T Z)U^T\right) + \operatorname{Tr}(U(F^T Z)^T(F^T Z)U^T) \\ &= \mathcal{G}(U_{ij}^t) + \mathcal{G}'(U_{ij}^t)(U_{ij} - U_{ij}^t) + (Z^T F F^T Z)_{jj}(U_{ij} - U_{ij}^t)^2.\end{aligned} \tag{31}$$

Lemma 2. *The auxiliary function of Eq. (31) on $\mathcal{G}(U)$ is*

$$\mathcal{R}\left(U_{ij}, U_{ij}^t\right) = \mathcal{G}(U_{ij}^t) + \mathcal{G}'(U_{ij}^t)(U_{ij} - U_{ij}^t) + \frac{(U^t Z^T F F^T Z)_{ij}}{U_{ij}^t}\left(U_{ij} - U_{ij}^t\right)^2. \tag{32}$$

Proof: Obviously, $\mathcal{R}\left(U_{ij}, U_{ij}\right) = \mathcal{G}(U_{ij})$ holds. Next, we show that $\mathcal{R}\left(U_{ij}, U_{ij}^t\right) \geqslant \mathcal{G}(U_{ij})$, which is equivalent to proving that

$$\frac{(U^t Z^T F F^T Z)_{ij}}{U_{ij}^t}\left(U_{ij} - U_{ij}^t\right)^2 \geqslant \left(Z^T F F^T Z\right)_{jj}\left(U_{ij} - U_{ij}^t\right)^2. \tag{33}$$

By matrix expansion, we have

$$\begin{aligned}\frac{(U^t Z^T F F^T Z)_{ij}}{U_{ij}^t} &= \frac{\sum\limits_{k=1}^{d} U_{ik}^t \times (Z^T F F^T Z)_{kj}}{U_{ij}^t} \\ &\geqslant \frac{U_{ij}^t \times (Z^T F F^T Z)_{jj}}{U_{ij}^t} = (Z^T F F^T Z)_{jj}.\end{aligned} \tag{34}$$

According to the above inequality, we can show that Eq. (32) is an upper bound auxiliary function of Eq. (31). Based on Lemma 1, we get that

$$U_{ij}^{t+1} = U_{ij}^t \frac{[XF^T Z]_{ij}}{[U^t Z^T F F^T Z]_{ij}}. \tag{35}$$

Similar to proving the convergence of the iterative formula for U, we can also prove the convergence of the iterative rules for Z and F.

4 Experiments

In this section, we perform comparison, accuracy, parameters and sensitivity experiments to verify the superiority of the algorithm. We will run NISNMF on four image datasets, including ORL, PIE, COIL20, MNIST. Table 1 summarizes the details of the above four datasets. In Fig. 2 , we show some samples from four datasets. The experimental results are compared with seven advanced algorithms, including four unsupervised algorithms Kmeans [21], NMF [5], GNMF [6], RNMF [7], and three supervised algorithms RSNMF [11], SNMFDSR [12], and CNMF [10].

Table 1. Description of the dataset.

Dataset	#Samples	#Feature	#Class	Type
ORL	400	1024	40	Face
PIE	2856	1024	68	Face
COIL20	1440	1024	20	Object
MNIST	70000	784	10	Digital

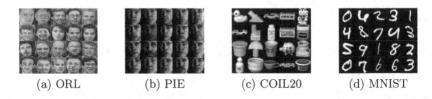

(a) ORL	(b) PIE	(c) COIL20	(d) MNIST

Fig. 2. Some samples from four datasets.

4.1   Experimental Setting

For experimental fairness, we uniformly set $p = 5$ and $\sigma = 1$ as the number of nearest neighborhood and the spread parameter. We randomly select k categories and mix samples from them as X, with k ranging from 2 to 10. In the SNMF model, the proportion of labeled data is set to 10%, i.e., 10% of the samples from each category are randomly selected. For ORL data, a single label has no practical significance, so we used 30%. The parameters of each method remain consistent across all comparison experiments, and these values are set according to the optimal recommendations in the original paper. We set the dimensionality of the low-dimensional space to the number of category, run each algorithm independently 20 times, set the maximum iteration number as 100 for all models and use Kmeans [21] as postprocessing clustering method to record average ACC and NMI.

In the paper, we use Accuracy (ACC) and Normalized Mutual Information (NMI) to evaluate the clustering results. ACC [6] is defined as shown below:

$$\text{ACC} = \frac{\sum\limits_{i=1}^{n} I\left(c_i, \text{map}\left(l_i\right)\right)}{n}, \tag{36}$$

where c_i and l_i represent the predicted label and real label respectively. $I(x, y)$ is the indicator function, which is 1 when $x = y$ and 0 otherwise. map($\cdot$) is the function which maps the predicted label to corresponding ground-truth label. NMI [17] is defined as

$$\text{NMI}(\mathcal{Q}, \tilde{\mathcal{Q}}) = \frac{\text{MI}(\mathcal{Q}, \tilde{\mathcal{Q}})}{\max\left(H(\mathcal{Q}), H(\tilde{\mathcal{Q}})\right)}, \tag{37}$$

where $\text{MI}(\mathcal{Q}, \tilde{\mathcal{Q}})$ is the mutual information metric. Entropy is denoted by $H(\cdot)$.

Table 2. Comparison of average clustering results across four datasets.

Datesets	ACC(%)				NMI(%)			
	ORL	PIE	COIL20	MNIST	ORL	PIE	COIL20	MNIST
Kmeans	88.21	37.44	78.84	66.70	89.47	26.28	74.78	55.58
NMF	85.92	51.68	77.06	61.67	85.94	44.04	71.37	48.34
GNMF	85.92	86.22	89.11	74.58	87.78	87.20	87.84	70.68
RNMF	30.73	24.47	30.95	28.52	13.13	3.38	11.19	5.43
RSNMF	47.74	26.18	43.96	45.70	43.38	4.54	33.03	25.77
SNMFDSR	78.83	78.17	73.53	66.90	80.32	76.75	71.95	61.80
CNMF	74.03	49.90	72.58	57.25	65.97	37.80	60.77	41.24
NISNMF	**93.13**	**94.48**	**93.36**	**94.63**	**93.36**	**92.38**	**92.85**	**87.24**

4.2 Clustering Comparision

To highlight the superiority of the NISNMF algorithm, we conduct comparative experiments. The average results are shown in Table 2, and the best performing method of each dataset is highlighted in bold. We can draw the following conclusions:

(1) Clustering on face datasets: Here we compare NISNMF with the second best algorithm. On ORL dataset, compared with Kmeans, NISNMF can achieve 4.92% and 3.89% improvement in ACC and NMI. On PIE dataset, NISNMF achieve 8.26% improvement in ACC and 5.18% improvement in NMI than GNMF.

(2) Clustering on object and digital datasets: Here we compare NISNMF with the second best algorithm. On COIL20 dataset, compared with GNMF, NISNMF can achieve 4.25% and 5.01% improvement in ACC and NMI. On MNIST dataset, NISNMF increase 20.05% and 16.56% in ACC and NMI than GNMF.

Based on the experimental results of the above clustering experiments, we explore three aspects to analyze the effectiveness of NISNMF:

(1) From the above comparative experiments, it is concluded that manifold learning and semi-supervised learning play an important role in the representation learning of NMF models to better exploit the local structure and supervised information of high-dimensional image data.

(2) NISNMF always achieves good performance on all these four datasets especially in the PIE and MNIST datasets. This demonstrates that by propagating relatively high NI label node, NISNMF can improve the clustering effect of NMF.

(3) Compared to other hard-constrained SNMF, NISNMF utilizes a predictive soft-constraint matrix to improve the flexibility of the model and better adapt to the complexity of real image datas.

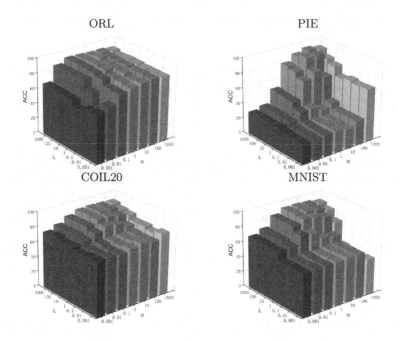

Fig. 3. ACC of NISNMF versus parameters α and λ.

4.3   Parameter Sensitivity Analysis

For graph construction and label propagation constraint terms in NMF models, the selection of appropriate parameters is crucial. In the NISNMF model, there are three different parameters (α and λ) and p-NN graph of (p). In this section, we analyze how to choose the appropriate parameters in the four datasets and give the corresponding parameter ranges.

The selection range of the parameters α and λ is set at $\{0.001, 0.01, 0.1, 1, 10, 100, 1000\}$. We randomly select 10% labeled information in each category as label node. (Note that for ORL, we randomly select 30%). In order to reflect the clustering performance more intuitively, we use ACC as the evaluation index in the parameter selection comparison. All experiments run 20 times and take the average value as final result. Specific results about parametric sensitivity analysis are presented in Fig. 3.

Figure 3 presents the clustering effect of different parameters in four datasets. A higher histogram indicates better clustering effect and better performance of the parameter combination. The parameter α controls the influence of neighboring labels during label propagation, and λ controls the consistency of the initial labels with the predicted labels during propagation. As α increases, the importance of graph regularization term increases, thus improving clustering performance. Especially in the ORL, and COIL20 datasets, the increase of α significantly improves the clustering performance, indicating the geometric manifold structure has the higher importance compared to the node importance in these three datasets. A larger λ corresponds to increasing the importance difference between the labels, which can make the larger NI node more important. In the PIE, and MNIST datasets, the clustering performance increases significantly when λ is greater than 10, indicating that the effect of NI is more important in these datasets. Through sensitivity experiments in different datasets, we conclude that the model of NISNMF performs better when α is from the range of [10,1000] and when λ is in [1, 100].

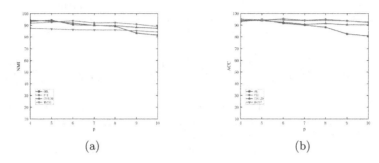

(a)   (b)

Fig. 4. Clustering results of NISNMF within parameter p. (a) ACC. (b) NMI.

Next, we investigate the influence of the graph construction parameter p for different datasets. Specifically, we explore the effects of the number of neighbors ranging from 4 to 10, and the results are recorded as the average of 20 replications in each case. Figure 4 presents the curves that plot the clustering performance against the number of neighbors across different datasets. Note that in our experiments we set other parameters to the optimal values explored above.

Figure 4 shows that the performance of all datasets slowly decreases with the increase of p, which indicates that the NISNMF model is robust to the number of neighbors parameter and can effectively alleviate the sensitivity of graph construction to the number of neighbors.

5 Conclusion

In this paper, we propose a new image clustering algorithm called semi-supervised nonnegative matrix factorization based on node importance (NIS-NMF). Our algorithm measures the importance of node by the overlap degree of shared neighbors of the labeled node from a local perspective, and then integrates node importance propagation with semi-supervised nonnegative matrix factorization into a unified framework. In addition, the model uses the predicted membership matrix as a soft constraint to better utilize the data information. Theoretically, we design an effective iterative method to solve the proposed optimization problem of NISNMF. Experimental results show that the method has better performance than other algorithms.

References

1. Wang, Y., Jia, Y., Hu, C.: Non-negative matrix factorization framework for face recognition. Int. J. Pattern Recognit. Artif. Intell. **19**(04), 495–511 (2005)
2. Xu W., Liu X., Gong Y.: Document clustering based on non-negative matrix factorization. In: Proceedings of the 26th Annual International ACM SIGIR Conference on Research and Development in Information Retrieval, pp. 267–273 (2003)
3. Zheng, X., Zhang, C.: Mirna-disease association prediction via non-negative matrix factorization based matrix completion. Signal Process. **190**, 108312 (2022)
4. Li, B., Huang, D.S., Wang, C.: Feature extraction using constrained maximum variance mapping. Pattern Recogn. **41**(11), 3287–3294 (2008)
5. Lee, D.D., Seung, H.S.: Learning the parts of objects by non-negative matrix factorization. Nature **401**(6755), 788–791 (1999)
6. Cai, D., He, X., Han, J.: Graph regularized nonnegative matrix factorization for data representation. IEEE Trans. Pattern Anal. Mach. Intell. **33**(8), 1548–1560 (2010)
7. Kong D., Ding C., Huang H.: Robust nonnegative matrix factorization using L21-norm. In: ACM Conference on Information & Knowledge Management, pp. 673–682. Association for Computing Machinery (2011)
8. Chapelle, O., Scholkopf, B., Zien, A.: Semi-supervised learning. IEEE Trans. Neural Netw. **20**(3), 542 (2009)
9. Lee, H., Yoo, J., Choi, S.: Semi-supervised nonnegative matrix factorization. IEEE Signal Process. Lett. **17**(1), 4–7 (2009)
10. Liu, H., Wu, Z., Li, X.: Constrained nonnegative matrix factorization for image representation. IEEE Trans. Pattern Anal. Mach. Intell. **34**(7), 1299–1311 (2011)
11. Li, Z., Tang, J., He, X.: Robust structured nonnegative matrix factorization for image representation. IEEE Trans. Neural Netw. Learn. Syst. **29**(5), 1947–1960 (2017)
12. Jia, Y., Kwong, S., Hou, J.: Semi-supervised non-negative matrix factorization with dissimilarity and similarity regularization. IEEE Trans. Neural Netw. Learn. Syst. **31**(7), 2510–2521 (2019)
13. Wang B., Tu Z., Tsotsos JK.: Dynamic label propagation for semi-supervised multiclass multi-label classification. In: Proceedings of the IEEE International Conference on Computer Vision, pp. 425–432 (2013)
14. Hoyer, P.O.: Nonnegative matrix factorization with sparseness constraints. J. Mach. Learn. Res. **5**(9), 1457–1469 (2004)
15. Zhang, L., Liu, Z., Pu, J.: Adaptive graph regularized nonnegative matrix factorization for data representation. Appl. Intell. **50**(2), 438–447 (2020)
16. Zhou D., Bousquet O., Lal T.: Learning with local and global consistency. Adv. Neural Inf. Process. Syst. **16**(3) (2003)
17. Xing, Z., Wen, M., Peng, J.: Discriminative semi-supervised non-negative matrix factorization for data clustering. Eng. Appl. Artif. Intell. **103**(1), 104289 (2021)
18. Xing, Z., Ma, Y., Yang, X.: Graph regularized nonnegative matrix factorization with label discrimination for data clustering. Neurocomputing **440**, 297–309 (2021)
19. Ye, X., Sakurai, T.: Robust similarity measure for spectral clustering based on shared neighbors. ETRI J. **38**(3), 540–550 (2016)
20. Belkin, M., Niyogi, P.: Laplacian eigenmaps and spectral techniques for embedding and clustering. Adv. Neural. Inf. Process. Syst. **14**(6), 585–591 (2001)
21. Chaudhuri, D., Chaudhuri, B.: A novel multiseed nonhierarchical data clustering technique. IEEE Trans. Syst. Man Cybern. **27**(5), 871–876 (1997)

An Empirical Study on the Impact of Environmental Policies on Green Total Factor Productivity of Manufacturing Industry in China

Yanru Cui[1]([✉]), Mingran Wu[2], Tao Wang[1], and Mengjun Ming[1]

[1] National University of Defense Technology, Changsha 410073, China
cuiyanru@nudt.edu.cn
[2] Nanjing University of Posts and Telecommunications, Nanjing 210003, China

Abstract. Based on the concept of green development, resource and environmental factors are incorporated into the traditional analysis framework of total factor productivity. The SBM-GML model is employed to measure the green total factor productivity and its decomposition value of the manufacturing industry using the panel data of 27 manufacturing sub-sectors in China from 2016 to 2020. Then to investigate the nonlinear relationship between environmental policy and green total factor productivity, linear and nonlinear panel data models are built. Based on empirical analysis, the subsequent conclusions have been drawn: the overall green total factor productivity of China's manufacturing industry is at an upward level, and there is a clear stage in the sample range, with gentle fluctuations in the initial period and gradually increasing fluctuations in the later stage. Furthermore, there are obvious industry differences in the growth of GTFP in the manufacturing industry. Finally, there are different nonlinear relationships between heterogeneous environmental policy instruments and green total factor productivity.

Keywords: Green Total Factor Productivity · Environmental Policy · SBM-GML

1 Introduction

Since the reform and opening up, China's national economy has developed vigorously. However, as the shortcomings of the long-term crude economic growth mode emerge, high input, high pollution and high energy consumption have gradually become the constraints on China's economic and social development. Therefore, it has become an inevitable choice for the high-quality development of China's economy to seek a sustainable development path for the manufacturing industry and to solve the contradiction between economic development, resource constraints, and ecological protection. The green total factor productivity-oriented economic development model has become one of the important means of China's current stage of green sustainable development path, in promoting economic development while taking into account both the reasonable consumption of energy resources and balancing the impact of environmental factors in the

Y. Tan and Y. Shi (Eds.): DMBD 2023, CCIS 2018, pp. 85–100, 2024.
https://doi.org/10.1007/978-981-97-0844-4_7

production process. However, the market mechanism alone is unable to address these external diseconomy issues due to the negative externality of the environment. Instead, the government must take active actions through environmental policy to compel businesses to change. Therefore, it is presently a hot topic of concern for people from all walks of life in the community to investigate how the environmental policy will influence the GTFP, whether to lead to its development in trouble or to push the manufacturing industry "phoenix nirvana".

About the issue of environmental policy and the development of the manufacturing industry, there are currently three mainstream views in the academic community: the first is the innovation compensation theory, which argues that appropriate environmental policies can be used to stimulate the innovation initiative of enterprises, so as to promote the development of enterprises and offset the increased cost caused by environmental policies (Poter and Linde, 1995; Lanoie et al., 2010) [1, 2]. The second is the following cost theory, which argues that the implementation of environmental policies will make enterprises spend more time, manpower, and financial resources to install and operate environmental protection facilities, etc. In turn, the policies negatively affect the economic performance (Wayne B. Gray, 1993; Ambec et al., 2013) [3, 4]. The third believes that there is uncertainty in the mechanism of the role of environmental policy on economic growth. For example, Zhang Tongbin (2017) found that strong environmental regulations can stimulate the "innovation compensation" effect of polluting firms, which transforms their short-term losses into long-term gains [5].

The aspects of environmental policy intensity, environmental policy type on GTFP impact, as well as its indirect impact mechanism, are important areas of current academic research. For example, in terms of the impact of environmental policy intensity on green productivity, Peuckert (2014) found that the impact of environmental regulation intensity on total factor productivity differs in the short and long term [6]. Johnstone et al. (2017) argue that the increase in the intensity of environmental regulatory policies boosts total factor productivity, but its impact is nonlinear and subjects to threshold effects [7]. In terms of the impact of various types of environmental policies on GTFP, Chaofan Chen et al. (2018) argue that there is an inverted U-shaped nonlinear impact between different types of environmental regulatory policies and GTFP [8]. Li et al. (2019) argue that command-and-control environmental policies don't have a significant impact on GTFP in the iron and steel industry, whereas there is a U-shaped impact of market-driven environmental policies [9]. In terms of the indirect impact of environmental policies on GTFP, some scholars believe that the mechanism of environmental policies on GTFP is mainly realized through technological progress and the improvement of technical efficiency (Martinez-Zarzoso et al., 2019; Zhou et al., 2020) [10, 11]. In addition, some scholars use factors such as foreign investment and industrial structure as mediating variables to explore the path of environmental policy on GTFP (Qiu, 2021; Li and Liu, 2020) [12, 13].

The existing research results provide a theoretical basis and a research method for reference for this study. Given this, this paper starts with the types of environmental policies to test whether various types of environmental policies can effectively promote the enhancement of GTFP in the manufacturing industry, and to explore the role of its mechanism with GTFP, to be able to provide the corresponding empirical results and policy recommendations.

2 Industry Classification and Green Total Factor Productivity Measurement

2.1 Industry Classification

This study refers to the national economy industry classification standard (GB/T4754–2011) to select 27 manufacturing sub-industries such as the food manufacturing industry as the object of study, and divides the 27 manufacturing industries into three categories of highly, moderately and heavily polluting industries according to the degree of pollution emission [14]. The specific methods are shown below:

1) Calculate pollution emissions:

$$UE_{ij} = E_{ij}/O_i \tag{1}$$

where E_{ij} is the pollution emission of the jth pollutant for the ith industry and O_i is the business revenue of each industry ($i = 1, 2, \cdots, m; j = 1, 2, \cdots, n$).

2) Standardized pollution emissions:

$$UE_{ij}^s = \frac{UE_{ij} - \min(UE_j)}{\max(UE_j) - \min(UE_j)} \tag{2}$$

3) Calculate the average score:

$$MUE_{ij} = \sum_{j=1}^{n} UE_{ij}^s/n \tag{3}$$

4) Calculate the pollution emission intensity in different industries:

$$Score_{ij} = \sum_{j=1}^{n} NUE_{ij}/t \tag{4}$$

where $Score_{ij}$ is the average annual pollution emission intensity.

The specific results are shown in Table 1. Influenced by the specific research intervals and so on, this paper has some discrepancies in the classification of specific subsectors, but the overall classification results are roughly the same as those of Li Ling (2012), indicating that the measurement results of this paper have a certain degree of reasonableness and scientificity.

Table 1. Classification of Manufacturing Industries.

categorization	Industry
Heavily polluting industries	Agricultural and sideline foodstuffs processing industry (I1); food manufacturing (I2); textile industry (I5); manufacture of paper and paper products (I10); oil processing, coking and nuclear fuel processing (I13); manufacture of raw chemical materials and chemical products (I14); nonmental mineral product industry (I18); ferrous metal smelting and calendering processing industry (I19); nonferrous metal smelting and rolling processing industry (I20)
Moderately polluting industries	Wine, beverage and refined tea manufacturing (I3); leather, fur, feather, and their manufacturing industry (I7); wood processing and manufacturing of rattan, bamboo, and palm grass (I8); pharmaceutical manufacturing industry (I15); chemical fiber manufacturing industry (I16); metal products industry (I21); automobile manufacturing industry (I24); electrical machinery and equipment manufacturing industry (I26); computer, communications and other electronic equipment manufacturing (I27)
Lightly polluting industries	Tobacco industry (I4); textile and clothing manufacturing industry (I6); furniture manufacturing industry (I9); printing and recording media reproduction (I11); arts, education, sports and entertainment goods manufacturing (I12); rubber and plastic products industry (I17); general equipment manufacturing industry (I22); special equipment manufacturing (I23); railway, shipbuilding, aerospace and other transportation equipment manufacturing (I25)

2.2 Green Total Factor Productivity Measurement.

SBM Model and GML Index. *SBM model.* Considering that the traditional DEA model does not take into account the non-expected outputs such as environmental pollution, this paper draws on the SBM model proposed by Tone (2001) that includes non-expected outputs. The SBM model overcomes the shortcomings of the radial model that cannot adequately take into account the slack of inputs and outputs, and carrying out the efficiency evaluation more accurately [15]. In this paper, each industry of manufacturing industry is taken as a production decision unit and the n input factors of each industry are set as $x_j = (x_{1j}, x_{2j}, \cdots, x_{nj})$, and the desired output of each industry is denoted as $y_j = (y_{1j}, y_{2j}, \cdots, y_{gj})$, while the non-desired output is denoted as $z_j = (z_{1j}, z_{2j}, \cdots, z_{bj})$, so the SBM model is expressed as:

$$\min \rho = \frac{1 - \frac{1}{n} \sum_{i=1}^{n} \frac{s_i^-}{x_{i0}}}{1 + \frac{1}{g+b} \left(\sum_{r=1}^{g} \frac{y_r^+}{y_{r0}} + \sum_{t=1}^{b} \frac{z_t^-}{z_{t0}} \right)} \tag{5}$$

$$s.t. \begin{cases} \sum_{j=1}^{n} x_{ij}\lambda_j + s_i^- = x_{i0} & i = 1, 2, \cdots, n \\ \sum_{j=1}^{n} y_{rj}\lambda_j - y_r^+ = y_{r0} & i = 1, 2, \cdots, g \\ \sum_{j=1}^{n} z_{tj}\lambda_j + z_t^- = z_{t0} & i = 1, 2, \cdots, b \\ \sum_{j=1}^{n} \lambda_j = 1 \\ \lambda_j, s_i^-, y_r^+, z_t^- \geqslant 0 \end{cases} \tag{6}$$

where ρ is the objective function, s_i^- is the input slack variable, y_r^+ is the desired output slack variable, and z_t^- is the non-desired output slack variable. When $\rho = 1$, it means the decision unit is valid; when ρ is between 0 and 1, it means the decision units invalid.

GML Index. In order to effectively solve the problem of linear programming without feasible solutions, OH (2010) constructed the Global-Malmquist-Luenberger productivity index (GML) based on the Malmquist-Luenberger index by combining its concept of productivity with the directional distance function [16]. Where x^t, y^t, b^t is the input factor, desired output and non-desired output of decision unit in period t, and $D^G(x^t, y^t, b^t)$ is the global directional distance function. Therefore the GML index formula is:

$$\begin{aligned} GML_t^{t+1} &= \frac{1 + D_0^G(x^t, y^t, b^t)}{1 + D_0^G(x^{t+1}, y^{t+1}, b^{t+1})} \\ &= \frac{1 + D_0^t(x^t, y^t, b^t)}{1 + D_0^{t+1}(x^{t+1}, y^{t+1}, b^{t+1})} \times \left[\frac{\frac{1 + D_0^G(x^t, y^t, b^t)}{1 + D_0^t(x^t, y^t, b^t)}}{\frac{1 + D_0^G(x^{t+1}, y^{t+1}, b^{t+1})}{1 + D_0^{t+1}(x^{t+1}, y^{t+1}, b^{t+1})}} \right] \\ &= EC_t^{t+1} + TC_t^{t+1} \end{aligned} \tag{7}$$

where when $GML > 1$ indicating that the industry GTFP development shows an increasing trend in the period, otherwise, it declines. The GML index can be decomposed into the change in technical efficiency (EC) and the change in technological progress (TC).

Input-Output Indicators. Input factor indicators: capital inputs, for the estimated value of the capital stock, the net fixed assets of enterprises above the designated size in 27 sub-industries of Chinese manufacturing are used, while the price index of fixed asset investment is used to adjust the data of capital stock with 2015 as the base period to minimize the impact of inflation; for manpower input, it is expressed by the annual average number of people employed in enterprises above designated size in the sub-industries; for energy input, it is expressed using the total energy consumption of enterprises in the manufacturing sub-industries and converted to 10,000 tons of standard coal according to the standard coal conversion factor.

Indicators of output elements: desired output, expressed by the main business income of enterprises above the scale of 27 manufacturing sub-industries, with 2015 as the base period and the main business income data adjusted by using the producer ex-factory price index of each industry; non-desired output, expressed by the pollution emissions of enterprises above the scale of the sub-industries, with the specific indicators including the emissions of chemical oxygen demand (COD) and the emissions of industrial sulfur dioxide (SO_2) and so on. In the process of measuring, environmental pollution indicators are further constructed by the entropy value method.

The above data are mainly from the "China Statistical Yearbook" and other sources as well as the website of the National Bureau of Statistics, and the missing data of individual years are made up by interpolation and autoregressive prediction. The descriptive statistics of each input-output variables are analyzed as shown in Table 2 below.

Table 2. Descriptive statistics of input-output data

Variable		Unit of Measure	Mean	SD	Max	Min
Input factor indicators	capital inputs	Billion	8647.05	7097.00	29671.73	1232.58
	manpower input	ten thousand person	280.31	191.89	914.84	16.16
	energy input	Mtce	9507.98	16231.96	66851.00	180.00
Desired outputs	revenue	Billion	37265.71	27725.50	117084.72	6634.63
Non-desired output	Environmental pollution indicators	No	0.0816	0.1336	0.6771	0.0011

Results of Green Total Factor Productivity Measurements. Based on the various input-output indicators set in the previous section, this paper measures the green total factor productivity (GTFP) of China's manufacturing industries as well as its decomposition terms using Maxdea and the SBM-GML model. Considering that the GTFP and its decomposition terms measured by Maxdea express the dynamic change process of adjacent years, this paper uses the end year of the adjacent period to represent the period, such as using 2017 to represent the period of 2016–2017.

Overall Industry Conditions in the Manufacturing Sector. Figure 1 represents the overall trend change of GTFP and its decomposition index technical efficiency and technical progress in manufacturing industry from 2016 to 2020. From the figure, it can be seen that the GTFP, TC and EC indexes in each year basically fluctuate around 1 up and down, and has an obvious stage in the sample range, with gentle fluctuations in the first period and gradually increasing fluctuations in the later stage.

In 2016–2018, the average value of GTFP in the manufacturing industry was 1.0378, the average value of the EC was 0.9635, and the average value of TC index was 1.1381. It can be seen that the increase in the green total factor productivity in this period mainly lies in the improvement of the level of technological progress. This can be attributed to the fact that with the "Made in China 2025" program, a series of guiding policy documents for the green and sustainable development of the manufacturing industry have been introduced to promote the transformation of more innovative achievements and their application to the development of the manufacturing industry. The decline in the level of EC indicates that the original enterprise management model is no longer adapted to the current level of production and market demand, so the technical efficiency of the manufacturing industry to a certain extent limits the development of GTFP.

During the 2019–2020 period, the GTFP development of the manufacturing sector is more volatile in this period, with a significant increase in the TC and a significant drop in the EC. This may be related to the initiation of various STI research projects brought about by the initial phase of the New Crown Epidemic and business mismanagement due to the shutdown of industries and work stoppages.

Analysis of Environmental Pollution Heterogeneity. By the above division of the manufacturing industry according to the degree of pollution emission, this paper calculates the change in the trend of GTFP for heavy, medium and light pollution industries as shown in Fig. 2. The average GTFP values of heavy, medium and light pollution industries are 1.0698, 1.1055 and 1.1782 respectively, which are all greater than 1. This indicates that the GTFP of the three types of industries shows a clear growth trend, and the development of light pollution industries is more mature, but the development is more similar in the early part of the analyzed period, and the difference is stronger in the later part. Among them, the GTFP of the heavy pollution industry shows a trend of first increasing and then decreasing, which plays a certain role in inhibiting the growth of the overall GTFP in later development. The main reason for this phenomenon may be the difference in industry types. Most of the highly polluting industries are heavy chemical industries, such as petroleum processing coking and nuclear fuel processing industries, which have a higher dependence on resources and produce more polluting emissions in the production process, hindering the development of GTFP.

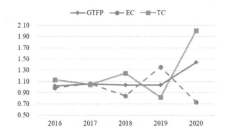
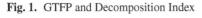
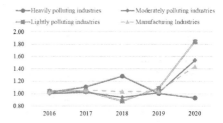

Fig. 1. GTFP and Decomposition Index   **Fig. 2.** GTFP Trend Chart by Industry

3 Empirical Analysis

3.1 Model Construction

In order to empirically test the relationship between environmental regulation and GTFP, this paper chooses a fixed-effect model to eliminate the effect of unobserved heterogeneity and constructs a linear model to analyze the correlation, as below:

$$\ln GTFP_{it} = \alpha_0 + \alpha_1 \ln ER_{it} + \vartheta X_{it} + \tau_t + \varepsilon_{it} \tag{8}$$

where α_0 is a constant term, α_1 is the coefficient of the core explanatory variable environmental policy on the explanatory variable GTFP, X_{it} is a control variable, τ_t is a time fixed effect, ε_{it} is a random error term.

Considering that there may be a nonlinear relationship between environmental policy and GTFP, and in order to study whether there is an optimal effect of environmental policy implementation efforts, this paper adds the quadratic term of the environmental policy variables to construct a nonlinear model. As shown in Eq. 9. Where α_2 is the coefficient of the effect of the quadratic term of the core explanatory variable environmental policy on the explanatory variable GTFP.

$$\ln GTFP_{it} = \alpha_0 + \alpha_1 \ln ER_{it} + \alpha_2 (\ln ER_{it})^2 + \vartheta X_{it} + \tau_t + \varepsilon_{it} \tag{9}$$

3.2 Index Selection and Data Declaration

Explained Variable. Green Total Factor Productivity. Considering that the value of the SBM-GML index measured in the previous section is the level of the growth rate of GTFP, which represents its change relative to the previous year's green productivity. This paper draws on Chen Chaofan's (2016) adjustment method [17], the actual GTFP value is obtained by serial multiplication of the measured GML index, such as assuming that the GTFP of 2015 as the base period is 1, the actual GTEP of 2016 is the base period value of 2015 multiplied by the GML index value of 2016.

Core Explanatory Variables. This paper measures environmental policies in terms of Command-Control environmental policies (CE) and market-driven environmental policies (ME). CE selects the operating costs of pollution control facilities in each industry as a proxy variable [18], which is calculated as follows:

$$CE_j = \sum_{i=1}^{n} c_{ij}/w_j \tag{10}$$

where c_{ij} is the cost of operating pollutant treatment facilities in various industries; w_j is the business income of each industry.

Market incentive-based environmental policies mainly include environmental protection tax, R&D subsidies and other policies. In this paper, we choose the natural logarithm of sewage charge/environmental protection tax to represent it. Since the sub-industry summary data on sewage charges cannot be found directly, this paper estimates the 2016–2017 sewage charge data. The specific methods are as follows.

(1) Calculate the emissions of various types of major industrial pollutants: this paper selects industrial wastewater and exhaust gas pollutants for calculation. Among them, industrial wastewater pollutants include ammonia nitrogen, etc.; industrial exhaust pollutants include industrial particulate matter, etc.
(2) Calculation of the number of pollution equivalents: this paper refers to the provisions of the "sewage charge levy standards and calculation methods" (hereinafter referred to as "Methods") for the calculation of the equivalent number of each pollutant:

$$\gamma_i = \frac{p_i}{\sigma_i} \tag{11}$$

where γ_i is the number of pollution equivalents number of a pollutant; p_i is a pollutant emission; σ_i is the pollution equivalents of the pollutant

(3) Determine the fee factor: then rank each pollutant equivalent number in descending order and determine the first three as the fee factor (it can be less than but not more than three).

(4) Calculation of sewage charges:

$$SC_i = u_i * \sum (\gamma_{ij})$$ (12)

where SC_i is a charge for the discharge of various pollutants; u_i is the standard price of the relevant sewage charge.

Finally, it is sufficient to sum the resulting sewage charges. Considering that it takes some time for CE to produce effects from lag, it is treated with a two-period lag in the empirical analysis.

Control Variables. (1) Labor force employment skill structure (LS). In this paper, the ratio of the high-skilled labor force to the low-skilled labor force is regarded as labor force employment skill structure [19]. Among them, the subindustry R&D personnel is taken as the indicator of a high-skilled labor force, and the difference between the number of employed persons and R&D personnel in each industry is taken as the low-skilled labor force. (2) Ownership structure (SC), which is measured by the ratio of business revenue of large and medium-sized state-controlled industrial enterprises to the revenue of large and medium-sized enterprises. (3) Independent Innovation (ZZCX). This paper selects internal expenditure on R&D and expenditure on digestion and absorption of each manufacturing industry as the proxy variables, and constructs the independent innovation index by entropy value method. Considering that independent innovation needs time investment, it will be treated with a two-period lag in the empirical analysis. (4) Size structure (GMIG). This is expressed by the ratio of the total revenue of large and medium-sized industrial enterprises in each industry to the total revenue of the industry. (5) Technology introduction level (JSYJ). In this paper, the expenditure on introducing technology and expenditure on purchasing domestic technology" of manufacturing enterprises are selected as proxies for this variable, and the index is constructed by the entropy value method.

All data are mainly from the "China Statistical Yearbook" and other sources, as well as the website of the National Bureau of Statistics. Missing data of individual years are filled in by linear interpolation. In order to eliminate the heteroscedasticity and multicollinearity of the data, the data required in the model are logarithmically processed. The descriptive statistics of the above variables are shown in Table 3.

3.3   Empirical Results Analysis

Empirical Test. *Multicollinearity test.* When carrying out multiple regression, it is usually necessary to carry out the test of multicollinearity first, to avoid the regression coefficients that cannot explain the regression model due to the excessive correlation between the independent variables. As can be seen from Table 4, the variance inflation

Table 3. Descriptive statistics

Variable	number	Mean	SD	Max	Min
lnGTFP	135	9.28	0.26	8.57	10.08
lnCE	135	4.67	1.06	2.37	6.36
lnME	135	2.19	0.17	1.81	2.52
lnLS	135	6.10	0.56	4.79	6.89
lnSC	135	7.36	1.03	4.82	8.84
lnZZCX	135	5.67	1.26	2.76	7.91
lnGMJG	135	8.60	0.32	7.53	9.10
lnJSYJ	135	4.86	1.56	2.42	8.40

factor (VIF) values of all variables are less than 10, and the 1/VIF values are between 0.15 and 0.9, which can basically determine that there is no multicollinearity between the variables.

Table 4. Variance inflation factor test

	lnCE	lnLS	lnSC	lnZZCX	lnGMJG	lnJSYJ	Mean
VIF	1.15	2.33	1.70	3.83	1.62	5.55	2.69
1/VIF	0.87	0.43	0.59	0.26	0.62	0.18	0.49
	lnME	lnLS	lnSC	lnZZCX	lnGMJG	lnJSYJ	Mean
VIF	1.99	2.70	2.08	5.80	1.64	5.80	3.34
1/VIF	0.50	0.37	0.48	0.17	0.61	0.17	0.38

Table 5. Panel cointegration test

Variable	Inspection indicators	Statistic	p-value
lnGTFP, lnCE, lnME	Augmented Dickey-Fuller	−5.2800	0.0000
	Unadjusted modified Dickey-Fuller	−1.9932	0.0231
	Unadjusted Dickey-Fuller	−2.0143	0.0220
lnGTFP, lnCE, lnME, lnLS, lnSC, lnZZCX, lnGMJG, lnJSYJ	Augmented Dickey-Fuller	−3.3898	0.0003
	Unadjusted modified Dickey-Fuller	−2.2549	0.0121
	Unadjusted Dickey-Fuller	−3.5187	0.0002

Cointegration Test. After conducting the panel unit root test, it is found that the industry data collected in this paper is non-stationary. In order to avoid pseudo-regression, a panel cointegration test is needed to determine whether there is a long-run equilibrium cointegration relationship between the variables. The specific results are shown in the Table 5. The Kao test rejects the original hypothesis of "there is no cointegration relationship" at the 5% significance level. Therefore, there is a cointegration relationship between the variables and the causal relationship between the variables can be discussed in depth.

Analysis of Regression Results. *Regression results on the impact of command-and-control environmental policies.* The data shows that the coefficients of the primary term of CE are positive in both linear and nonlinear models, while the R-squared and adjusted R-squared of the regression results of the nonlinear model (9) are higher than those of the linear model (8). Therefore, it is straightforward to assume that CE has an inverted "U" shaped effect on GTFP. Specifically, as the implementation of environmental policy increases, it will first promote and then inhibit GTFP.

Table 6. Regression results

Variable	(1)	(2)	Variable	(3)	(4)
	lnGTFP	lnGTFP		lnGTFP	lnGTFP
lnCE	0.334**	1.849**	lnME	9.982**	−59.81*
	(0.160)	(0.867)		(3.777)	(35.02)
lnCE2	–	−0.171*	lnME2	–	16.23*
		(0.0965)			(8.267)
lnLS	−1.255***	−1.167**	lnLS	−1.076**	−0.654
	(0.463)	(0.455)		(0.462)	(0.410)
lnSC	0.173	0.237	lnSC	0.440	0.600**
	(0.244)	(0.241)		(0.281)	(0.232)
lnZZCX	0.222	0.259	lnZZCX	0.231	0.612***
	(0.231)	(0.226)		(0.300)	(0.221)
lnGMJG	−2.428***	−2.461***	lnGMJG	−2.439***	2.090***
	(0.864)	(0.844)		(0.831)	(0.730)
lnJSYJ	0.253**	0.232**	lnJSYJ	0.195*	0.167*
	(0.0984)	(0.0969)		(0.0998)	(0.0935)
_cons	32.64***	28.64***	_cons	9.542	39.31
	(10.37)	(10.38)		(14.16)	(36.60)
time effect	control	control	time effect	control	control
R2	0.632	0.657	R2	0.647	0.697
adj. R2	0.361	0.389	adj. R2	0.387	0.461

Based on the regression results in Table 6, this paper plots the nonlinear impact analysis of CE on GTFP in Fig. 3. When the innovation compensation effect is stronger, it will promote the development of GTFP; when the cost effect and crowding out effect are stronger, CE may lead to problems such as increased production costs, high market entry thresholds, and insufficient investment funds, which will harm the city's economic returns. With the increase in the intensity of the implementation of environmental policies, enterprises will increase the cost of emission reduction and environmental protection in order to meet the environmental protection requirements. If enterprises do not actively carry out pollution control because of the high cost, this will damage the interests of the community. At this time, the enterprise's private marginal cost will be less than the social marginal cost, thus generating a negative externality of production, which in turn inhibits the enhancement of enterprise efficiency. Therefore, the government's reasonable and effective policy system is an important guarantee to drive the green development of the manufacturing industry.

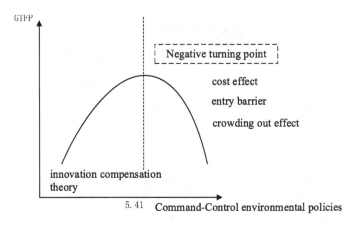

Fig. 3. The nonlinear impact analysis of CE on GTFP

Regression Results on the Impact of Market-Incentivized Environmental Policies. Table 6 demonstrates the fixed-effects regression results of ME and GTFP. The regression coefficients of the primary term of their linear model are positive; however, the regression coefficients of the primary term of the nonlinear model are negative, and the regression coefficients of the secondary term are positive.

Considering that the primary term coefficients of ME have opposite positive and negative signs in the linear and nonlinear models, this paper utilizes stata16 to further plot the linear and nonlinear fitting graphs (e.g., Fig. 4), and it can be found that the scatter plots have a more obvious U-shape trend. Due to the right side of the inflection point has more scatter distributions than the left side, the results of the positive effect will appear in the linear fitting. Meanwhile, the R-squared and adjusted R-squared of the regression results of the nonlinear model (8) are higher than those of the linear model (9), which indicates that the influence of ME on GTFP shows a "U" shape. Increasing the ME level within a moderate range can enhance the constraints on energy conservation and emission reduction in various industries, which is conducive to the improvement of GTFP.

Based on the regression results in Table 6, this paper plots the nonlinear impact analysis as shown in Fig. 5. When the cost effect, entry barrier and crowding out effect of ME are strong, environmental policy will inhibit the enhancement of GTFP. When the innovation compensation effect and the factor allocation effect are stronger, the ME will incentivize and guide enterprises to reduce pollution emissions and promote the R&D and innovation of new environmental products through the market mechanism, thus promoting the positive development of GTFP.

Robustness Analysis. This research chooses the decomposition term EC of GTFP to replace it to substitute into the model for the robustness test to verify the reliability of the regression results. Table 7 shows that the linear and quadratic terms of the key explanatory variables CE and ME's positive and negative regression coefficients pass the test at the 10% significance level and are consistent with the outcomes of the benchmark regression. Additionally, the finding that there are U-shaped and inverted U-shaped connections for the impacts of each form of environmental policy on GTFP is still valid. As a result, it is possible to conclude the relationship between different environmental policy instruments and green total factor productivity.

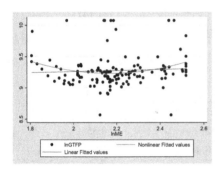

Fig. 4. Plot of linear vs. nonlinear fit of ME to GTFP

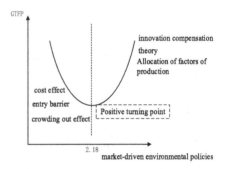

Fig. 5. The nonlinear impact analysis of ME on GTFP

Table 7. Robustness analysis

Variable	(5)	Variable	(6)
	lnEC		lnEC
lnCE	3.245***	lnME	−74.41*
	(0.981)		(42.54)
lnCE2	−0.343***	lnME2	20.55**
	(0.105)		(10.20)
lnLS	−0.989	lnLS	−1.130*
	(0.707)		(0.652)
lnSC	−0.978**	lnSC	−1.166**
	(0.453)		(0.512)
lnZZCX	0.362	lnZZCX	−0.458
	(0.299)		(0.316)
lnGMJG	0.803	lnGMJG	−2.152*
	(0.809)		(1.141)
lnJSYJ	0.106	lnJSYJ	0.108
	(0.117)		(0.119)
_cons	5.472	_cons	109.0**
	(10.44)		(47.61)
time effect	control	time effect	control
R2	0.553	R2	0.555
adj. R2	0.205	adj. R2	0.209

Note: t-values in parentheses, *, **, and *** indicate significance at the 10%, 5%, and 1% significance levels, respectively.

4 Conclusion

Based on the concept of green development, this paper combines energy and environmental issues with traditional total factor productivity analysis. Utilizing the 2016–2020 panel data of China's 27 manufacturing industry, this paper studies the mechanism of the impact of environmental policies on GTFP in manufacturing. It is found that China's manufacturing GTFP as a whole is at an increasing level, and has an obvious stage in the sample interval, with flat fluctuations in the early stage and gradually increasing fluctuations in the later stage. At the same time, there are obvious industry differences in the growth of GTFP in the manufacturing industry, the average annual growth rate of GTFP is the highest in medium and lightly polluted industries, followed by medium polluted industries; the average productivity value of heavily polluted industries has decreased. Finally, there are different nonlinear relationships between heterogeneous environmental policy instruments and GTFP. There is an inverted U-shaped nonlinear relationship between command-and-control environmental policy and GTFP, while the impact of market incentive environmental policy on GTFP shows a U-shaped relationship. With the increase of policy intensity, the enhancement of GTFP shows the impact of inhibition followed by promotion.

Combined with the findings of this paper, the following policy recommendations are put forward: firstly, at the enterprise level, enterprises should proactively carry out enterprise management mode and scale efficiency improvement, building a scientific and effective enterprise management mode with clear responsibilities and keep pace with the times, to promote the overall high-quality development of the industry. Secondly, according to the degree of pollution in the industry, it should formulate enterprise segmentation environmental protection standards and strengthen the promotion of enterprise clean production mode. Third, at the national level, the development status of different industries should be taken into account and the implementation intensity of various environmental policy tools should be adjusted accordingly. Due to the manufacturing industry segments having obvious heterogeneity, the formulation of policy can't blindly take "one size fits all" policy measures. It should be formulated by the characteristics of different industries and the current state of development, and environmental protection taxes, technological upgrading and other forms of policies should be adopted in a coordinated manner, so as to gradually promote the green development of enterprises and advance the process of carbon peak attainment and carbon neutrality in a steady and orderly manner.

References

1. Poter, M.E., Linde, C.V.D.: Green and competitive: ending the stalemate. Harv. Bus. Rev. **73**(5), 120–133 (1995)
2. Lanoie, P., Luccheti, J., Johnstone, N., Ambec, S.: Environmental policy, innovation and performance: new insights on the porter hypothesis. J. Econ. Manage. Strategy **20**(3), 803–842 (2011)
3. Ambec, S., Cohen, M.A., Elgie, S., et al.: The porter hypothesis at 20: can environmental regulation enhance innovation and competitiveness? Rev. Environ. Econ. Policy **7**(1), 2–22 (2013)
4. Gray, W.B.: Environmental regulation and manufacturing productivity at the plant level. Nberworking paper, No. 4321. Cambridge, Mass. (1993)
5. Tongbin, Z.: Can enhancing the environmental regulation intensity address both current and long-term needs? Financ. Trade Econ. **38**(03), 116–130 (2017)
6. Peuckert, J.: What shapes the impact of environmental regulation on competitiveness? evidence from executive opinion surveys. Environ. Innov. Soc. Trans. **10**, 77–94 (2014)
7. Johnstone, N., Managi, S., Rodriguez, M.C., et al.: Environmental policy design, innovation and efficiency gains in electricity generation. Energy Econ. **63**, 106–115 (2017)
8. Chaofan, C., Jing, H., Yuanlong, M.: Environmental regulation, industrial heterogeneity and industrial green growth in china—a nonlinear test from the perspective of total factor productivity. J. Shanxi Univ. Financ. Econ. **40**(03), 65–80 (2018)
9. Li, H., Zhu, X., Chen, J., Jiang, F.: Environmental regulations, environmental governance efficiency and the green transformation of China's iron and steel enterprises. Ecol. Econ. **165**, 106397 (2019)
10. Martínez Zarzoso, I., Bengochea-Morancho, A., Morales, L.R.: Does environmental policy stringency foster innovation and productivity in OECD countries? Energy Policy **134**, 110982 (2019)

11. Zhou, X., Xia, M., Zhang, T., Du, J.: Energy-and environment-biased technological progress induced by different types of environmental regulations in China. Sustainability **12**(18), 7486 (2020)

12. Li, Q., Liu, S., Yang, M., et al.: The effects of China's sustainable development policy for resource-based cities on local industrial transformation. Resour. Policy **71**, 101940 (2021)

13. Qiu, S., Wang, Z., Geng, S.: How do environmental regulation and foreign investment behavior affect green productivity growth in the industrial sector? An empirical test based on Chinese provincial panel data. J. Environ. Manage. **287**, 112282 (2021)

14. Li, L., Tao, F.: Selection of optimal environmental regulation intensity for chinese manufacturing industry—based on the green TFP perspective. China Ind. Econ. **290**(05), 70–82 (2012)

15. Tone, K.: A slacks-based measure of efficiency in data envelopment analysis. Eur. J. Oper. Res. **130**(3), 498–509 (2001)

16. Oh, D.: A global Malmquist-Luenberger productivity index. J. Prod. Anal. **34**, 183–197 (2010)

17. Chen, C.: China's industrial green total factor productivity and its determinants—an empirical study based on ML index and dynamic panel data mode. Stat. Res. **33**(3), 53–62 (2016)

18. Zhang, X., Liu, J., Li, B.: Environmental regulation, technological innovation and the green development of manufacturing. J. Guangdong Univ. Financ. Econ. **35**(05), 48–57 (2020)

19. Lyu, Y., Yang, F.: Study on the impact of environmental regulation on the labor employment skill structure. J. Stat. Inf. **37**(03), 86–96 (2022)

Digital Simulation Methods

Construction of Digital Twin Battlefield with Command and Control as the Core

Fang Wang[✉], Ling Ye, Shaoqiu Zheng, Haiqing Wang, Chenyu Huang, and Lingyun Lu

Nanjing Research Institute of Electronic Engineering, Nanjing 210007, China
caoerzhu@163.com

Abstract. With the development of networking information-centric system of systems (SoS), the complexity and fidelity requirements of digital twin battlefield construction are gradually increasing. Currently, we are facing with the problem that the models with command and control elements in digital twin battlefield are relatively weak. The combat process in real battlefield can't be fully mapped by digital twin battlefield. The method of command and control system digital twin modeling is studied intensively, and then the operation architecture of the digital twin battlefield with command and control system as the core and serial key technologies are proposed, the typical application scenarios supporting the combat decision-making and SoS optimization design are analyzed. Finally, the ideas of digital twin battlefield construction and application are brought up.

Keywords: Digital Twin Battlefield · Command and Control · Modeling

1 Introduction

In recent years, with the development and application of emerging science and technology such as the Internet of Things, Cloud Computing, Artificial Intelligence, Virtual Reality, Augmented Reality and so on, digital twin technology has moved from concept to reality. In the military field, digital twin technology has been gradually applied in the fields of Equipment Manufacturing, Simulation & Training and Maintenance & Logistics. Further, digital twin technology will be expanded to support the construction of digital twin for a real battlefield space. Command and control system as the "brain" and "nerve center" of the modern combat system of systems (SoS) is a key element in the networking information-centric SoS. In the construction and application of digital twin battlefield, the digital twin model of the command and control system plays an important role in improving the realism of the digital twin battlefield.

This paper firstly introduces the current situation of the digital twin battlefield and the digital twin model of the command and control system in foreign countries, and then aiming at the indispensable role of the command and control elements in the digital twin battlefield, researches the specificity and importance of constructing the command and control system digital twin model. It puts forward the operation architecture of the digital twin battlefield with command and control system as the core and serial key technologies, and analyzes the typical application scenarios. At last, it provides a better solution for the construction of the digital twin battlefield.

Y. Tan and Y. Shi (Eds.): DMBD 2023, CCIS 2018, pp. 103–114, 2024.
https://doi.org/10.1007/978-981-97-0844-4_8

2 Digital Twin Battlefield Status

The concept of digital twin can be traced back to 2002, Professor Grieves [1] of the University of Michigan in the United States, put forward the real space, virtual space, as well as from the real space to the virtual space of data flow and from the virtual space to the real space of information flow. After that, Prof. Grieves successively used the "Mirror Space Model", "Information Mirror Model" and other names in the treatise. In 2010, NASA released the "Modeling, simulation, information technology & processing roadmap" [2], which specified the development vision of digital twin. In 2011, NASA engineer John Vickers named it "digital twin". The significance of the digital twin is to realize the feedback of the real physical system to the digital model of the virtual space, and the various types of simulation, analysis, data accumulation, data mining, and even the application of artificial intelligence that grow out of this feedback can ensure its applicability to the real physical system [3]. According to the U.S. Army, digital twin is an effective method to realize the interaction and communion between the physical world and the information world, which can portray the physical world, simulate the physical world, optimize the physical world, and enhance the physical world by the information world. The core concept and mode of digital twin are introduced into the military field, especially the field of battlefield construction. The concept of digital twin battlefield is giving birth.

Digital twin battlefield is the digitalization, virtualization and intelligence of each physical element and physical system in real battlefield, and its core is the realistic simulation of the real combat environment [4]. The construction and application of digital twin battlefield in foreign countries is being gradually carried out. From February to March 2022, the U.S. Navy conducted the first demonstration experiment of the "Advantageous Digital Ecosystem for Naval Aggregation (ADENA)" project [5]. ADENA is also known as "sandbox", which is a virtual digital twin battlefield for technology research, mission planning, and experimental training that supports multi-domain, multi-task, and multi-use case applications. Users only need a shared portal to discover the required tools, models, data and other resources, and can use digital tools for on-demand construction and cloud deployment. It supports users to create personalized digital twin battlefield instances, and carry out all kinds of operational and technological issues research. Plugging in new equipment for a series of systematic test and evaluation is supported.

3 Command and Control System Digital Twin

3.1 Modeling Characteristics

According to the definition in the 2011 edition of «Military Language» [6], the command and control system is an information system that guarantees the commanders and command organizations to implement command and control of combatants and weapon systems. Command and control systems include joint operation command and control systems at all levels, as well as command and control systems of military services and specialized fields. Its development has experienced the process from simple to complex, from low level to high level, from single function to comprehensive function, from simple interconnection to high degree of networking, and from the independent construction of each military service to the integrated construction. The command and control system is soft-based, with the characteristics of human-computer integration, multi-dimensional and system linkage [7].

As a real entity in the physical world, command and control system also has a digital mirror in digital world, that is, the digital twin model. However, for the above characteristics of the command and control system, the construction of command and control system digital twin model, compared with the current aerospace, intelligent manufacturing, smart cities and other fields, there are many differences: ① Twin object is different. The industrial digital twin modeling object is the specific hardware equipment whose geometric characteristics, physical attributes, functional performance indicators, operational processes, etc., are more clearly. However, the command and control system digital twin modeling object is mainly software system but few general hardware. The method of describing the industrial digital model of physical entity characteristics, such as fluid dynamics model, structural mechanics model, thermodynamic model, fatigue damage model, and so on, is not fully applicable to the construction of the command and control system digital twin model. You need to grasp the core elements of the command and control system for abstract modeling; ② Fidelity requirements are different. Generally speaking, the digital twin in virtual space replicates as much as possible the various details of the physical entity in real space, using the digital modeling methods of multi-physical characteristics and the multi-scale integration. The digital twin model accurately reflects the state and behavior of the physical entity. However, the command and control system itself is a digital form mainly, and if its digital twin model infinitely is convergent or equivalent to the actual load, but also the significance of the twin is lost. So, the digital twin model of the command and control system should not only reflect the main features of the actual equipment, but also reduce the scale and refine the functions; ③ The personnel modeling needs are different. Based on the information of the physical entity in the virtual space, the digital twin model is built, and receives data synchronized with the physical entity. It operates and feeds back the information according to the rules in the virtual space, and the whole process does not require the participation of human beings. However, the operation of the command and control system, which is related to the cognitive level of the commanders, is not the same as the physical entity. It can be said that the command and control activities are jointly completed by human and machine. According to the requirement that the digital twin should comprehensively characterize the characteristics, states and behaviors of the physical entity, the digital twin model of the command and control system should contain the digital mirror of the commanders. The complexity of human thought and behavior makes abstract modeling very difficult.

The U.S. military has carried out relevant research and tests in digital twin modeling of command and control system. In March 2019, the U.S. Navy's "Arleigh Burke" class destroyer "Thomas Hudson" successfully conducted its first live-fire intercept test using the "virtual Aegis" system. This is a milestone event in the application of digital twin technology to complex information system. The "Virtual Aegis" system is consisted of the "Aegis" combat system software code and part of the core hardware for virtualization. It used the ATRT equipment and special protocols to access real-battlefield data, conducted online testing and evaluation of new tactical algorithms, and then rapidly deployed the new tactical algorithms to physical ships without affecting the actual combat. In 2020, the U.S. Naval Undersea Warfare Center, Newport Division, created and demonstrated a virtualized AN/BYG-1 submarine combat control system, which provided equivalent submarine combat control system functionality with a quarter of the hardware of an actual system. The Navy also developed and deployed a new machine learning application on the virtual system, validating the ability of virtual-reality interaction and the rapid deployment of new technologies.

3.2 Important Role

In today's information warfare age, the networking information-centric SoS has become the basic form of combat. It integrates all kinds of combat forces, combat units and combat elements, with the complexity and diversity of the war situation. The combat space is broad and multidimensional and the combat forces are new and diverse [8]. The command and control equipment is the adhesive of all kinds of combat elements in the networking information-centric SoS, and it is the core and soul of achieving victory. The command and control equipment has penetrated fully to situational awareness, fire striking, comprehensive protection and other combat areas, fused the intelligence, force, firepower, logistics, equipment and other types of combat elements in the land, sea, air, sky, electricity, network and other battlefield space together. The command and control equipment drives combat elements orderly operation around the common combat objectives, and all of them constitute a tight "observation-adjustment-decision-making-action" (OODA) combat ring, and support "detection, control, resistance, fight, evaluation" combat process. As a result, the combat capabilities of networking information-centric SoS are formed, and the "$1 + 1 > 2$" overall emergence effect is realized.

Digital twin battlefield is a realistic virtual environment or simulation mirror system that runs in parallel with the real battlefield, driven by new technologies such as digital twin, parallel simulation and AI. With the evolution of the real combat system to the networking information-centric SoS, the real battlefield has changes significantly, and the interaction of reconnaissance equipment, communication equipment, combat equipment, electrical resistance equipment, accusation equipment, and security equipment is complex. The composition of networking information-centric SoS and the flow of information are constantly changing along with the process of combat. The command and decision-making process is reflected in the design of the design in the traditional simulation the simplified rules of combat are replaced by a simplified design. The command and decision-making process is reflected in the simulation design in traditional simulation, or is instead of the simplified rules in simulation deduction. That can't support the construction of a digital twin battlefield that truly reflects the real battlefield situation. Therefore, the digital twin battlefield for networking information-centric SoS must include the digital twin model of the command and control system. The command and control system digital twin model simulates the command and control behavior against the real equipment, hinges on other equipment models to form a closed-loop system, supports intelligent decision-making and "human in the loop" dynamic adjustment. So that, the dynamism and complexity of the combat system are reflected fully. The command and control system digital twin model is an important factor for improving the realism of digital twin battlefield.

4 Operation Architecture

The operation architecture of digital twin battlefield with command and control as the core, is based on the construction of the standard specification system, supported by the digital twin foundation platform. It provides services for the construction and application of the digital twin battlefield through the digital twin service-supply mode. The operation architecture is shown in Fig. 1, which includes four layers from the bottom to top: the foundation layer, the platform layer, the service layer and the application layer.

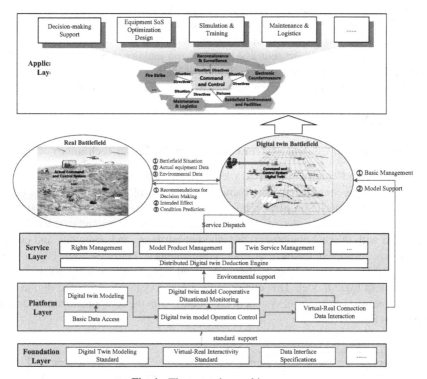

Fig. 1. The operation architecture.

(1) Foundation layer. The foundation layer is the overall specification for the operation of the digital twin battlefield. It identifies the standards in the construction and operation of the digital twin battlefield from the top, which includes the command and control system, reconnaissance equipment, combat platforms, and other digital twin modeling. In addition this, the interaction standards between physical elements of the real battlefield and the virtual elements of the digital twin battlefield, and interface specifications between the virtual and real equipment for the communication and business layer are all included.

(2) Platform layer. The platform layer provides basic management and model support capabilities for the digital twin battlefield, including the construction of digital twin

models for various types of equipment, as well as the core basic services supporting the operation of the digital twin battlefield, such as data access, virtual and real interaction, operation control, situational monitoring and so on.

(3) Service layer. The service layer provides all kinds of service supply and scheduling to the application, utilizing distributed digital twin deduction engine, on-demand scheduling for all kinds of different application scenarios. It provides safe and stable services, and is the bridge between the support platform and the user applications. Various types of supply models for twin service integration and using, meet the needs of different applications, and achieve the reasonable distribution of service resources and on-demand construction of twin environment.

(4) Application layer. The application layer is oriented to the requirements of different types of users and scenarios. Using digital tools and twin models in digital twin battlefield, users can carry out assisted decision-making support, equipment SoS optimization design, Simulation & Training, Maintenance & Logistics, and other applications, empowering the real battlefield and the development of real equipment.

5 Key Technologies

5.1 Command and Control System Digital Twin Modeling Technology

The command and control system is a kind of physical equipment with both hardware and software components. The command and control system digital twin model is constructed from basic properties, business logic and intelligent decision-making in accordance with the principles of componentization, aggregation and extensibility. In comparison with the real equipment, the inherent attributes and command and control behaviors are abstracted, the basic attribute components and business logic components are established respectively. The intelligent decision-making component is a supplement to the business logic model. This components are aggregated to form the digital twin model of command and control system in accordance with the componentized modeling, as shown in Fig. 2.

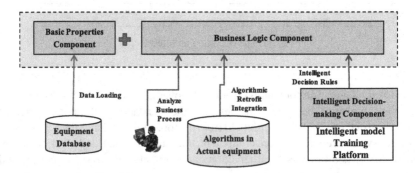

Fig. 2. Command and control system digital twin modeling.

Among them, the basic attribute component mainly focuses on the description of static capabilities of the command and control system, including the external physical characteristics, overall capability, war technology performance, etc. from the perspective of physicalized equipment. The modeling elements include the basic information of the equipment and the information of the system deployment, which are represented in the form of parameterization.

The business logic component mainly focuses on the description of the dynamic characteristics of the command and control system, including the feedback of the external state and the business processing flow. The business logic component is generally constructed by the combination of multiple atomic behaviors and atomic conditions. Among them, the atomic behavior refers to the accusing business process, and the atomic condition refers to the judgment conditions of state transition between atomic behaviors. If necessary, the actual core algorithm can be embedded in atomic behaviors.

The intelligent decision-making component focuses on the description of intelligent characteristics, which is based on business logic and adds the part of intelligent decision-making. It includes the simulation of human decision-making behavior characteristics. The main idea is to combine big data, machine learning and other technologies to form an intelligent decision-making model with the ability of self-optimization, self-learning and self-evolution. The intelligent decision-making component needs to rely on a special intelligent platform for training.

5.2 Command Elements Drive Digital Twin Battlefield Operation Technology

Command and control system is the core element of the networking information-centric SoS. In the digital twin battlefield, the command and control system digital twin model also interacts closely with the reconnaissance equipment model, communication equipment model, combat platform model, weapon and ammunition model, etc. It drives the to the OODA closed loop in joint combat system. Specifically, it includes the synergistic interaction between internal equipment of our army, as well as the confrontational interaction with the enemy forces, as shown in Table 1.

Table 1. Interaction of the command and control system digital twin model with other models.

Interaction Type	Interaction subcategory	Source of Information A	Receiver of Information B	Direction	Business Information	Note
Equipment Synergistic Interaction	Awareness Interaction	Red Force Reconnaissance Equipment Models	Red Force Command and Control System Models	A → B	Intelligence Information	Relying on models of Communication Equipment
				A ← B	Detection Mission Command, Targeted Indicator Messages	

(*continued*)

Table 1. (*continued*)

Interaction Type	Interaction subcategory	Source of Information A	Receiver of Information B	Direction	Business Information	Note
	Command Interaction	Red Force Command and Control System Models	Red Force Battle Platform Models	A → B	Force Deployment Directive, Strike Command, Withdrawal Orders, etc	Relying on models of Communication Equipment
				A ← B	Battle Platform Statuses, Strike Effectiveness, etc	
Equipment confrontational Interaction	Weapons Killing Interaction	Blue Force Weapons and Ammunition Models	Red Force Command and Control System Models	A → B	Probability of Damage for Red Force	Relying on Arbitration Rules

Awareness Interaction refers to the interaction between our command and control system model and our reconnaissance equipment model, interacting with the detection task command, detection intelligence, and target indication information. Command Interaction refers to the interaction between our command and control system model and our combat platform model, interacting with the force deployment command, strike command, withdrawal command, as well as the status of the combat platform, the strike effect report and other information. Weapons killing Interaction refers to the interaction between our command and control system model and the enemy weapon and ammunition model, obtaining the result of our destruction probability according to the engagement arbitration rules in digital twin battlefield. The interaction between our command and control system model and other equipment models relies on the channel simulated by our communication equipment model for information transmission.

5.3   Command and Control System Digital Twin Virtual-Reality Connection and Interaction Technology

Connection and interaction are the important components of the digital twin, and their main function is to realize the data transmission and information exchange between the virtual and real elements of the digital twin [9]. Through the virtual-reality connection and interaction channel, the digital twin model of the command and control system in the digital twin battlefield shares information with the real equipment in real battlefield. That can improve the accuracy of the digital twin model of the command and control system, and provide decision-making suggestions for the actual combat through digital projection. Ultimately, the effects of controlling, previewing, and optimizing the real battlefield by the virtual battlefield are achieved.

Command and control system digital twin virtual-real connection interaction is shown in Fig. 3, mainly including: ① From reality to virtual. That is, the static and dynamic data that perceives from the actual equipment is set to the input of the digital twin model in the digital space after processing. These data drives the model to run and update, so as to realize the digital twin model accurately reflecting the real physical state of the real equipment; ② From virtual to reality. That is, the decision-making recommendations, the effect of destruction, the future state of the real equipment and other information, from the command and control system digital twin model in digital twin battlefield, are sent accurately in real time to the real equipment of real battlefield. In this way, we can achieve the dynamic adjustment of the real combat process, as well as the maintenance of the real equipment; ③ The connection and interaction with human. That is, the command and control system digital twin model in digital battlefield space needs to have the ability to interact with human. This ability is determined by the characteristics of the command and control system human-computer fusion. Especially when artificial intelligence has not completely replaced the commander's cognitive decision-making, "human in the loop" is a suitable mode for participating in digital simulation and deduction in the appropriate time. The decision-making process of the actual battlefield can be reflected more realistically. In addition to this, the digital twin model of the command and control system also needs to receive information on the operational posture and the battlefield environment, which provides data input for command decision-making.

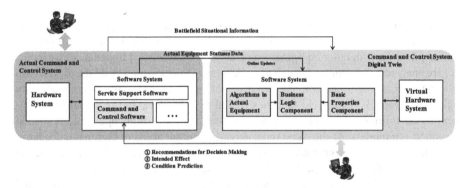

Fig. 3. Command and control system digital twin virtual-real connection interaction.

6 Application

6.1 Assisted Decision-Making Support

With the development of new types of combat forces, combat styles and emerging technologies, the operational tempo of information war is accelerating, the combat range is expanding, and the battlefield is becoming more and more complex and changeable. The fog of war continues to increase, which puts forward higher requirements for the commanders to analyze the battlefield situation and make the right decision. Relying on the experience and brain power of the commanders, it is much more difficult to optimize the combat action program and plan, as well as predict the effect of confrontation between the enemy and us. The emergence of digital twin battlefield provides a new technical way to solve the above problems. By constructing combat scenarios in the digital battlefield, we can form a closed loop of the joint operation system in digital space with command and control system as the core. Through the large-sample digital simulation and deduction, various possibilities are explored continuously to minimize the probability of battlefield emergencies, and provide support for the commanders' combat command decision-making. The application process is shown in Fig. 4.

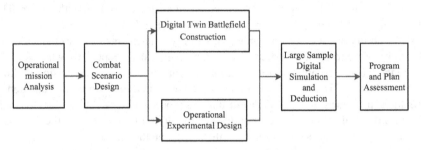

Fig. 4. Assisted decision-making support application process.

First, we can analyze the combat mission, combat attempts, equipment deployment, and combat operations. With the joint command and control equipment as the core, the joint application with other equipment such as sensors, electrical impedance, weapons, etc. are analyzed, the combat scenarios are designed. Then, we can build the digital twin battlefield according to the combat scenarios, including various types of combat entity digital twin models, battlefield facilities digital twin models, and battlefield environment models. Equipment data, environment data, and rules of engagement are loaded to support the models. At the same time, according to the needs of command decision-making, we can select experimental factors and design multiple sets of experimental programs. Finally, through the large sample digital simulation and deduction, we will get the results of executing the program plan under different battlefield postures, and quantitatively evaluate the program plan according to the simulation data. At last, assisted decision-making suggestions for the commanders are provided.

6.2 SoS Optimization Design

With the accelerated evolution of war patterns, single-platform confrontation has become a thing of the past, and the overall confrontation between enemy SoS and our SoS has become the mainstream. In the era of networking information-centric SoS, the equipment SoS is required to have the ability of open structure, dynamic adaptation and continuous evolution. The equipment construction mode of first development and then integration, first installation and then verification is constrained by a variety of factors. In the face of the increasingly large and complex equipment SoS, it has been difficult to continue this mode which results in high test costs, long equipment improvement cycle, and slow enhancement of system capabilities. Based on the digital twin battlefield to build a combination of virtual and real research environment, on the one hand, the current equipment SoS problems will be reproduced and analyzed. On the other hand, the research environment provides many means of iterative testing, improvement and optimization. The application process is shown in Fig. 5.

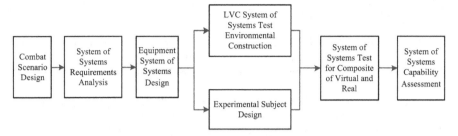

Fig. 5. Application flow of equipment SoS optimization design.

First, we can design the typical scenarios of equipment SoS application, analyze the winning mechanism under the scenarios based on the combat scenarios, and establish the equipment SoS capability framework. After analyzing the capabilities, we can form the system capability requirements. Then, the design of equipment SoS architecture, system composition, and node relationship, is carried out according to the requirements. We can build the "real + simulator + digital simulation" (LVC) SoS test environment, and design the test subjects. Finally, using the combination of virtual-real test and verification environment, the testes of inter-node communication, command relationship adjustment, and rapid detection of strikes are carried out. The LVC test environment will be able to help us analyze and evaluate the SoS capability, and find out the system blocking points, short boards and weaknesses of equipment SoS. The LVC test environment provides many digital support tools for the optimization and development of the equipment SoS.

7   Conclusion

At present, digital twin technology has entered a rapid development stage, it is promoting the construction of digital twin battlefield to go deeper gradually. As a key element in the networking information-centric SoS, the command and control system plays an important role in the construction and utilization of digital twin battlefield. This paper focuses on the characteristics of command and control system, studies the construction of digital twin model of command and control system, as well as the operation architecture and key technologies of digital twin battlefield with command and control as the core. Research results can provide researchers in the industry with ideas and references. Subsequently, we will further deepen the practical application of the digital twin model of the command and control system, and pull the construction of a digital twin battlefield that is closer to the real battlefield and fully reflects the characteristics of the networking information-centric SoS.

References

1. Grieves, M., Vickers, J.: Digital twin: mitigating unpredictable, undesirable emergent behaviour in complex systems. In: Kahlen, J., Flumerfelt, S., Alves, A. (eds.) Transdisciplinary Perspectives on Complex Systems, pp. 85–113. Springer, Cham (2017). https://doi.org/10.1007/978-3-319-38756-7_4
2. Shafto, M., Conroy, M., Doyle, R.: Modeling, simulation, information technology & processing roadmap. National Aeronautics and Space Administration (2010)
3. Zhou, J., Xue, J., Li, H.: Thinking on digital twin for weapon system. J. Syst. Simul. **23**(4), 539–552 (2020)
4. Wu, Y., Fu, C., Zhang, N.: Construction of agent modeling framework for digital twin battlefield. Command Inform. Syst. Technol. **13**(4), 19–25,31 (2022)
5. Hu, Q.: U.S. Navy uses virtual digital battlefield to dolve operational problems. Retrieved from zhkzyfz. https://mp.weixin.qq.com/s/g8JYrPrVHIihIzMoi8djRw. Accessed 30 Sep 2022
6. Academy of Military Sciences. Military dictionary of the Chinese people's liberation army. Beijing: Military Science Press (2011)
7. Zhang, W., Wang, F., Lu, L.: Analysis on simulation modeling of command and control system. In: 8th Proceedings on China Command and Control Conference, pp. 146–151. Chinese Institute of Command and Control, Beijing (2020)
8. Fu, C., Zhou, F., Wu, Y.: Engagement effect adjudication method for digital twin battlefield. Command Inform. Syst. Technol. **13**(4), 26–31 (2022)
9. Tao, F., Ma, X., Qi, Q.: Theory and key technologies of digital twin connection and interaction. Comput. Integr. Manuf. Syst. **29**(1), 1–10 (2022)

A Joint Method for Combat Intent Recognition and Key Information Extraction

Jinhao Zhang[1,2]([✉]), Lingyun Lu[2], Guoxin Jiang[1], Chi Yuan[1], Haoqian Zhang[1], and Shaoqiu Zheng[2]

[1] School of Computer and Information, Hohai University, Nanjing, China
zjinhao2022@126.com
[2] Nanjing Research Institute of Electronic Engineering, Nanjing, China

Abstract. To alleviate the problems of poor quality and low efficiency in traditional combat plan making, we propose an intelligent combat plan generation method based on Bert pre-trained language model. First, we studied practical combat scenarios and military related websites, and constructed a military domain combat intent dataset that includes structured information such as combat categories, objects, and scenarios. Second, we utilize Bert pre-trained language model for semantic analysis of requirements, TextCNN (Convolutional Neural Network for Text) for combat intent recognition, and BiLSTM (Bidirectional Long Short-Term Memory) for key information extracting and entity normalization. Thus, based on the intent and key information, candidate schemes can be retrieved from the knowledge graph in the field of military operations in the future. Compared with traditional methods, the scheme quality and generation efficiency are significantly improved. This study provides an effective approach for intelligent decision support in the military field, and also offers references for intelligent scheme generation in other domains.

Keywords: Combat Intent Recognition · Key Information Extraction · Bert

1 Introduction

Military operational planning is a crucial process in modern military operations, directly relating to the effectiveness of troops completing combat missions [1–5]. However, the traditional process of combat planning relies on personal experience, resulting in unsatisfactory quality and efficiency of generated plans. In order to achieve intelligent generation of military operational plans, this study has constructed a military domain combat intent dataset, designed an end-to-end combat intent recognition and key information extraction system based on Bert pre-trained language models. The system integrates structured knowledge in the military domain and leverages advanced natural language processing techniques to provide high-quality, intelligent combat instructions. Candidate schemes can be retrieved from the knowledge graph in the field of military operations in the future. An overview of the model is shown in Fig. 1.

In the military domain, we construct a high-quality dataset containing key information including combat categories, combat objects, and combat scenarios, in order to

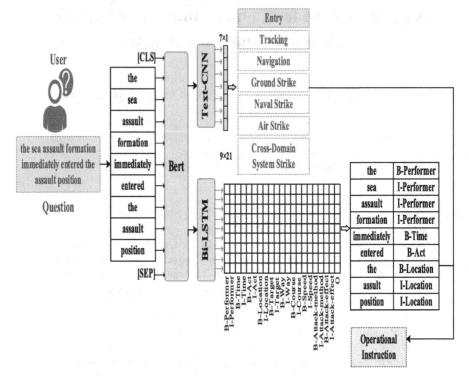

Fig. 1. An overview of the proposed model.

integrate rich structured military knowledge. First, the user's military question is input into the Bert pre-trained language model and CLS special token pairs are extracted to obtain semantic information of the whole sentence. TextCNN performs further semantic extraction for intent identification. The remaining tokens are utilized for more fine-grained semantic analysis through a Bidirectional LSTM (BiLSTM) to fill slots and normalize entities. After two processing steps based on the user's combat intent recognition and key information extraction, the system analyzes the corresponding operational instructions for the generation of subsequent combat plans.

This approach fully exploits structured military data and natural language understanding capabilities of Bert pre-trained language models. Not only does it improve the quality of generating operational instructions, but it also makes the entire process intelligent. It provides an effective technical means for decision-making and judgment in the military field.

We believe that by utilizing the extensive prior knowledge contained in pre-trained language model and the military dataset used in this study, combined with fine-tuning of joint extraction downstream tasks, satisfactory combat instruction results can be achieved. Thus, we can promote the transformation of combat planning from experience-driven to intelligent generation, and achieve a leap in combat planning capabilities. The main contributions of this study include:

1. Constructed a military domain dataset containing combat categories, combat objects, combat scenarios etc., applying structured information to operational instructions generation.
2. An intelligent generation method based on Bert pre-trained language model, including intention recognition and key information extraction, facilitating the generation of a high-quality combat plan.
3. Achieved integration of military domain knowledge and pre-trained language models, combining structured data with natural language understanding, and providing effective technical means for decision support.

2 Related Works

2.1 Operational Intent Recognition

The current work mainly focuses on using deep learning to analyze intelligence to identify enemy combat intentions, playing an important role in military operations and providing strategic and tactical guidance. For example, Guo et al. [6] designed an attention-based model using time convolutional networks and bidirectional gated recurrent units (Attention-TCN-BIGRU) [7] for air combat scenarios, improving recognition of air target combat intent. Xue et al. [8] proposed PCLSTM, a deep learning method that captures essential intelligence information characteristics, overcoming limitations of traditional methods. PCLSTM was used to simulate tests on truncated intelligence data sets to analyze optimal lengths for different intents. Some existing methods utilize BERT-based pre-trained models, first trained on general data then fine-tuned on military datasets [14–18].

2.2 Combat Information Extraction

Operational information extraction is another significant military task, aiming to extract useful structured intelligence to support analysis and decisions. This includes named entity recognition, relationship extraction, and joint extraction of intent slots. For operational plan generation, we discuss named entity recognition and joint intent-slot extraction. For example, L et al. [12] proposed a Chinese NER method using BERT-BiLSTM-Att-CRF, utilizing BERT for context-aware word embeddings, BiLSTM-Att to capture key semantics, and CRF for optimal label sequences. Recently, some joint extraction methods have been proposed using BERT, like Zheng et al. [9] who transformed it to a labeling problem and studied end-to-end models. Xue et al. [10] integrated BERT via dynamic attention to improve representation. Qiao et al. [11] proposed BERT-BiLSTM-LTM using BERT embeddings and applied it to datasets like NYT and AgriRelation. Tavares et al. [13] designed a multi-task model for user intent extraction in dialog by sharing parameters for intent and slot extraction, learning richer interactions.

3 Methods

3.1 Combat Intent Recognition

Combat intent recognition refers to identifying the user's operational intent and requirements from the user's natural language query, which is an important step to realize the generation of intelligent operational plans. Specifically, we first input natural language queries from the military domain into the BERT pre-trained language model, and the BERT model adds special CLS tags at the beginning of the sentence to extract semantic information from the entire input sentence. Then, we take the CLS tag representation corresponding to BERT output and input it into the TextCNN text classification model as the feature expression of the whole sentence. It maps the semantic features to seven different operational intents, including entry, tracking, navigation, land strike, air strike, sea strike, and cross-domain system strike. In this way, the end-to-end mapping approach is implemented from military language query to precise operational intent classification. It provides important information for subsequent retrieval for operational plans in the military knowledge graph. Ultimately, the classification problem of operational intent recognition is achieved.

3.2 Key Information Extraction

Entity extraction is a natural language processing (NLP) technique aimed at identifying and extracting entities with specific meanings from text. Entities can be concrete things or abstract concepts. The use of entity extraction technology for entity recognition of military instructions is a technique that automatically recognizes and extracts specific types of entities from text. In military instructions, entities can be elements related to military operations such as location, organization, person, time, etc. In this article, a complete sentence of military query tokens are first input into the Bert pre-trained language model to get the feature representation of each token. They are fed into the BiLSTM to obtain even finer grained and richer word semantic information. Finally, to ascertain the entity type of each token, a probability distribution for the sequence annotations is derived by the softmax function, and the label with the highest probability is determined by the argmax function. This article utilizes the "BIO" (Beginning, Inside, Outside) labeling scheme for annotation. For example, for the location entity in the instruction, the location where the entity appears can be marked as B-LOC (start position) and I-LOC (internal position), and the non-entity part can be marked as O (external position).

Through entity extraction technology, important information in operational instructions can be automatically identified and extracted, which helps to accelerate the interpretation and understanding process of military instructions, provide decision support and intelligence analysis.

3.3 Joint Extraction Method

Combat intent recognition is a classification problem for predicting intent categories. Key information extraction is a sequence labelling problem giving a sequence of input words $X = (x_1, x_2, \ldots, x_N)$ labelled with labels $Y = (y_1, y_2, \ldots, y_M)$. A general joint extraction approach to combat intent recognition and key information extraction is to exploit the dependencies between these two tasks, integrate them to improve the performance of the whole model. In our joint extraction approach, the military text is first encoded by the Bert pre-trained language model. The resulting output consists of pooler output corresponding to semantic representation of the entire sentence marked with [CLS] and the Last Hidden State corresponding to each token. For combat intent recognition, the semantic representation of the entire sentence marked with [CLS] is classified by TextCNN to obtain the probability distribution vector of the intent. Then, the label with the highest probability is output by argmax function. For key information extraction, the result of Bert's Last Hidden State, Which is the hidden state corresponding to each position, is exploited as the input vector of BiLSTM. Then, combining it with the output of combat intent recognition for vector superposition, so as to achieve the effect of enhanced its own information extraction. Finally, the probability distribution of the sequence labelling is derived to determine the entities and their categories. The total loss is computed by summing the losses of the two tasks(combat intent recognition and key information extraction) for joint optimisation. The framework diagram of the whole method is shown in Fig. 2.

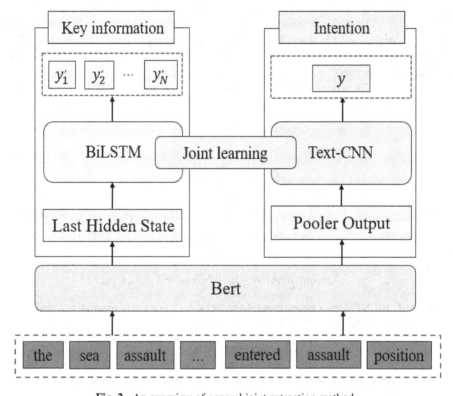

Fig. 2. An overview of general joint extraction method.

3.4 Concrete Methods

Overall, the Bert pre-training model extracts the contextual and semantic information of a sentence. For the task of combat intent recognition, Pooler Output is the semantic representation of the entire sentence obtained by pooling the [CLS] tag, which can be used for text classification. For the task of key information extraction, Last Hidden State contains the hidden states of each layer. Each position contains the information learned by the model when processing input sequences. Therefore, Pooler Output and Last Hidden State are exploited as inputs for TextCNN and BiLSTM respectively.

TextCNN can capture local features in input text through convolutional operations, which gives it advantages in expressing phrases and vocabulary. Therefore, it is suitable for combat intent recognition tasks that require capturing features for short text classification.

The long-distance dependency structure of BiLSTM enables the model to learn long-distance dependency relationships, which is beneficial for understanding the semantic structure of the entire sentence. For key information extraction involving marking each input marker, BiLSTM is better for sequence level information extraction.

The Bert pre-training model is input with a sequence of words $X = (x_1, x_2, \ldots, x_N)$. Then, text feature vectors are encoded as output through Bert. Among them, $H_O = (h_O^1, h_O^2, \ldots, h_O^N)$ encodes the token sequence of the text corresponding to Pooler Output. $H_L = (h_L^1, h_L^2, \ldots, h_L^N)$ is the [CLS] vector corresponding to Last Hidden State. The former is utilized for combat intent recognition, while the latter is employed for key information extraction.

First, TextCNN processes input sequences H_O. The operation description of this process is as follows:

$$c_i = \text{ReLU}(W_i \cdot x + b_i) \tag{1}$$

$$p_i = MaxPool(c_i) \tag{2}$$

Among them, $x \in H_O^{batch\_size \times sequence\_length}$, c_i is the feature vector after the i-th convolution operation and p_i is its maximum pooling result. Then, all pooling results are concatenated into a one-dimensional vector $[p_1, p_2, \ldots, p_k]$. Therefore, for combat intent recognition, the objective function can be defined as follows:

$$y^i = soft\max(W_{fc} \cdot p_i + b_{fc}), \ i = 1, \ldots, k \tag{3}$$

Second, BiLSTM processes input sequences H_L. For each time step t and each sample i, the calculation of BiLSTM is as follows:

$$h_{it} = BiLSTM(x_{it}, h_{i,t-1}) \tag{4}$$

Among them, $x_{it} \in H_L^{batch\_size \times sequence\_length \times hidden\_size}$, h_{it} is the hidden state at time step t, and $h_{i,t-1}$ is the hidden state at time step $t-1$. BiLSTM includes LSTMs in both forward and backward directions, with their hidden states represented by $\overrightarrow{h_{it}}$ and $\overleftarrow{h_{it}}$ respectively. Connect the forward and backward hidden states to obtain the final hidden state matrix $H_t = [\overrightarrow{h_{1t}}, \overrightarrow{h_{2t}}, \ldots, \overrightarrow{h_{Nt}}, \overleftarrow{h_{Nt}}, \ldots, \overleftarrow{h_{1t}}]$, where $h_t \in H_t^{batch\_size \times 2*hidden\_size}$. Therefore, for key information extraction, the objective function can be defined as follows:

$$y_n^s = soft\max(h_n^s), \ n = 1, \ldots, N \tag{5}$$

So, for the joint extraction function, the objective function can be defined as follows:

$$p(y^i, y^s|x) = p(y^i|x)\Pi_{n=1}^{N}p(y_n^s|x) \tag{6}$$

Joint loss function

Combat Intent Recognition. The Cross Entropy Loss function is used to calculate the loss of the combat intent recognition task:

$$L_{intent} = -\sum_i y_{intent_i} \log(p(intent_i|X)) \tag{7}$$

Here, i represents the index of the intent category label, y_{intent_i} is the one-hot encoding of the true intent label, $p(intent_i|X)$ is the probability that the model predicts the intent label i.

Key Information Extraction. For key information extraction task, the Cross Entropy Loss function can also be used to calculate the loss of the slot label for each token, and then the loss for all tokens can be added together. The total loss of all tokens is defined as follows:

$$L_{slots} = -\sum_{j=1}^{N}\sum_k y_{slots_{j,k}} \log(p(slot_{j,k}|X)) \tag{8}$$

Here, j represents the jth token, k represents the index of the slot label, $y_{slots_{j,k}}$ is the one-hot encoding of the true slot label k of the jth token, $p(slot_{j,k}|X)$ is the probability of the model predicting the slot label k of the jth token.

Joint Extraction Method. The total loss is computed by summing the losses of the two tasks (combat intent recognition and key information extraction) for joint optimisation.

$$L_{joint} = \lambda_{intent} \cdot L_{intent} + \lambda_{slots} \cdot L_{slots} \tag{9}$$

where λ_{intent} and λ_{slots} are hyperparameters for controlling the weights of the two.

4 Experiments

4.1 Dataset

By studying actual combat scenarios and military-related websites, we have summarized 7 combat intentions: Naval Strike, Air Strike, Ground Strike, Navigation, Tracking, Entry and Cross-Domain System Strike. These categories integrate relevant corpora, containing different key information. For the task of key information extraction, 21 slot categories are designed, such as performer, time, act, location, speed, course, altitude, etc. These standardized slots are sufficient to constitute military instructions. We have generated approximately 3, 300 pieces of military data in JSON format, and ultimately divided training, testing, and validation sets in a 7:2:1 ratio. The information for each intent category and its corresponding key information extraction examples are shown in Table 1 and Table 2.

Table 1. The information of each intent category in dataset.

Category	Amount	examples
Naval Strike	871	1200 air-to-sea assault formation artillery attack on enemy underwater targets
Air Strike	842	Land-based air defence group fires Red Arrow missiles to counter incoming drones from the south-east
Ground Strike	685	The Standing Guide Assault Group captured the forward armoured vehicle one hour later
Navigation	223	Patrol formation heading 300 speed 20 knots altitude 18554
Tracking	147	The jamming group is tracking the Nimitz-class carriers at a safe distance
Entry	243	Maritime assault formations take up assault positions immediately
Cross-Domain System Strike	275	Combined fire support group strikes on enemy position 4 with 50 per cent reduction in reconnaissance capability

Table 2. Key information extraction examples

Text	Operational slot extraction
The sea assault formation immediately entered the assault position.	{" performer ": "The sea assault formation", "time": "immediately", act": "entered", "location": "the assault position"
Joint Fire Strike Group Strike Taiwan Island Command System, Reduced Investigation Capability by 50%.	{"performer": "Joint Fire Strike Group", "attack_target": "Taiwan Island Command System", "attack_effect": "Reduced Investigation Capability by 50%"}
Assault formation heading 300, speed 20 knots, altitude 7000 meters.	{"performer": "Assault formation", "course": "heading 300", "speed": "speed 20 knots","high": "altitude 7000 meters"}
One hour later, the sea assault formation launched artillery fire on the enemy ship.	{"performer": "the sea assault formation", "time": "One hour later", "attack_method": "artillery fire"}
At 1200 hours, air to sea assault formation artillery attacks enemy underwater targets.	{"performer": "air to sea assault formation", "time": "At 1200 hours", "attack_target": "enemy underwater targets", "attack_method": "artillery"}

4.2 Experimental Environment

Our experimental environment is Python3.8, Pytorch1.12.1. The experimental equipment is NVIDIA GeForce RTX 3090Ti. And the detailed experimental setup for each task is briefly shown below.

Entity recognition using Bert pre-trained model: After continuous adjustment of hyperparameters, a set of hyperparameters is derived to make the model have the best performance. The model uses Bert for parameter initialization. In this task, set the epoch size to 30, the batch size to 16, and the maximum statement length to 80.

Combat intent recognition using the Bert-TextCNN model: After comparing the performance of various models, set the epoch size to 30, the learning rate to 5e−5, the batch size to 16, and the optimizer to Adam.

Key information extraction using the Bert-BiLSTM model: After comparing the performance of various models, set the epoch size to 30, the learning rate to 5e−5, the batch size to 16, and the optimizer to Adam.

Joint extraction combines the above two for learning: after comparing the performance of various models, set the epoch size to 30, set the learning rate to 5e−5, set the batch size to 16, and set the optimizer to Adam.

4.3 Experimental Results

(See Tables 3, 4 and 5).

Table 3. Combat intent recognition

	Precision	Recall	F1-score
Bert-Linear	0.9365	0.9493	0.9424
Bert-BiLSTM	0.9279	0.9436	0.9346
Bert-TextCNN	0.9382	0.9439	0.9672

Table 4. Key information extraction

	Precision	Recall	F1-score
Bert-Linear	0.8337	0.8572	0.8452
Bert-TextCNN	0.8385	0.8741	0.8553
Bert-BiLSTM	0.8548	0.8829	0.9152

Table 5. Joint extraction

	Intent	Slot
Precision	0.9565	0.8776
Recall	0.9647	0.8899
F1-score	0.9596	0.8850

The two tasks of combat intent recognition and key information extraction are compared with the Bert-Linear baseline method, respectively. For combat intent recognition, the experimental results indicate that TextCNN has better performance than BiLSTM for simple text classification tasks. For key information extraction involving long-distance dependencies, BiLSTM is more capable of capturing fine-grained lexical relationships. As envisioned, the outputs of the two are vectorized to enhance the effectiveness of total information extraction.

5   Conclusion

In this paper, we first construct a military dataset containing seven types of operational intents. Then, to obtain the important elements of combat intent and key information, combining the prior knowledge of Bert pre-trained language model and fine tune it based on the joint extraction task. Afterwards, the joint extraction of operational instructions includes entity information such as operational categories and scenarios for subsequent retrieval of detailed plans in the military knowledge graph. Through the verification of experimental results, we prove that the system has accuracy, effectiveness, intelligence and powerful interactivity. This scientific combat plan generation system makes an important contribution to the intelligent development of the combat field. In the future, we will contemplate leveraging data in various languages and employing multimodal approaches to further refine our system, enhancing its performance and versatility. Concurrently, the original query intent and pertinent key information will be fed into large-scale language models (e.g., ChatGlm), harnessing their formidable semantic comprehension capabilities to select the most fitting singular operational strategy.

Acknowledgements. This work was supported by Key Laboratory of Information System Requirements, No: LHZZ 2021-M04.

References

1. Chou, K.-P., et al.: Robust feature-based automated multi-view human action recognition system. IEEE Access **6**, 15283–15296 (2018). https://doi.org/10.1109/ACCESS.2018.280 9552
2. Chou, K.-P., et al.: Automatic multi-view action recognition with robust features. In: Liu, D., Xie, S., Li, Y., Zhao, D., El-Alfy, E.S. (eds.) Neural Information Processing. ICONIP 2017. LNCS, vol. 10636, pp. 554–563. Springer, Cham (2017). https://doi.org/10.1007/978-3-319-70090-8_56
3. Qararyah, F., Daraghmi, Y.A., Daraghmi, E., Rajora, S., Lin, C.T., Prasad, M.: A time efficient model for region of interest extraction in real time traffic signs recognition system. In: 2018 IEEE Symposium Series on Computational Intelligence (SSCI), Bangalore, India: IEEE, pp. 83–87, November 2018. https://doi.org/10.1109/SSCI.2018.8628874
4. Li, D.L., Prasad, M., Liu, C.-L., Lin, C.-T.: Multi-view vehicle detection based on fusion part model with active learning. IEEE Trans. Intell. Transport. Syst. **22**(5), 3146–3157 (2021). https://doi.org/10.1109/TITS.2020.2982804
5. Cheng, E.-J., et al.: Deep sparse representation classifier for facial recognition and detection system. Pattern Recogn. Lett. **125**, 71–77 (2019). https://doi.org/10.1016/j.patrec.2019.03.006

6. Guo, Y., et al.: ESIE-BERT: Enriching Sub-words Information Explicitly with BERT for Joint Intent Classification and SlotFilling (2022)
7. Teng, F., Yafei, S.: Attention-TCN-BiGRU: an air target combat intention recognition model. Mathematics **9**(19), 2412 (2021). https://doi.org/10.3390/math9192412
8. Xue, J., Zhu, J., Xiao, J., Tong, S., Huang, L.: Panoramic convolutional long short-term memory networks for combat intension recognition of aerial targets. IEEE Access **8**, 183312–183323 (2020). https://doi.org/10.1109/ACCESS.2020.3025926
9. Zheng, S., Wang, F., Bao, H., Hao, Y., Zhou, P., Xu, B.: Joint Extraction of Entities and Relations Based on a Novel Tagging Scheme. ArXiv abs/1706.05075 (2017)
10. Xue, K., Zhou, Y., Ma, Z., Ruan, T., Zhang, H., He, P.: Fine-tuning BERT for joint entity and relation extraction in Chinese medical text. In: IEEE International Conference on Bioinformatics and Biomedicine (BIBM), San Diego, CA, USA, pp. 892–897 (2019). https://doi.org/10.1109/BIBM47256.2019.8983370.(2019)
11. Qiao, B., Zou, Z., Huang, Y., et al.: A joint model for entity and relation extraction based on BERT. Neural Comput. Appl. **34**, 3471–3481 (2022). https://doi.org/10.1007/s00521-021-05815-z
12. Daiyi, L., Yaofeng, T., Xiangsheng, Z., et al.: End-to-end chinese entity recognition based on BERT-BiLSTM-ATT-CRF. ZTE Commun. **20**(S1), 27–35 (2022)
13. Tavares, D., Azevedo, P., Semedo, D., Sousa, R., Magalhaes, J.: Task Conditioned BERT for Joint Intent Detection and Slot-filling. ArXiv abs/2308.06165 (2023)
14. Li, Z., Lifeng, W., Yaoming, Z.: Evaluation method of operation scheme based on recurrent neural networks. In: IEEE International Conference on Information and Automation (2018)
15. Xiang, Y., Meng, Z., Mengqiao, C.: Combat intention recognition of the target in the air based on discriminant analysis. J. Projectiles Rockets Missiles Guidance (2018)
16. Li, Y., Wu, J., Li, W., Dong, W., Fang, A.: A hierarchical aggregation model for combat intention recognition. J. Northwestern Polytech. Univ. (2023)
17. Bingtao, H., Zhixiang, Y., Weimin, X., et al.: Joint slot filling and intent detection with BLSTM-CNN-CRF. Comput. Eng. Appl. (2019)
18. Lihua, W., Wenzhong, Y., Miao, Y., Ting, W., Shanshan, L.: Bidirectional association model for intent detection and slot filling. Comput. Eng. Appl. **57**(3), 196–202 (2021)

Theory-Assisted Deep Learning Weapon System Combat Effectiveness Prediction

Jiahao Zhou[1], Xuekang Yang[1], Weiran Guo[2], Xiang Huang[2], and Jie Zhang[1(✉)]

[1] Nanjing University of Science and Technology, Nanjing 210094, China
NineOvOzhou@njust.edu.cn
[2] Science and Technology on Information Systems Engineering Laboratory, Nanjing 210007, China

Abstract. Combat effectiveness prediction is of very importance throughout the entire process of weapon equipment design, production, and actual combat. This paper proposes a theory-assisted deep learning combat effectiveness prediction algorithm that incorporates knowledge from weapon foundation models as auxiliary drivers. The paper provides a brief overview of the general construction form of weapon system foundation models. Based on this foundation, it elaborates on the training method that integrates theoretical knowledge into conventional deep learning models. This process does not require specific knowledge of the underlying physical model, while retaining the advantages of direct and efficient data-driven techniques. Addressing the multidimensional time series prediction involved in combat effectiveness prediction, a GA-CNN-LSTM hybrid prediction model is proposed, which adaptively learns temporal and spatial features of the data. This approach effectively mitigates the problem of poor generalization performance in deep learning large models caused by insufficient training data. The effectiveness and utility of the method are validated through a case study on combat simulation performance evaluation of a certain type of radar equipment. The results demonstrate that the hybrid prediction model improves the R2 score performance metric by approximately 2.9% compared to the original model.

Keywords: Theory-driven · Data-driven · Combat Effectiveness Prediction

1 Introduction

The weapon equipment system is a complex system composed of multiple functional resources, and there is a tight coupling relationship between the functional subsystems. Combat effectiveness analysis, which is a measure of the effects produced by weapon equipment in accomplishing specific tasks under specific conditions, provides a basis for the inspection and optimal selection of weapon equipment. It evaluates the performance indicators and deployment arrangements of weapon equipment, and analyzes the combat effectiveness to achieve the intended mission objectives. This evaluation has significant theoretical and practical significance.

The evaluation of the combat effectiveness of traditional weapon equipment systems mainly relies on expert knowledge to construct an index system as guidance. Representative methods include the ADC method [1], Analytic Hierarchy Process (AHP) [2], and

© The Author(s), under exclusive license to Springer Nature Singapore Pte Ltd. 2024
Y. Tan and Y. Shi (Eds.): DMBD 2023, CCIS 2018, pp. 126–140, 2024.
https://doi.org/10.1007/978-981-97-0844-4_10

expert evaluation method. These methods have the advantages of simplicity, intuitiveness, and good interpretability of evaluation results. However, the reliance on expert experience in these methods results in subjectivity, and their operability decreases as the complexity of the weapon equipment systems deepens. This makes it difficult to meet the requirements of large-scale data processing and rapid evaluation. With the development of artificial intelligence technology, classic machine learning methods such as BP neural network [3] and support vector machine [4] have been introduced into the field of combat effectiveness evaluation of weapon equipment. Along with the increasing complexity of combat systems, the evaluation data accumulated from combat simulations and exercises show a trend of big data. The data-driven evaluation concept provides a new and effective solution for evaluating the effectiveness of weapon equipment.

One of the representative research achievements is the use of machine learning or deep learning models for combat effectiveness evaluation. By deeply mining data features, these methods reduce various problems caused by human involvement [5]. These data-driven methods not only bypass the problem of causality that is difficult to discover due to factors such as nonlinearity and uncertainty in the weapon system but also allow model-driven analysis based on relevant data that characterizes combat effectiveness. The core idea is to transform combat effectiveness evaluation into a classification or prediction problem. [6] In order to predict the combat effectiveness of the equipment system of systems, an improved Stacking Ensemble learning model is proposed. The model is validated using simulation combat data. [7] For regression prediction, the fully connected Deep Neural Network (DNN) model is chosen. The network parameters are then adjusted using the genetic algorithm to optimize and evaluate the combat effectiveness of the system. [8] A multi-morphological parallel neural network is constructed using one-dimensional Convolutional Neural Network (CNN) to adaptively learn the original operation data of equipment. This neural network is employed to evaluate the index system of complex equipment.

There is a significant gap in the existing research on data-driven combat effectiveness prediction. Current studies primarily focus on developing advanced model architectures to accurately depict the potential connections between multidimensional state data and long-term temporal information. However, they neglect to address the data scarcity problem, which could hinder practical applications. Collecting effectiveness evaluation data remains challenging and expensive. To accurately model the high nonlinearity of weapon equipment, high-order intelligent models are necessary. However, the complexity of these models and algorithms necessitates a large amount of training data [9]. In reality, the available measured data, even when combined with data augmentation algorithms, is much smaller than what is required for model parameter training. As a result, deep learning models are prone to overfitting, leading to a decrease in their ability to generalize. In conclusion, it is crucial to research algorithm models that are tailored to the characteristics of the military-industrial field. This will facilitate the application of data-driven thinking to predict weapon combat effectiveness.

In this paper, we propose a theory-assisted deep learning model for predicting weapon equipment combat effectiveness by incorporating prior knowledge from weapon basic model theory. This is done to overcome the problem of poor model generalization performance due to lack of extensive data support.

The structure of this paper is as follows: First, a brief overview of the general modeling paradigm for weapon basic models is provided. Then, we explain in detail how the physical equations involved can be used as constraints to assist model training. To address the multidimensional time series prediction problem involved in combat effectiveness prediction, we propose an adapted hybrid model structure that explores the feature information of data in both the time and space domains. Finally, we conduct an experiment using a simulated combat effectiveness assessment of a radar equipment type to validate the effectiveness of the proposed theory-assisted algorithm in improving model performance.

2 Theory-Assisted Model Training

2.1 Basic Model Description

The construction of a physical model for a weapon system involves searching for a model solution in the hypothesis space that minimizes the output error [10]. This process can be described as solving a nonlinear equation with multiple objective inputs, which can be described as the following mathematical model:

$$\begin{cases} object\ Function\ F(X) \\ s.t.\ g_j(X) \le 0, j = 1, 2, \cdots, M \\ h_k(X) = 0, k = 1, 2, \cdots, P \end{cases} \tag{1}$$

where $X = (x_1, x_2, \cdots, x_n)^T \in R^n$ is the set of weapon system evaluation indicators, which comes from an evaluation index system constructed for a performance problem; R^n is an n-dimensional real vector space; $F(X)$ is a nonlinear objective function in the model hypothesis space; $g_j(X)$, $h_k(X)$ are the inequality constraints and equality constraints of the objective function, respectively.

The analytical modeling method for evaluating the operational effectiveness objective function $F(X)$ has been developed to a relatively mature stage for some weapon systems, which has resulted in the formation of some theoretically sound and practically valuable physical models [11–13]. However, as the complexity of weapon equipment deepens and modern weapon systems become increasingly large in scale, the interconnection and complexity among subsystems often cannot be described by specific mathematical expressions, making them "black box systems." Although the operational effectiveness objective function for these weapon systems cannot be directly obtained, their operational logic still follows classical physics properties. Therefore, it is possible to derive certain constraints for these systems, including both equality and inequality constraints. The following section will discuss these two scenarios in detail.

2.2 Theory-Driven and Data-Driven Hybrid

Here is an example that utilizes a general form of a machine learning loss function, demonstrating the process of designing deep learning model loss functions with theoretical guidance. The typical definition of the loss function for deep learning methods is as follows:

$$L_c = \frac{1}{N} \sum_{i=1}^{N} \left\| F(X_i)^* - F(X_i) \right\| \tag{2}$$

where N is the number of training samples; $F(X_i)^*$ and $F(X_i)$ respectively denote the model's predicted output and the true values; $\|\cdot\|$ is an arbitrary metric function, such as the commonly used mean squared error criterion in regression prediction tasks.

If we can establish a physical model for the weapon system, meaning we can obtain the mathematical expression $F'(X_i)$ for $F(X)$ in Eq. (1), then we can create a theory-assisted machine learning loss function:

$$L = \lambda L_p + (1 - \lambda) L_c \tag{3}$$

where $L_p = \frac{1}{N} \sum_{i=1}^{N} \left\| F'(X_i) - F(X_i) \right\|$ is the loss function driven by theory; L_c is the loss function driven by data; λ is the theoretical confidence factor.

The concept of physics-informed machine learning [14] can be introduced if it is not possible to obtain the specific mathematical expression or precise description of the model. By incorporating the equality and inequality constraints required by the weapon system's nonlinear equations into the loss function design, the trained model can further satisfy the fundamental physical law constraints of the weapon system's operational effectiveness. In other words, the trained model not only approximates the actual data but also automatically adheres to the classical physical properties followed by the weapon system. We can construct the following loss function driven by theory:

$$L_p = \sum_{j=1}^{M} \frac{1}{N} \sum_{i=1}^{N} \left\| \mathrm{relu}(g_j(X)) \right\| + \sum_{k=1}^{P} \frac{1}{N} \sum_{i=1}^{N} \left\| \mathrm{relu}(h_k(X)) \right\| \tag{4}$$

where the first two terms correspond to the inequality constraints and equality constraints in Eq. (1); $\mathrm{relu}(x) = x \otimes 1_{x \geq 0}$ represents the rectified linear unit and $\otimes$ is the Hadamard product, representing the element-wise multiplication operation on tensors.

Equation (4) transforms the discrete comparison of inequalities into a popular non-linear activation function in deep learning models. This enables efficient execution and handling of operations during both forward computation and backward gradient propagation in the program.

By integrating the data-driven component and theory-assisted component, we can achieve the overall training objective:

$$\mathrm{Min}\, L = L_c + L_p \tag{5}$$

3 Model Based on GA-CNN-LSTM

A hybrid prediction model called GA-CNN-LSTM is proposed to address the evaluation data with multiple dimensions, long time spans, and diverse samples in the data-driven method for predicting the operational effectiveness of weapon equipment. This model includes a Convolutional Neural Network (CNN) [15] for feature extraction, a Long Short-Term Memory (LSTM) network [16] for time series prediction, and a Genetic Algorithm (GA) [17] for optimizing network parameters during training.

The implementation of operational effectiveness prediction is primarily accomplished by the CNN-LSTM part. Specifically, the CNN module consists of convolutional layers, pooling layers, and flattening layers. Feature extraction is performed on data from different time periods by setting the size of the convolutional kernel, and the number of convolutional kernels in each layer is used as an input to the genetic algorithm. To improve training efficiency, batch normalization is added before the pooling layer. Subsequently, the data is flattened to extract global features. Finally, the data is input into the LSTM module for prediction. The overall model structure is illustrated in Fig. 1.

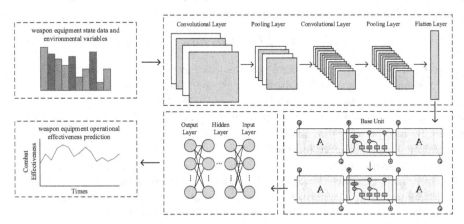

Fig. 1. The specific structure and training process of the model

Increasing the number of LSTM neurons has been found to improve the predictive ability of the model, as indicated by several experimental studies conducted by different scholars [18]. Therefore, in this study, the number of neurons in each layer of LSTM is treated as an individual gene input to the genetic algorithm. To prevent overfitting, dropout is employed in LSTM. Finally, the output representing the predicted value of resource aggregation capability is generated in a specified format through a fully connected layer.

Many papers [19–21] have validated the effectiveness of the CNN-LSTM model, especially in the field of prediction. The CNN-LSTM model utilizes data extracted from CNN as input for LSTM prediction, and LSTM exhibits unique advantages in time series data prediction. In long-term time series prediction, LSTM avoids the problems of vanishing gradients and exploding gradients. However, for parameter selection in the CNN-LSTM model, most studies use exhaustive methods such as grid search, which is time-consuming and challenging to find the most suitable parameters. Therefore, this paper adopts the GA algorithm and utilizes the genetic and mutation processes in the genetic algorithm to select the number of convolutional kernels and neurons in the CNN-LSTM model, thereby improving the model's efficiency. By iteratively training the model until reaching the preset number of iterations or meeting the requirements, the fittest individual is obtained, and the individual's genes are used as parameters to predict the capability value in CNN-LSTM. The proposed GA-CNN-LSTM model is an improvement over the CNN-LSTM model. The fitness function for the individuals in the algorithm is shown as follows:

$$F = \frac{1}{E}\left(1 + \alpha\left(1 - \frac{n_{conv}}{n_{all}}\right) + \beta\left(1 - \frac{n_{lstm}}{n_{all}}\right)\right) \tag{6}$$

where F is individual fitness; E is the error, in which the hybrid-driven loss function described earlier is chosen; α represents the impact of CNN on model performance; β represents the impact of LSTM on model performance, taken as $\alpha = 0.8$, $\beta = 0.2$ in this case; n_{conv} is the number of convolutional kernels; n_{lstm} is the number of neurons; n_{all} is the total number of CNN convolutional kernels and LSTM neurons.

From the perspective of time efficiency, the GA-CNN-LSTM model takes much less time compared to the exhaustive method of selecting the best model parameters. In this model, individual fitness is inversely proportional to the hybrid-driven loss function, which is obtained by calculating the loss function to evaluate the model's performance. This fitness value serves as the basis for determining the final parameters.

4 Empirical Study

This paragraph takes a specific type of strategic warning radar system as the evaluation example. The experimental data used in this study is derived from the weapon equipment operational simulation system. The simulation system data consists of multidimensional time-series sample data generated during the simulation deduction process. It represents combat simulation data produced under a comprehensive multi-party game scenario and serves as the closest approximation to real combat training data in the absence of actual combat data support. To evaluate the operational effectiveness of the weapon equipment, multiple simulation experiments are conducted using the simulation system. Based on the operational deployment and tasks determined by the simulation system, the experimental data obtained from these simulation experiments are used for model training.

4.1 Theoretical Modeling

According to [22, 23], this paper takes the radar detection probability as the specific quantitative indicator of the operational effectiveness of this type of strategic Early-warning radar system. The specific modeling process is described in detail below. To predict the operational effectiveness of this type of strategic Early-warning radar system, the model diagram is shown in Fig. 2. The paper establishes a hybrid-driven loss function of the training target model according to the method described in the second chapter of this paper.

The power density of the returned radar receiving antenna Q_r can be determined by considering the total peak power generated by the radar transmitter P_t and the gain of the radar transmitting antenna in the target direction G_t:

$$Q_r = \frac{P_t G_t \sigma}{(4\pi)^2 R^4} \tag{7}$$

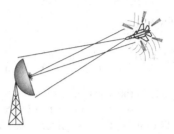

Fig. 2. Schematic diagram of strategic Early-warning radar model

where R is the distance between the target and the radar, and σ is the monostatic radar cross-section of the target.

The radar antenna's receiving power P_r can be determined by multiplying the gain G_r of the radar receiving antenna in the target direction:

$$P_r = \frac{P_t G_t G_r \lambda^2 \sigma}{(4\pi)^3 R^4} \tag{8}$$

where λ is the radar working wavelength.

Consider the input noise of the radar receiver, including external antenna noise and internal noise generated during receiver operation. The external antenna noise includes the radio noise reflected from the earth's surface, the radio noise radiated from the earth's atmosphere, and the cosmic Background radiation radiation noise. The internal noise comes from the random noise generated by the Thermal motion of electrons in the receiver circuit. Here, the internal noise in the receiver is taken as the dominant noise, and the power of the thermal noise in the radar receiver P_n is:

$$P_n = kT_s B = kT_0 FB \tag{9}$$

where $k = 1.38 \times 10^{-23} J/K$ is the Boltzmann constant; $T_s = T_0 F$ is the equivalent noise temperature of the antenna, and $T_0 = 290k$ is the standard temperature, F is the noise coefficient of receiver subsystem; B is the working bandwidth of the radar receiver.

The signal-to-noise ratio of radar target detection SNR is:

$$\text{SNR} \triangleq \frac{P_r}{P_n} = \frac{P_t G_t G_r \lambda^2 \sigma}{(4\pi)^3 R^4 k T_0 FB} \tag{10}$$

Considering the coherent accumulation of radar and signal loss caused by atmospheric absorption, component resistance loss, and non ideal signal processing conditions, the radar equation for a single station is represented as follows:

$$\text{SNR} = \frac{P_t G_t G_r \lambda^2 \sigma n_p}{(4\pi)^3 R^4 k T_0 FB L_s} \tag{11}$$

where n_p is the number of pulses emitted by the radar; L_s is the comprehensive loss of the radar system.

Let r(t) represents the envelope of the received signal in the radar receiver. The detection probability P_D is the probability that the sample R of r(t) exceeds the threshold voltage in the presence of both noise and signal, denoted as:

$$P_D = \int_{V_T}^{\infty} \frac{r}{\psi^2} I_0\left(\frac{rA}{\psi^2}\right) \exp\left(-\frac{r^2+A^2}{2\psi^2}\right) dr \qquad (12)$$

where $I_0(\beta) = \frac{1}{2\pi} \int_0^{2\pi} e^{\beta\cos\theta} d\theta$ is the modified zero-order Bessel function; A is the amplitude of the target echo signal; ψ is the variance of signal noise, and V_T is the threshold voltage.

Given that the radar signal is a sinusoidal waveform with amplitude A, the false alarm probability is P_{fa}, with SNR $= A^2/2\psi^2$ and $V_T^2/2\psi^2 = \ln(1/P_{fa})$ combined, Eq. (12) can be rewritten as follows:

$$\begin{aligned} P_D &= \int_{\sqrt{2\psi^2\ln(1/P_{fa})}}^{\infty} \frac{r}{\psi^2} I_0\left(\frac{rA}{\psi^2}\right) \exp\left(-\frac{r^2+A^2}{2\psi^2}\right) dr \\ &= Q\left[\sqrt{2SNR}, \sqrt{2\ln\left(\frac{1}{P_{fa}}\right)}\right] \end{aligned} \qquad (13)$$

where $Q[\alpha, \beta] = \int_{\beta}^{\infty} \xi I_0(\alpha\xi) e^{-(\xi^2+\alpha^2)/2} d\xi$ is the Marcum Q function.

This article addresses the complexity of integrating Eq. (13) by employing a precise approximation method suggested in [24]:

$$P_D \approx 0.5 \times \mathrm{erfc}\left(\sqrt{-\ln P_{fa}} - \sqrt{SNR+0.5}\right) \qquad (14)$$

where $\mathrm{erfc}(z) = 1 - 2\int_0^z e^{-v^2} dv/\sqrt{\pi}$ is the complementary error function.

In conclusion, the operational effectiveness of the strategic Early-warning radar system is measured by the target detection probability, which serves as a specific quantitative index. To achieve this, the radar mechanism model is established and utilized to obtain:

$$P_D = F'\left(P_t, G_t, G_r, \lambda, \sigma, n_p, R, B, F, L_s, P_{fa}\right) \qquad (15)$$

4.2 Data Set Construction

The combat effectiveness evaluation index system shown in Table 1 is obtained according to the basic theoretical model of strategic Early-warning radar. Then, the effectiveness evaluation data is collected. In order to measure the effectiveness of weapons and equipment in completing target tasks under specific conditions, it is necessary to add relevant data reflecting the battlefield situation to model training.

Setting the Background: In a military operation, a strategic Early-warning radar was deployed at a position of (9°S, 161°E), which is 0.65 km away from an island in Solomon Islands. The radar's main objective is to detect and track enemy aircraft entering the responsible area. The responsible area, which the radar is tasked to monitor,

Table 1. Strategic Early Warning Radar Combat Effectiveness Evaluation Index System

Combat unit	Characteristic		Combat unit	Characteristic	
our side radar	location	latitude (°)	counterparty jammer	location	latitude (°)
		longitude (°)			longitude (°)
		altitude (°)			altitude (°)
	input peak power (W)			input peak power (W)	
	working frequency (Hz)			bandwidth (Hz)	
	antenna gain (dB)			antenna gain (dB)	
	bandwidth (Hz)			losses (dB)	
	total losses (dB)		detect target	location	latitude (°)
	number of samples per unit time				longitude (°)
					altitude (°)
	false alarm probability			RCS (m^2)	
	noise figure			target type	

is a square area composed of (8°S-10°S, 160°E-162°E). In the operational scenario, the simulation involves the crossing of the responsible area airspace by one enemy jamming aircraft and one enemy aircraft. Both aircraft can enter the airspace in any direction and fly out of it in any direction. The enemy jamming aircraft has a flying altitude range of 8 km–12 km, while the enemy aircraft has a flying altitude range of 9 km–20 km. These two aircraft will appear synchronously and fly out of the responsible area simultaneously in each simulation.

Figure 3 displays the schematic diagram of the simulation system experiment. The collected data for combat effectiveness evaluation is based on the combat readiness evaluation index system. This data primarily consists of the local azimuth information of the radar and enemy jammer during battle, utilizing the AER coordinate system to acquire the azimuth, elevation, and distance of the target object. Additionally, the data includes the local azimuth information of the radar and enemy aircraft, performance indicators of the radar system state, performance indicators of the enemy jammer state, and performance parameter indicators of the enemy aircraft. In total, 100 experimental simulations were conducted, with each simulation collecting sequence information over 100 time steps, resulting in a total of 10,000 sample data. These simulations generated 21 indicators related to the comprehensive performance of radar resources. The specific quantitative indicator used to measure the operational effectiveness of the strategic Early-warning radar was the target detection probability. The remaining 20 indicators were utilized as the initial index set to construct the data sample set $T = \{I_1, I_2, \cdots, I_{20}\}$.

The proposed prediction model is the GA-CNN-LSTM hybrid model. It utilizes the time series feature map as input and implements the word vector method from Natural Language Processing for reference. The design includes a two-dimensional sample vector, where the dataset's feature dimensions correspond to the number of

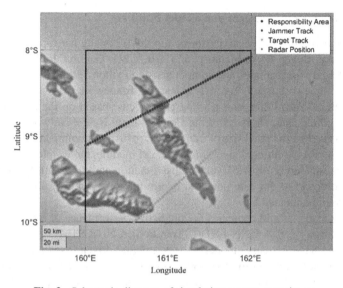

Fig. 3. Schematic diagram of simulation system experiment

indicators. Thus, a vector is formed to represent a series of related features collected within a time step. This resulting vector constitutes a completely new time series data. The joint characterization of the probability of target detection at each moment is based on its relevant features. The next step involves inputting the feature map generated from the time series data into the CNN module through window sliding. The sliding window width is set to 20, the step size is set to 1, and the size of the unit feature map is 20×20 to facilitate subsequent computations. The characteristic map data, as shown in Table 2, is then inputted. These characteristic maps are arranged chronologically to form the original data sample. Lastly, to minimize the impact of multiple simulation experiments, 81 unit feature maps were obtained for each period using 100 sample data as the dividing period. This means that a total of 81 * 100 experimental samples were gathered.

Table 2. Sample Data Table of Unit Characteristic Map

Sample Number	Feature 1	Feature 2	......	Feature 20	Detection Probability
1	4.0611	0.0356		0.3164	0.7580
2	4.0723	0.0363		0.2980	0.7396
3	4.0837	0.0369		0.3189	0.7667
4	4.0953	0.0375		0.2877	0.8078
......	......	......	......	......	......
20	4.3090	0.0472		0.3135	0.8993

4.3   Experimental Environment and Model Building

The experiments in this article are performed in the following hardware environment: CPU: Intel Xeon Silver 4210, Memory: 157 GB, GPU: GeForce RTX 2080 Ti. The relevant models are programmed and computed using Python 3.9 and the PyCharm tool. The software framework is a PyTorch deep learning framework.

Two layers of convolution and pooling are selected based on the size of the unit feature map and the characteristics of the Convolutional Neural Network (CNN). The convolutional layer has a kernel size of 2 and a stride of 1. The pooling layer has the same parameters as the convolutional layer. In the LSTM module, the weights are initialized with the mean squared error (MSE) as the loss function and the Adam function as the optimizer. Moreover, to mitigate potential overfitting during model training, Dropout operations are implemented.

This paper analyzes and compares the predictive performance of five models: GA-CNN-LSTM (Theory), GA-CNN-LSTM (Tradition), CNN-LSTM, LSTM, and CNN. The GA-CNN-LSTM (Theory) model utilizes a mixed-driven loss function, which is called as theory-assisted. On the other hand, the GA-CNN-LSTM (Tradition) model employs the L2 loss criterion for its fitness function error. The experiments involve training and evaluating each model using the selected dataset. Furthermore, a search strategy is employed to determine the optimal hyperparameters for the neural network sizes of all models.

5   Result and Discussion

This study employs mean absolute error (MAE), R-squared score (R2 score), Pearson correlation coefficient (r), and index of agreement (IA) as the criteria for measuring the pros and cons of the model. The primary evaluation metric is the R2 score.

Under the optimal parameter settings, GA-CNN-LSTM (Theory) and GA-CNN-LSTM (Tradition) demonstrate the best performance. Tables 3, 4, 5 and 6 show the comparison results of MAE, R2 score, r, and IA, respectively. From these tables, CNN exhibits poor performance in fitting multi-dimensional time series data, whereas LSTM surpasses CNN but still has scope for improvement. CNN-LSTM effectively utilizes CNN's spatial feature extraction capability and LSTM's powerful time series data processing ability to explore relevant information in the dataset and identify potential connections between disparate data points. The GA-CNN-LSTM model selects the number of neurons in the CNN-LSTM model using a genetic algorithm. Despite its remaining errors, it is more effective and accurate than CNN-LSTM. Refer to Tables 3, 4, 5 and 6 for further specific details. Based on the MAE performance data, GA-CNN-LSTM (Theory) consistently outperforms the other four models, displaying a 6.6% decrease compared to GA-CNN-LSTM (Traditional). The R2 score is a reliable indicator to assess the quality of regression model predictions. In this case, GA-CNN-LSTM (Theory) outperforms GA-CNN-LSTM (Traditional) with a 2.9% improvement, achieving the highest score. This study shows that incorporating theory-assisted models for training can improve the fitting ability and optimality of regression models. In tasks with limited sample sizes, the inclusion of explicit functional relationships in the data aids in improving model stability and reducing the likelihood of overfitting. By incorporating this theoretical term as an additional penalty in the objective function, the model's ability to generalize is enhanced. Although GA-CNN-LSTM (Theory) shows the greatest performance in the r and IA metrics, substantial improvements were not achieved.

Table 3. The experimental results in terms of Mean Absolute Error (MAE)

Test	GA-CNN-LSTM (Theory)	GA-CNN-LSTM (Tradition)	CNN-LSTM	LSTM	CNN
1	4.430	4.576	4.869	5.296	5.686
2	4.231	4.681	4.733	5.394	5.587
3	4.320	4.629	4.777	5.370	5.596
4	4.376	4.698	4.901	5.259	5.660
5	4.275	4.583	4.826	5.392	5.621
Average	4.326	4.633	4.821	5.342	5.630

Table 4. The experimental results in terms of R-squared score (R2 score)

Test	GA-CNN-LSTM (Theory)	GA-CNN-LSTM (Tradition)	CNN-LSTM	LSTM	CNN
1	0.842	0.820	0.783	0.767	0.733
2	0.847	0.823	0.780	0.761	0.734
3	0.845	0.813	0.781	0.771	0.733
4	0.846	0.829	0.773	0.771	0.742
5	0.845	0.818	0.783	0.762	0.738
Average	0.845	0.821	0.780	0.766	0.736

Table 5. The experimental results in terms of Pearson correlation coefficient (r)

Test	GA-CNN-LSTM (Theory)	GA-CNN-LSTM (Tradition)	CNN-LSTM	LSTM	CNN
1	0.925	0.915	0.906	0.900	0.887
2	0.925	0.921	0.903	0.901	0.895
3	0.924	0.912	0.906	0.905	0.887
4	0.929	0.918	0.904	0.903	0.885
5	0.923	0.919	0.901	0.897	0.886
Average	0.925	0.917	0.904	0.901	0.888

Table 6. The experimental results in terms of Index of Agreement (IA)

Test	GA-CNN-LSTM (Theory)	GA-CNN-LSTM (Tradition)	CNN-LSTM	LSTM	CNN
1	0.960	0.953	0.941	0.942	0.927
2	0.961	0.958	0.949	0.945	0.922
3	0.961	0.955	0.950	0.939	0.936
4	0.964	0.958	0.950	0.944	0.937
5	0.961	0.958	0.945	0.934	0.927
Average	0.961	0.956	0.947	0.941	0.930

Figure 4 shows a comparison between the predicted results of each model using the Test2 parameters and the corresponding actual values in a single experiment. The table shows CNN's predicted results fluctuating greatly, with a significant gap compared to the true values. The predicted trends of CNN and LSTM significantly differ from the true values, with CNN generally yielding lower predicted results. GA-CNN-LSTM (Theory), GA-CNN-LSTM (Traditional), and CNN-LSTM demonstrate superior prediction accuracy compared to the others. The GA-CNN-LSTM theory effectively captures the probability of target detection from start to finish. Nevertheless, the model's predictions exhibit inadequacy and larger errors during the initial time steps, underscoring the need for additional research.

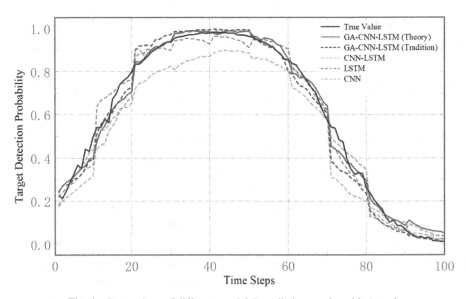

Fig. 4. Comparison of different models' prediction results with Actual.

6 Conclusions

The prediction of combat effectiveness for weapon systems is of significant theoretical and practical importance in military strategic planning and decision-making. This paper proposes a deep learning combat effectiveness prediction algorithm that incorporates weapon basic model theory knowledge as an auxiliary driver. By constructing the weapon basic model modeling paradigm, physical constraints are added as regularization terms to the design model optimization objective. This assists the model in training while retaining the advantages of conventional deep learning models as simple, direct, and low-threshold proxy models. To address the multi-dimensional time series prediction involved in combat effectiveness prediction, a GA-CNN-LSTM hybrid forecasting model is designed. Experimental results demonstrate that the hybrid model with theoretical assistance can achieve excellent generalization capability even with fewer training samples. It exhibits a 2.9% improvement in R2 score compared to purely data-driven models. This study provides a new approach to alleviate the issue of data scarcity faced by data-driven models in practical applications. It is hoped that this approach will facilitate the implementation of more cutting-edge and advanced deep learning algorithms and models in the defense industry, enabling them to demonstrate their exceptional performance.

References

1. Dacheng, L., Jianfeng, C., Zongfu, L.: Research on operational effectiveness evaluation method of anti-radiation UAV based on improved ADC model. Ship Electron. Eng. **40**(08), 130–133 (2020)
2. Changdong, H., Nan, H., Dijiu, Y., Yongshun, Z.: Effectiveness evaluation of mobile communication system based on Gray-AHP. Fire Control Command Control **45**(11), 106–112 (2020)
3. Changpeng, P., Zhongfa, W., Haitao, W., et al.: Operational effectiveness evaluation of carrier-based aircraft attacking land based on BP neural network. Ordnance Ind. Autom. **41**(12), 9–12 (2022)
4. Chen, X., Hu, N.: Research on operational effectiveness assessment for reconnaissance UAV based on the improved SVM. Fire Control Command Control **43**(10), 31–34 (2018)
5. Ziwei, Z., Qisheng, G., Zhiming, D., et al.: Review of system of systems combat effectiveness evaluation and optimization methods. J. Syst. Simul. **34**(02), 303–313 (2022)
6. Li, C., Miao, J., Shen, B.: Operational effectiveness prediction of equipment system based on improved stacking-ensemble-learning method. Acta Armamentarii:1–12[2023-05-24]
7. Ni, L., Yuhong, L., Guanghong, G., Xiaodong, H.: Intelligent effectiveness evaluation and optimization on weapon system of systems based on deep learning. J. Syst. Simul. **32**(08), 1425–1435 (2020)
8. Li, C., Chen, H., Li, J.: An effectiveness evaluation indicator system based on multi-scale parallel convolution neural network. Electron. Opt. Control **28**(11), 31–34+93 (2021)
9. Yu, X., Xiong, W., Han, C.: A survey of effectiveness evaluation methods based on neural network. Ordnance Ind. Autom. **42**(03), 1–8+43 (2023)
10. Lu, Y., Qian, X., Chen, W., et al.: Research on construction method of data-driven equipment effectiveness evaluation model. J. Syst. Simul. **30**(12), 4587–4594+4601 (2018)
11. Fuling, M., Pengcheng, L., Jinglun, Z.: Study on air force campaign simulating system based on analytical models. J. Syst. Simul. **08**, 1723–1726 (2007)

12. Changhai, F., Keli, H., Li, T., et al.: Assess damage effectiveness for warhead to complex targets. J. Syst. Simul. **19**, 5971–5976 (2009)
13. Xinqi, L., Hongxia, L., Yanfen, Q.: System modeling and analysis of operational effectiveness on conventional missile blocking airport runway based on SEA. J. Ballist. **35**(01), 94–102 (2023)
14. Meng, C., Seo, S., Cao, D., et al.: When physics meets machine learning: a survey of physics-informed machine learning. arXiv preprint arXiv:2203.16797 (2022)
15. LeCun, Y., Bottou, L., Bengio, Y., et al.: Gradient-based learning applied to document recognition. Proc. IEEE **86**(11), 2278–2324 (1998)
16. Hochreiter, S., Schmidhuber, J.: Long short-term memory. Neural Comput. **9**(8), 1735–1780 (1997)
17. Holland, J.H.: Adaptation in Natural and Artificial Systems: An Introductory Analysis with Applications to Biology, Control, and Artificial Intelligence. MIT Press, Cambridge (1992)
18. Yang Li, W., Yuxi, W.J., et al.: Research on recurrent neural network. J. Comput. Appl. **38**(A02), 1–6 (2018)
19. Barzegar, R., Aalami, M.T., Adamowski, J.: Short-term water quality variable prediction using a hybrid CNN–LSTM deep learning model. Stoch. Env. Res. Risk Assess. **34**(2), 415–433 (2020)
20. Zha, W., Liu, Y., Wan, Y., et al.: Forecasting monthly gas field production based on the CNN-LSTM model. Energy 124889 (2022)
21. Livieris, I.E., Pintelas, E., Pintelas, P.: A CNN–LSTM model for gold price time-series forecasting. Neural Comput. Appl. **32**, 17351–17360 (2020)
22. Scheer, J., Holm, W.A.: Principles of Modern Radar. SciTech Pub., Raleigh, NC, USA (2010)
23. Mahafza, B.R.: Radar Systems Analysis and Design Using MATLAB. CRC press, Boca Raton (2022)
24. North, D.O.: An analysis of the factors which determine signal/noise discrimination in pulsed-carrier systems. Proc. IEEE **51**(7), 1016–1027 (1963)

Aerial Scene Understanding Based on Synthetic Data

Zhiyuan Zhao[1,2(✉)] and Ke Xie[1,2(✉)]

[1] Science and Technology on Information Systems Engineering Laboratory,
Nanjing, China
tuzixini@163.com, xieke3@cetc.com.cn
[2] Nanjing Research Institute of Electronic Engineering, Nanjing, China

Abstract. Public area monitoring will always be a key aspect of great concern. Its development has greatly promoted rapid innovation in many fields, such as public safety supervision, intelligent transportation analysis, and urban planning. Many researchers have made efforts on public area monitoring. However, most of these studies are based on the traditional monitoring perspective, which suffers high construction costs and is hard to update. In recent years, rapidly developing drone technology demonstrates superiority in convenience, flexibility, and low cost compared to traditional monitoring systems. Nevertheless, it is not widely employed in public area monitoring. Therefore, we build a framework for diversified aerial view data collection based on virtual scenes and name it as Synthetic Drone. To verify its effectiveness, we construct a virtual aerial view public safety monitoring dataset named SynthDrone. It contains 300 video clips under various scenes with annotations includes location, identification and depth *etc.* In addition, we also build a Depth Aware Target Distribution estimation Network (DATDNet) that takes cross-modal input data and orients multiple tasks in public safety monitoring. Based on the newly constructed dataset and DATDNet, we design experiments to verify their effectiveness and discuss the domain gap between synthetic and real-world data.

Keywords: Aerial Scene Understanding · Synthetic Data · Public Safety · Artificial Intelligence

1 Introduction

Drone monitoring has made expeditious developments in recent years, and it has been rapidly applied to various fields. The most typical examples are geological surveying and mapping, agricultural assistance, group detection, as well as emergency relief and security monitoring [19]. The new flexible drone equipment greatly reduces the cost of these jobs, and completes many tough tasks quickly. With the development of the social economy and the continuous growth of population density, the threats to public security are becoming more and more complex and diverse. More attention has been paid to the social public safety monitoring and analysis system based on drone technology.

Y. Tan and Y. Shi (Eds.): DMBD 2023, CCIS 2018, pp. 141–156, 2024.
https://doi.org/10.1007/978-981-97-0844-4_11

The public safety monitoring and analysis system mainly depends on the detection and state analysis of the crowds and vehicles. Thus, target density estimation, traffic jam detection, and target trajectory analysis have become the most basic tasks of public safety monitoring and analysis system. Most of the previous monitoring and analysis systems are based on the images collected from the closed-circuit television monitoring cameras, such as UCSD [16] and WorldExpo'10 [29], which leads to a single data scene and limits the generalization ability of the algorithm. In order to solve this problem, free view datasets like NWPU-Crowd [25], JHU-CROWD++ [21] are collected which uses widely collected data from different sources and increases the complexity of the scene covered by the data. However, due to the perspective effect, those captured image suffers a significant "near big, far small" problem, that is to say, for the same target, there will be a large scale variation when it is close to or away from the acquisition end. On the one hand, the existence of this problem will affect the performance of the detection and analysis algorithm, on the other hand, it is not consistent with the data characteristics collected by drone equipment.

To better serve the requirements of public safety monitoring and analysis from the view of drones, some researchers try to use drones to collect and construct related aerial view datasets [14]. However, there are still some problems in building such datasets. First of all, the cost of collecting this kind of data is high. Secondly, the collected data need to go through a complex labeling process before it can be used, which consumes a lot of manpower and material resources.

Considering all the challenges suffered by the public safety analysis task under the aerial view mentioned above, we try to promote the development of this area from the data level. The main contribution can be summarized into the following three aspects:

1) Based on the realistic Rockstar Game Grand Theft Auto V (GTAV), a diversified drone monitoring data collection framework named Synthetic Drone is built. Which designs and renders the data acquisition scene, collects the raw data during the rendering process, and rebuilds after the capture work.
2) Construct a large-scale aerial view public safety analysis video dataset, namely SynthDrone. It contains 306 video clips collected from 51 different locations and a total of 18,360 frames and provides accurate annotations on density estimation, detection, identification, depth, segmentation map, and tracking of variant pedestrians and vehicles.
3) Serval state-of-the-art public safety analysis methods are tested under the proposed dataset. The experimental results prove the proposed synthetic dataset enhances the performance of existing algorithms. At the same time, we analyze the internal principle focus on why synthetic data brings improvement to the final results. We also designed the Depth Aware Target Distribution Estimation Network (DATDNet) to provide a simple cross-modal multi-task baseline.

2   Related Work

Here, we put the image acquisition equipment, acquisition height, scene illumination, capture angle, sensors [24] *etc.* together and call it acquisition environment. Different datasets lean on different acquisition environments and finally lead to images with variant characteristics. Dataset from different perspectives suffers different advantages and disadvantages, we will introduce it here separately. Table 1 shows the statistical data analysis of some common public safety monitoring datasets. All those datasets will be introduced below.

Table 1. Statistical data analysis of some common public safety monitoring datasets.

Name	V¹	I	D	M	View	Avg Resolution	Avg Entity	Frames
UCF_CC_50 [10]					Free	2101 × 2888	1,279	50
Shanghaitech A [30]					Free	589 × 868	501	482
UCF-QNRF [11]					Free	2013 × 2902	815	1535
NWPU-Crowd [25]					Free	2191 × 3209	418	5109
Shanghaitech B [30]					Surveillance	768 × 1024	123	716
GCC [26]					Surveillance	1920 × 1080	501	15,211
UCSD [4]	✓				Surveillance	158 × 238	25	2000
Mall [5]	✓				Surveillance	480 × 640	31	20000
DroneCrowd [27]	✓	✓			Aerial	1920 × 1080	145	33,600
SynthDrone	✓	✓	✓	✓	Aerial	1920 × 1080	121	18,000

¹ V means Video, I means Identification, D means Depth, M means Multi-Object

Surveillance View: The datasets under this view collect images from closed-circuit televisions or capture devices with similar heights, which are often applied under different public scenes like markets, streets, traffic stations, etc. UCSD [4] collects 2,000 crowd images on a sidewalk within the university campus. It contains annotations for pedestrian location and motion tracks. Mall [5] also captures 2,000 crowd images inside a shopping mall with slightly better resolution compared with UCSD. These two datasets all build upon one single monitoring scenario, so they both suffer from the lack of data diversity. To enrich the data scenarios, increase the diversity and generalization ability, WorldExpo'10 [29] and CityUHK-X [12] build crowd analysis datasets with 108 and 55 fixed scenes separately. Furthermore, datasets like ShanghaiTech Part B [30] and Crowd Surveillance [28] were proposed based on surveillance view images from lots of sources with much higher resolutions compared with former datasets mentioned above. Besides collecting crowd images for public safety monitoring, projects like Next Generation Simulation (NGSIM) [1] constructs variant traffic scenes with annotations for each vehicle inside the target scene. VSCrowd [15] consists of 634 videos, and contains 62,938 samples.

Aerial View: To alleviate the problems existing in the above surveillance view, some researchers propose to monitor and analyze the scene from the aerial view and use drones or specific flight equipment to collect the corresponding data. In addition to improving the problems mentioned earlier, the images under aerial view have the advantages of a much flexible and broader field of view because of its higher acquisition position. Therefore, it can be better applied to the security monitoring requirements of large-scale activities and large scenes. For crowd analysis, Bahmanyar et al. [2] collect 33 large aerial images involving mass scenes like sports events, city centers. The VisDrone team focuses on building datasets with cameras carried by drones. They propose the DroneCrowd [33] and Drone-eVehicle [23] for aerial view crowd and vehicle analysis separately. Eckstein *et al.* are devoted to the analysis of traffic scenes. They collect variant datasets with different and unique characteristics. For example, the Highway Drone Dataset (highD) [14] records traffics at six locations, which involves more than 110,500 vehicles with type, size, and speed information.

Free View: To better serve images from variant sources and improve the application scope of the algorithm. Some researchers proposed to build datasets not based on specific views, namely free view datasets. Those datasets usually collect images from the internet or a variety of other publicly accessible sources. No specific scenarios are required during the collecting process. Therefore, such datasets usually contain complex and diverse data, which means both surveillance and bird-eye views are involved here. As early as 2013, Idrees *et al.* [10] collects UCF_CC_50 contains only 50 images, which is a very insufficient amount at present. However, it speeds up the study of crowd analysis at that age. Following datasets like ShanghaiTech Part A [30] and UCF-QNRF [11] enlarges the datasets into the number of hundreds and thousands of samples. The JHU-CROWD++ [21] increases the dataset size into 4,372 samples with average resolution of 1430×910. The NWPU-Crowd [25] collected by Wang *et al.* broke through 5,000 samples with average resolution up to 2191×3209. FUDAN-UCC [6] provides dataset without labeling.

3 Synthetic Drone Raw Data Generation Framework and SynthDrone Dataset

Grand Theft Auto V (GTAV) is a first-person free scene sandbox game built among the Rockstar Advanced Game Engine(RAGE) and released by Rockstar Game in the year 2013. It has achieved an excellent effect in scene modeling, texture processing, and 3D simulation. The main scene of the game is concentrated in a virtual city called Los Santos, San Andreas which is built based on the real city Los Angeles, California, USA. Many scenes in virtual cities are modeled based on the real world. At the same time, a large number of real vehicles and interactive logic are provided in the game, which makes it possible to use this software to build a virtual dataset for scientific research.

Fig. 1. Working flow of the Synthetic Drone raw data generation framework.

The game manufacturer allows players to use the plug-in MODs to intervene in the software in the off-line mode for non-commercial use. Alexander Blade builds the C++ runtime library named Script Hook V [3] for MOD development. He also tests and creates the native function database for parsing and modifying the running software. On this basis, Crosire*et al.* build Script Hook Dot Net to run script files written by .NET languages. They also integrate some reverse parsing methods for the contents inside the memory, which makes it more convenient for users to get useful data from the memory. Therefore, we build the Synthetic Drone raw data generation framework based on the Script Hook Dot Net library. Under this framework, we can set the game content, control different entities, adjust game environments, and record the raw data with simple precessing. Compared with the previous real datasets that relied on manual collection and annotation, this construction method consumes almost no manpower and saves a lot of time and resources. Figure 1 shows the raw data generation working flow.

3.1   Raw Data Generation

In this part, we introduce the raw data generation process, which can be split into two stages, namely scene generation and data collection stage.

Scene Generation: The software contains a large-scale map including a variety of topography and scenes, like city, desert, and beaches. To obtain a more reasonable dataset, we manually select the caption location, which encompasses the following three kinds of public safety monitoring scenarios:

- **Pure traffic scene** focuses on the most common public areas, namely road areas. It involves several different types of concerns, including variance vehicles on the main trunk road and pedestrians on the edge of the road.
- **Enclosed areas** like parks, campus, courtyards, beaches, and playgrounds encounter no vehicles, thus they mainly focus on analyzing the state of crowds.
- **Boundary scene** may involve both situations mentioned above, including fast-passing vehicles and crowds. The target status suffers considerable differences under such a scene. Such examples usually appear at the entrance of parks, edges of pedestrian streets, and areas near the shopping mall.

Considering the diversity and effectiveness of the data collection scenes, we selected 50 locations within all three types listed above. Due to the differences in the state and topography of different areas, we also manually select the preset acquisition height for each location, and the subsequent acquisition process will dynamically adjust the actual height in each process based on the preset height. The complete map and all acquisition locations and corresponding heights are shown in Fig. 2. Limited by the hardware and the interactive logic, during the software normal running there are few appearances for the targets we really pay attention like crowds and vehicles. Thus, in addition to the natural targets in the system itself, we made independent planning at each acquisition location, marking out the areas suitable for adding target instances.

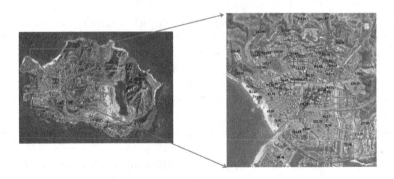

Fig. 2. Caption Locations.

Data Collection: The camera status, weather, and time need to be set for each location. Those key settings will be introduced one by one. The camera height of each acquisition is randomly selected within the range of five meters above or below the preset height of the position, the camera is vertically facing the ground and the field of view is set to a fixed value of 50. The weather of the scene is selected from Extra Sunny, Clear, Foggy, Raining, and Thunderstorm. We divide one day into six time periods starting from zero o'clock. For each location, a total of six capture processes are made to cover each time period and weather condition. Then, additional targets need to be placed in separate steps. The main target here is the pedestrians inside the current scene. The character is constructed based on the random model provided by the software and uniformly placed in the areas set in the previous stage. Automatic tasks are added to each additional character to drive it to move freely in the scene.

The depth and texture are the intermediate information intercepted from the engine rendering process using the GTAVisionExport native tools [9]. For the target information, the data collector first acquires all the pedestrians and vehicles within the range of 2 km for the acquisition location from the memory and then dumps all the data that may be useful into XML files with a specific format for each instance. For each location, we collect six video clips under different time and weather conditions, and each video clip contains 60 frames, so we have obtained 300 video clips and 18000 frames for 50 locations.

3.2 Dataset Post Processing and Statistical Analysis

During the collection process, we only record the raw data, and then further process the data after completing all the collection work. The original scene, depth, and texture files use a non-universal save format, which cannot be used directly. In the post-processing, the scene image is converted into normal PNG/JPEG files together with the segmentation map. As for the depth, we save it with a 32-bit NumPy float format for convenience. All target instance whose location is not within the display area of the screen is removed, and the bounding boxes of the instances is calculated using the recorded boundary points.

In this task, we mainly focus on two types of targets, namely pedestrians and vehicles, together we call them entities. Finally, we collect this synthetic dataset with 50 locations, 300 video clips, 18,000 frames, and 2,171,133 entities. Each frame contains a 1920 × 1080 scene image and their corresponding segmentation map, depth map with the same resolution. There is also the location, bounding box, and id information for each entity on the scene. Figure 3 (a) displays the entity distribution for each acquisition location. As shown in Fig. 3 (b) and (c), simple statistical analysis on the final dataset demonstrates that the randomly generated scenes obey uniform distribution for the weather and time interval.

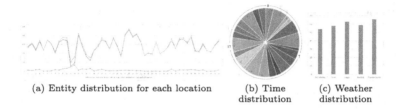

(a) Entity distribution for each location   (b) Time distribution   (c) Weather distribution

Fig. 3. Simple statistical analysis on the final dataset.

To better analyze the generalization ability of the dataset and algorithms, we split the dataset according to acquisition location. We first sort the locations according to a total entity, pedestrians and vehicles quantities, and then divide the sorted list into two high-density and low-density location groups. For each group, we randomly select 70% as the training set and the remaining 30% as the test set. So we got a training set of 210 video clips for 35 locations and a test set with 90 video clips collected from 15 locations. All subsequent experiments on this dataset are carried out under this split mode.

4   Depth Aware Target Distribution Estimation Network

To take the inter-frame sequence information and depth information into account, we designed the Depth Aware Target Distribution Estimation Network(DATDNet). As shown in Fig. 4, the DATDNet consists of feature extraction parts and multiple target distribution analysis heads.

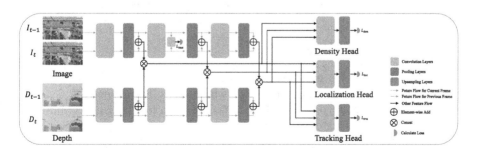

Fig. 4. The architecture of Depth Aware Target Distribution Estimation Network.

Feature Extraction Stage: This stage consists of RGB image path and the depth information path. The encoder structure of the two paths is similar, but the parameters are not shared. Each encoder consists of three-layer encoding blocks, the size of the features will be compressed once by each coding block, and the different levels of features encoded by the three coding blocks of the two branches will be spliced together for subsequent use in the analysis stage. It can only accept the current frame or together with the previous one at the same time. The branch used to process depth information can also be freely plugged in as needed. The working model of this branch is similar to that of the RGB image branch, and it can also receive single-frame input or multi-frame input.

Distribution Analysis Heads: This stage estimates target distribution based on the features extracted by the previous stage. To be specific, the distribution information contains not only basic target density but also localization and tracking clues. All three heads consist of a simple convolution layer and the upsampling layer to recover output size, but the shape and state of their output are different. Different heads face different tasks, so we design independent loss functions for each head.

Loss Functions: For the target density estimation and localization task, the ground truth is generated by the Gaussian filtering operation. The density map generation process works with kernel size 15 and variation value set to 4. For the generation of localization map, we follow the methods proposed in [32] use fixed Gaussian kernel to filter all input dot maps and only keeps the maximal one for the overlapped areas. The density map loss and localization map loss can be formulated by following equation:

$$\mathcal{L} = \sum_{i=1}^{H} \sum_{j=1}^{W} ||\mathcal{M}(i,j) - \hat{\mathcal{M}}(i,j)||_2, \tag{1}$$

where $\mathcal{L}$ is the density or the localization loss, H and W is the height and width of current scene. $\mathcal{M}(i,j)$ is the ground truth value with coordinate (i,j), $\hat{\mathcal{M}}(i,j)$ is the predicted one. $||\cdot||_2$ is the 2-norm operation.

Different from the density estimation and localization tasks, the tracking head focus on the target identification between adjacent frames. So we modify the triplet loss proposed by Hermans *et al.* [8,17] to maximize the feature distance between different target instance and minimize the distance for the same instance. The tracking loss can be calculated by following equation:

$$\mathcal{L}_{trc} = \frac{1}{N} \sum_{p,q=1}^{N} max(\mathcal{D}_s(p,q) - \mathcal{D}_d(p,q) + \tau, 0), \tag{2}$$

where N is the instance number, p,q is the instance belong to current frame or last frame. τ is the distance threshold which set to 0.2 during the training process. $\mathcal{D}_s(p,q)$ and $\mathcal{D}_d(p,q)$ are the distance function for the same or different class defined by following equations:

$$\mathcal{D}_s(p,q) = max(max(\sqrt{(\mathcal{F}_p - \mathcal{F}_q)^2}), \tau_{max}), if \quad p = q, \tag{3}$$

$$\mathcal{D}_d(p,q) = min(min(\sqrt{(\mathcal{F}_p - \mathcal{F}_q)^2}), \tau_{min}), if \quad p \neq q. \tag{4}$$

$\mathcal{F}_p$ is the feature vector represents instance p, τ_{max} and τ_{min} are the distance thresholds to prevent outliers, which set to 2000 and 0.01 during the training process.

To further mine the inside information difference between two adjacent frames, we add an auxiliary loss function to guide the encoder. This $\mathcal{L}_{aux}$ simply calculates the distance between two input frames after they pass through the first encoding block, we also set a threshold to avoid excessive deviations:

$$\mathcal{L}_{aux} = min(||\mathcal{F}_t - \mathcal{F}_{t-1}||_2, \tau_{aux}), \tag{5}$$

where $\mathcal{F}$ also represents the feature vector, and $\tau_{aux} = 2000$ is the threshold.

The total loss used for the training process is:

$$\mathcal{L} = \alpha\mathcal{L}_{den} + \beta\mathcal{L}_{loc} + \gamma\mathcal{L}_{trc} - \delta\mathcal{L}_{aux}, \tag{6}$$

$\mathcal{L}_{den}$ and $\mathcal{L}_{loc}$ is the density and location loss, α, β, γ and δ are the weights for different sub loss functions, which can set to zero when it is not under use.

5   Experimental Results

This section focuses on analyzing the experimental results on the proposed synthetic dataset and corresponding results adapted to real-world datasets.

5.1   Evaluation Metrics

For the evaluation of target density estimation, we follow the previous work like [10,11] use Mean Absolute Error (MAE) and Mean Squared Error (MSE) to measure the prediction error. For the evaluation of target localization, we use Average Precision (AP) with distance threshold m pixels represented as $L@m$. Threshold m indicates if the distance between the predicted instance and the ground truth is less than m pixels, this instance is considered to be a correct true positive prediction. We calculate mean Average Precision (L-mAP) with distance thresholds within $\{5, 6, 7, \ldots, 25\}$ pixels to measure the overall localization performance. In addition to the overall results, we measure the results under three specific distances represented as $L@5$, $L@15$, and $L@25$.

For the evaluation of target tracking, we follow the trajectory definition given by Eunbyung et al. [20]. Each predicted trajectory contains a series of target center points under each frame with a confidence level. For tracks with the same identity index, we sort it according to their average confidence level among all frames and then try to match it with the given ground truth. For the center point in each frame, if it is located within 30 pixels from the label, we take it as a correct prediction. If the correct center point ratio inside one trajectory exceeds a specific threshold, it is considered to be a matched one. Here we set three groups of thresholds for evaluation (0.1, 0.2, 0.3). The tracking scores are represented as $T@0.1$, $T@0.2$, and $T@0.3$ for three given thresholds and T-mAP for the average score.

5.2   Experiment Results on the SynthDrone Dataset

For the evaluation of target density estimation, we build experiments based on the C^3F [7] crowd counting framework. All the experiments are constructed on the Ubuntu 18.04 operating system, Xeon(R) Silver 4110 CPU @ 2.10 GHz, and the NVIDIA TITAN RTX GPU. The Adam is used to optimize the proposed DATDNet, the learning rate is set to $1e-5$ and decreases 0.5% after each epoch.

Considering the data splitting manner of the SynthDrone dataset, we use the training set for network optimization and evaluate the model performance on the validation set. For the methods like MCNN [30], CSRNet [18], SASNet [22] and DroneNet [13] *etc.*, they only use single RGB image as the input, we also use the proposed DATDNet work with the single image mode, and named as DATDNet**. For methods that use sequential information, we compare it with BVCC [31]. We use DATDNet* to represent DATDNet in this working model.

Table 2. Target density estimation result on the SynthDrone validation set for DATD-Net and serval contrast algorithms. The **bold** or underlined result represent the one ranked **first** or second.

Method	RGB	Sequential	Depth	Crowd			Vehicle		
				MAE	MSE	NAE	MAE	MSE	NAE
MCNN	✓			21.78	32.44	1.30	5.14	**7.50**	0.74
VGG	✓			19.63	28.14	1.24	5.15	7.55	0.73
CSRNet	✓			18.17	25.97	1.28	5.15	7.53	0.73
SASNet	✓			15.16	24.07	0.90	5.14	<u>7.52</u>	0.74
DroneNet	✓			15.32	23.09	0.97	5.13	7.54	0.75
DATDNet**	✓			15.73	23.61	1.13	<u>5.13</u>	7.58	**0.72**
BVCC	✓	✓		17.33	27.09	**0.47**	5.15	7.54	<u>0.73</u>
DATDNet*	✓	✓		<u>13.54</u>	<u>22.68</u>	<u>0.52</u>	5.14	8.01	0.77
DATDNet	✓	✓	✓	**12.63**	**21.31**	0.72	**5.12**	7.63	0.79

Table 2 show the target density estimation results for serval methods. The first part is the density estimation algorithms that only uses RGB images as input, the second is the methods that can analyze temporal information, and finally, it is the method that can use all types of input data provided by Synth-Drone data sets at the same time. The complete version of the proposed DATD-Net achieves MAE of 12.63 and MSE of 21.31 on the crowd density estimation task, which is the best among all the tested methods. On the evaluation of NAE, our DATDNet performance slightly fall behind, the best one is BVCC, which reached 0.47. In the task of vehicle density estimation, because of the characteristics of the dataset itself, that is to say, the vehicle density of the whole dataset is on a low-lever, the final results of all methods are relatively close. DATDNet got the best result of 5.12 on MAE, but not the best on MSE and NAE.

Through the comparison of the three categories of methods in Table 2, especially under the three different working modes of DATDNet, we can see that no matter which targets it is, the addition of sequence and depth information can effectively improve the performance of density estimation methods.

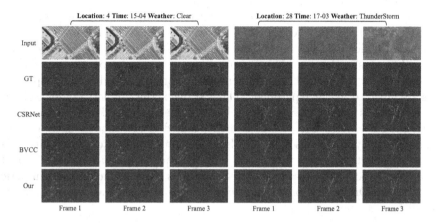

Fig. 5. The visualization of three selected crowd density estimation methods from different groups.

Figure 5 visualizes the results of serval methods on the crowd density estimation task. To better show the impact of sequential and depth information on the crowd density estimation task, we select one method from each category listed in Table 2 to visualize. The first line of the graph is the original input image, the second line is the ground truth of the crowd density map. The third line is the result for CSRNet, which just uses RGB images for input. The fourth line is BVCC which takes sequential information into account. The proposed DATDNet is shown in the last line. On the left and right sides are two groups of different video clips. Due to space limitations, each group only contains three consecutive frame slices. The first group uses the data collected at location 4, under the clear weather condition, and the second group is location 28 under thunderstorm weather. By comparing the density map below, we can see that in the clear weather of the first scene, the performance of all methods is good, and there is no significant difference between the density map. In the second scene, due to the influence of thunderstorm weather, the light in the scene is weak and abnormal, as shown in the third frame on the right. At this time, our method shows obvious advantages. It can be seen that there is a serious false detection of CSRNet under the influence of abnormal light, and the performance of BVCC in false detection is slightly better, but it suffers lots of miss detection. Our method maintains a good balance between false detection and miss detection and achieves the best results.

5.3 Cross Domain Density Estimation

We design the following experiments to verify what changes the proposed SynthDrone dataset can bring to the performance of existing methods on the real datasets. Putting aside those redundant domain adaptation processes, we directly mine the improvements through a simple pre-train mechanism. We use MCNN, CSRNet, and VGG-C3F to construct experiments on UCF-QNRF [11] and Shanghai Tech Part A [30] datasets respectively and fine-tune the model parameters under different initialization modes. Considering the higher density of crowd targets in the SynthDrone dataset, here we mainly focus on the task of crowd density estimation. Three different initialization methods of model parameters are involved in the experiment. The first one is the simplest random initialization, which is usually used in some relatively small models. Then the ImageNet pre-training is carried out, which is mainly aimed at the models using general backbones. They usually use the models trained on ImageNet classification tasks as the initialization parameters of the network backbone and initialize the rest parameters randomly. Finally, the pre-training is carried out on the synthetic dataset SynthDrone. All pre-trained models will be fine-tuned on the specific dataset for 100 epochs.

Table 3. Cross domain crowd density estimation results by different parameter initialization mechanism. All results are shown in the arrangement of MAE/MSE.

Dataset Methods	UCF-QNRT			Shanghai Tech Part A		
	MCNN	CSRNet	VGG-C3F	MCNN	CSRNet	VGG-C3F
Random	281.2/445.0	–	–	139.3/206.9	–	–
ImageNet	–	238.9/356.9	212.8/366.6	–	157.8/246.9	141.7/219.2
SynthDrone	201.4/347.5	198.2/322.7	182.4/298.9	136.5/197.4	131.2/200.9	126.8/190.5

Table 3 show the experiment results for server methods under different parameter initialization mechanisms. The models pre-trained on the SynthDrone dataset perform better than the one on ImageNet. There has been a considerable improvement in each combination of methods and datasets, and the best one achieves an improvement of 28.5% compared to the original MAE.

5.4 Target Localization and Tracking

As programmed in Table 4 we construct experiments to compare the crowd localization results of the proposed DATDNet with serval density estimation-based localization methods. For those methods like MCNN, CSRNet, and VGG-C3F, they do not have the localization head, so we directly apple their predicted density map as the localization map and filter the peak values to get the final crowd localization predictions.

Table 4. Crowd localization and tracking results on SynthDrone (% in the data is omitted).

Methods	L@5	L@15	L@25	L-mAP	T@0.1	T@0.2	T@0.3	T-mAP
MCNN	9.90	13.42	14.87	12.73	12.89	9.77	6.19	9.62
CSRNet	12.06	13.73	14.89	13.56	16.78	13.08	11.35	13.74
VGG-C3F	15.31	16.45	18.62	16.79	17.48	14.00	13.46	14.98
DATDNet**	18.89	20.34	21.78	20.34	16.21	13.95	11.80	13.99
DATDNet*	35.78	39.45	41.86	39.03	32.07	25.20	**21.81**	26.36
DATDNet	**38.91**	**40.78**	**42.38**	**40.69**	**32.62**	**26.58**	20.39	**26.53**

Compare to the results reported in Table 4, we can find the complete version of DATDNet achieves the best in the task of crowd localization with the mAP of 40.69%. The simplest version of the DATDNet does not show a significant advantage over normal crowd density estimation methods. The addition of time-series information greatly improves the performance of the original method (20.35% in mAP). In comparison, the use of depth information does not have such a significant effect (1.66% in mAP).

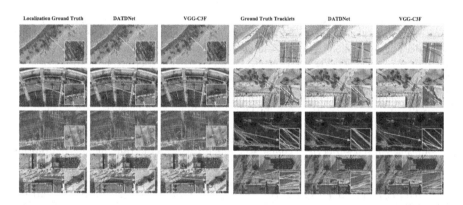

Fig. 6. The visualization of tracking and localization results.

As mentioned in the evaluation metrics part, we build the tracklets for each instance based on the localization results for the normal density estimation methods. Then we try to match it with ground truth trajectories and calculate the match ratio. Figure 6 visualizes the tracking and localization results. The tracking results show a tendency to be acquainted with the localization results. The complete version of DATDNet achieves almost the best one among all methods. For the tracking task, the influence of sequential information is more significant.

6   Conclusion

An efficient synthetic aerial view data acquisition and generation framework are proposed in this paper, it can deal with various kinds of data types and is highly customizable. We construct a large-scale synthetic public safety monitoring dataset SynthDrone under this framework. This dataset provides a wide range of available data types, including sequence, depth, bounding box, segmentation, center point, and other information. Aiming at the SynthDrone dataset, we also propose the DATDNet, which can simultaneously accept multiple inputs and predict the target density, position, and trajectory at the same time. Through sufficient experiments and visualization results, we prove the effectiveness of DATDNet and the improvement that the SynthDrone dataset can bring to the existing methods in the real world. In the future, we will further improve both the data acquisition framework and the predict method at the same time to improve the target density estimation, localization, and tracking performance in the real world.

References

1. Administration, F.H.: Next generation simulation. https://ops.fhwa.dot.gov/trafficanalysistools/ngsim.htm
2. Bahmanyar, R., Vig, E., Reinartz, P.: MRCNet: crowd counting and density map estimation in aerial and ground imagery. arXiv preprint arXiv:1909.12743 (2019)
3. Blade, A.: Script hook v. http://www.dev-c.com/gtav/scripthookv/
4. Chan, A., Liang, Z., Vasconcelos, N.: Privacy preserving crowd monitoring: counting people without people models or tracking. In: IEEE Conference on Computer Vision and Pattern Recognition, pp. 1–7. IEEE (2008)
5. Chen, K., Loy, C., Gong, S., Xiang, T.: Feature mining for localised crowd counting. In: BMVC, p. 3 (2012)
6. Gao, J., Huang, Z., Lei, Y., Wang, J.Z., Wang, F.Y., Zhang, J.: S ^{2} FPR: crowd counting via self-supervised coarse to fine feature pyramid ranking. arXiv preprint arXiv:2201.04819 (2022)
7. Gao, J., Lin, W., Zhao, B., Wang, D., Gao, C., Wen, J.: C$\hat{}$ 3 framework: an opensource pytorch code for crowd counting. arXiv preprint arXiv:1907.02724 (2019)
8. Hermans, A., Beyer, L., Leibe, B.: In defense of the triplet loss for person re-identification. arXiv preprint arXiv:1703.07737 (2017)
9. IanKirwan, C.: Gtavisionexport. https://github.com/umautobots/GTAVisionExport/
10. Idrees, H., Saleemi, I., Seibert, C., Shah, M.: Multi-source multi-scale counting in extremely dense crowd images. In: Proceedings of the IEEE Conference on Computer Vision and Pattern Recognition, pp. 2547–2554 (2013)
11. Idrees, H., et al.: Composition loss for counting, density map estimation and localization in dense crowds. In: Proceedings of the European Conference on Computer Vision, pp. 532–546 (2018)
12. Kang, D., Dhar, D., Chan, A.: Incorporating side information by adaptive convolution. In: The International Conference on Neural Information Processing Systems, pp. 3870–3880 (2017)

13. Khan, M.A., Menouar, H., Hamila, R.: DroneNet: crowd density estimation using Self-ONNs for drones. In: 2023 IEEE 20th Consumer Communications & Networking Conference (CCNC), pp. 455–460. IEEE (2023)

14. Krajewski, R., Bock, J., Kloeker, L., Eckstein, L.: The highD dataset: a drone dataset of naturalistic vehicle trajectories on German highways for validation of highly automated driving systems. In: International Conference on Intelligent Transportation Systems, pp. 2118–2125 (2018). https://doi.org/10.1109/ITSC.2018.8569552

15. Li, H., et al.: Video crowd localization with multifocus gaussian neighborhood attention and a large-scale benchmark. IEEE Trans. Image Process. **31**, 6032–6047 (2022)

16. Li, W., Mahadevan, V., Vasconcelos, N.: Anomaly detection and localization in crowded scenes. IEEE Trans. Pattern Anal. Mach. Intell. **36**(1), 18–32 (2013)

17. Li, X., Chen, M., Nie, F., Wang, Q.: Locality adaptive discriminant analysis. In: IJCAI, pp. 2201–2207 (2017)

18. Li, Y., Zhang, X., Chen, D.: CSRNet: dilated convolutional neural networks for understanding the highly congested scenes. In: Proceedings of the IEEE Conference on Computer Vision and Pattern Recognition, pp. 1091–1100 (2018)

19. Niu, G., Gu, J., Chen, Z.: Multi-object quantity estimation based on multi-view convolution neural network. Command Inf. Syst. Technol. **13**(5), 71–79 (2022)

20. Park, E., Liu, W., Russakovsky, O., Deng, J., Li, F.F., Berg, A.: Large scale visual recognition challenge 2017 (2017)

21. Sindagi, V., Yasarla, R., Patel, V.M.: JHU-CROWD++: large-scale crowd counting dataset and a benchmark method. IEEE Trans. Pattern Anal. Mach. Intell. (2020)

22. Song, Q., et al.: To choose or to fuse? Scale selection for crowd counting. In: Proceedings of the AAAI Conference on Artificial Intelligence, vol. 35, pp. 2576–2583 (2021)

23. Sun, Y., Cao, B., Zhu, P., Hu, Q.: Drone-based RGB-infrared cross-modality vehicle detection via uncertainty-aware learning. arXiv e-prints pp. arXiv-2003 (2020)

24. Tang, Z., Cai, Y., Wang, H.: Multi-sensor data fusion method based on adaptive weighting algorithm. Command Inf. Syst. Technol. **13**(5), 66–70 (2022)

25. Wang, Q., Gao, J., Lin, W., Li, X.: NWPU-CROWD: a large-scale benchmark for crowd counting and localization. IEEE Trans. Pattern Anal. Mach. Intell. **43**(6), 2141–2149 (2020)

26. Wang, Q., Gao, J., Lin, W., Yuan, Y.: Learning from synthetic data for crowd counting in the wild. In: IEEE Conference on Computer Vision and Pattern Recognition, pp. 8198–8207 (2019)

27. Wen, L., et al.: Detection, tracking, and counting meets drones in crowds: a benchmark. In: IEEE Conference on Computer Vision and Pattern Recognition, pp. 7812–7821 (2021)

28. Yan, Z., et al.: Perspective-guided convolution networks for crowd counting. In: Proceedings of the IEEE International Conference on Computer Vision, pp. 952–961 (2019)

29. Zhang, C., Li, H., Wang, X., Yang, X.: Cross-scene crowd counting via deep convolutional neural networks. In: IEEE Conference on Computer Vision and Pattern Recognition, pp. 833–841 (2015)

30. Zhang, Y., Zhou, D., Chen, S., Gao, S., Ma, Y.: Single-image crowd counting via multi-column convolutional neural network. In: Proceedings of the IEEE Conference on Computer Vision and Pattern Recognition, pp. 589–597 (2016)

31. Zhao, Z., Han, T., Gao, J., Wang, Q., Li, X.: A flow base bi-path network for cross-scene video crowd understanding in aerial view. In: Bartoli, A., Fusiello, A. (eds.) Computer Vision – ECCV 2020 Workshops. ECCV 2020. LNCS, vol. 12538, pp. 574–587. Springer, Cham (2020). https://doi.org/10.1007/978-3-030-66823-5_34
32. Zhou, X., Wang, D., Krähenbühl, P.: Objects as points. arXiv preprint arXiv:1904.07850 (2019)
33. Zhu, P., et al.: Detection and tracking meet drones challenge. IEEE Trans. Pattern Anal. Mach. Intelli. **01**, 1–1 (2021)

A New Approach for Ontology Generation from Relational Data Design Patterns

Xiang Li, Rui Luo, Kun Liu, Fan Li, Chengjun Wang, and Qiang Wang[(✉)]

Advanced Institute of Big Data, Beijing, China
wangq@aibd.ac.cn

Abstract. Knowledge graphs can effectively manage domain knowledge such as entities, properties, relations and events. Recent years have witnessed quite a few successful AI applications with the help of knowledge graphs. High-quality knowledge graphs are often built with a domain ontology, which is known to be a tedious and manual intensive task. Well-designed Relational Databases (RDBs) is an important source for obtaining ontologies and knowledge graphs. For this reason, designing automatic algorithms to generate ontologies from data has been a hot research topic. However, existing methods only consider basic ontology elements directly encoded in the RDB metadata, such as table names and foreign keys. This not only leads to erroneous or meaningless ontology classes, but also overlooks a large portion of hidden relations. As we know, database design patterns (DDP) often contain hidden semantics, which should be reconstructed into the ontology. This paper studies how typical DDPs could be recognized and how to extract ontologies from such DDPs. We focus on the JC3IEDM database, a rigorously-designed RDB in the field of joint operation, which is a widely-accepted industrial standard. Through analysis, we summarize 5 representative relational DDPs and identify their metadata characteristics. Based on these characteristics, we propose a new approach to automatically recognize and classify these patterns. Finally, we derive a rule-based method to generate OWL-format ontologies according to the identified DDPs. Empirically, we verify our approach using the whole JC3IEDM database, which contains more than 200 tables and thousands of data columns. The experimental results show that our method can automatically generate the ontology for this large-scale database, and the resultant ontology has improved quality compared to existing methods.

Keywords: Ontology Generation · Database Design Patterns · Semantic Integration of Databases

1 Introduction

Ontology refers to the standard semantic description of a specific set of concepts and their internal logical relationships of a specific domain. It can provide a basic

---

X. Li and R. Luo—Contributed equally to this work.

Y. Tan and Y. Shi (Eds.): DMBD 2023, CCIS 2018, pp. 157–172, 2024.
https://doi.org/10.1007/978-981-97-0844-4_12

classification framework and associative description mechanism for the domain data, thereby organizing the semantic implications of the data reasonably. An ontology can be seen as an abstraction of the human knowledge, serving as a semantic bridge to connect humans and machines.

Recent years have witnessed many successful AI applications using knowledge graphs. As we know, high-quality knowledge graphs are often built from a well-designed domain ontology. Moreover, obtaining a semantic ontology for data silos is an effective approach towards data governance, integration and sharing [3]. For example, semantic ontology has been used as the intermediate layer for data virtualization, which virtually integrates various data sources and provide a unified query interface such that traditional data warehousing (physical integration and centralized storage) are no longer mandatory.

Building a semantic ontology from scratch is often tedious and manual intensive. Relational Databases (RDBs) is an important structural data source for obtaining ontologies. In the academia, many research efforts [4,8] have been made towards automatic ontology generation from various types of data, including RDB. For a given RDB source, these methods could automatically parse the metadata, extract the ontology features and generate the ontology axioms. The final results are usually presented in the W3C recommended OWL2 format.

However, existing methods can only identify basic ontology elements encoded in the RDB metadata, such as table names as class and foreign keys as object properties. Such apporach has two fundamental problems. Firstly, existing generators only consider RDB metadata which inevitably ignores classes and relations hidden in the content of the data, such as the class names contained in a dictionary table or a *type* column. This often lead to an incomplete and or coarse-grained ontology. Secondly, existing generators are unaware of the Database Design Patterns (DDPs) used, which often generate meaningless classes and overlook relations. Specifically, the RDB table and ontology class may not have a one-to-one correspondence since some tables describe relations rather than classes. Moreover, existing methods cannot discover hidden classes and relations which can only be collectively modeled by a group of RDB tables. These detailed semantics can only be extracted from the DDP used. Unfortunately, none of the existing ontology generator support the identification of DDP. In this paper, we aim at the second problem and propose a novel DDP-aware RDB ontology generator.

Unlike object-oriented design patterns [1] that are extensively used by the developer community, DDPs are scarcely talked about. There are still no standard definition and classification of DDPs. However, DDPs are in fact widely-used in the software industry. In this paper, we take an empirical approach and focus on a well-designed RDB in the field of Multinational Joint Operation, i.e., the JC3IEDM database. The JC3IEDM database is widely-recognized by the industry and its design is a result of rigorous development with extensive discussions and negotiations among different parties [6]. Unlike other databases that are prone to anti-patterns [5], JC3IEDM is known to be of high-quality and may contain well-designed and reusable DDPs.

By studying the DDPs in JC3IEDM, we design a new DDP-aware approach to extract these ontology semantics, which consists of three steps: 1. RDB metadata extraction, 2. DDP recognition and classification, 3. ontology semantics reconstruction. We empirically verify our approach on the ontology generation task for the whole JC3IEDM RDB. The experiment results show that our method is effective in automatically generating a correct ontology in presence of the DDPs. Our approach has great potential to fasten the ontology generation process in practice.

2   Background: Ontology Automation

There are existing methods for automatically generating ontologies from RDBs, for example, IncMap [8], bootOX [4]. These algorithms and tools are difficult to support the dynamic and agile ontology modeling process, especially in aspects of agility, completeness and usability.

The agility of ontology construction refers to the ability of an ontology system to support quick construction or update of ontologies with minimal human efforts. Current ontology modeling tools, such as Protege [7] cannot effectively support the rapid construction of dynamic ontologies. It only has limited automatic ontology generation capability, and users often need to manually edit the mapping between ontology and relational data. At the same time, ontology modeling and mapping settings are usually regarded as two independent steps, which increases human workload and can lead to unmatched mapping and ontology.

The correctness of ontology construction reflects the ability to discover the accurate semantics of an RDB. Existing ontology automation tools only consider a simple correspondence between RDB metadata and the target ontology. For example, the Bootstrap plugin in Protege [7,9] simply reuse RDB table names as ontology classes names and column names as data properties. Meanwhile, all foreign keys are treated as object properties with no domain or range specified. As a result, the generated ontology contains mistaken semantics while loses a large proportion of implicit relations that are intended by the RDB design. Another popular RDB-ontology generator [4] designs 15 rules for extracting ontology axioms for different RDB features. However, they often lead to fragmented or meaningless ontology elements since the rules are not compatible with commonly used DDPs.

Finally, the usability of the generated ontology refers to whether the ontology complies with the terms and semantics commonly used by the domain users. As current ontology automation tools ignore many hidden semantics, the resultant ontologies often have poor usability, which increases the burden of manual editing and verification. More importantly, most of the aforementioned ontology automation tools are close-sourced, and some of them are no longer available.

3   Ontology Generation from Relational Databases

In this section, we describe our approach for automatic ontology generation from RDBs. We first describe a basic ontology generator which follows the traditional approach while ignores DDPs. In contrast, we later derive a new algorithm to extract ontologies from the DDPs found in JC3IEDM.

3.1   A Basic Ontology Generator

For a given RDB data source, an ontology generation algorithm is responsible for automatically parsing the metadata of the RDB and generating the ontology axioms. We follow the traditional methods [4,8] and propose a rule-based ontology generator, as described by Table 1.

As can be seen from Table 1. The above method only extracts common ontological elements that are general to almost all RDB metadata. However, the adoption of DDPs may include more specialized hidden semantics. Since there is no authoritative listing nor classification of common DDPs, we seek the JC3IEDM data model for high-quality and generalisable DDPs.

3.2   The JC3IEDM Data

JC3IEDM, or Joint Consultation, Command and Control Information Exchange Data Model is a relational data model managed by the Multilateral Interoperability Programme (MIP), NATO. The JC3IEDM model defines the standard elements of information that enables interoperability between automated Command and Control Information Systems (C2ISs), To capture the massive heterogeneous information in the Joint Operation domain, JC3IEDM models the data space from 3 different levels: the conceptual model, the logical model, and the physical model. All are responsible for describing the entities and their features, states, positions and inter-relationships, as well as expressing the dynamic activities of entities in a Joint Operation. The JC3IEDM model focuses on covering information activities such as situational awareness, action planning, task execution, and reporting during the Joint Operation process. JC3IEDM was evolved from NATO standards such as C2IEDM and ATCCIS, which dates back to the early 90 s. Since 2004, the JC3IEDM model has become a NATO standard itself. We choose JC3IEDM as our target database since it is a delicately designed RDB model which has a rigorous development process and full-fledged documentation.

3.3   Ontology Generation from Relational DDPs

In version 3.1.4 of the JC3IEDM conceptual model, the basic concept is an *Entity*, which refers to any distinguishable person, place, thing, event, and other related concepts. The characteristics of an entity are modeled as *Attributes*. These attributes specify the data to be recorded for each business related concept. The JC3IEDM physical model contains a total of 276 SQL tables. As shown

Table 1. A basic ontology generator for common RDB

No.	RDB characteristics	generation process	ontology axioms
1	Table T is a regular entity table	Create ontology class C_T	Class: C_T
2	The data column a in Table T corresponds to the SQL value type t	1. Create a data attribute Ra with a definition domain of ontology class C_T and a value domain of $d(t)$, where $d(t)$ is the RDFS type corresponding to t 2. Create a parent-child relationship between class C_T and virtual class (Ra some $d(t)$)	DataProperty: R_a Ra Domain: C_T Ra Range: $d(t)$ C_T SubClassOf: R_a some $d(t)$
3	Foreign key f referencing T_x in Table T	1. Create an object attribute P_f with a definition domain of ontology class C_T and a value domain of ontology class C_{T_x}, assuming that class C_{T_x} has been created 2. Create a parent-child relationship between class C_T and virtual class (P_f some C_{T_x})	ObjectProperty: P_f P_f Domain: C_T P_f Range: C_{T_x} C_T SubClassOf: P_f some C_{T_x}
4	The data column a in Table T is of type t, and there is a unique constraint on a	Create a key axiom Ra for the ontology class C_T, where it is assumed that the data attribute Ra has been created	C_T HasKey: R_a
5	The foreign key f referencing T_x in Table T has a unique constraint on f	Create a key axiom P_f for the ontology class C_T, where it is assumed that the object attribute Pf has been created	C_T HasKey: P_f
6	There is a composite master in Table T, which can contain multiple non foreign key data columns and multiple foreign keys	Assuming that the data columns contained in the composite primary key correspond to data attributes $R_1 \ldots R_n$, and the foreign keys contained correspond to object attributes $P_1 \ldots P_m$. Create key axioms for ontology class C_T, covering ($R_1 \ldots R_n$ and $P_1 \ldots P_m$)	C_T HasKey: $R_1 \ldots R_n$ $P_1 \ldots P_m$
7	Several data tables $T_1 \ldots T_n$ in the same data source contain columns $a_1 \ldots a_n$ with the same name, and the same datatype t	1. Create a data attribute R_a with a definition domain of virtual ontology class (C_{T_1} or ... or C_{T_n}) and a value domain of $d(t)$ 2. Using data attributes $R_1 \ldots R_n$ as sub attributes of R_a, it is assumed that the data attributes $R_1 \ldots R_n$ have been generated by rule 2 3. Create a parent-child relationship between class C_{T_i} and virtual class (P_f some $d(t)$) for each T_i	R_a Domain: C_{T_1} or ... or C_{T_n} R_a Range: $d(t)$ R_i SubPropertyOf: R_a C_{T_i} SubClassOf: R_a some $d(t)$

in its E-R model, JC3IEDM RDB only explicitly depicts the *one-to-many* and *many-to-many* between entity tables. However, implicitly, different DDPs may entail hidden semantic relationships. As we delve into the design of JC3IEDM, we identify 5 representative DDPs.

In the following part of the paper, all RDB table names are presented in hyphen connected uppercase letters such as RULE-OF-ENGAGEMENT, while the ontology class names are given as Title case connected by underscores, such as Rule_of_engagement.

Independent Entities DDP. In JC3IEDM, independent entities are those conceptual entities at the top-level of the ontology hierarchy. Their identification does not rely on or refer to any other entity, hence the primary key in their RDB table does not contain any foreign keys. As can be seen in Fig. 1, the RULE-OF-ENGAGEMENT table is an independent entity. In total, JC3IEDM has 19 independent entities. Ontology modeler should be aware that these independent entity tables represent the most basic or high-level concept of the domain.

RULE-OF-ENGAGEMENT
rule-of-engagement-id
rule-of-engagement-name-text
rule-of-engagement-description-text
owning-organisation-id (FK)

Fig. 1. The RULE-OF-ENGAGEMENT table which represents the Independent Entity DDP. The upper part of the box indicates primary key.

Class Table Inheritance DDP. When the primary key of a SQL table T_1 is also a foreign key referencing T_2, it indicates that T_1 represents a subclass concept of T_2. In this DDP, the subclass is depicted in a different table, hence the name Class Table Inheritance. As can be seen in Fig. 2, the design of ACTION-AIRCRAFT-EMPLOYMENT table is a typical Class Table Inheritance DDP, where the referenced parent table is ACTION-RESOURCE-EMPLOYMENT. The columns in the sub-table (ACTION-AIRCRAFT- EMPLOYMENT) usually denotes the attributes that are specific to the subclass (Action_aircraft_employment). Meanwhile, the subclass also inherits all attributes in the parent class Action_resource_employment.

Multi-value Attribute Dependency DDP. Multi-value Attribute Dependency is a DDP for storing multi-valued attribute. Traditionally, storing attributes which may contain several co-appearing values in one RDB table has been a problem for data designers. Using several columns for the target attribute is not a good idea especially when the number of co-appearing values is also a variable. The solution provided by the Multi-value Attribute Dependency is to create a dependent table with one column for the multi-value attribute, a foreign key referencing the original table and usually a sub-index used for distinguishing the co-appearing attribute values. As can be seen in Fig. 3, the design of

ACTION-AIRCRAFT-EMPLOYMENT

action-id (FK)
action-resource-index (FK)
action-resource-employment-index (FK)
action-aircraft-employment-approach-offset-code
action-aircraft-employment-deplanement-method-code
action-aircraft-employment-egress-direction-angle
action-aircraft-employment-inflight-report-requirement-indicator-code
action-aircraft-employment-ingress-direction-angle
action-aircraft-employment-crew -composition-code
action-aircraft-employment-general-role-code

Fig. 2. The ACTION-AIRCRAFT-EMPLOYMENT table which represents the Class Table Inheritance DDP. The upper part of the box indicates primary key, which is also a foreign key referencing ACTION-RESOURCE-EMPLOYMENT, which corresponds to the parent class.

ACTION-OBJECTIVE table represents a typical Multi-value Attribute Dependency DDP. In the ACTION-OBJECTIVE table each row is a different instance of Action_objective, which naturally captures the semantics that an Action can have multiple Objectives.

According to the intended semantics of this DDP, it is important for ontology modelers to have a directed relational edge (object property) that starts from the main entity class (Action) to the dependent class (Action_objective), which enables user semantic queries such as *List all the Objectives that a certain Action may have.*

ACTION-OBJECTIVE

action-id (FK)
action-objective-index
action-objective-category-code
action-objective-qualifier-code
action-objective-authorising-organisation-id (FK)

Fig. 3. The ACTION-OBJECTIVE table in JC3IEDM which represents the Multi-value Attribute Dependency DDP. Eacn Action can have several Action_objective. The upper part of the box indicates primary key.

Association Bridge DDP. Association bridge or associative table is a standard DDP for representing many-to-many correspondence. The association bridge table usually has two foreign keys in its primary key, each referencing a different entity table. As can be seen in Fig. 4, the ACTION-REQUIRED-CAPABILITY table represents a association bridge, where each Action may require several Capabilities, and vice versa.

When building the ontology for this DDP, it is more important to have a bi-directional edge (2 object properties) that connect the 2 referred entities, i.e., Action and Capability.

ACTION-REQUIRED-CAPABILITY

action-id (FK)
capability-id (FK)
action-required-capability-quantity

Fig. 4. The ACTION-REQUIRED-CAPABILITY table which represents the Association Bridge DDP. Each Action may require several Capabilities and one Capability can be required by several Actions. The upper part of the box indicates primary key.

Association Bridge with Multi-value Attribute Dependency DDP. This DDP is a combination of Association Bridge and Multi-value Attribute Dependency DDPs, which represents the case where the many-to-many correspondence itself has Multi-value attributes as its detailed specification.

As can be seen in Fig. 5, the ACTION-LOCATION table in JC3IEDM represents a Association Bridge with Multi-value Attribute Dependency, where the Action-Location binary relation has several descriptive attributes, i.e., action-location-accuracy-dimension, action-location-bearing-angle and reporting-data-id. Meanwhile, it is allowed that each Action-Location pair has several sets of values on these descriptive attributes.

ACTION-LOCATION

action-id (FK)
location-id (FK)
action-location-index
action-location-accuracy-dimension
action-location-bearing-angle
reporting-data-id (FK)

Fig. 5. The ACTION-LOCATION table which represents the Association Bridge with Multi-value Attribute Dependency DDP. The upper part of the box indicates primary key

Based on the above observations, we propose a simple rule-based DDP recognition algorithm, as shown in Algorithm 1. Note that some RDB table in JC3IEDM and other database may not follow any of the 5 concerned DDPs, which is indicated by *No DDP*. More DDPs will be considered in our future work.

Algorithm 1. The DDP recognition algorithm

Require: M_T: the metadata of the RDB table T
Ensure: DDP_T: the database design patterns of T
  1: $DDP_T \leftarrow$ No DDP
  2: **if** M_T has no Foreign key in the primary key **then**
  3:     $DDP_T \leftarrow$ Independent Enitity DDP
  4: **else if** M_T has exactly 1 Foreign key in the primary key **then**
  5:     **if** no non-FK column left in the primary key **then**
  6:        $DDP_T \leftarrow$ Class Table Inheritance DDP
  7:     **else if** M_T has exactly 1 non-FK column left in the primary key **then**
  8:        $DDP_T \leftarrow$ Multi-value Attribute Dependency DDP
  9:     **end if**
10: **else if** M_T has exactly 2 Foreign keys in the primary key **then**
11:     **if** no non-FK column left in the primary key **then**
12:        $DDP_T \leftarrow$ Association Bridge DDP
13:     **else if** M_T has exactly 1 non-FK column left in the primary key **then**
14:        $DDP_T \leftarrow$ Association Bridge with Multi-value Attribute Dependency DDP
15:     **end if**
16: **end if**

After we detect and classify the Database Design Pattern that a target RDB table participates, we further derive the automatic ontology extraction method for the each of the 5 DDPs. The method is a delicately designed rule based procedure, as shown in Tables 2, 3, 4, 5 and 6.

4 Experiments

To demonstrate that our method can generate high-quality ontology from RDB. In this section, we choose JC3IEDM dataset version 3.1.4 for empirical study. We consider all 276 RDB tables and their foreign key and primary key indexes.

4.1 Comparing Against the Baselines

To verify that our method can generate better ontologies by supporting the DDPs, we compare with 2 baseline methods in the experiment, i.e., BootOX [4] and the ontop Bootstrap Plugin [9]. While the ontop Bootstrap Plugin can be accessed through the Protege software [7], BootOX has limited availability. In fact, BootOX is integrated into the Optique system [2], which is no longer maintained or publicly available. For this reason, we have re-implemented BootOX following the 15 rules proposed in its original paper. For the implementation of our method, we use Algorithm 1 for DDP recognition and the rule-based ontology extraction described in the previous section. We implement our algorithm using the OWLApi java library.

As can be seen from Table 7, because of the ignorance of the DDPs, the baseline methods generate too many data properties while misses a significant

Table 2. Automatic Ontology Generation Rules for the Independent Entity DDP

No.	Generation Step	Detailed Process	Ontology Axioms
1	Define ontology class for the entity table	for table T (RULE-OF-ENGAGEMENT), create a corresponding ontology class C_T	Class: C_T
2	Define key properties for the ontology class	for the primary key in T, create one or several data properties on each columns of the primary key (e.g., *rule-of-engagement-id*) their domains are class C_T. Add a key axiom on these data properties.	DataProperty: $R_1 \ldots R_n$ $R_1 \ldots R_n$ Domain: C_T C_T HasKey: $R_1 \ldots R_n$
3	Define object properties for foreign keys outside of the primary key	for each foreign key outside of the primary key, in this case *owning-organisation-id*, creates an object property p_f (fk_organisation) who's domain in the current table class (Rule_of_engagement) while the range is the referenced table class (Organization). Add the inverse object property q_f (has_rule_of_engagement) of p_f, define it as Inverse functional	ObjectProperty: P_f ObjectProperty: Q_f P_f Domain: C_T P_f Range: C_{T_x} Q_f InverseOf: P_f P_f Functional Q_f InverseFunctional C_T SubClassOf: P_f some C_{T_x}
4	Define data properties for data columns outside the primary key	for each data column (non-Fk) outside of the primary key (*rule-of-engagement-name-text*, etc.) creates a data property with the same column name who's domain is the current table class (Rule_of_engagement), and range is inferred from the SQL datatype of this data column, e.g., string	DataProperty: R_a Ra Domain: C_T Ra Range: $d(t)$ C_T SubClassOf: R_a some $d(t)$

Table 3. Automatic Ontology Generation Rules for the Class Table Inheritance DDP

No.	Generation Step	Detailed Process	Ontology Axioms
1	create an ontology class C_T for the entity table (Action_aircraft_employment), which is the same as the rule 1 of Independent Entity		
2	Define key properties for ontology classes, this is the same as rule 2 of Independent Entity. The key properties in this case are (*action-id, action-resource-index, action-resource-employment-index*)		
3	create the class inheritance relation in the ontology	for the primary key columns (*action-id, action-resource-index, action-resource-employment-index*), if they are also foreign key referencing table T_2 (ACTION-RESOURCE-EMPLOYMENT), creates a class subsumption relation in the ontology that C_{T2} (Action_resource_employment) is the subclass of C_{T1} (Action_aircraft_employment)	C_{T2} SubClassOf: C_{T1}
4	Define data properties for data columns outside of the primary key	for each data (non-Fk) column outside of the primary key, in this case *action-aircraft-employment-approach-offset-code* etc., creates a data property with the same column name who's domain is the current table class (Action_aircraft_employment), and range is inferred from the SQL datatype of this data column, e.g., string	DataProperty: R_a R_a Domain: C_T R_a Range: $d(t)$ C_T SubClassOf: R_a some $d(t)$

Table 4. Automatic Ontology Generation Rules for the Multivalue Attribute Dependency DDP

No.	Generation Step	Detailed Process	Ontology Axioms
1	create an ontology class C_T for the entity table (Action_objective), which is the same as the rule 1 of Independent Entity		
2	Define an object property for the foreign key inside the primary key	for the foreign key in the primary key, in this case *action-id*, creates an object property p_f (fk_action) who's domain in the current table class (Action_objective) while the range is the referenced table class (Action). Add the inverse object property q_f (has_action_objective) of p_f, define it as Inverse functional	ObjectProperty: P_f P_f Domain: C_T P_f Range: C_{T_x} Q_f InverseOf: P_f P_f Functional Q_f InverseFunctional C_T SubClassOf: P_f some C_{T_x}
3	Define a data property for the non-Fk data column inside the primary key	for the non-Fk data column in the primary key, in this case *action-objective-index*, creates a data property with the same column name who's domain in the current table class (Action_objective), and range is inferred from the SQL datatype of this data column, e.g., string.	DataProperty: R_a Ra Domain: C_T Ra Range: $d(t)$ C_T SubClassOf: R_a some $d(t)$
4	Define key properties for the ontology class	since the data column in the primary key has already been defined as data property R_a (*action-objective-index*), and the foreign key in the primary key has already been defined as object property p_f (fk_action). Now we only need to add key axioms on these ontology properties	C_T HasKey: R_a P_f
5	Define object properties for foreign keys outside of the primary key (i.e., *action-objective-authorising-organisation-id*), using rule 3 of the Independent Entity DDP		
6	Define data properties for data columns outside of the primary key (i.e., *action-objective-category-code* and *action-objective-qualfier-code*). The process is the same as rule 4 of the Independent Entity DDP		

Table 5. Automatic Ontology Generation Rules for the Association Bridge DDP

No.	Generation Step	Detailed Process	Ontology Axioms
1	create the object property for the pair of foreign keys in the primary key	Inside the primary key, for the foreign key referencing T_1 (Action) and another foreign key referencing T_2 (Capability), create an object property P_f (action_required_capability) whose domain is T_1 and range is T_2, and also creates its inverse object property Q_f (capability_action).	ObjectProperty: P_f ObjectProperty: Q_f P_f Domain: C_{T_1} P_f Range: C_{T_2} Q_f InverseOf: P_f
2	Define data properties for data columns outside of the primary key (i.e., *action-required-capability-quantity*). The process is the same as rule 4 of the Independent Entity DDP		

Table 6. Automatic Ontology Generation Rules for the Association Bridge with Multivalue Attribute Dependency DDP

No.	Generation Step	Detailed Process	Ontology Axioms
1	create the object property for the pair of foreign keys in the primary key	Inside the primary key, for the foreign key referencing T_1 (Action) and another foreign key referencing T_2 (Location), create an object property P_f (action_location) whose domain is T_1 and range is T_2, and also creates its inverse object property Q_f (location_action)	ObjectProperty: P_f ObjectProperty: Q_f P_f Domain: C_{T_1} P_f Range: C_{T_2} Q_f InverseOf: P_f
2	Define a data property R_a (*action_location_index* in this case) for the data column inside of the primary key, same as rule 3 of the multi-value attribute dependency DDP		
3	Define object properties for foreign keys outside of the primary key (i.e., *reporting-data-id*), using rule 3 of the Independent Entity DDP.		
4	Define data properties for data columns outside of the primary key (i.e., *action-location-accuracy-dimension* and *action-location-bearing-angle*). The process is the same as rule 4 of the Independent Entity DDP		

Table 7. JC3IEDM ontology generation results for different methods.

Methods	Classes	Data Properties	Relations
bootOx-re	276	1640	400
protege-bootstrap	276	2045	400
ours	261	863	436

portion of entity relations (object properties). Specifically, the excessive data properties are caused by the identical column names scattered in different RDB tables. Baseline methods are unaware of the fact that many of these columns are actually involved in an inheritance relationship. Moreover, the baseline methods can only identify the simplest many-to-many table and are unable to find other cases of association bridge. As a result, they have overlooked quite a few relations during the ontology generation process.

4.2   A Graphical View of the Generated Ontology

We also demonstrate a graphical view of the whole ontology we have generated for JC3IEDM data. As can be seen from Fig. 6, ontological elements such as object properties and data properties have been correctly reconstructed. Since JC3IEDM contains hundreds of tables and thousands of data columns, which result in a large-scale ontology. In fact, the generated ontology contains 261 classes, 863 data properties (attributes) and 436 object properties (relational edges). For ease of presentation, we only demonstrate the object properties while filtering out the data properties.

5   Discussion and Future Work

In this work, we have studied how parsing the RDB DDPs can help boost the performance of an RDB ontology generator. However, the inability to identify DDPs is only one of the drawbacks of existing ontology automation methods. How to find hidden classes and hidden relations which do not appear in the RDB schema is also an important research direction.

As we know, dictionary RDB tables might contain class names. Meanwhile, in the Single Table Inheritance DDP a type column could be used without an explicit dictionary table, which might also contain class-level information. A discriminative statistical model for finding such type columns and dictionary tables has potential to further improve the performance of ontology generation.

Besides, since class relations marked by the RDB foreign keys can be seen as edges of a semantic ontology graph. It is also interesting to study the transitivity of these edges for inducing hidden relations (i.e. multi-hop edges). As can be expected, there is always the caveat that many hidden edges might be meaningless to reconstruct. Therefore, a data-dependent prediction model for determining and reconstructing the valid hidden relations will probably be an important research direction.

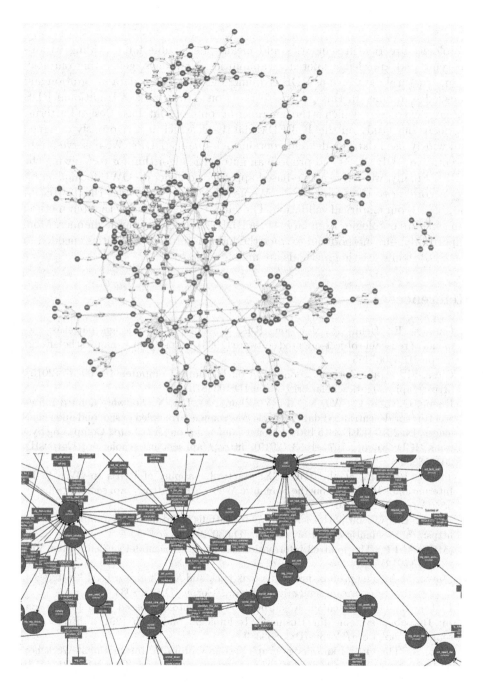

Fig. 6. Upper part is the whole entire JC3IEDM ontology fully automatically generated by our method. The lower figure is a zoomed-in part of the whole generated JC3IEDM ontology. For ease of presentation, the data properties are not shown in the figure.

6 Conclusion

Ontologies are rich in semantics and meanwhile flexible for providing various querying and knowledge inference capabilities. Nowadays, generating ontology from structural data such as RDB is a fundamental step for data integration and knowledge mining. In this paper, we focus on a drawback of traditional RDB ontology extractors, which is the ignorance of common Database Design Patterns. We focus our study on the JC3IEDM database, which is a rigorously designed and widely used data model and contain high-quality DDPs. We observe 5 representative RDB DDPs and propose an automatic algorithm for recognizing the DDPs. Finally, we derive a rule-based approach to generate OWL-format ontology according to the found DDPs. We use the whole 276 tables the JC3IEDM database as our empirical validation. The validation results show that our method can generate ontologies from large-scale RDB in a fully automatic manner. More importantly, our method can extract the hidden ontology semantics encoded in the DDPs while existing methods are unable to do so.

References

1. Gamma, E., Helm, R., Johnson, R.E., Vlissides, J.M.: Design patterns: elements of reuseable object-oriented software (1994). https://api.semanticscholar.org/CorpusID:54007465
2. Giese, M., et al.: Optique: zooming in on big data. Computer **48**, 60–67 (2015). https://api.semanticscholar.org/CorpusID:10348732
3. Huang, G., Luo, C., Wu, K., Ma, Y., Zhang, Y., Liu, X.: Software-defined infrastructure for decentralized data lifecycle governance: principled design and open challenges. In: 2019 IEEE 39th International Conference on Distributed Computing Systems (ICDCS), pp. 1674–1683 (2019). https://api.semanticscholar.org/CorpusID:207758658
4. Jiménez-Ruiz, E., et al.: BOOTOX: practical mapping of RDBs to OWL 2. In: International Workshop on the Semantic Web (2015). https://api.semanticscholar.org/CorpusID:2287280
5. Karwin, B.: SQL antipatterns: avoiding the pitfalls of database programming (2010). https://api.semanticscholar.org/CorpusID:63072457
6. (MIP), M.I.P.: The joint c3 information exchange data model (jc3iedm main ipt3 v3.1.4) (2012)
7. Musen, M.A.: The protégé project: a look back and a look forward. AI Matters **14**, 4–12 (2015). https://api.semanticscholar.org/CorpusID:13208034
8. Pinkel, C., et al.: Incmap: a journey towards ontology-based data integration. In: Datenbanksysteme für Business, Technologie und Web (2017). https://api.semanticscholar.org/CorpusID:38803389
9. Xiao, G.: The virtual knowledge graph system Ontop. In: International Workshop on the Semantic Web (2020). https://api.semanticscholar.org/CorpusID:221317578

Mining Maximal High Utility Co-location Patterns from Large-Scale Spatial Data

Muquan Zou[1,2], Vanha Tran[3]($\boxtimes$) (iD), Ducanh Khuat[3], Thanhcong Do[3], and Jinpeng Zhang[4,5,6]

[1] Kunming University, Kunming 650214, China
[2] Postdoctoral Research Workstation of Fudian Bank, Kunming 650200, China
[3] FPT University, Hanoi 155514, Vietnam
{hatv14,anhkd3}@fe.edu.vn, congdthe150385@fpt.edu.vn
[4] Yunnan University of Finance and Economics, Kunming 650221, China
zjp@ynufe.edu.cn
[5] Yunnan University, Kunming 650091, China
[6] Yunnan Key Laboratory of Service Computing, Kunming 650221, China

Abstract. High utility co-location patterns (HUCPs), which are groups of spatial features considering the utility values of these spatial features, can effectively expose valuable relationships and knowledge from spatial data. However, the mining result normally contains too many HUCPs, this makes it difficult for users to absorb and apply the mining result. This work proposes a concise representation of the mining result, maximal HUCPs. A HUCP is maximal iff it has no supersets that also are HUCPs. A straightforward way to discover maximal HUCPs is to first find all HUCPs and then filter maximal HUCPs. However, at present, the methods of mining HUCPs employ a common generation-test candidate level-wise traversal mining framework combined with some pruning strategies. These methods are relatively inefficient and require a large storage when dealing with large-scale spatial data. In order to efficiently discover maximal HUCPs, this work adopts a clique-hash table-based top-down traversal mining method. First, all neighboring instances are enumerated by a set of maximal cliques. Then these cliques are further arranged into a hash table structure. After that, the mining process iterates all the keys of the hash table structure beginning from the largest keys. If the keys are maximal HUCPs, the mining process continues with the next sizes of keys. While the keys are not maximal HUCPs, the directed subsets of the keys are generated and examined in the next iterator. Experimental results on both synthetic and real spatial data sets show that the proposed method is effective and efficient.

Keywords: High utility co-location patterns · Maximal co-location patterns · Level-wise traversal mining framework · Top-down traversal mining method

© The Author(s), under exclusive license to Springer Nature Singapore Pte Ltd. 2024
Y. Tan and Y. Shi (Eds.): DMBD 2023, CCIS 2018, pp. 173–188, 2024.
https://doi.org/10.1007/978-981-97-0844-4_13

1   Introduction

Nowadays, a large amount of data including spatial information is recorded and collected every day. For example, users check in on Facebook every day whenever they come to a place, users order food from online systems daily, and so on. How to discover valuable knowledge from massive spatial data sets is extremely important. Discovering spatial prevalent co-location patterns (SPCPs) is an important branch of spatial data mining. A SPCP refers to a set of spatial features whose instances occur frequently in close proximity to each other [14]. For example, Fig. 1(a) shows the distribution of a point-of-interest (POI) data set in Shanghai, China [10]. There are twenty points of interest that are called spatial instances, e.g., a hotel located in the intersection between Wulumiqi Road and Hengshen Road, three bus stops along Huaihai Road, etc. The twenty instances are grouped into four categories namely bus stops, hotels, fast food restaurants, and public spaces. The four categories are called spatial features. Assuming we consider within 200 m, if the distance between two different feature instances is smaller than this 200 m, they have a neighboring relationship and are connected by a solid line as shown in Fig. 1(b). We found that within 250 m, buses, fast food restaurants, and hotels frequently appeared together. We call Buses, Fast food restaurants, Hotels a SPCP. This pattern hides a lot of useful information. If you are a businessman who operates a fast food restaurant and you want to expand your business scale, you are planning to open a new fast food restaurant in the city, site selection should be the most crucial step for you. This SPCP, Buses, Fast food restaurants, Hotels, can serve as a reference for you. Your new fast food restaurant should be located within a 200-meter radius of buses and hotels. Since taking advantage of the convenience of traffic brought by bus stops and high passenger volume from hotels, the footfall of your new restaurant should be high. SPCPs have been applied in many fields such as business [9], ecology [6], agriculture science [2], public health [7], and so on.

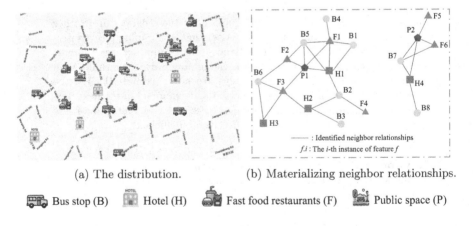

(a) The distribution.   (b) Materializing neighbor relationships.

🚌 Bus stop (B)   🏨 Hotel (H)   🍔 Fast food restaurants (F)   🏛 Public space (P)

Fig. 1. A POI data set and its neighbor relationship materialization.

It can be seen that the traditional SPCP does not consider the distinction between spatial features, it regards the features in spatial data as equally important. However, in reality, the importance of spatial features is totally different. For example, the importance of hotels is completely different from that of bus stops. SPCPs lose their meaning if the importance of features is not considered. Therefore, each spatial feature is assigned a utility value to reflect its importance. A concept of high utility co-location patterns (HUCPs) has been proposed [12]. The utility value of a pattern is measured by a pattern utility ratio (PUR) which is the ratio of the total utility of all features participating in the pattern to the utility of the entire spatial data set. If the PUR of the pattern is greater than a minimum utility threshold set by the user, the pattern is a HUCP.

Usually, the minimum utility threshold is difficult to give. If the threshold is small, too many patterns are discovered, while if its value is large, only common knowledge patterns are discovered. These common sense patterns generally carry very little valuable information. Therefore, in order to discover more valuable information hidden in spatial data sets, the minimum utility threshold should be set as small as possible. However, it leads to too many HUCPs being returned to users, which can interfere with their absorption, understanding, and application. To overcome this, this work proposes the concept of mining maximal HUCPs. If a pattern is maximal, it is a HUCP and it does not have any supersets that are also HUCPs.

In traditional SPCP mining, unnecessary candidates can be effectively pruned since the measurement prevalence of a co-location pattern (that is participation index, PI) satisfies the downward closure property. Thus, many mining PCP algorithms using this property have been proposed and they follow a common mining framework, generation-test candidate level-wise traversal mining framework, such as joinless [15], clique candidate-based [14], instance clique-based [1], and so on. However, in HUCP mining, PUR does not meet the downward closure property any longer. The current common approach is to design pruning strategies to reduce candidate search space, such as extended pruning algorithm [12], subsume index-based [8], EHUCM [5]. However, the pruning effect is limited, so the mining efficiency of these algorithms is not high, especially they cannot handle large datasets. Although many excellent algorithms for mining maximal PCPs have been proposed, e.g., MaxColoc [14], sparse-graph and condensed tree-based [13], MCHT [10], their premise is to utilize downward closure property to quickly find candidates of maximal patterns. However, these algorithms cannot be directly applied to discover maximal HUCPs. A straightforward approach to mining maximal HUCPs is to first discover all HUCPs and then filter maximal HUCPs. However, the algorithms for mining HUCPs themself are not efficient, so the efficiency of discovering maximal HUCPs also is definitely low.

To avoid this, this work adopts a new mining framework, clique-hash table-based top-down traversal mining method. First, neighboring instances are enumerated by a set of cliques. Then a hash table structure is constructed based on these cliques to further compress neighboring instances. After that, the process of mining maximal HUCPs begins from the largest keys of the hash table. The largest keys are exactly candidates. If the keys are maximal HUCPs, the mining process continues with the next sizes of keys. While the keys are not maximal HUCPs, the directed subsets of them are generated and examined in the next iterator.

In summary, the contributions of this work are as follows.

1) Propose the concept of maximal HUCPs that can significantly reduce the number of HUCPs and give a concise representation to users to conveniently understand and apply.
2) Employ a clique-hash table-based top-down traversal mining method to efficiently discover maximal HUCPs without designing any pruning strategies.
3) The effect and efficiency of the proposed method are proved by extensive experiments on both synthetic and real spatial data sets.

The remainder of this paper is organized as follows. The concepts of HUCPs and maximal HUCPs are described in Sect. 2. Section 3 presents the clique-hash table-based top-down traversal mining method. An extensive experimental study is shown in Sect. 4. Section 5 concludes our work.

2 High Utility Co-location Patterns and Their Maximal Representation

Given a spatial data set $S = \{o_1, ..., o_n\}$, each spatial instance $o_i \in S$ is a three-element vector, i.e., $< f_t, \text{ID}, (x, y) >$, where f_t is the feature type that o_i belongs to, ID is its identification using to distinguish between it and other instances that also belong to f_t, and $F = \{f_1, ..., f_m\}$ is the set of all features in S, the HUCP and maximal HUCP mining problems are defined as follows.

Definition 1 (Spatial feature utility and external utility). *The utility of a spatial feature f_t is a positive value that is assigned to the feature to reflect its importance according to the reference of users and is denoted as $u(f_t)$. The spatial feature utility is also called external utility.*

Definition 2 (Utility of a spatial data set). *The utility of a spatial data set is the sum utility value of all features involved in it and is denoted as $u(S) = \sum_{\forall f_t \in F} u(f_t) * |f_t|$, where $|f_t|$ represents the number of instances of it in S.*

For example, in Fig. 1, a user set the utility values of the four feature are $u(\text{B}) = 21$, $u(\text{F})=24$, $u(\text{H})=38$, $u(\text{P})=42$. The numbers of instances of B, H, F, and P are 8, 6, 4, and 2, respectively. Thus, $u(S) = 21 \times 8 + 24 \times 6 + 38 \times 4 + 42 \times 2 = 548$.

Definition 3 (Candidate high utility co-location pattern). *A candidate high utility co-location pattern, c, is a subset of the feature type set F, i.e., $c = f_1, ..., f_k \subseteq F$. The number of features in c is k and it is called the size of c, i.e., c is a size k candidate.*

Definition 4 (Neighbor relationship and neighboring instance set). *Given two instances o_i and o_j, if the distance between them (could be Euclidean, Manhattan, etc. distance) is less than a user-set distance threshold d, they have a* *neighbor relationship, i.e., $R(o_i, o_j)$. The neighboring instance set of an instance o_i is a set of all instances that have the neighbor relationship with it and is denoted as $NB(o_i) = \{o_j | R(o_i, o_j)\}$*

As shown in Fig. 1(b), the neighbor relationship instances are connected by solid lines. Table 1 lists the neighboring instance sets of all these instances.

Table 1. The neighboring instance sets.

o_i	$NB(o_i)$	o_i	$NB(o_i)$	o_i	$NB(o_i)$	o_i	$NB(o_i)$
B1	F1, H1	B6	F2,F3,H3	F3	B6,H2,H3,P1	H2	B2,B3,F3
B2	F4,H1,H2	B7	F6,H4,P2	F4	B2	H3	B6,F3
B3	H2	B8	H4	F5	P2	H4	B7,B8
B4	F1	F1	B1,B4,B5,H1,P1	F6	B7,H4,P2	P1	B5,F1,F2,F3,H1
B5	F1,F2,H1,P1	F2	B5,B6,P1	H1	B1,B2,B5,F1,P1	P2	B7,F5,F6,H4

Definition 5 (Co-location instances and participating instance). *Given a candidate $c = \{f_1, ..., f_k\}$, a co-location instance of c is a set of instances that belong to all feature types in c and they have a neighbor relationship to each other. A co-location instance also is a clique. The participating instance of a feature $f_t \in c$ is a set of all instances of f_t that are collected from all co-location instances of c and is denoted as $ParI(f_t, c)$.*

Definition 6 (Internal utility). *The internal utility of a feature f_t in a candidate c is its cardinality and is denoted as $q(f_t) = |ParI(f_t)|$.*

Definition 7 (Pattern utility). *Given a candidate $c = \{f_1, ..., f_k\}$, the utility of it is denoted as*

$$u(c) = \sum_{\forall f_t \in c} u(f_t) \times q(f_t) \tag{1}$$

Definition 8 (Pattern utility ratio, PUR). *The pattern utility ratio of c is the ratio of the utility of c to the utility of S and is denoted as*

$$PUR(c) = \frac{u(c)}{u(S)} \tag{2}$$

Definition 9 (High utility co-location pattern). *A candidate $c = \{f_1, ..., f_k\}$ is a high utility co-location pattern if its pattern utility ratio is not smaller than a minimum utility threshold μ given by users, that is, $PUR(c) \geq \mu$.*

Definition 10 (Maximal high utility co-location pattern). *A high utility co-location pattern is maximal if it has no supersets that also are high utility co-location patterns.*

Figure 2 illustrates the process of mining HUCPs from the data set in Fig. 1(b). For example, after collecting all co-location instances of candidate $c = \{B,F,H\}$, we

Size 2 candidates

B	F	B	H	B	P	F	H	F	P	H	P
B1	F1	B1	H1	B5	P1	F1	H1	F1	P1	H1	P1
B4	F1	B2	H1	B7	P2	F3	H2	F2	P1	H4	P2
B5	F1	B2	H2			F3	H3	F3	P1		
B5	F2	B3	H2					F5	P2		
B6	F3	B3	H3					F6	P2		
B7	F6	B6	H3								
		B7	H4								
		B8	H4								

Candidate ← Co-location instances

Size 3 candidates

B	F	H	B	F	P	B	H	P	F	H	P
B1	F1	H1	B5	F1	P1	B5	H1	P1	F1	H1	P1
B5	F1	H1	B5	F2	P1	B7	H4	P2			
B6	F3	H3	B7	F6	P2						

Size 4 candidates

B	F	H	P
B5	F1	H1	P1

Fig. 2. Illustration of discovering HUCPs based on the generation-test candidate level-wise traversal mining framework.

obtain $ParI(B,c) = \{B1,B5,B6\}$, $ParI(F,c) = \{F1,F3\}$, and $ParI(H,c) = \{H1, H3\}$. The pattern utility of this candidate is equal to $u(c) = u(B)\times|ParI(B,c)| + u(F)\times|ParI(F,c)| + u(H)\times|ParI(H,c)| = 21\times3 + 24\times2 + 38\times2 = 270$. Thus, the pattern utility ratio of this pattern is $PUR(c) = \frac{u(c)}{u(S)} = \frac{270}{548} = 0.34$. If a user sets a minimum utility threshold $\mu = 0.25$, since $PUR(c) = 0.34 \geq \mu = 0.25$, $c = \{B,F,H\}$ is a HUCP.

Similar calculations allow us to obtain all HUCPs as follows: $\{B,F\}$, $\{B,H\}$, $\{F,H\}$, $\{F,P\}$, $\{B,F,H\}$, $\{B,F,P\}$, and $\{B,H,P\}$. Applying Definition 9, we can obtain that the maximal HUCPs are $\{B,F,H\}$, $\{B,F,P\}$, and $\{B,H,P\}$. It can be seen that the number of patterns can be reduced by 50%, from 6 patterns to 3 patterns. This is beneficial for users to understand and apply.

3 The Clique-Hash Table-Based Top-Down Traversal Mining Method

From the mining process of the above example, it is easy to find that the prerequisite for calculating the PUR of a candidate is to collect all co-location instances of the candidate. This step has been proven to be the most time-consuming part in the entire mining process [10,15]. Therefore, quickly collecting all co-location instances of candidates is the most critical step in improving mining efficiency. In addition, it is difficult to determine the upper bound of candidates because PUR does not hold the downward closure property. For example, if the data set includes m features, in the worst-case scenario, the longest candidate is the size m candidate, i.e., $c \equiv F = \{f_1, ..., f_m\}$ and we need to examine $(2^m - 1)$ candidates. When processing large-scale datasets, the mining efficiency is extremely inefficient. Moreover, from Fig. 2 we also find that for a candidate to be considered, it must have at least one co-location instance.

Therefore, based on the above observation, if we first obtain cliques (including maximal cliques and non-maximal cliques) and then use some data structure to

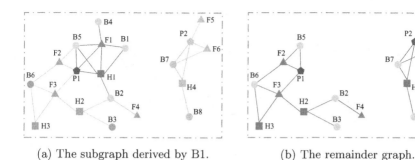

(a) The subgraph derived by B1.   (b) The remainder graph.

Fig. 3. An illustration of subgraph partitioning.

arrange these cliques to obtain all participating instances of candidates from the structure. This can avoid the two shortcomings mentioned above, that is, reducing candidate search space and quickly collecting participating instances.

3.1 Maximal Clique Enumeration

Although maximal clique (MC) enumeration is an NP-hard problem, numerous efficient enumerating maximal cliques have been proposed [3,4,11]. In this work, we adopt the algorithm proposed by Chen et al. for enumerating maximum cliques [16]. The algorithm is divided into two steps. First, it constructs a candidate map to obtain maximal and non-maximal cliques. Then, it designs an inverted clique tree to filter out non-maximal cliques and only output maximal cliques. For details of the algorithm, please refer to [16].

However, when the data set is large and dense, the algorithm cannot be directly applied. Since the candidate map preserves all maximal and nonmaximal cliques, as the processing progresses, each clique header will induce a large number of clique bodies, the candidate map will quickly become large, and its storage cost will be very expensive. Therefore, in this work, we designed a graph partitioning approach to efficiently apply this algorithm.

Definition 11 (Subgraph). *Given an instance o_i and a threshold $0 < g \leq 1$, the subgraph induced by o_i is denoted as $G_{sub} = (V_{sub}, E_{sub})$ where $V_{sub} = \{o_j | o_j \in NB(o_i)\}$. If the size of V_{sub} is smaller than $g \times |S|$, G_{sub} continues to be expanded by placing instances that are neighbors of the current vertices in V_{sub}.*

For example, in Fig. 1, we randomly chose $o_i = B1$ and set $g = 0.3$. At the initial stage, $S_{sub} = \{B1,F1,H1\}$, since $|V_{sub}| = 3 < g \times |S| = 0.3 \times 20 = 6$, G_{sub} is expanded by adding the neighboring instance sets of B1, F1, and H1, i.e., $G_{sub} = \{B1,B2,B4,B5,F1,H1,P1\}$ and it is highlighted in Fig. 3(a). Since now $|V_{sub}| = 7 \geq 6$, the maximal clique enumeration algorithm is executed.

After enumerating the maximal cliques on the subgraph derived from o_i, the subgraph is deleted, and we continue to enumerate maximal cliques from other subgraphs until no more subgraphs are generated. Figure 3(b) illustrates the result when deleting the subgraph derived from B1.

Table 2. The maximal cliques listed in Fig. 1(b).

MCs	MCs	MCs	MCs
{B1,F1,H1}	{B5,F2,P1}	{F3,H2}	{B8,H4}
{B4,F1}	{B6,F2}	{B2,H2}	{B7,F6,P2}
{B5,F1,H1,P1}	{B6,F3}	{B3,H2}	{B7,H4,P2}
{B2,H1}	{B6,F3,H3}	{B2,F4}	{F5,P2}

The proposed subgraph partitioning method can ensure that the amount of data processed is not much different each time the algorithm for enumerating maximal cliques is executed, which can effectively prevent excessive memory consumption. Table 2 lists all maximal cliques that are enumerated in Fig. 1(b).

3.2   The Hash Table Structure

Definition 12. *The hash table structure is constructed as follows: these maximal cliques whose instances belong to the same feature type are arranged to an item of the hash table structure. The item also is a hash table with its keys are the independent feature of each instance in the maximal cliques and its values are the set of the instances of these maximal cliques that belong to the same feature type.*

Figure 4 shows the hash table structure that is constructed based on the maximal cliques listed in Table 2. As can be seen, we convert neighboring instances into a compact hashtable. The next step is how to discover maximal HUCPs from this structure.

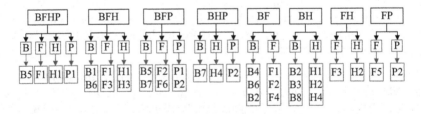

Fig. 4. The hash table constructed form the maximal cliques in Table 2.

3.3   Top-Down Traversal Mining Maximal HUCPs

Algorithm 1 describes the top-down traversal mining algorithm to discover maximal HUCPs. First, the algorithm materializes the neighbor relationship between instances (Step 1). Then, it enumerates maximal cliques through the graph partitioning method (Step 2). Next, it constructs the hash table structure based on these maximal cliques (Step 3). After that, it takes out all the keys from this hash

---

Algorithm 1 Top-down traversal mining HUCP algorithm

    Input: S, d, μ, g
    Output: a set of maximal HUCPs, MPs
 1: $NBs \leftarrow$ materializingNeiborRelationship(S, d)
 2: $MCs \leftarrow$ enumerateMaximalClique(S, NBs, g)
 3: $HT \leftarrow$ constructHashtable(MCs)
 4: $KEYs \leftarrow$ getAllKeys(HT)
 5: $MPs \leftarrow \emptyset$
 6: $VCs \leftarrow \emptyset$ ▷ Visited candidate set
 7: **while** $KEYs \neq \emptyset$ **do**
 8:     $CANDs \leftarrow$ getLongestKey$(KEYs)$
 9:     **for** $c \in CANDs$ **do**
10:         **if** c is a subset of any patterns in MPs **then**
11:             $VCs \leftarrow VCs \cup c$
12:             Break
13:         **end if**
14:         **if** $c \in VCs$ **then**
15:             Break
16:         **end if**
17:         **for** $key \in HT$ **do**   ▷ Travel each keys in the hash table
18:             **if** $c \subseteq key$ **then**
19:                 $ParI(f, c) \leftarrow$ getValue(c, HT) ▷ Get the participating instances
20:             **end if**
21:         **end for**
22:         $PUR(c) \leftarrow$ computePUR$(ParI(f, c))$
23:         **if** $PUR(c) \geq \mu$ **then**
24:             $MPs \leftarrow MPs \cup c$
25:         **else**
26:             $newCands \leftarrow$ generateDirectSubset(c) ▷ Generate new candidates
27:             $KEYs \leftarrow KEYs \cup newCands$
28:             $VCs \leftarrow VCs \cup c$ ▷ Remark visited candidates
29:         **end if**
30:     **end for**
31: **end while**

---

structure and these keys are the initial candidate set for discovering maximal HUCPs (Step 4). The algorithm first considers the longest keys as candidates for mining maximal HUCPs (Step 8). It traverses the entire hash table structure, if a key is a superset of the candidate, it takes out the corresponding value as the participating instances of each feature in the current candidate (Steps 17–21). The algorithm then proceeds to calculate the PUR of the candidate according to Definitions 6–8 (Step 22). If the PUR of the candidate is greater than the minimum utility threshold, it is a maximal HUCP and is put into the result set (Steps 23–25). If the PUR of the candidate is less than the threshold, the algorithm generates its direct subset as new candidates and puts them into the candidate set (Steps 26–27). At the same time, the candidate is also put into the visited candidate set (Step 28).

Note that when the algorithm calculates PUR for each new candidate, it first needs to check that if the candidate is a subset of maximal HUCPs in the result set, MPs, the candidate does not need to be calculated (Steps 10–13). When the candidate is not a subset of any maximal HUCPs in the result set, it also needs to be verified in the visited candidate set. If it has been visited, we also do not compute the PUR of it (Steps 14–16). This avoids repeated processing of candidates and ensures that each candidate is calculated only once.

For example, suppose we calculate the PUR value of candidate $c = \{B,F,H\}$, we traverse the hash structure to find these keys that are supersets of c, i.e., BFHP and BFH. From the value of key BFHP we get $ParI(B,BFHP) = \{B5\}$, $ParI(F,BFHP) = \{F1\}$, and $ParI(H,BFHP) = \{H1\}$. From key BFH we obtain $ParI(B,BFH) = \{B1,B6\}$, $ParI(F,BFH\ ) = \{F1,F3\}$, and $ParI(H,BFH) = \{H1,H3\}$. Merging the participating instances that are obtained from the values of the two keys above, we get the entire participating instances of the features in c, i.e., $ParI(B,c) = ParI(B,BFHP)\ \cup\ ParI(B,BFH) = \{B1,B5,B6\}$, $ParI(F,c) = ParI(F,BFHP)\ \cup\ ParI(F,BFH) = \{F1,F3\}$, and $ParI(H,c) = ParI(H,BFHP)\ \cup\ ParI(H,BFH)=) = \{H1,H3\}$. This are also exactly the participating instances of the features that we obtain by collecting form all independent co-location instances as shown Fig. 2.

4   Experimental Study

4.1   Experimental Environment

Compared Algorithms: To demonstrate the effectiveness and efficiency of the proposed method, we performed a series of experiments. Our algorithm is compared with the EPA algorithm [12] which can discover complete HUCPs from spatial data sets and adopts the generation-test candidate level-wise traversal mining framework. At the same time, the SGCT algorithm [13] which discovers maximal PCPs and the IDS algorithm [1] which adopts a clique-based mining framework to find PCPs, are also considered. All algorithms are coded in C++ and executed on a Windows 10 OS with Intel(R) Core i7-3770 and 16 GB of RAM.

Data Sets: Both synthetic and real data sets are used in our experiments. First, to generate synthetic data sets, a synthetic data generator is employed [15]. Then, we extract the point of interest (POI) data set of Las Vegas city, USA from the Yelp data set[1]. The feature utility values of this data set are assigned by the average of the number of check-ins in instances of them. Moreover, a vegetation data set collected from the Three Parallel Rivers of Yunnan Protected Area is also used in our experiments [1]. The utility value of each feature in this data set is the price of each type of vegetation. Table 3 summarizes the primary parameters of our data sets.

4.2   The Effectiveness of Maximal HUCPs

In the first experiment, we prove the effectiveness of the maximal HUCP representation, that is, it can effectively reduce the number of patterns and provide

---

[1] https://www.yelp.com/dataset.

Table 3. A summary of our experimental datasets (1k = 1000, * : variable).

Name	Spatial size	# features	# instances	Nature
Real data sets				
Las Vegas	38,649 × 62,985	17	22,725	Dense, clustering
Vegetation	71,920 × 66,443	15	408,945	Dense, big
Synthetic data sets				
Fig. 6	5k × 5k	15	20k	Dense
Figs. 8, 10	5k × 5k	15	50k	Dense
Fig. 12	5k × 5k	15	*	Dense, big

users with a concise mining result. Figures 5 and 6 show the number of all HUCPs and the number of maximal HUCPs on synthetic and Las Vegas data sets with different distance thresholds and minimum utility thresholds, respectively. Note that, since the mining performance of the compared algorithm varies greatly, in order to complete this mining task and give the mining results, we only conduct experiments on 50% of the Las Vegas data set.

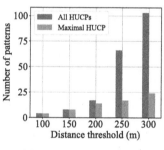
(a) Las Vegas ($\mu = 0.1$)

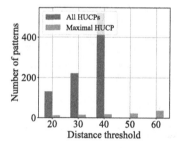
(b) Synthetic data set ($\mu = 0.1$)

Fig. 5. The number of patterns in different distance thresholds.

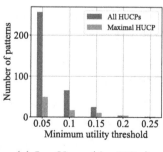
(a) Las Vegas ($d = 250$m)

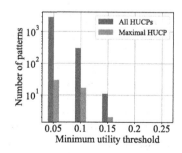
(b) Synthetic data set ($d = 35$)

Fig. 6. The number of patterns in different minimum utility thresholds.

As can be seen, the number of HUCPs is significantly reduced by using maximal representation. This makes it easy for users to understand, absorb, and apply mining results. In addition, when the distance threshold increases or the utility threshold becomes smaller, correspondingly, more HUCPs can be found, but at this time, the maximal representation can more effectively reduce the number of patterns.

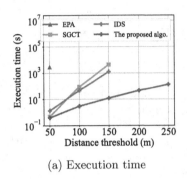
(a) Execution time

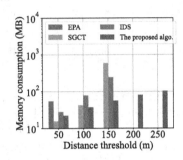
(b) Memory consumption

Fig. 7. The execution time and memory consumption of the compared algorithms in different distance thresholds on the Las Vegas data set. ($\mu = 0.1$)

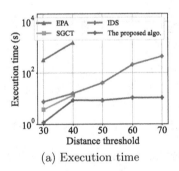
(a) Execution time

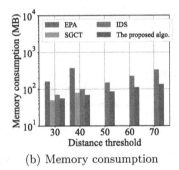
(b) Memory consumption

Fig. 8. The execution time and memory consumption of the compared algorithms in different distance thresholds on the synthetic data set. ($\mu = 0.1$)

4.3 The Efficiency of the Proposed Algorithm

In the following experiments, we investigate the efficiency of the proposed mining method by using several workloads, i.e., different values of distance thresholds, minimum utility thresholds, and different numbers of instances.

Different Distance Thresholds: Figures 7 and 8 show the changes in execution time and memory consumption of the four algorithms on the Las Vegas and synthetic data sets as the distance threshold increases, respectively. It is easy to see that when the distance threshold increases, the performance of EPA that employs the generation-test candidate level-wise traversal mining framework rapidly deteriorates. Although two algorithms, SGCT and IDS, also use the top-down mining style, it is relatively inefficient to collect candidate co-locations in SGCT, and IDS does not use the downward closure property to reduce the candidate search space, so the performance of the two algorithms also deteriorates rapidly. While the proposed algorithm gives good performance when the distance threshold increases.

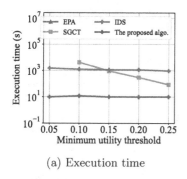

(a) Execution time

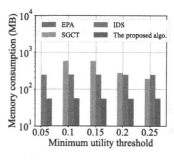

(b) Memory consumption

Fig. 9. The execution time and memory consumption of the compared algorithms in different minimum utility thresholds on the Las Vegas data set. ($d = 150\,\mathrm{m}$)

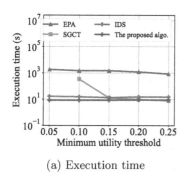

(a) Execution time

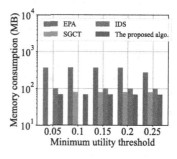

(b) Memory consumption

Fig. 10. The execution time and memory consumption of the compared algorithms in different minimum utility thresholds on the synthetic data set. ($d = 40$)

Different Minimum Utility Thresholds: Figures 9 and 10 plot the changes in execution time and memory consumption of the compared algorithms as the minimum threshold changes, respectively. It can be seen that EPA is completely ineffective on the Las Vegas data set. At small values of the minimum utility thresholds (e.g., $\mu = 0.05$), SGCT also fails because too many candidates are generated. Although IDS can complete the mining task with a small threshold, its execution time and memory consumption are always more than our algorithm. In addition, on synthetic data sets, our algorithm also gives better performance.

Different Number of Instances (different sizes of data sets): In the last experiment, we examine the performance of the proposed algorithm when changing the size of data sets. To create different sizes of real data sets, we perform different sampling on the Vegetation data set. The performance of the compared algorithms on different sizes of spatial data sets is depicted in Figs. 11 and 12. It can be seen that EPA and SGCT fail rapidly as the size of the data set increases. When dealing with particularly large-scale data sets (e.g., more than 80% of real data sets, larger than 160,000 instances of synthetic data sets), IDS is also incompetent. While the proposed algorithm shows scalability to large-scale spatial data sets. It is worth noting that our algorithm can avoid memory overflow by tuning the subgraph threshold g when dealing with large-scale datasets.

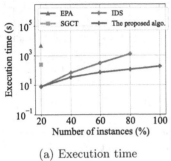 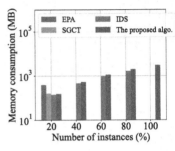

(a) Execution time   (b) Memory consumption

Fig. 11. The execution time and memory consumption of the compared algorithms in different numbers of instances (Vegetation, $d = 800\,\mathrm{m}$, $\mu = 0.1$)

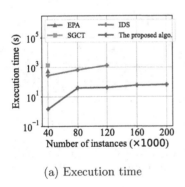 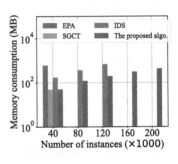

(a) Execution time   (b) Memory consumption

Fig. 12. The execution time and memory consumption of the compared algorithms in different numbers of instances (Synthetic data sets, $d = 25, \mu = 0.1$)

5   Conclusion

This paper proposes a concise representation of HUCPs, maximal HUCPs. In order to efficiently discover maximal HUCPs, a top-down traversal mining method is adopted. This method first keeps neighboring instances into a set of maximal cliques, and then it reasonably organizes these maximal cliques into a special hash table structure to quickly collect the participating instances of candidates. This method completely abandons the traditional mining method in which the participating instances of each candidate are collected through each independent co-location instance of the candidate. Experimental results on both real and synthetic data sets show that the proposed method can effectively reduce the number of patterns and give users a concise result. At the same time, the proposed method can also efficiently discover maximal HUCPs in large-scale spatial data sets.

It is easy to find that in our algorithm, the step of enumerating maximal cliques in subgraphs can be parallelized. Our further work is to parallelize the proposed algorithm to handle larger-scale spatial data sets.

Acknowledgements. This work is supported by the Special Basic Cooperative Research Programs of Yunnan Provincial Undergraduate Universities' Association(grant NO.202101BA070001-152), the National Natutal Science Foundation of China of funder(grant NO. 62066023, 62106024), the Scientific Research Project of Kunming University (No. XJZZ1706), and the Foundation of Yunnan Key Laboratory of Service Computing(No.YNSC23109).

References

1. Bao, X., Wang, L.: A clique-based approach for co-location pattern mining. Inf. Sci. **490**, 244–264 (2019)
2. Cai, J., Liu, Q., Deng, M., Tang, J., He, Z.: Adaptive detection of statistically significant regional spatial co-location patterns. Comput. Environ. Urban Syst. **68**, 53–63 (2018)
3. Eppstein, D., Löffler, M., Strash, D.: Listing all maximal cliques in sparse graphs in near-optimal time. In: Cheong, O., Chwa, K.Y., Park, K. (eds.) Algorithms and Computation. ISAAC 2010. LNCS, vol. 6506 pp. 403–414. Springer, Berlin, Heidelberg (2010). https://doi.org/10.1007/978-3-642-17517-6_36
4. Eppstein, D., Löffler, M., Strash, D.: Listing all maximal cliques in large sparse real-world graphs. J. Exp. Algorithmics (JEA) **18**, 3–1 (2013)
5. Li, Y., Wang, L., Yang, P., Li, J.: EHUCM: an efficient algorithm for mining high utility co-location patterns from spatial datasets with feature-specific utilities. In: Strauss, C., Kotsis, G., Tjoa, A.M., Khalil, I. (eds.) Database and Expert Systems Applications. DEXA 2021. LNCS, vol. 12923, pp. 185–191. Springer, Cham (2021). https://doi.org/10.1007/978-3-030-86472-9_17
6. Liu, Q., Liu, W., Deng, M., Cai, J., Liu, Y.: An adaptive detection of multilevel co-location patterns based on natural neighborhoods. Int. J. Geogr. Inf. Sci. **35**(3), 556–581 (2021)
7. Shu, J., Wang, L., Yang, P., Tran, V.: Mining the potential relationships between cancer cases and industrial pollution based on high-influence ordered-pair patterns. In: Chen, W., Yao, L., Cai, T., Pan, S., Shen, T., Li, X. (eds.) Advanced Data Mining and Applications. ADMA 2022. LNCS, vol. 13725, pp. 27–40. Springer, Cham (2022). https://doi.org/10.1007/978-3-031-22064-7_3

8. Song, W., Qiao, Q.: Mining high utility co-location patterns using the maximum clique and the subsume index. In: Proceedings of the 2020 2nd International Conference on Big Data Engineering, pp. 1–6 (2020)
9. Tran, V.: Meta-PCP: a concise representation of prevalent co-location patterns discovered from spatial data. Expert Syst. Appl. **213**, 119255 (2023)
10. Tran, V., Wang, L., Chen, H., Xiao, Q.: MCHT: a maximal clique and hash table-based maximal prevalent co-location pattern mining algorithm. Expert Syst. Appl. **175**, 114830 (2021)
11. Wu, Q., Hao, J.K.: A review on algorithms for maximum clique problems. Eur. J. Oper. Res. **242**(3), 693–709 (2015)
12. Yang, S., Wang, L., Bao, X., Lu, J.: A framework for mining spatial high utility co-location patterns. In: 2015 12th International Conference on Fuzzy Systems and Knowledge Discovery (FSKD), pp. 595–601. IEEE (2015)
13. Yao, X., Peng, L., Yang, L., Chi, T.: A fast space-saving algorithm for maximal co-location pattern mining. Expert Syst. Appl. **63**, 310–323 (2016)
14. Yoo, J.S., Bow, M.: A framework for generating condensed co-location sets from spatial databases. Intell. Data Anal. **23**(2), 333–355 (2019)
15. Yoo, J.S., Shekhar, S.: A joinless approach for mining spatial colocation patterns. IEEE Trans. Knowl. Data Eng. **18**(10), 1323–1337 (2006)
16. Yu, T., Liu, M.: A linear time algorithm for maximal clique enumeration in large sparse graphs. Inf. Process. Lett. **125**, 35–40 (2017)

Research on the Meta Synthesis Model of Strategic Risk Management for the Complex Weapon Equipment Systems Development

Xinfeng Wang[(⊠)] and Tao Wang

College of Systems Engineering, National University of Defense Technology, Changsha, China
wxf_nudt@126.com

Abstract. The strategic management of the complex weapon equipment systems development must carry out effective strategic risk management. Firstly, the concept and process of strategic risk management for the complex weapon equipment systems were analyzed development. Then, the Hall three-dimensional structure theory was used to construct the three-dimensional system structure of strategic risk management for the complex weapon equipment systems development. Based on this, a Meta Synthesis Model for strategic risk management for the complex weapon equipment systems development was established, and applied to the practice of strategic risk management for a certain type of complex weapon equipment system development, The results indicate that this model can provide effective theoretical support and methodological guidance for the practical application of strategic risk management in the complex weapon equipment systems development.

Keywords: Complex weapon equipment system development · Strategic risk management · Hall's three-dimensional structure theory · Meta synthesis model

1 Introduction

Strategic management for the complex weapon equipment systems development is the process of introducing strategic management theory and methods into the field of complex weapon equipment system development, scientifically planning and developing complex weapon equipment systems from a global and strategic perspective, and conducting a series of activities such as prediction, decision-making, planning, implementation, and evaluation to formulate and implement complex weapon equipment system development strategies. Due to the wide range, large scale, complex internal structure, rapid changes in external environment, high cost, and relatively new technology involved in the construction and development of complex weapons equipment systems, there are inevitably various strategic risks in their strategic management process, that is, the possibility of insufficient or non-existent conditions required to achieve strategic goals that cannot guarantee their achievement. The existence of strategic risks may lead to problems such as cost overruns, progress delays, and construction failures in the complex weapon

© The Author(s), under exclusive license to Springer Nature Singapore Pte Ltd. 2024
Y. Tan and Y. Shi (Eds.): DMBD 2023, CCIS 2018, pp. 189–201, 2024.
https://doi.org/10.1007/978-981-97-0844-4_14

equipment systems development. To ensure the achievement of construction goals and the smooth implementation of strategic management processes, it is necessary to carry out strategic risk management for the complex weapon equipment systems development. Strategic risk management is an effective combination of strategic management and risk management, and has become an important branch in the field of strategic management [5–7]. The strategic management of the complex weapon equipment systems development has a comprehensive, systematic, and dynamic nature, and its risks are highly complex. The strategic management of the complex weapon equipment systems development must attach great importance to risk management issues.

At present, relevant research has been conducted in the field of risk management in the complex weapon equipment systems development. However, most of the risk management research is conducted from a specific process of the complex weapon equipment systems development, such as system demonstration, procurement of complex weapon equipment systems, development of complex weapon equipment systems, and use of complex weapon equipment systems [8–12]. However, there is almost no research on risk management at the strategic level. The management of strategic risks in the complex weapon equipment systems development is a complex systematic process that must be studied using scientific and systematic methods. Comprehensive integration is aimed at solving complex system problems, using a combination of qualitative and quantitative methods to conduct holistic and integrated analysis of complex systems [13, 14]. This article adopts a comprehensive integration method to systematically analyze the strategic risk management of the complex weapon equipment systems development, and constructs a comprehensive integration model for the strategic risk management of complex weapon equipment system construction and development that is suitable for the strategic management of complex weapon equipment system construction in the new era. It has important theoretical and application value for the current development of complex weapon equipment system.

2 Concept and Process of Strategic Risk Management for the Complex Weapon Equipment Systems Development

There is currently no unified consensus at home and abroad on the definition of strategic risk. One side believes that strategic risk is a strategic risk, which refers to the risk that affects the implementation of strategic design and planning; The other party believes that strategic risk refers to the risk of strategy, which refers to the risks that exist in the process of strategic implementation and affect the implementation of strategic design and planning. From these two definitions, because strategic implementation can be seen as a behavior after strategic design and planning, the risks of the strategy will inevitably be unified into strategic risks. The basic definition of risk is the uncertainty of losses, therefore, the uncertainty of losses caused by strategic implementation behavior can be considered as strategic risk. The losses here include losses of economic benefits (such as overspending, loss, etc.) and non economic benefits (such as delay, failure, etc.).

Risk management refers to a series of activities that include developing risk management plans, identifying risks, analyzing risks, evaluating risks, responding to risks, monitoring risks, etc., with the aim of reducing the likelihood of risk occurrence and reducing or avoiding losses caused by risk occurrence [15–17]. Strategic risk management for the complex weapon equipment systems development is a systematic process of planning, identifying, analyzing, evaluating, responding to, and monitoring strategic risks that exist in the complex weapon equipment systems development, as shown in Fig. 1. The purpose of strategic risk management is to control the strategic risks of the complex weapon equipment systems development to an acceptable level, in order to improve and ensure the achievement of the development goals of complex weapon equipment system construction and the smooth implementation of the management process.

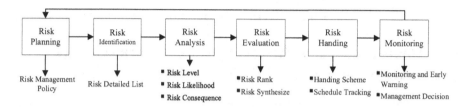

Fig. 1. Strategic Risk Management Process for the complex weapon equipment systems development

1) Risk planning: Risk planning refers to the process of planning and designing risk management activities. This process includes defining action plans and methods for organizational and member risk management, selecting risk management methods, determining risk judgment criteria, establishing monitoring risk requirements, and equipping risk management activities with sufficient resources.

2) Risk identification: Risk identification is the process of discovering, identifying, and describing risks. This process includes identifying, identifying, and describing potential risk events that may have an impact on the target, analyzing the sources, causes, scope and nature of risk consequences, as well as corresponding current control measures, preparing a risk list, providing input and laying a foundation for the risk analysis process.

3) Risk analysis: Risk analysis is the process of further understanding risk characteristics and confirming risk levels, which is the foundation of risk assessment and risk response. Strategic managers for the construction and development of complex weapons and equipment systems should use quantitative and qualitative methods to analyze the likelihood and potential impact of risks based on risk identification results, and determine the magnitude of risks accordingly, providing input for risk assessment.

4) Risk assessment: Risk assessment is the process of comparing risk analysis results with risk criteria to determine whether risks and their magnitude are acceptable or tolerable. The strategic risk assessment of the complex weapon equipment systems development not only needs to achieve the evaluation of individual risks in each stage, but also needs to comprehensively evaluate the possible outcomes of overall risks.

5) Risk response: Risk response is based on the results of risk assessment, proposing, evaluating, and selecting risk response plans, preparing and implementing risk

response plans, and controlling risks at an acceptable level under given constraints. Risk response can be addressed through various coping strategies, including changing the nature of risk factors, the probability of risk occurrence, or the magnitude of risk consequences. These strategies typically include risk avoidance, risk mitigation, risk retention, risk transfer, and risk contingency.

6) Risk monitoring: Risk monitoring is the dynamic tracking, monitoring, and adjustment of risk influencing factors, risk events, and response measures based on risk management plans, actual risk events, and risk response results at any time, in order to implement comprehensive dynamic management of risks. The risk monitoring results provide a basis for developing risk response plans and identifying new risks. It is an important task in the implementation process of strategic management.

3   A Three-Dimensional System Structure for Strategic Risk Management in the Complex Weapon Equipment Systems Development

The "Hall 3D Structure" model is a system engineering methodology proposed by American system engineer Hall in 1969. It effectively reflects the overall content of the system through three dimensions: time dimension, knowledge dimension, and logical dimension, providing a unified thinking method for solving complex system problems [18, 19]. In the strategic risk management of the complex weapon equipment

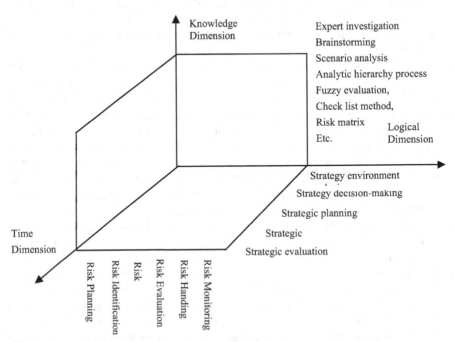

Fig. 2. 3D System Structure of Strategic Risk Management for the Complex Weapon Equipment Systems Development

systems development, the "Hall three-dimensional structure" is used to divide the management system into time dimension, knowledge dimension, and logical dimension, and a three-dimensional system structure diagram is established as shown in Fig. 2.

3.1 Time Dimension

The time dimension corresponds to the entire lifecycle of strategic management for the complex weapon equipment systems development. Generally speaking, its strategic management mainly includes three key stages: strategic design, strategic implementation, and strategic evaluation. The tasks of the strategic design stage mainly include strategic environment analysis, strategic decision-making, and strategic planning.

1) Strategic environment analysis: Strategic environment analysis mainly includes the equipment construction development external environment and internal environment analysis, the external environment analysis is to understand the armaments system development of external threats and opportunities for development, realize the equipment construction development is the purpose of the internal environment analysis of the existence of internal advantages and disadvantages, through strategic environment analysis to understand the equipment construction development environment and relative competitive position ", It lays the foundation for strategic decision making and embodies the forward-looking strategic management

2) Strategic decision-making: Strategic decision-making is the process of selecting and establishing major issues such as the development goals, development paths, and development priorities of complex weapon equipment systems based on strategic environmental analysis and clear strategic needs. Strategic decision-making is the process of establishing development goals and directions, mainly solving the problem of "where to develop" and reflecting the long-term nature of strategic management.

3) Strategic planning: Strategic planning is the process of decomposing and refining strategic goals and tasks based on strategic decision-making, optimizing strategic resource allocation with planning as the leading factor, clarifying development measures, methods, and steps, and forming policy documents such as development plans, plans, or plans. Strategic planning is the concretization of strategic decision-making, mainly solving the problem of "how to develop", reflecting the overall nature of strategic management.

4) Strategic implementation: The main task of the strategic implementation stage is to improve the organizational system and mechanism through the construction and development of complex weapons and equipment systems, inspect, supervise, guide, and regulate the implementation process of strategic planning, ensure the implementation of strategic decision-making and planning, and reflect the entire process of strategic management.

5) Strategic evaluation: The tasks of the strategic evaluation stage include the evaluation of the strategy itself, the execution of the strategy, and performance evaluation. The evaluation of strategy itself mainly refers to the argumentation and evaluation of strategic decisions and planning plans. Its task is to propose improvement suggestions around the weak links and problems in strategic decisions, planning, and planning, and enhance the scientificity and feasibility of planning; The evaluation of

strategic implementation mainly refers to the evaluation of the progress of strategic planning implementation, providing reference for strategic adjustment; Performance evaluation is an evaluation of the implementation effect of the development strategy for the construction of complex weapon equipment systems. Strategic assessment and environmental changes are the main basis for strategic adjustment, reflecting the environmental adaptability of the strategy.

3.2 Logical Dimension

The logical dimension corresponds to the process of strategic risk management for the complex weapon equipment systems development. The strategic risk management process for the complex weapon equipment systems development includes risk planning, risk identification, risk analysis, risk assessment, risk response, and risk monitoring. At each time dimension stage, there are six work processes to go through, namely risk planning, risk identification, risk analysis, risk assessment, risk handling, and risk monitoring. The main inputs and outputs of each process are described as follows:

1) Strategic risk planning for the complex weapon equipment systems development: This module mainly inputs the risk management plan for the complex weapon equipment systems development, existing management practical experience, system description, known historical risks, etc. The output mainly includes the overall strategy of risk management, including methods, roles and responsibilities, type levels and descriptions, benchmarks, reporting forms, and tracking.
2) Strategic risk identification for the complex weapon equipment systems development: This module mainly inputs risk cases and risk knowledge bases for the complex weapon equipment systems development, and outputs risk levels, risk types, risk factors, risk impacts, risk status descriptions, etc.
3) Strategic risk analysis for the complex weapon equipment systems development: This module mainly inputs risk level criteria, risk knowledge base, etc., and outputs risk likelihood, risk consequence degree, risk level description, etc.
4) Strategic risk assessment for the complex weapon equipment systems development: This module mainly inputs risk benchmarks, risk knowledge bases, etc., and outputs risk ranking results and evaluation results of various risk selection schemes.
5) Strategic risk response for the complex weapon equipment systems development: This module mainly inputs risk response objectives, and outputs risk response plans and progress.
6) Strategic risk monitoring for the complex weapon equipment systems development: This module mainly inputs monitoring strategies, monitoring standards, etc., and outputs contingency measures, control actions, change requests, and modification plans.

3.3 Knowledge Dimension

The knowledge dimension represents the knowledge, theory, and experience involved in completing the above stages and steps. The complex weapon equipment systems development require common knowledge such as systems science, information science, military complex weapon equipment systems science, military operations research, and professional technical methods for risk management, mainly including risk planning, identification, analysis, evaluation, response, and monitoring. Currently, there are many specific technical methods related to risk identification, analysis, evaluation, response, and monitoring, in practical applications, it is necessary to find methods that are suitable for the strategic risk management characteristics of the construction and development of specific complex weapon equipment systems.

Due to the systematicity, dynamism, and complexity of the development process of complex weapon equipment systems, it is determined that the risk management methods for the construction and development of these complex weapon equipment systems should also pay attention to the following two points in their application: firstly, combined with the risk management process of complex weapon equipment system construction and their interrelationships, based on various models such as knowledge models, relationship models, mathematical models, and management models of each module, Conduct research by comprehensively utilizing various methods of risk planning, analysis, evaluation, response, and monitoring; The second is the comprehensive integration of qualitative and quantitative analysis methods. Qualitative analysis should be conducted first, followed by simplification for quantitative calculation. Finally, based on the quantitative calculation results, further system analysis and optimization should be carried out.

4   A Meta Synthesis Model for Strategic Risk Management in the Complex Weapon Equipment Systems Development

On the basis of the three-dimensional system structure of strategic risk management for the complex weapon equipment systems development, a meta synthesis model of strategic risk management for the complex weapon equipment systems development is established, as shown in Fig. 3. This model reveals and describes the integration relationship between various systems in the complex weapon equipment systems development, and describes the information input and output of each module in the comprehensive integration model of risk management in the complex weapon equipment systems development, reflecting the relationship between various elements and processes of risk management in the complex weapon equipment systems development, And the work basis and results of risk management in various stages of the complex weapon equipment systems development.

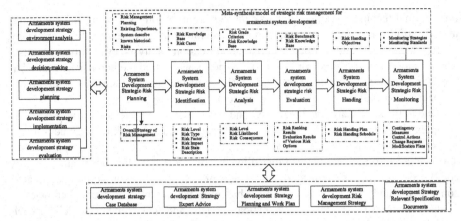

Fig. 3. Meta Synthesis Model for Strategic Risk Management of Complex Weapon Equipment System Construction and Development

This risk management comprehensive integration model has the following three characteristics:

Firstly, it organically integrates the strategic management process of complex weapon equipment system construction and development, and its risk management is mainly based on the overall strategic management needs and strategies. At the same time, the results of risk management will feedback and affect the specific implementation and improvement of strategic management in each stage;

Secondly, this model changes the commonly used single loop serial risk management method and provides a continuous risk management and feedback mechanism. The six work processes of risk management are interdependent and constantly communicate and provide information feedback, enabling continuous and dynamic management of risks in the management process.

Thirdly, this model organically combines expert opinions on the complex weapon equipment systems development, historical data and information on strategic management of complex weapon equipment system construction and development (including strategic management case library, strategic planning and work plan, risk management strategy, relevant normative documents, etc.) with computing machines, achieving a comprehensive and systematic overall understanding of the strategic risks of complex weapon equipment system development, Provide scientific basis and decision-making support for strategic risk management of complex weapon equipment systems.

5 An Example of Strategic Risk Integrated Management for a Certain Type of Complex Weapon Equipment Systems Development

5.1 Strategic Risk Characteristics of a Certain Type of Complex Weapon Equipment Systems Development

This type of complex weapon and equipment system is air defense and anti-missile weapon system, which includes main system and many subsystems, comprehensive system-wide research and balanced coordination should be carried out in its construction and development, therefore, the strategic risk of the this type of weapon equipment systems development not only has the characteristics of objectivity, universality, Chance and Necessity and manageability, but also presents the following characteristics:

1) The multi-level and diversity of strategic risks in the construction and development of the complex weapon equipment system of this model. The strategic risks of this complex weapon equipment system can be divided into performance risks, schedule risks, and cost risks according to its development goals. From the perspective of risk factors, they can be divided into external strategic environmental risks, internal strategic resource risks, and strategic implementation capability risks; External strategic environmental risks mainly include national security strategic environmental risks, socio-economic environmental risks, combat environmental risks, and competitive environmental risks of complex weapon equipment systems. Internal strategic resource risks mainly include human resource risks, financial resource risks, material resource risks, technical resource risks, cultural resource risks, etc. Strategic implementation capability risks mainly include organizational management risks, human resource management risks financial management risks, project organization risks, internal supervision risks, etc. Although the strategic risks present diversity throughout the entire lifecycle of the construction and development of this type of complex weapon equipment system, the hierarchical nature of the strategic risks in the construction and development of this type of complex weapon equipment system can be clearly delineated using fault tree analysis and analytic hierarchy process based on the development goal risks, risk factor sources, and risk factor influencing factors.

2) The dynamic nature of strategic risks in the complex weapon equipment systems development for this model. With the changes in factors such as the development stage and internal and external environment of the complex weapon equipment system construction of this model, as well as the improvement of strategic risk management level of implementing personnel and the execution and implementation of risk management measures, the development risks of the complex weapon equipment system construction of this model have shown dynamic changes, which are highlighted in the following three aspects: first, changes in the nature of strategic risks. Some strategic risk events have changed with the development process, and the original strategic risk events or factors have no longer become risks; Secondly, changes in the magnitude of strategic risks. As personnel's understanding, prediction, and prevention level of strategic risks change, the probability of risk events occurring and the losses caused will also change; Thirdly, the life and death turnover of risk factors. With the

improvement of management level, technological progress, and the application of corresponding risk control measures, the original risk factors will change, some risk factors may be eliminated, and some new risk factors will emerge.

3) The correlation of strategic risks in the complex weapon equipment systems development for this model. The entire life cycle of the construction and development of the complex weapon equipment system of this model is divided into stages such as strategic environment analysis, strategic decision-making, strategic planning, strategic implementation, and strategic evaluation. The procurement risks of each stage are not independent of each other, but interconnected and mutually influencing, and form a series of risk systems as a whole.

5.2 Comprehensive Risk Management Model for a Certain Type of Complex Weapon Equipment System Development

According to the strategic risk characteristics of the construction and development of the complex weapon equipment system of this model, its strategic risk management is an open and complex system process. Drawing on the three-dimensional system structure of strategic risk management for the complex weapon equipment systems development and the Meta Synthesis Model of strategic risk management for the complex weapon equipment systems development, a comprehensive risk management model for the construction and development of this type of complex weapon equipment system is established. The results are shown in Fig. 4.

Compared with traditional risk management models, the comprehensive risk management model for the construction and development strategy of the complex weapon equipment system shown in the above figure has the following characteristics:

1) This comprehensive management model breaks through the traditional sequential single cycle risk management concept (risk planning, risk identification, risk analysis, risk evaluation, risk response, risk monitoring), and adopts a concurrent multi cycle risk management concept;

2) Under the guidance of the concept of concurrent multi cycle risk management, this integrated management model is not simply a systematic understanding and research approach using comprehensive integration methods, avoiding non systematic approaches or using simple systems to deal with complex risk management object systems, but rather constitutes a sufficiently complex strategic risk management entity for the construction and development of a certain type of complex weapon equipment system, Make it more complex than or equivalent to the strategic risk management object being studied;

3) The integrated management model organically combines the data and information of the complex weapon equipment system, the comprehensive expert group consultation opinions on the construction and development of the complex weapon equipment system, and computers, combining scientific theories and human knowledge from various disciplines to form a system, leveraging the overall and comprehensive advantages of this system, and achieving a combination of empirical research and empirical judgment, Ultimately, a comprehensive and systematic overall understanding of the risks associated with the construction and development of this type of

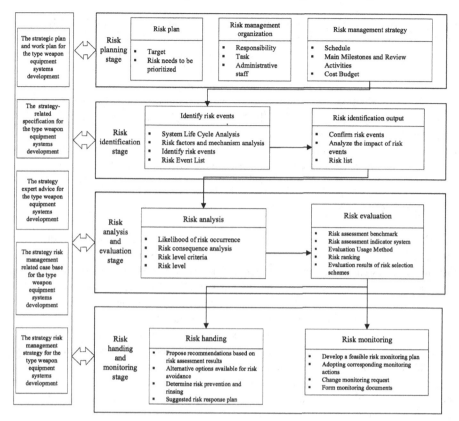

Fig. 4. Meta Synthesis Model of Strategic Risk Management for a Certain Type of Complex Weapon Equipment Systems Development

complex weapon equipment system can be formed, combining qualitative and quantitative analysis, providing scientific basis and decision-making support for strategic risk management in the construction and development of this type of complex weapon equipment system.

5.3 Use of a Comprehensive Risk Integration Model for the Construction and Development of a Certain Type of Complex Weapon Equipment System

Based on the comprehensive risk management model for the construction and development of a certain type of complex weapon equipment system, a comprehensive risk management process was carried out according to risk planning, risk identification, risk analysis and pre-evaluation, risk response and monitoring. Firstly, based on the risk planning process method, develop a scientific strategic risk plan, including project risk plan, project management organization, and risk management strategy; Secondly, in response to the advantages and disadvantages of risk identification methods in each knowledge dimension, combined with the characteristics of strategic risks in the complex weapon equipment systems development, a system dynamics based strategic identification method for the complex weapon equipment systems development is proposed; Then conduct risk analysis and evaluation, use scenario analysis method to conduct strategic risk analysis, construct a strategic risk evaluation index system, establish a fuzzy hierarchical comprehensive evaluation model for strategic risk, and calculate the results of strategic risk evaluation for the construction and development of a certain type of complex weapon equipment system; Finally, based on the evaluation results, a dynamic and adaptable strategic risk response and monitoring framework is established, and countermeasures and measures for risk management in the construction and development of this type of complex weapon equipment system are provided, achieving good results.

6 Epilogue

Based on the analysis of the concept and process of strategic risk management in the complex weapon equipment systems development, this article establishes a three-dimensional system structure for strategic risk management in the complex weapon equipment systems development. On this basis, a Meta Synthesis Model for strategic risk management in the complex weapon equipment systems development is further constructed, and applied to the practice of risk management in the construction and development of a certain type of complex weapon equipment system. The research shows that: This model provides methodological guidance for the engineering practice of strategic risk management in the complex weapon equipment systems development, effectively ensuring the achievement of strategic goals in the complex weapon equipment systems development, and focusing on improving the development efficiency of complex weapon equipment systems.

References

1. Li, M., Liu, P., et al.: Demonstration Method and Application of Military Complex Weapon Equipment System Development System. National Defense Industry Press, Beijing (2000)
2. Ding, B.C.: Systematic thinking on the development strategy of modern weapon complex weapon equipment system. Military Oper. Res. Syst. Eng. 3, 24–26 (2002)
3. Zhang, J., Guo, D., Yang, G.G.: Overview of the development strategy for complex weapon equipment systems. Firepower Command Control 9, 1–5 (2009)
4. Bu, G.Z., Lv, S.Q.: Evaluation and analysis of system capability in the development strategy of complex weapon equipment systems. Firepower Command Control 12, 6–9 (2014)
5. Li, J.: A review of strategic risk management theory, models, and applications. Manag. Theory 01, 123–125 (2014)
6. Zhang, C.Y., Xu M.J.: Research on strategic risk management of enterprises in the new era. Coop. Econ. Technol. 7s, 114–115 (2020)
7. Yang, H.J.: Research on the evolution of company strategy and strategic risk management theory. Sci. Decis.-Making 7, 124–135 (2021)
8. Zhang, Z.J.: Research on Risk Management in the Development of Complex Weapon Equipment Systems. Tianjin University (2007)
9. Bai, F.K.: Risk Management for the Acquisition of Military Complex Weapon Equipment Systems. National Defense Industry Press, Beijing (2010)

10. Di, P., Hu, T., Huang, T.: Research on risk analysis and evaluation model for the construction of complex weapon equipment system of systems. J. Nav. Eng. Univ. **3**, 71–76 (2008)
11. Li, J., Li, H., Ning, J.S.: Research on the risk management model for the use of complex weapon equipment systems. China Saf. Prod. Sci. Technol. **4**, 140–144 (2010)
12. Ji, W.F., Chen, X.W.: The current situation and inspiration of risk management in US military testing and appraisal. Value Eng. **28**, 172–173 (2019)
13. Dai, R.W.: The formation and modern development of the comprehensive integration method from qualitative to quantitative. J. Nat. **6**, 311–314 (2009)
14. Li, Z.M., Tang, S.C., Chen, S.F., et al.: Risk management for emergency procurement of complex weapon equipment systems based on comprehensive integration methods. Syst. Eng. Electron. Technol. **10**, 1761–1762, 1780 (2005)
15. Gu, M.D., Lei, P.: Risk Management. Tsinghua University Press, Beijing (2005)
16. Shen, J.M.: Project Risk Management. Mechanical Industry Press, Beijing (2004)
17. Chapman, C., Ward, S.: Project Risk Management, Process, Technology and Insight. Wiley, Hoboken (2003)
18. Zhao, Y.C.: Research and Application of Project Risk Dynamic Management Based on 3D Structure. Shandong University of Science and Technology (2010)
19. Gui, X., Chen, C.L., Zhang, S.X., et al.: A system engineering research method for the allocation and scheduling of maintenance tasks in wartime complex weapon equipment systems. Sci. Technol. Bull. **7**, 80–87 (2018)

A Service-Oriented Data Sharing and Exchange Model

Qian Li[1], Xinyu Jiang[1], Jianwei Sun[1], Hongyu Guo[1], Yulong Liu[1], Zi Wang[2], and Dan Liu[3]($\boxtimes$)

[1] The 15th Research Institute of China Electronics Technology Group, Beijing, China
[2] Bank of Beijing, Beijing, China
[3] National University of Defense Technology, Beijing, China
danliu@nudtedu.cn

Abstract. With the development of the times, data plays an increasingly important role in government business. Due to the differences in data formats, interfaces, and security access requirements between different systems, cross-system data sharing and exchange face various difficulties in reality. To this end, we propose a service-oriented data sharing and exchange model aimed at solving the difficulties encountered in data sharing and exchange. This model is based on the original basic data services, and coordinates business services between different systems through a shared switching center, thereby realizing data intercommunication between systems. Using this model can reduce the degree of coupling between systems, eliminate barriers between business systems, and improve the efficiency of government business development.

Keywords: Data Sharing Exchange Model · Service Orientation · Heterogeneous Data Sources

1 Introduction

With the advancement of society and science and technology, Chinese government departments actively adopt computer information management systems to improve management levels and replace complex manual business processes [1]. However, in the initial stage of system construction, due to the lack of unified planning, most business systems were developed, managed and used independently, which led to significant differences in platform selection, development language, database type and version, etc. In addition, this decentralized system construction method has led to the formation of closed "data islands" in the business systems of various departments [2–4]. This leads to difficulties in data exchange inside and outside the department, and it is impossible to effectively realize cross-departmental business collaboration. At the same time, the work efficiency is extremely low, and serious management loopholes may appear. In order to solve the existing problems among current business systems, we need

Y. Tan and Y. Shi (Eds.): DMBD 2023, CCIS 2018, pp. 202–212, 2024.
https://doi.org/10.1007/978-981-97-0844-4_15

to propose a new data sharing and exchange model. The goal of this model is to carry out development iterations on the basis of retaining the original business system, and at the same time, it is not intrusive to the original business system, and has strong applicability and guiding significance. Specifically, the characteristics of this model include the following aspects: (1) Retain the original business system to reduce secondary development costs and workload. (2) Solve the "data island" problem caused by multi-source heterogeneous data, provide solutions for multi-source heterogeneous databases, and ensure data sharing and interoperability. Among them, data service is an effective solution, which can standardize and encapsulate data in various business systems to ensure data consistency and interoperability. This paper proposes a service-oriented data sharing and exchange model as a centralized platform for data sharing and exchange among business systems. Through this model, different business systems can share each other's data, realize data intercommunication, promote business expansion, and reduce the coupling between business systems

2   Related Work

2.1   Digital Government

The concept of "digital government" first evolved from the "Digital Earth" proposed by the United States in 1998, that is, the government collects and integrates relevant data information through the flexible use of information technologies such as earth information systems, networks, and virtual simulations, and implements social management based on this. It is an important basis for the research and practice of government data sharing. From the perspective of comparison with public governance, scholars have reached a consensus that the fundamental goal of digital government is to defend and enhance public values. After comparing the similarities and differences between the two academic communities of public governance and digital government, Gil-Garcia et al. [8] pointed out that digital government is related to public governance in a substantive way. Innovative ways in which technology can be used to facilitate the generation of public value. From the perspective of the relationship between digital government and sustainable development, digital government is of great significance for promoting the sustainable development of developing and transitional economies, and the degree of construction of digital government can provide information for measuring sustainable development. Castro et al.'s [9] research analysis of 103 countries shows that e-government development is a positive determinant of a country's sustainable development. Because the development of digital government is a way to promote the efficiency of public administration, which can help economies support sustainable development in a more balanced manner.

2.2   Data Sharing

Since the beginning of the new century, "data governance" has become the governance concept of many countries. European and American countries started research on the open sharing of government data earlier, leading in theoretical research and practical application. The potential value, influencing factors, and privacy protection of government data sharing have been comprehensively discussed. Anne [10] pointed out that the public sector is an authoritative source of various types of big data, and its shared and open data for reuse will have an important impact on big data analysis in various industries. Sheshadri et al. [11] believe that security and privacy issues are important reasons why data sharing subjects are unwilling to share, and they believe that these data will be abused and damage their rights and interests. The use of artificial intelligence may improve the security of private data to a certain extent in the future.

3   Model

Different from the traditional monolithic design architecture, the service-oriented data sharing and exchange model aims to output services, and the model is based on the data sharing and exchange center to complete the interaction between data services. This can effectively reduce the overall complexity of the system, effectively eliminate data barriers, and greatly improve the efficiency of government affairs.

3.1   Overall Architecture

The overall architecture design of the service-oriented data sharing model is shown in Fig. 1. The overall model consists of three parts, namely service access layer, shared exchange layer and business collaboration layer. The delivery of messages between the platforms of the model is based on HTTPS requests to ensure the effective dissemination of messages. The advantages of this model can be summarized in the following three points:

1) The focus of the business interaction platform is to obtain the corresponding business service interface information from the shared switching center according to the business data requirements. By requesting these service interfaces, the business interaction platform can obtain the required data information. At the same time, the service layer does not have to worry about data security and format issues, because these issues are determined by the business interaction platform. The service layer will return data in a unified data format, and the business interaction platform will encapsulate the data according to business requirements. In order to ensure the consistency and reliability of system message delivery, the system uses the HTTPS protocol for message transmission.

2) The existence of a shared exchange platform eliminates the differences between data sources and reduces the complexity of data integration and sharing. It provides a centralized data standard, so that all basic services can process data in the same way, thereby avoiding data consistency problems caused by multi-source heterogeneous data. This unified data processing method helps to improve the overall efficiency and accuracy of the system, enabling the system to better cope with complex data environments.

3) The system is easy to maintain and has high scalability. By encapsulating data source information and basic application information into basic services, the system can expand its functions more flexibly. Adding or replacing an underlying service does not have a significant impact on other functions, because the dependencies between them are limited to the shared exchange level. This design simplifies system maintenance and reduces the cost and risk of developing new functions.

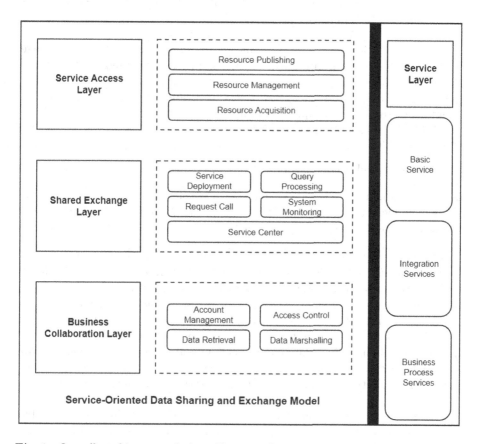

Fig. 1. Overall architecture design diagram of service-oriented data sharing and exchange mode.

3.2   Business Collaboration Layer

As shown in Fig. 1, the business collaboration layer consists of four parts, namely account management module, access control module, data retrieval module and data marshalling module.

1) Account management module. This module provides user registration function, and can give users different system access rights according to user needs, which is convenient for user management.
2) Access control module. This module has two main functions: one is responsible for the verification of user login, preventing illegal user login, and ensuring the security of the system; the other is responsible for the data security of the system, and different users have different access rights, if the user accesses the service beyond the level, it is not allowed. In order to prevent data information leakage, it is necessary to authenticate the user's authority and filter out illegal user requests for services.
3) Data retrieval module. This module is mainly responsible for the service access interaction with the data sharing exchange center. Users can make service requests according to the service information released by the sharing exchange center.
4) Data marshalling module. This module can encapsulate the data information obtained from the data query module according to user needs, and convert it into formats such as xml and json.

3.3 Shared Exchange Layer

As shown in Fig. 1, the shared exchange layer consists of five parts, namely service deployment module, query processing module, request call module, system monitoring module and service center module.

1) Service deployment module. The Service deployment module mainly provides relevant service information to the business interaction layer, so as to facilitate the business interaction module to access services.
2) Query processing module. The Query processing module mainly analyzes the service request sent by the business interaction layer, and provides the analyzed service specific information to the service request module.
3) Request call module. The Request call module is mainly responsible for requesting data services from specific services, and the corresponding services can directly return data to the business interaction module, which functions as a route.
4) System monitoring module. The System monitoring module is responsible for monitoring the status information of each service. It adopts the heartbeat mechanism [5]. Once the service status is found to be abnormal, it will issue a service warning and tell the administrator to troubleshoot the abnormality.
5) Service center module. The Service center module contains the basic information and interface services of each service. If other services want to call the data of the service, they only need to query the detailed information of the service through the registration center, call the interface module of the corresponding service, and obtain the corresponding service data. The coupling between services facilitates service expansion and maintenance.

3.4 Service Access Layer

As shown in Fig. 1, the service access layer consists of three parts, namely resource publishing module, resource management module and resource acquisition module.

1) Resource acquisition module. This module integrates the data resources of the original business module to adapt to different data management systems.
2) Resource management module. This module is mainly for the convenience of data interaction between basic services, composite services and business process services. The above concepts will be described in detail below.
3) Resource publishing module. This module publishes the function and interface information of each resource to the shared exchange center to facilitate future business inquiries and calls between services

4 Process

The process of data sharing and exchange is mainly divided into two parts: one is how to connect services to the system, and the other is how system visitors use services. This article will design the process from two aspects of creating services and using services.

4.1 Creating Services

Service Features. Each service represents some definite business functions. The new system creates services and integrates them into a service network that can call each other. The system has high flexibility and changes will not affect the entire system. Each service consists of two properties. First of all, each service has a complete definition and clear interface [6, 7]. The interface can be divided into two categories, one is the service definition interface, which is used to define the service, and the other is the service call interface, which is used to call service; secondly, each service can hide the internally executed business logic and specific implementation details through an interface.

Service Type. Services are divided into basic services, business process services and integration services by function.

Basic Service. The basic service is mainly responsible for accessing other systems. At the same time, if conditions permit, the basic service can directly connect to the data source, as shown in Fig. 2. This method of directly connecting data sources can effectively reduce the links of data transmission and improve the efficiency of data acquisition. By directly connecting to data sources, basic services can obtain the latest data in real time and make it available to other systems. This method can not only speed up the update speed of data, but also avoid the problems of delay and inconsistency during data transmission.

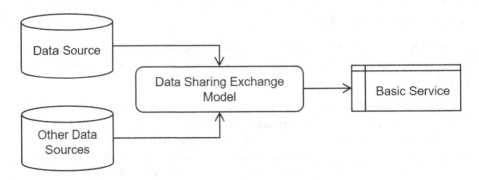

Fig. 2. Basic service flow chart.

Business Process Service. As the processor of actual business requirements, business process services are responsible for directly returning the results to users. Its main responsibility is to call related basic services and other services according to the needs of users, and return the processed results directly to users.

Integration Service. In actual production, because the services provided by basic services are too simple, it often happens that multiple business process services call the same basic service combination. In this way, business process services often need to write redundant and repeated codes to handle the same logic and operations when invoking basic services, which increases the workload and is not conducive to code maintenance. For this situation, we can provide more flexible and rich integration services by extending the functions of the basic services to reduce duplication of code in business process services.

Integration services can provide more advanced service composition and encapsulation functions, and combine some common service operations into a unified interface for business process service calls, as shown in Fig. 3. In this way, the business process service only needs to call this high-level interface, and does not need to care about the specific implementation details of the underlying layer, thus reducing the writing and maintenance of redundant codes.

Service Access System. In the service access system, the resource access module at the service access end is responsible for connecting different data sources into the system, which may involve various data sources such as databases, file systems, and Web services. The resource publishing module is responsible for registering and sharing the service interface information to the registration center, so that other systems or services can discover and use these interfaces.

In order to support the realization of composite services, the resource call module plays an important role in the composite service access system. It is responsible for obtaining the service interface information table (Table 1) from the registration center, which records all registered service interfaces and related information. Developers can freely combine these service interfaces according to

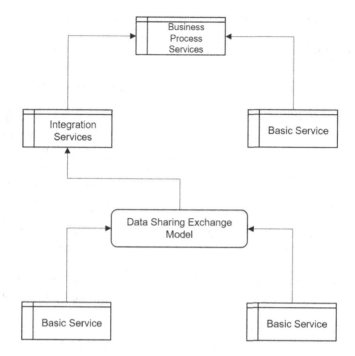

Fig. 3. Basic-integration-business process service flow chart.

business needs to form composite services with specific functions. The resource call module can call the corresponding basic service according to the combination request of the developer, and return the result to the caller.

Through the collaborative work of the above processes and modules, the service access system can effectively realize the access and release of basic services, and support flexible combined service calls. In this way, the business process service can obtain the required basic services from the service access system, and then meet the actual business needs, and return the results to the user.

The process of accessing the system for business process services and composite services is similar, but also different. When publishing services, business process services not only provide interface information to the service center to form a service interface information table, but also provide service information to the service publishing module of the shared exchange center to form a business service information table, which is convenient for service users to perform services call.

4.2   Use of Services

If the user wants to use the system, he needs to go through the following steps of using the service, as shown in Fig. 4.

The user registers through the user management module of the business interaction layer, and applies to the system administrator for corresponding usage

Table 1. Registry service interface information table.

Number	Field name	Example	Explanation
1	Service ID	404	Unique service number.
2	Service Name	Equipment Info Service	The specific name of the service.
3	Service Type	2	0: basic service; 1: integration service; 2: business process service
4	Server Address	https://www.abc.cn	The address required to access the service.
5	Access Method	1	0: GET request; 1: POST request
6	Web API	/device/info/list	Restful style API information of the interface.
7	Interface Parameter	page: 1; size: 200	Parameters that need to be provided by the access interface.
8	Interface Description	Equipment details	The specific function of the interface.
9	Return Parameter	{ "code":23, "msg":xxx, "data":xxx}	Parameter information returned by the service.
...	...	...	...

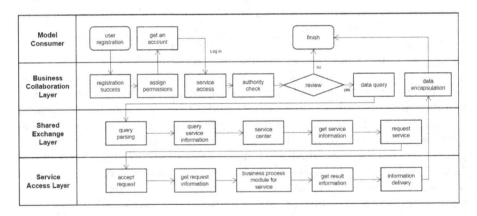

Fig. 4. Service usage flow chart.

rights. After obtaining the administrator's affirmation, the user can use the corresponding system. After the user logs in to the system, he will see the information table about the service, and the user can access the data according to the needs. However, at this time, the authority verification module will check the user's authority. If the user's authority does not meet the requirements of the current service, then Users cannot access related services. After the user obtains the relevant permissions, the business interaction layer can request services from the shared switching center through the data query module. The query analysis of the shared switching center will query the service information of the registration center according to the service information, and the service request will request the corresponding service according to the service information. After the service obtains the corresponding request, it will return the data to the business interaction layer according to the request information. The data encapsulation module of the business interaction layer will encapsulate the data into the form required by the user and return it to the user. At this point, the user's access to the service is completed.

5 Conclusion

This paper proposes a service-oriented data sharing and exchange model, which connects the original business systems in series in the form of services. This model is based on the original basic data services, and coordinates business services between different systems through a shared switching center, thereby realizing data intercommunication between systems. The service layer provides data source adaptation functions and can solve multi-source heterogeneous data source problem. At the same time, each service calls between services through the model, which reduces the coupling of the system, facilitates the interaction between the systems, and reduces the development cost of the system. It has been proved by practice that the system solves the "data island" problem in the government's business data interaction, greatly improves the government's work efficiency, and contributes to the expansion of government data services.

References

1. Balsari, S., et al.: Reimagining health data exchange: an application programming interface-enabled roadmap for India. J. Med. Internet Res. **20**(7), e10725 (2018)
2. Castro, C., Lopes, C.: Digital government and sustainable development. J. Knowl. Econ. **13**(2), 880–903 (2022)
3. Chatterjee, S., Sreenivasulu, N.: Personal data sharing and legal issues of human rights in the era of artificial intelligence: moderating effect of government regulation. Int. J. Electro. Gov. Res. (IJEGR) **15**(3), 21–36 (2019)
4. Durrant, A., Markovic, M., Matthews, D., May, D., Leontidis, G., Enright, J.: How might technology rise to the challenge of data sharing in agri-food? Global Food Security **28**, 100493 (2021). https://doi.org/10.1016/j.gfs.2021.100493. https://www.sciencedirect.com/science/article/pii/S2211912421000031
5. Gil-Garcia, J.R., Dawes, S.S., Pardo, T.A.: Digital government and public management research: finding the crossroads. Public Manag. Rev. **20**(5), 633–646 (2018)
6. Lu, X., Phang, K.: An enhanced hadoop heartbeat mechanism for mapreduce task scheduler using dynamic calibration. China Commun. **15**(11), 93–110 (2018). https://doi.org/10.1109/CC.2018.8543052

7. Martens, B., de Streel, A., Graef, I., Tombal, T., Duch-Brown, N.: Business-to-business data sharing: an economic and legal analysis. Electr. Eng. eJournal (2020). https://api.semanticscholar.org/CorpusID:225361918

8. Turoń, K.: From the classic business model to open innovation and data sharing-the concept of an open car-sharing business model. J. Open Innov.: Technol. Market Complex. **8**(1), 36 (2022)

9. Washington, A.L.: Government information policy in the era of big data. Rev. Policy Res. **31**(4), 319–325 (2014)

10. Zhang, A., Lv, N.: Research on the impact of big data capabilities on government's smart service performance: empirical evidence from China. IEEE Access **9**, 50523–50537 (2021). https://doi.org/10.1109/ACCESS.2021.3056486

11. Zhou, H., Zhao, Y., Shen, Q., Yang, L., Cai, H.: Risk assessment and management via multi-source information fusion for undersea tunnel construction. Autom. Constr. **111**, 103050 (2020)

Integrated Organization and Sharing Method and Platform for AI Computing Resources Based on Digital Object

Yishuai Zhao, Zhihui Ma, Shan Jiang, and Kun Liu[✉]

Advanced Institute of Big Data, Beijing, China
liukun@aibd.ac.cn

Abstract. This paper proposes an integrated organization and sharing method for AI computing resources based on digital object to address the lack of unified integration and management capabilities of computing power, data, algorithm, and AI framework required for AI computing. It also tackles the difficulty of sharing, discovery, and flexible scheduling of distributed computing resources under the condition of storage-computing separation architecture. This method encapsulates AI computing resources, such as computing power, data, algorithm, and AI framework into a digital object, which comes from the Digital Object Architecture. Leveraging the interconnectivity and interoperability of digital object resources under the data network, this method enables widespread discovery and shared use. Furthermore, an AI computing and sharing platform is designed to implement and verify this method. The platform's operation mode and application scenarios are also studied and analyzed in this paper.

Keywords: AI Computing Resources · Digital Object Architecture · Digital Object Encapsulation · Data Network · Distributed Operation Mode

1 Introduction

The advancement of hardware chip technology, for instance Graphics Processing Unit (GPU), in addition to vast data from the Internet and the Internet of Things has facilitated the realization of Artificial Intelligence (AI) through machine learning and deep learning algorithms. Consequently, the utilization of AI technology to implement data analysis has become a primary focus in big data. The unevenness in generation, storage, and utilization of big data, alongside the growing demand for AI data analysis, has seriously impeded the development of AI computing, due to low usage of AI computing resources including computing power, data, algorithm, and AI framework resources.

In the big data environment, data generation, storage and computation often happen in different business scenarios and involve independent nodes. The traditional approach of centrally deploying storage and computing resources leads to a waste of storage and computing resources. Splitting storage and computing resources into independent modules for construction offers significant advantages in the utilization rate of respective resources and deployment flexibility. This approach forms data center storing large amounts of data and computing center providing powerful computing services. Using storage-computing separation architecture for data storage and computation has become a mainstream idea for the country's coordinated use of computing power and data resources.

One of the main challenges faced in the current research of AI computing under big data, is how to integrate and manage various AI computing resources, as well as how to give distributed computing power resources the ability to be shared and used by a wide range of users under the storage-computation separation architecture. So that the computing power resources can be flexibly and efficiently dispatched to improve the efficiency and service capacity, and data and computing power resources can be coordinated for efficient AI computing under the storage-computation separation architecture.

One straightforward approach to creating an AI computing platform is to establish a local computing power environment and install an AI computing framework to process computation. However, this workshop-based AI computing platform may not be capable of delivering systematic AI computing services. For this purpose, several AI computing solutions are proposed.

Shreyas S Rao et al. [1] introduced Machine Learning as a Service (MLaaS) [2]. The MLaaS is deployed in a PaaS container-based environment, it separates model preparation, training, and prediction as individual services in AI computing. This design offers flexibility in model design, parameter configuration, and deployment through loosely-coupled architecture, thereby creating an end-to-end AI computing microservice for web-based applications in the cloud.

Sankie, a scalable general-purpose AI platform that extracts data from databases or data services and trains models, was proposed by Rahul Kumar et al. [3]. Sankie is built and deployed on Microsoft's Azure cloud, and its data extraction and model training are performed through Azure Batch. Additionally, Azure Cloud Service-Web Role is used for model prediction.

To better meet the performance requirements of AI computation, Philipp Moritz et al. [4] proposed Ray, a high-performance distributed computing engine. Ray's Master-Slave framework is similar to Hadoop and Spark, but Ray uniquely employs distributed bottom-up two-level task scheduling to enhance its efficiency. Within the entire cluster, Ray gives priority to employing local resources for executing AI computations, and schedules tasks to remote nodes based on the scheduling policy only when local resources are inadequate, thus realizing the automated management of AI computation resources.

The AI computing solutions listed above prioritize the organization and management of the AI computing training process, with emphasis on integrated management of computing resources. The Sankie platform goes a step further by including data resource management. However, all of the above solutions manage AI computing resources within the same computing center or cluster without considering the autonomous sharing of distributed computing resources across multiple centers, nor the integrated management of other AI computing resources, including data, algorithms, AI frameworks, and other related resources.

Digital Object Architecture (DOA) is a software architecture introduced by Professor Robert Kahn, the Turing Award laureate and the pioneer of the Internet [5]. It aims to resolve the issue of interoperability between information system resources in an open environment centred around Digital Object (DO). DOA efficiently overcomes the significant problem of interconnection and interoperability between heterogeneous information systems in the Internet environment [6]. It also offers a mechanism for discovering and sharing digital object resources. Gang Huang et al. [7] separated the data and applications and made the data as application independent resources using Digital Object.

To address the issues of discovering and scheduling computing power across different computing centers, as well as the absence of unified integration management of different types of AI computing resources in the current AI computing platform, this paper proposes an integrated method for organizing AI computing resources based on digital object. It combines DOA digital object with AI computing resources and organizes AI computing resources such as computing power, algorithm, data and AI framework as digital object, in accordance with the standards of DOA. Unlike the traditional cloud-centralized management of computing power, the method proposed in this paper enables distributed and autonomous computing power centers to not only unify and integrate the management of computing power, algorithm and data resources locally, but also realize AI computing resources can be widely discovered and used in the form of digital object under the storage-computation separation architecture.

The comparison of the digital object-based AI computing resource organization method proposed in this paper and the existing AI computing resource processing platforms mentioned above is presented in Table 1.

Table 1. Comparison table of the above AI computing platforms.

Capability	Proposed method	MLaaS	Sankie	Ray
Managing computing power resource	Yes	Yes	No	Yes
Managing data resource	Yes	No	Yes	No
Discovering computing power resource	Yes	No	No	No
Cross-cluster resource scheduling	Yes	No	No	No
Managing multiple AI computing resources	Yes	No	Yes	No
Executing AI computing directly	No	Yes	No	Yes
Dependence on cloud services	No	No	Yes	No

Based on this, the paper has designed a platform that integrates and shares AI computing resources using digital object. Through the platform, the research has achieved unified management of computing power, data, algorithm, and AI framework resources, as well as the sharing, discovery and use of AI computing resources in distributed operation mode, thus achieving efficient utilization of AI computing resources.

2 Organization of AI Computing Resources Based on Digital Object

2.1 Key Technology

Digital Object Architecture

The Digital Object Architecture that proposes the concept of digital object is one of the key technologies of the AI computing resource organization method proposed in this paper.

The DOA comprises one fundamental model, two essential protocols, and three core systems. The fundamental model denotes Digital Object, representing a unified abstraction of any possible data resources that can be classified into four constituents: identifier (DOID), metadata, status information and entity. Among these constituents, the DOID points to a digital object uniquely and irreversibly and remains a fundamental attribute of the digital object, regardless of the owner, storage location or the access method. The metadata describes the information about the digital object and is used for discovering and retrieving the digital object. The digital object's current location, usage status, access method, and other information for locating and accessing are described by status information; while the entity refers to the actual content of the digital object.

There are two essential protocols in DOA: The Digital Object Interface Protocol [8] (DOIP) is used to interact with digital objects or information systems that manage them, while the Digital Object Identifier Resolution Protocol [9] (DO-IRP) is used to create, assign, update, delete, and resolve identifiers.

The three core systems are the Digital Object Repository System, the Digital Object Registration System and the Digital Object Identification System. The Digital Object Repository System is mainly responsible for encapsulating, storing, accessing, and destroying digital objects. The Digital Object Registration System is primarily responsible for registering, releasing, modifying, and deleting metadata of digital object. Finally, the Digital Object Identification System is mainly responsible for creating, resolving, modifying, and destroying digital object identifiers.

The DOA's Digital Object Repository System and Digital Object Registration System respectively store the entities and metadata of digital objects. The Digital Object Registration System enables the sharing and discovery of digital objects by storing metadata, thereby addressing the challenge of data silos hindering sharing and discovery. The data network is the interconnection and interoperability network created through the DOA system between digital objects.

The digital object's encapsulation, search, and discovery techniques for AI computing resources are the focus of the research presented in this paper and serve as the foundation for AI computing resource sharing and use based on Digital Object Architecture.

The encapsulation is the process of creating digital objects from structured or unstructured resources in heterogeneous data source, in accordance with digital object standard. The goal of encapsulation is to import diverse resources into the data network to enable their sharing and use. This process converts physical data resources into digital objects and publishes them for use on the data network.

The search and discovery of digital object is a fundamental capability enabled by the data network, closely linked to digital object's metadata. The digital object's metadata represents a multi-dimensional feature description of the digital object aiding search and discovery of the digital object on the data network. After publication on the data network, users may search for a digital object using its DOID or search for the object's metadata using keywords to obtain results sorted by relevance. Users may then select the appropriate digital object to complete their operation.

Virtualization and Container Technology
The virtualization and container technologies are crucial supporting technologies for this paper.

The virtualization technology creates multiple virtual machines by partitioning the hardware resources of a single physical machine through software or hardware partitioning. Each virtual machine exhibits the same characteristics as a physical machine, allowing users to operate directly as if they were using a physical machine [10].

The resource pooling technology refers to the conversion of hardware, such as the Central Processing Unit (CPU), GPU, memory, disk, and network, into a dynamic resource pool that can be managed using software virtualization. This allows the resource integration and enhances the utilization rate. The virtualization of different types of resources serves as the foundation of pooling technology.

The container technology comprises container running and container orchestration technologies. The container running technology is a lightweight virtualization technology operating at the kernel level of the operating system, based on the Namespace and Cgroup technologies of the Linux kernel to encapsulate the process. The Namespace technology isolates the kernel resources, such as process number, filesystem, network, etc., whereas the Cgroup technology allocates, isolates, and restricts the group of processes' physical resources, such as CPU, memory, disk, IO, etc. [11]. In contrast to the traditional virtual machine technology, the container technology doesn't require virtualization of hardware devices or operating system as it runs processes directly in the host's kernel. So that the container has lower resource consumption, efficient resource utilization, faster boot time, and improved portability.

In a production environment, the container orchestration technology is necessary for managing the relationship between multiple containers. As the number of containerized applications increases, it becomes essential to coordinate container resources across multiple physical hosts, monitor the running state of each container, and manage the deployment and discovery of containers. The container orchestration technology provides the necessary solutions for these challenges.

The proposed AI computing resource organization method uses virtualization and pooling technology to transform physical computing power resources into resource pools. This allows digital object to select resources and encapsulate them without being restricted by the size of the physical resources. Additionally, a real AI computing runtime environment entity is created using container technology to perform AI computations when users employ the AI computing resource digital object.

2.2   AI Computing Resource Digital Object Encapsulation Implementation

An AI computing resource digital object is a digital encapsulation of computing power, algorithm and AI framework resources on the computing resources side, such as computing centers, in accordance with Digital Object Architecture standard. It comprises four parts: identification, metadata, status information, and entity. The metadata consists of discovery metadata and application metadata. The discovery metadata describes relevant information about the digital object that users can search and discover, and the application metadata describes how the digital object is used.

In the specific implementation, using resource pooling technology convert hardware like CPU, GPU, memory, disk, network, etc. into a resource pool that can be dynamically managed by software. The computing center obtains the AI computing resource digital object by encapsulating it in accordance with preset encapsulation standard based on pooled computing power resources, as well as AI algorithm and AI framework resources provided by the computing center.

In an AI computing resource digital object, the identification is used to uniquely identify the AI computing resource digital object. The discovery metadata provides descriptions of the maximum memory, maximum CPU, and maximum GPU resources that are available at the computing center, along with lists of available AI algorithm and AI framework resources. The application metadata describes how the AI computing resource digital object is used. The status information indicates the usage state of the AI computing resource digital object. The entity of the AI computing resource digital object is the runtime environment in which the AI computation runs, and it does not necessarily exist at the time of encapsulation.

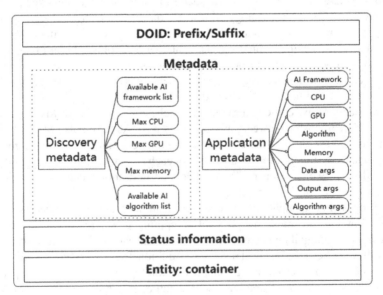

Fig. 1. AI computing resource digital object Illustration.

The AI computing resource digital object constructed in this paper is shown in Fig. 1, the DOID is an identifier, which consists of prefix and suffix according to the standard of DOA. The application metadata owns specific fields such as AI framework, CPU, GPU, algorithm, memory, data arguments, output arguments, algorithm arguments and so on, to describe how to use the DO to accomplish AI computation. The discovery metadata has available AI framework list, max CPU, max GPU, max memory, and available AI algorithm list, which provides the fields and information for search. The status info is the status information, and the entity is runtime environment, which is a container if it really exists.

According to the DOA theory, the metadata information and entity information of digital objects are independent of each other. Metadata provides information about the digital object, and users can comprehend the requisite information about digital objects through metadata without accessing the entity data.

The discovery metadata of the AI computing resources digital objects in this paper provides search information. After selecting a relevant AI computing resources digital object via discovery metadata information, the user inputs specific parameters for their AI computing task, including computing power parameters, algorithm parameters, data parameters, and input/output parameters based on the application metadata description. Subsequently, the user requests the computing center where the AI computing resources belong by using the parameters, and the computing center generates an entity to execute the AI computing task.

In practical terms, the Digital Object Identification System registers and assigns DOID, while the encapsulating party (such as the computing center) fills in the metadata and status information according to the standard of encapsulation and usage of the AI computing resources. Additionally, the container technology is leveraged to create the entity of the AI computing resource digital object, which is an AI computing runtime environment and generally generated when the user initiates AI computation.

3 AI Computing Platform Based on Digital Object

3.1 Design of AI Computing Platform

Figure 2 shows the AI computing platform based on digital object, which is divided into four layers starting from the bottom. The physical resource layer is at the bottom, followed by the container service layer at the second layer, the digital object management layer at the third layer, and the platform function layer at the top.

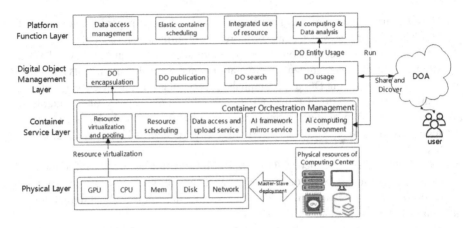

Fig. 2. Platform Architecture.

The physical resource layer deploys resources such as GPUs, CPUs, memory, hard disk and network. In an actual environment, the computing centers usually offer services and resources as clusters. This platform's physical resource layer utilizes the master-slave node arrangement to organize the whole distributed cluster, with one master node and N slave nodes in the entire cluster. The master node is a centralized management and scheduling module for the whole cluster. All other nodes directly or indirectly connect to the master node through the network to keep information synchronization and heartbeat with it. All the physical resource information of other nodes, such as IP address, GPU information, CPU information, memory information, and application task information, etc., is aggregated to the master node. Slave nodes are in charge of discovering and managing resources like GPUs on their physical nodes. They provide functions that include discovering and managing physical GPU resources, abstracting physical GPUs into elastic virtual GPUs, and executing GPU computing tasks for AI applications.

The container service layer is a crucial component of the platform that enables resource virtualization and pooling, resource scheduling, data access and upload service, AI framework mirror services, creation of the AI computing runtime environment, and other necessary functions through container technology. In a cluster environment, the platform services are typically provided by multiple containers running on various nodes. Manually deploying and managing these containers is impractical. To achieve efficient scheduling and management of containers, container orchestration management software is incorporated into the container service layer. This software enables resource scheduling, deployment management, service discovery, expansion, contraction, monitoring, and maintenance of containerized applications.

The digital object management layer executes various operations on digital objects. The encapsulation, publication, search, and usage of digital objects are part of this layer. The platform connects to the data network via the digital object management layer. An encapsulated AI computing resource digital object is shared by being published on the data network through this layer. Furthermore, other digital objects on the data network can also be searched and found. Encapsulating AI computing resource digital object within the digital object management layer is correlated with container service layer's resource virtualization and pooling function. The virtualization and pooling of physical resources, such as GPUs and CPUs, serves as the foundation for encapsulating AI computing resource digital object.

The platform function layer enables various AI computing-related business functions like data access management, elastic container scheduling, integrated use of resource, and AI computing and data analysis. The AI computing and data analysis refers to the specific application of AI computing resource digital object, and their final operation is conducted in the AI computing runtime environment established within the container service layer.

3.2 Key Capabilities

The AI computing platform based on digital object comprises the key capabilities as follows:

(1) The capabilities of unified resource management. It enables unified management of computing power, data, algorithm, and AI framework resources. GPU and other computing power resource virtualization and pooling is achieved through resource pooling technology, which enables on-demand allocation and scheduling management of resources. The platform utilizes container service to enable access and upload of data and algorithm code, ensuring a unified management of data and algorithm. Through container technology, we also can upload and manage different AI framework images effectively.

(2) The capabilities of AI computing resource digital object encapsulation. The platform guides the encapsulation of AI computing resource digital object. During the encapsulation process, the user provides specific information regarding discovery metadata and application metadata based on the available resources. The platform creates AI computing resource digital objects by encapsulating computing power, data, algorithm, and framework resources with DOID, metadata, and status information according to DOA digital object standard and the information provided by the user.

(3) The capabilities of sharing and discovering. The platform shares its own AI computing resource digital object on the data network. Other data network users can search for appropriate digital objects via the discovery metadata. After receiving the request of its own digital object, the platform can respond to users' requests for use of AI computing resource digital objects.

(4) The capabilities of creating an AI computing runtime environment and executing AI computing. The platform selects the corresponding computing power resources and user-specified AI framework from a variety of uniformly managed resources to create an AI computing runtime environment through container technology based on the user's request to use AI computing resources. The runtime environment carries out AI computation using data and algorithm specified in the request and output the corresponding AI computation results.

4 Operation Mode and Usage Scenarios

4.1 Operation Mode

The AI computing operation mode based on digital object is a data network distributed operation mode in which every computing center is both autonomous and distributed. Each center encapsulates and publishes its own AI computing resource digital objects, which are then shared through the data network to form a shared use of AI computing resources.

The distributed operation mode of AI computing based on digital object includes three main steps. In step 1, the computing center encapsulates AI computing resource digital objects and publishes them for sharing. In step 2, the user searches and discovers AI computation resources digital object to utilize them for AI computation. Finally, in step 3, the computing center creates an AI computing runtime environment to execute the computation as per the user's request with AI computing resource digital object.

The flowchart of the distributed operation mode is illustrated in Fig. 3. The computing center provides resource pooling service, container service, and AI framework image repository using the platform designed in this paper. The step 1 consists of the actions ① and ② depicted in Fig. 3, wherein the computing center encapsulates the AI computing resources as digital object.

In action ①, AI computing resource digital objects are encapsulated according to the DO standard. It describes resources in the discovery metadata of the AI computing resource digital object based on free quantity and combination rationing strategies of resources such as the maximum memory, maximum CPU, and maximum GPU computing resources, as well as the available AI algorithms and AI frameworks provided by the computing center. It describes the usage of the AI computing resource digital object in the application metadata and the use status in the status information. The AI computing resource digital object's entity is a runtime environment that is not necessarily materialized during encapsulation. When DOID is assigned, the encapsulation of digital object is completed. In action ②, the computing center publishes the AI computing resource digital object on the network, which the users can discover and use through the data network.

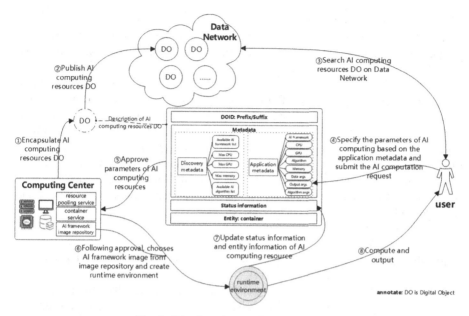

Fig. 3. Distributed Operation Mode Flow.

The step 2 of the distributed operation mode is the user to search for and use AI computing resource digital objects, which consists of actions ③ and ④ in Fig. 3. In action ③, the users search for AI computing resource digital objects on the data network using DOIDs or keywords, based on their specific needs for AI computing. In action ④, users select the appropriate AI computing resource digital object, specify the necessary parameters such as computing power, algorithm, AI framework, data address, result output path, and then submits the AI computation request.

The step 3 of the distributed operation mode involves the computing center response to the user's computing request for AI computing resource digital object, as summarized in actions ⑤ to ⑧ in the Fig. 3. Once the user submits an AI computing request, the computing center receives it for approval in action ⑤. Following approval in action ⑥, the center selects computing resources from the pool of resources, chooses an AI framework image from the AI framework image repository with user-given AI framework parameters, and creates a runtime environment by container technology. Then the status information of the relevant AI computing resource digital object is changed to occupied in action ⑦. In action ⑧, the AI computation is proceeded using the user-selected or user-provided algorithm and data in runtime environment. Once the AI computation is complete, the computing center sends the AI computation results to the user-specified address, and changes the status information of the relevant AI computing resource digital object to idle.

4.2 Application Scenarios

Application Scenarios for Unified Convergence of Computing Resources

In scenarios such as computing centers or self-built machine rooms that provide local

AI computing, this paper proposes an integrated organization and shared management platform for AI computing resources. This platform enables the unified integration of computing power, data, algorithm, and AI framework, provides better support for the unified management of resources in AI computing, and enables the AI computing service with rapid data access, flexible resource scheduling, and rapid environment construction.

In this scenario, users can benefit from the AI computing resources integrated organizational and sharing management platform proposed in this paper. They won't need to worry about data access and storage and they can directly use the different AI frameworks pre-integrated into the platform, instead of having to manually build each one. Additionally, the resource pooling technology and container technology enable the flexible scheduling and maximum utilization rate of computing resources such as GPUs and CPUs. These advantages have significant practical implications for improving the efficiency of local AI computing platforms, reducing redundant construction efforts, and conserving computing power resources.

Application Scenarios for the Shared Use of Computing Resources Under Storage-Computation Separation Architecture

Aiming at the scenario of AI computing under the storage-computing separation architecture. The distributed computing centers have a wealth of computing power resources, but lack the ability to widely share them. By using the AI computing platform proposed in this paper, the computing centers can encapsulate computing power, algorithm, and AI framework resources as digital objects, publish them on the data network to promote the sharing and usage of autonomous, distributed computing power resources through the platform.

This scenario involves users searching and discovering AI computing resources through the data network, using relevant resources with guide of application metadata, and requesting computation for the distributed computing center which the resources belong to. The computing center then selects appropriate computing power, algorithm, and AI framework resources to create an AI computing environment that completes the computation. This approach facilitates the discovery and sharing of AI computing resources autonomously across distributed computing centers. This method is not only critical in organizing and scheduling AI computing resources flexibly and efficiently under a storage-computing separation architecture, but also in improving utilization rate of resources in distributed computing centers.

Example of Application Scenarios in the Financial Sector

The AI computing has various applications in the financial sector, including risk assessment, fraud detection, algorithmic trading models, and other fields. However, financial institutions may not have a robust computing center, one specific application scenario proposed in this paper is to search for AI computing resource digital objects on the data network and use them for AI computation in the financial field.

As shown in Fig. 4, assuming that a financial institution intends to implement the TensorFlow framework for running DNN models to evaluate customer risk levels through AI computation, it should begin by searching for AI computing resource digital object on the data network using "TensorFlow" or "DNN" as a keyword. After selecting the appropriate idle status digital object, the financial institution chooses the GPU, CPU, memory, and other resource parameters as well as the TensorFlow AI framework according to the description of the application metadata and fills in algorithm address, data address, and result output address. After receiving the AI computing request, the computing center will review and approve the request. Once the approval is granted, the computing center will select appropriate computing resources and AI framework based on the parameters provided by the financial institution. Then the center employs container technology to create the AI runtime environment with a TensorFlow framework. This environment uses the specific data and algorithm from the financial institution to complete the AI computing. The results are then delivered to the designated output address.

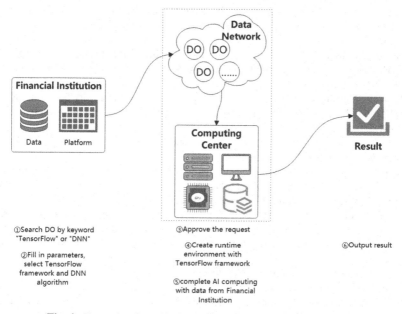

Fig. 4. Example of Application Scenarios in the Financial Sector.

In this application scenario, the financial institutions do not need to construct local computing centers. They can leverage the TensorFlow framework to evaluate customer risk levels through AI computing resource digital object discovered via the data network. This process lowers AI computing expenses for financial institutions and enhances computing center resource utilization.

5   Conclusion

This paper proposes a flexible method for encapsulating AI computing resources such as computing power, algorithms, and AI frameworks into schedulable digital objects. The paper explores the mechanism for realizing cross-domain discovery and sharing of AI computing resources under the unified protocol and standard of DOA. Building on this method, we designed and implemented an AI computing platform that integrates computing power, algorithm, data and AI framework of AI computing resources based on digital objects. Additionally, we studied and analyzed the operation mode and application scenarios of the AI computing platform to provide methodological references for more efficient AI computing under the storage-computing separation architecture.

References

1. Rao, S.S., Pradyumna, S., Kalambur, S., Sitaram, D.: Bodhisattva - rapid deployment of AI on containers. In: IEEE International Conference on Cloud Computing in Emerging Markets (CCEM), pp. 100–104. IEEE (2018)
2. Li, L.E., Chen, E., Hermann, J., Zhang, P., Wang, L.: Scaling machine learning as a service. In: Proceedings of the 3rd International Conference on Predictive Applications and APIs, pp. 14–29 (2017)
3. Kumar, R., Bansal, C., Maddila, C., Sharma, N., Martelock, S., Bhargava, R.: Building sankie: an AI platform for DevOps 2019. In: IEEE/ACM 1st International Workshop on Bots in Software Engineering (BotSE), pp. 48–53. IEEE (2019)
4. Moritz, P., Nishihara, R., Wang, S., et al.: Ray: a distributed framework for emerging {AI} applications. In: 13th USENIX Symposium on Operating Systems Design and Implementation (OSDI) 2018, pp. 561–577 (2018)
5. Kahn, R., Wilensky, R.: A framework for distributed digital object services. Int. J. Digit. Librar. 6(2), 115–123 (2006)
6. Sharp, C.: Overview of the digital object architecture (DOA). An Internet Society Information Paper, Internet Society. https://www.internetsociety.org/resources/doc/2016/overview-of-the-digital-object-architecture-doa. Accessed 31 Aug 2023
7. Huang, G., Luo, C., Wu, K., Ma, Y., Zhang, Y., Liu, X.: Software-defined infrastructure for decentralized data lifecycle governance: principled design and open challenges. In: IEEE 39th International Conference on Distributed Computing Systems (ICDCS), pp. 1674–1683 (2019)
8. Digital Object Interface Protocol Specification version 2.0. https://www.dona.net/sites/default/files/2018-11/DOIPv2Spec_1.pdf. Accessed 31 Aug 2023
9. Digital Object Identifier Resolution Protocol Specification version 3.0. https://www.dona.net/sites/default/files/2022-06/DO-IRPV3.0--2022-06-30.pdf. Accessed 31 Aug 2023
10. Creasy, R.J.: The origin of the VM/370 time-sharing system. IBM J. Res. Dev. 25(5), 483–490 (1981)
11. Zhuang, Z., Tran, C., Weng, J., Ramachandra, H., Sridharan, B.: Taming memory related performance pitfalls in Linux Cgroups. In: International Conference on Computing, Networking and Communications (ICNC), pp. 531–535. IEEE (2017)

Machine Learning for Medical Applications

Review of Machine Learning Algorithms for Breast Cancer Diagnosis

Man Chen, Wuyue Fan, Weiye Tang, Tianhao Liu, Daren Li,
and Omar Dib(✉) iD

Department of Computer Science, Wenzhou-Kean University, Wenzhou, China
{cheman,fanwu,tangwei,tiliu,lidar,odib}@kean.edu

Abstract. Breast cancer remains a global health challenge, contributing significantly to mortality worldwide. Addressing this critical issue, we review existing machine-learning algorithms for accurate breast cancer diagnosis. Our research employs an ensemble of algorithms, including Gaussian Naive Bayes, XGBoost, Support Vector Machine, Logistic Regression, Principal Component Analysis, Linear Discriminant Analysis, k Nearest Neighbors, Random Forest, Decision Tree Classifier, and an ensemble classifier. This study relies on specialized data preprocessing and balancing techniques, ensuring the reliability of the analysis. Our approach utilizes two prominent datasets, the Wisconsin Breast Cancer Diagnosis (WBCD) and the Wisconsin Diagnostic Breast Cancer (WDBC) dataset, carefully partitioned with a 5-fold cross-validation strategy. The evaluation protocol is comprehensive, spanning diverse performance metrics. We explore confusion matrices, accuracy, precision, recall, F1 score, the area under the curve (AUC), and Receiver Operating Characteristic (ROC) curves. Notably, in classifying benign and malignant tumors using the WBCD dataset, the SVM model stands out with a detection accuracy of 99.27%, complemented by precision, recall, and F1-score, all achieving 99.28%. Transitioning to the WDBC dataset, the XGBoost model emerges as the optimal choice, attaining accuracy, precision, recall, and F1-score values of 98.25%.

Keywords: Medical Diagnosis · Breast Cancer · Machine Learning Algorithms · Classification · Hyperparameter Optimization

1 Introduction

Breast cancer (BC) has surpassed lung cancer as the most often diagnosed disease and the fifth leading cause of cancer deaths worldwide. The International Agency for Research on Cancer released GLOBOCAN 2020 data from 185 countries showing 2.3 million new cases of BC (11.7%) and a mortality rate of 6.9% [18]. However, many individuals do not show symptoms in the early stages of the disease. Regular breast screenings can help detect and treat BC early, especially for individuals with a high risk. Hence, developing efficient and accurate diagnostic and detection tools for BC is paramount in medical research and healthcare

Y. Tan and Y. Shi (Eds.): DMBD 2023, CCIS 2018, pp. 229–243, 2024.
https://doi.org/10.1007/978-981-97-0844-4_17

[19]. The American Cancer Society identifies several types of BC, such as ductal carcinoma in situ, invasive ductal carcinoma, inflammatory BC, and metastatic BC. Some invasive BCs are characterized by unique features or developmental patterns that can influence their treatment and prognosis. These cancer types are less common but may present more severe health risks than others [15].

Thanks to their ability to extract knowledge from complex datasets, using machine learning (ML) algorithms to diagnose and classify BC variants can significantly improve healthcare outcomes. ML techniques have demonstrated significant potential in predicting, classifying, and prognosis BC [11,12]. They enable medical practitioners to differentiate benign from malignant tumors, enhancing the accuracy of BC classification. This technological advancement is particularly pertinent given the variety of BC types. In addition to their direct medical advantages, ML techniques greatly lower the costs of conventional diagnostic techniques [9]. ML algorithms have also found extensive application beyond medical sectors, notably in tuberculosis detection [8] and gene-based understanding of Autism [14]. Moreover, their utilization extends into non-medical domains like agriculture [23].

Building a ML system involves gathering sensitive data. This can be challenging in the medical field since it requires protecting patient privacy and data security while addressing ethical concerns. Patient data must be safeguarded to ensure privacy and prevent unauthorized use [13]. Moreover, the collection, archiving, and use of such data must strictly abide by legal and ethical requirements. Fortunately, Wisconsin Breast Cancer Diagnostic (WBCD), along with the Wisconsin breast cancer (WDBC) dataset, have become recognized as a benchmark dataset for BC detection and classification and are accessible online at the UCI ML repository [21,22].

This study leverages ML's potential and optimization techniques to refine the efficiency of BC classification. Based on various models, including the Gaussian Naive Bayes, XGBoost, Logistic Regression, Linear Discriminant Analysis, K-Nearest Neighbor, Support Vector Machine, Decision Tree Classifier, Random Forest Classifier, and Voting Classifier, we undertook a thorough assessment of each model's performance in classifying BC. The performance of these models was evaluated based on accuracy, precision, recall, and F1 score. Furthermore, a receiver operating characteristic (ROC) diagram was used to compare the models. Our study thoroughly examines two widely used BC datasets: WBCD and WDBC. Our comprehensive performance evaluation assesses the effectiveness of ML algorithms and data preprocessing techniques in BC classification. The ultimate goal is to identify the most efficient ML methods, contributing to advancements in early detection and intervention strategies for BC.

The paper is organized as follows: Sect. 2 reviews critical BC detection studies conducted from 2015 to 2022. Section 3 presents the datasets. We detail the ML-based framework for BC in Sect. 4. Section 5 presents the experimental results. Finally, Sect. 6 concludes the paper and outlines future directions.

2 Literature Review

Numerous investigations have leveraged ML models for BC analysis, specifically focusing on the Wisconsin Breast Cancer Dataset (WBCD) and the Wisconsin Diagnostic Breast Cancer (WDBC) dataset. For example, S. Kharya and S. Soni [12] proposed a predictive model called "Weighted Naive Bayes Classifier (WNBC)" in 2016 for BC detection, using the WBCD dataset. The model achieves 92% accuracy without using any sampling strategy. This indicates that the WNBC method may not be able to handle complex data relationships. In 2018, Bayes et al. [7] introduced a Naïve Bayes method and adopted a 10-fold cross-validation sampling strategy to measure the unbiased estimate, achieving a significantly improved accuracy of 97.36%. In the same year, Amrane et al. [4] proposed a KNN model, which used 60% of the data for training and 40% for testing, achieving an accuracy of 97.51%. Despite its high accuracy, The KNN method may be computationally expensive for large-scale datasets. The MLP model proposed by A. F. Agarap [1] uses 70% of the data for training and 30% of the data for testing, achieving 99.04% accuracy. The MLP algorithm performs well in terms of accuracy, surpassing most existing algorithms in BC detection. However, training the deep neural network requires large data and computing resources and might be prone to overfitting issues. The TAN model proposed by Ponniah et al. [20] achieves 94.11% accuracy using a 70–30 train-test split. The TAN model combines Naive Bayes and Tree Augmented Naive Bayes methods, allowing it to handle feature dependencies and correlations. However, in some cases, it may suffer from overfitting the data. In 2019, Bayrak et al. [6] used SVM for detecting pancreatic cancer. They partitioned the dataset into a 66–33 training-testing split and employed 10-fold cross-validation. The final accuracy achieved was 97%. In the same year, Omondiagbe et al. [17] introduced a novel BC diagnostic method that utilizes Linear Discriminant Analysis (LDA) to reduce dimensionality on high-dimensional features. The reduced dataset was then applied to SVM. Experimental results demonstrated the significant innovation of this approach, achieving an accuracy of 98.82%.

In the following years, researchers continued to optimize models, leading to substantial advancements in cancer detection. In 2020, P. Gupta and S. Garg [11] introduced the Adam Gradient Descent model, which achieved a satisfactory accuracy of 98.24% without employing any sampling strategies. This indicates that the method addresses BC prediction tasks well and does not require additional data processing or sampling. However, the performance of this method may be sensitive to the characteristics of the data, and the presence of noise or outliers in the dataset might affect the model's performance. Furthermore, Ak et al. [2] proposed the Logistic Regression (LR) model in the same year, using 80% of the dataset for training and 20% for testing, resulting in an accuracy of 98.1%. LR exhibits good scalability for large-scale datasets and provides information about the contribution of different features to BC prediction. Nevertheless, LR's handling of complex relationships between features may be less flexible, limiting its performance on certain complex problems.

In 2022, Ogundokun et al. [16] proposed a cancer diagnosis system based on ANN that can accurately differentiate between malignant and benign tumors. The ANN model achieved a high accuracy of 99.2% using 10-fold cross-validation and a 65–35 training-testing split. Similarly, Alshayeji et al. [3] utilized an ANN model to diagnose and predict BC, splitting their data into 80% for training and 20% for testing. They conducted various evaluations using 5-fold cross-validation on the model and achieved an accuracy of 99.85%. ANN can automatically learn and extract features from the data, reducing the feature selection burden. However, it demands computational resources and may require considerable time and computational power during training.

The above models possess both strengths and limitations. Many studies focus solely on a single dataset, often facing class imbalance and reproducibility challenges. Some models lack effective sampling strategies, and their performance metrics may not be comprehensively assessed. Applying advanced models to limited datasets can also lead to overfitting and compromised generalizability. Thus, selecting the most suitable model for BC prediction requires weighing factors such as data features, sampling techniques, performance evaluation, prediction requirements, and computational resources. Achieving a reproducible, precise, and robust BC prediction solution entails thoroughly considering these aspects and advocating for reproducibility through an open-source code framework.

3   Breast Cancer Dataset

This study employs the Wisconsin Breast Cancer (WBCD) and Wisconsin Diagnostic Breast Cancer (WDBC) datasets. These contain labeled malignant and benign instances to train ML algorithms for tumor classification. The datasets encompass features extracted from digitized breast mass fine needle aspirates (FNA) images. These features offer insights into cell nuclei characteristics within the images. The WBCD consists of 699 instances, each represented by a nine-feature vector. Each feature, drawn from a Fine Needle Aspiration (FNA) sample of a suspicious breast mass, is assigned a value between 1 and 10 based on the diagnosis. A 1 indicates normal or benign cases, whereas a score of 10 represents the most abnormal or potentially malignant instances [21]. Malignant cases are confirmed through biopsy examination, while benign cases are determined by biopsy or periodic examination. The Wisconsin Diagnostic Breast Cancer Dataset (WDBC) comprises 569 instances, each encapsulating 30 features. The attributes constitute ten primary real-valued features. Each attribute is further detailed by the mean, standard error, and the "worst" or largest value (mean of the three largest values).

Figure 1 illustrates a disparity in the WBCD and WDBC datasets. The WBCD encompasses 444 benign tumors, amounting to 65.01% of its total content, and 239 malignant tumors, forming the residual 34.99%. Conversely, the WDBC contains 357 benign tumor instances, making up 63% of its total instances, and 212 malignant instances, contributing the remaining 37%. The

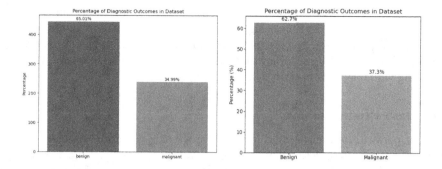

Fig. 1. Benign vs malignant tumors in 1)WBCD 2)WDBC

distinctive composition of each dataset underscores the need for a tailored approach in applying ML models to ensure reliable and accurate classifications.

4   Breast Cancer Classification Framework

We present the Breast cancer framework that utilizes different ML algorithms to detect malignant and benign cancers. Figure 2 shows the architecture including two main stages: data pre-processing and model training.

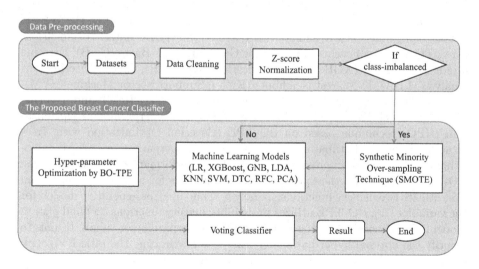

Fig. 2. A Breast Cancer Classifier Framework

Firstly, selecting a well-curated and standardized dataset is essential, followed by pre-processing steps, including data cleaning, normalization, and addressing class imbalance issues. Multiple ML models are then employed for training and testing. A voting classifier combines the predictions from these models, and hyper-parameter optimization using BO-TPE (Bayesian optimization and tree-structured Parzen estimator) is performed. Finally, the classifier's results are presented, enhancing the accuracy and performance of BC classification, thereby providing valuable assistance in clinical diagnosis.

4.1   Data Pre-processing

We first perform data cleaning during pre-processing to handle missing values, outliers, or erroneous data. Next, we apply Z-score normalization, transforming the data into a mean of 0 and a standard deviation of 1. In addition, we address class imbalance issues, as the cleaned and normalized datasets might exhibit distribution disparities among the classes. This imbalance can lead to poor training performance for minority classes. To tackle this, we employ the Synthetic Minority Over-sampling Technique (SMOTE) to generate artificial samples and increase the number of samples in the minority class. Unlike traditional sampling methods, SMOTE operates in the feature rather than the data space. This allows it to preserve the distribution of original data features better and generate more representative synthetic samples. By considering the features of neighboring samples, SMOTE demonstrates higher accuracy and effectiveness in addressing class imbalance problems.

4.2   The Breast Cancer Classifiers

This study presents two ML systems for BC diagnosis: one based on the WBCD dataset using nine features and another based on the WDBC dataset using 30 features. The models of each system include Gaussian Naive Bayes (GNB), Extreme Gradient Boosting (XGBoost), Logistic Regression (LR), Linear Discriminant Analysis (LDA), K-Nearest Neighbors (KNN), Support Vector Machine (SVM), Decision Tree Classifier (DTC), Random Forest Classifier (RFC), and a Voting ensemble model. Furthermore, this study employs a Hyperparameter Optimization (HPO) technique based on BO-TPE (Bayesian Optimization with Tree-structured Parzen Estimator) to fine-tune the hyperparameters of ML algorithms. This process improved the algorithms' performance and effectiveness. BO-TPE aims to find the optimal hyper-parameters for a given ML algorithm that utilizes two density functions, namely $l(x)$ and $g(x)$, as generative models for the variables [10]. BO-TPE utilizes probability density functions $l(x)$ and $g(x)$ to model the likelihood of finding good and poor hyperparameter values. It aims to identify the optimal hyper-parameter values by maximizing the ratio $l(x)/g(x)$, effectively guiding the search towards promising regions in the hyper-parameter space. Additionally, BO-TPE is versatile and capable of simultaneously optimizing various types of hyper-parameters. This makes it particularly well-suited for optimizing hyper-parameters in ML models that often have multiple hyper-parameters to tune. By leveraging the probabilistic modeling and efficient search strategy of BO-TPE, we can significantly enhance the performance of ML models. This leads to more accurate and effective models for tasks such as our BC classification research. Ultimately, we seize the advantages of ensemble learning, combining several models to classify BC. This paradigm exploits the distinctive strengths of a diverse suite of algorithms, thereby yielding a classification decision that generally outperforms individual models [5]. The ensemble technique deployed encapsulates a soft voting strategy for classification, incorporating all the aforementioned models. This approach considers the individual predictions of each model for every data sample and adjudicates the final prediction predicated on the averaged probability. This assembly strategy effectively amalgamates the individual strengths of the constituent models, thereby augmenting the overall performance and dependability of classification.

5   Experimental Study

Our development of the BC classifiers uses Python libraries to perform feature engineering, ML training, hyperparameter optimization, and data visualization. We employ Pandas for data manipulation and pre-processing, Scikit-learn for implementing ML algorithms and evaluating their performance, Matplotlib for data visualization, and XGBoost for harnessing the capabilities of the gradient-boosting model.

We employed a robust server computer, the Dell Precision 3660 Tower, to conduct experiments and train the models. This machine had a high-performance i9-12900 central processing unit (CPU) featuring 16 cores and a base clock speed of 2.40 GHz. Furthermore, the server boasted ample memory capacity, specifically 64 GB, ensuring the system's capability to handle the computationally intensive demands of the training process. To ensure reproducibility, we have made the complete source code of our project publicly available on GitHub. The repository can be accessed using the following URL: https://github.com/odib/ Breast_Cancer_Classification.

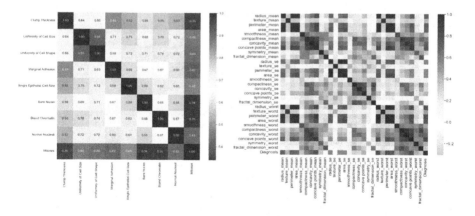

Fig. 3. Correlation heatmap of features 1) WBCD 2) WDBC

This section evaluates the ML system's performance in identifying benign and malignant BC tumors for the WBCD and the WDBC datasets. Each dataset is split into two parts: 80% for training and 20% for testing. To further enhance the reliability of our results, we employ 5-fold cross-validation during the training and testing processes.

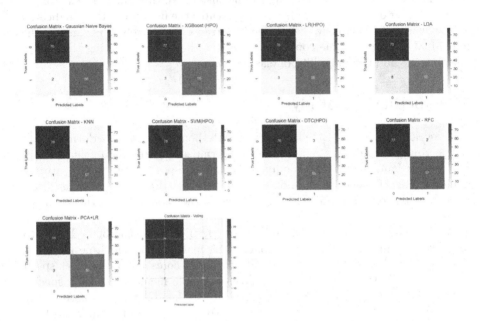

Fig. 4. Confusion Matrices of models for WBCD Dataset

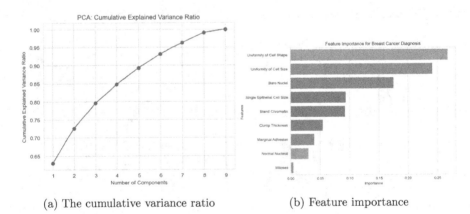

(a) The cumulative variance ratio   (b) Feature importance

Fig. 5. Cumulative variance and Feature importance for the WBCD Dataset

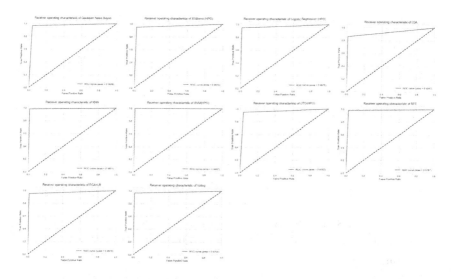

Fig. 6. ROC curves of models for WBCD

Analysis for WBCD Dataset. The WBCD dataset has 699 instances with 9 features per instance. We excluded 16 instances, each with missing feature values. SMOTE was applied only to the training data to address the class imbalance issue. The class distribution was assessed before and after applying SMOTE. Initially, the training data had 365 instances of the benign class and 181 instances of the malignant class. After SMOTE, the training data achieved a balanced distribution of 365 instances for each class. The features were normalized using the StandardScaler method to ensure fair comparisons and reliable evaluations.

The exploratory data analysis for the WBCD dataset began with comparing the feature distributions for benign and malignant instances. Each feature's histograms were analyzed, revealing distinctive attribute patterns. For instance, the distribution of 'uniformity of cell size' and 'uniformity of cell shape' for benign instances generally skewed towards lower values, whereas malignant cases showed a more dispersed distribution. Similarly, differences were observed for 'marginal adhesion', 'single epithelial cell size', 'bare nuclei', 'bland chromatin', and 'normal nucleoli'.

Next, we assessed the correlation between different tumor features. This analysis, visualized as a heatmap in Fig. 3, elucidates the linear relationships between variables. The correlation analysis yielded several pairs of features with a strong correlation value. Below are these pairs along with their correlation coefficients: 'Uniformity of Cell Size' and 'Uniformity of Cell Shape' with a correlation of 0.907. 'Uniformity of Cell Size' and 'Bland Chromatin' correlate with 0.756. 'Uniformity of Cell Size' and 'Single Epithelial Cell Size' with a correlation of 0.754. 'Uniformity of Cell Shape' and 'Bland Chromatin' correlate with 0.735. 'Uniformity of Cell Shape' and 'Single Epithelial Cell Size' with a correlation of 0.722. These strong correlations indicate a high degree of interdependence between

Table 1. Performance Metrics of classification Models for WBCD Dataset

Model	Accuracy	Precision	Recall	F1-score	5-fold CV average accuracy	ROC-AUC
GNB	96.35%	96.37%	96.35%	96.35%	96.16%	96.38%
XGBoost	96.35%	96.35%	96.35%	96.35%	96.85%	96.15%
LR	97.08%	97.11%	97.08%	97.07%	96.30%	96.78%
LDA	93.43%	93.81%	93.43%	93.36%	96.30%	92.47%
KNN	98.54%	98.54%	98.54%	98.54%	96.85%	98.51%
SVM	99.27%	99.28%	99.27%	99.27%	96.99%	99.37%
DTC	95.62%	95.62%	95.62%	95.62%	96.30%	95.52%
RFC	97.81%	97.83%	97.81%	97.81%	97.12%	97.87%
PCA-LR	97.08%	97.11%	97.08%	97.07%	96.44%	96.78%
Voting	97.81%	97.82%	97.81%	97.81%	97.12%	97.64%

these features. Recognizing this, we accounted for multicollinearity in our subsequent model selection and training process, as it could otherwise adversely affect the model performance and interpretability. The identified highly correlated feature pairs were carefully considered during the feature selection process, often choosing to include only one feature from each correlated pair to avoid redundancy in our feature space.

As the initial evaluation step, the confusion matrices and ROC curves using five-fold cross-validation are depicted in Fig. 4 and Fig. 6, respectively. Table 1 summarizes the performance metrics of the various ML models applied to the WBCD dataset. As can be noticed, the ML models successfully classified BC tumors using the WBCD dataset. The average accuracy across all models was found to be 97.25%, indicating high predictive capability. Additionally, the precision, recall, and F1-score metrics were consistently high across the models, indicating a good overall balance between true positives, true negatives, false positives, and false negatives in the classification results. The 5-fold cross-validation average accuracy also yielded an average of 96.82%, further supporting the robustness and generalizability of the models.

PCA was applied to the WBCD dataset to reduce the feature space while maximizing the total variance. Retaining 7 principal components captured over 95% of the total variance, enabling improved efficiency in subsequent ML models by reducing computational complexity as shown in Fig. 5a. Retraining the model using PCA-LR showed highly similar results to the original model without PCA. This similarity in performance indicates that PCA's dimensionality reduction had minimal impact on classification performance, making PCA-LR a computationally efficient alternative with comparable predictive capabilities.

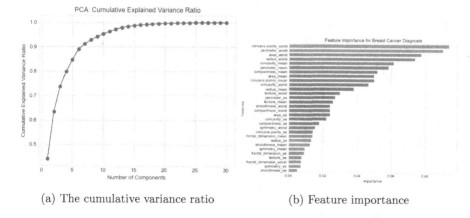

(a) The cumulative variance ratio   (b) Feature importance

Fig. 7. Cumulative variance and Feature importance for the WDBC Dataset

Results also indicate that the SVM model emerged as the most accurate model among all the evaluated models, achieving a high accuracy of 99.27%. The SVM demonstrated high precision, recall, and F1-score, all at a remarkable level of 99.28%, 99.27%, and 99.27%, respectively. These metrics further validate the SVM's ability to accurately identify malignant and benign tumors while minimizing false positives and negatives. In addition, the SVM model exhibited high discriminative power, as evidenced by its ROC-AUC value of 99.37%, underlining its robustness in making reliable predictions.

The RFC model was trained on the dataset, and its feature importances were extracted. To visualize the importance of each feature, we created a bar plot that ranked the features based on their importance scores. The bar plot provides insights into which features are crucial in BC diagnosis prediction, as shown in Fig. 5b. This allows researchers to identify the most influential features, which may help in feature selection and understanding the significance of each feature in the classification task.

Analysis for WDBC Dataset. The WDBC dataset consists of 569 instances, each comprising 30 features. This dataset has no missing feature values, rendering it complete and suitable for analysis. Before applying SMOTE, the training data comprised 286 benign and 169 malignant instances. After applying SMOTE, the training data achieved a balanced distribution, with 286 instances for each class. Then we normalized the features using the StandardScaler method.

We analyzed further by generating histograms to compare tumor features between benign and malignant cases. The histograms were created for each tumor characteristic and reported in Fig. 3. Furthermore, we calculated the correlation of the features with a correlation coefficient greater than 0.7. Some highly correlated feature pairs in the WDBC dataset are: 'radius_mean' and 'perimeter_mean', 'radius_worst' and 'perimeter_worst', 'radius_mean' and 'area_mean',

240   M. Chen et al.

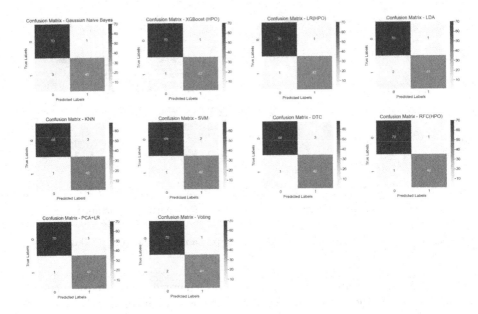

Fig. 8. Confusion Matrices of models for the WDBC dataset

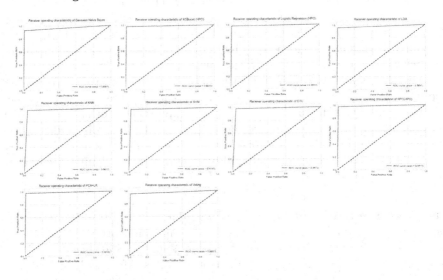

Fig. 9. ROC curves of models for the WDBC dataset

and 'perimeter_mean' and 'area_mean'. These high correlation values indicate a strong linear relationship between the features and may impact model performance due to multicollinearity.

Table 2. Performance Metrics of Models for the WDBC dataset

Model	Accuracy	Precision	Recall	F1-score	5-fold CV average accuracy	ROC-AUC
GNB	96.49%	96.52%	96.49%	96.47%	94.23%	95.81%
XGBoost	98.25%	98.25%	98.25%	98.24%	96.33%	98.13%
LR	98.25%	98.25%	98.25%	98.25%	97.73%	98.13%
LDA	97.37%	97.37%	97.37%	97.36%	97.21%	96.97%
KNN	96.49%	96.58%	96.49%	96.51%	97.73%	96.72%
SVM	97.37%	97.40%	97.37%	97.37%	94.25%	97.43%
DTC	96.49%	96.58%	96.49%	96.51%	94.06%	96.72%
RFC	98.25%	98.25%	98.25%	98.25%	97.03%	98.13%
PCA-LR	98.25%	98.25%	98.25%	98.25%	97.73%	98.13%
Voting	97.37%	97.37%	97.37%	97.36%	98.25%	96.97%

The performance of various ML models on the WDBC dataset is reported in Fig. 8 and 9. Furthermore, the average performance metrics of the WDBC models were calculated in Table 2. Results indicate that the models achieved an average accuracy of 97.78%, precision of 97.80%, recall of 97.78%, and F1-score of 97.77%, and the ROC-AUC score averaged at 97.40%. Among the models, XGBoost and Logistic Regression (LR) achieved the highest accuracy of 98.25%, demonstrating their superior ability to classify BC cases effectively. Both models also exhibited high precision, recall, and F1-score, confirming their superiority. In addition, the 5-fold cross-validation average accuracy for LR was 97.73%, showcasing its consistency and robustness across different data subsets.

PCA-LR, a model trained using Principal Component Analysis to reduce feature space while maintaining information content, achieved performance metrics similar to the original LR model without PCA. This suggests that PCA effectively reduced dimensionality without compromising classification accuracy. We use the cumulative explained variance ratio shown in Fig. 7a to calculate the number of principal components to keep in PCA. The number of components kept in PCA was 10, as it captured a significant portion of the dataset's variance. The RFC model was fitted on the BC dataset, and the feature importances were obtained and depicted in Fig. 7b. The top 5 features with the highest importance are: concave points_worst, perimeter_worst, area_worst, radius_worst, concavity_mean.

6   Conclusions

This study employed various data preprocessing and machine-learning techniques for breast cancer (BC) diagnosis. Each model has been fine-tuned through an advanced hyperparameter optimization technique. Rigorous testing has been conducted using the Wisconsin Breast Cancer Diagnosis (WBCD) and the Wisconsin Diagnosis Breast Cancer (WDBC) datasets. Results indicate that when tasked with discerning benign from malignant tumors within the WBCD dataset, the SVM model exhibited a remarkable performance, achieving an Accuracy of 99.27%, Precision of 99.28%, Recall of 99.27%, F1-score of 99.27%, and ROC-AUC of 99.37%. For the WDBC dataset, the XGBoost model emerged as the optimal choice, demonstrating high Accuracy, Precision, Recall, and F1-score, all at 98.25%, with a ROC-AUC of 98.13%. These findings aid healthcare practitioners and researchers in categorizing BC cases, thereby enriching decision-making precision. For future works, we have planned to explore novel optimization and feature selection techniques to elevate further the accuracy and robustness of BC classification models. Furthermore, broadening the scope of this study to include assessments on more extensive and diverse datasets would enhance the validation of these models' adaptability and resilience in real-world situations.

References

1. Agarap, A.F.M.: On breast cancer detection: an application of machine learning algorithms on the Wisconsin diagnostic dataset. In: Proceedings of the 2nd International Conference on Machine Learning and Soft Computing, ICMLSC 2018, pp. 5–9. Association for Computing Machinery, New York (2018)
2. Ak, M.F.: A comparative analysis of breast cancer detection and diagnosis using data visualization and machine learning applications. In: Healthcare, vol. 8, p. 111. MDPI (2020)
3. Alshayeji, M.H., Ellethy, H., Abed, S., Gupta, R.: Computer-aided detection of breast cancer on the Wisconsin dataset: an artificial neural networks approach. Biomed. Signal Process. Control **71**, 103141 (2022)
4. Amrane, M., Oukid, S., Gagaoua, I., Ensari, T.: Breast cancer classification using machine learning. In: 2018 Electric Electronics, Computer Science, Biomedical Engineerings' Meeting (EBBT), pp. 1–4. IEEE (2018)
5. Atallah, R., Al-Mousa, A.: Heart disease detection using machine learning majority voting ensemble method. In: 2019 2nd International Conference on new Trends in Computing Sciences (ICTCS), pp. 1–6 (2019). https://doi.org/10.1109/ICTCS. 2019.8923053
6. Bayrak, E.A., Kırcı, P., Ensari, T.: Comparison of machine learning methods for breast cancer diagnosis. In: 2019 Scientific Meeting on Electrical-Electronics & Biomedical Engineering and Computer Science (EBBT), pp. 1–3. IEEE (2019)
7. Chaurasia, V., Pal, S., Tiwari, B.: Prediction of benign and malignant breast cancer using data mining techniques. J. Algorithms Comput. Technol. **12**(2), 119–126 (2018). https://doi.org/10.1177/1748301818756225
8. Dou, W., et al.: An AutoML approach for predicting risk of progression to active tuberculosis based on its association with host genetic variations. In: Proceedings of the 2021 10th International Conference on Bioinformatics and Biomedical Science, pp. 82–88 (2021)
9. Fatima, M., Pasha, M.: Survey of machine learning algorithms for disease diagnostic. J. Intell. Learn. Syst. Appl. **9**(1), 1–16 (2017)
10. Garrido-Merchán, E.C., Hernández-Lobato, D.: Dealing with categorical and integer-valued variables in Bayesian optimization with gaussian processes. Neurocomputing **380**, 20–35 (2020)

11. Gupta, P., Garg, S.: Breast cancer prediction using varying parameters of machine learning models. Procedia Comput. Sci. **171**, 593–601 (2020). Third International Conference on Computing and Network Communications (CoCoNet 2019)
12. Kharya, S., Soni, S.: Weighted Naive Bayes classifier: a predictive model for breast cancer detection. Int. J. Comput. Appl. **133**(9), 32–37 (2016). https://doi.org/10.5120/ijca2016908023
13. Kobayashi, S., Kane, T.B., Paton, C.: The privacy and security implications of open data in healthcare. Yearb. Med. Inform. **27**(01), 041–047 (2018)
14. Liu, Z., et al.: Machine learning approaches to investigate the relationship between genetic factors and autism spectrum disorder. In: Proceedings of the 2021 4th International Conference on Machine Learning and Machine Intelligence, pp. 164–171 (2021)
15. TACS medical, editorial content team: Types of breast cancer (2021). https://www.cancer.org/cancer/types/breast-cancer/about/types-of-breast-cancer.html. Accessed 6 July 2023
16. Ogundokun, R.O., Misra, S., Douglas, M., Damaševičius, R., Maskeliūnas, R.: Medical internet-of-things based breast cancer diagnosis using hyperparameter-optimized neural networks. Future Internet **14**(5), 153 (2022)
17. Omondiagbe, D.A., Veeramani, S., Sidhu, A.S.: Machine learning classification techniques for breast cancer diagnosis. In: IOP Conference Series: Materials Science and Engineering, vol. 495, no. 1, p. 012033 (2019). https://doi.org/10.1088/1757-899X/495/1/012033
18. Sung, H., et al.: Global cancer statistics 2020: GLOBOCAN estimates of incidence and mortality worldwide for 36 cancers in 185 countries. CA Cancer J. Clin. **71**(3), 209–249 (2021)
19. Thagaard, J., et al.: Pitfalls in machine learning-based assessment of tumor-infiltrating lymphocytes in breast cancer: a report of the international immuno-oncology biomarker working group. J. Pathol. (2023)
20. Thirumalaikolundusubramanian, P., et al.: Comparison of Bayes classifiers for breast cancer classification. Asian Pac. J. Cancer Prev.: APJCP **19**(10), 2917 (2018)
21. Wolberg, W.: Breast Cancer Wisconsin (Original). UCI Machine Learning Repository (1992). https://doi.org/10.24432/C5HP4Z
22. Wolberg, W., Street, W., Mangasarian, O.: Breast cancer Wisconsin (diagnostic). UCI Machine Learning Repository (1995). https://doi.org/10.24432/C5DW2B
23. Zhenghan, N., Dib, O.: Agriculture stimulates Chinese GDP: a machine learning approach. In: Tang, L.C., Wang, H. (eds.) BDET 2022. LNDECT, vol. 150, pp. 21–36. Springer, Cham (2023). https://doi.org/10.1007/978-3-031-17548-0_3

Integrated Patient Care Optimization Model: A Novel Model to Enhancing Medical Alliance Efficiency

Hong Wang[1,2], Xinyu Li[1,2], Xiaolong Ou[1,2], Yaofa Su[1,2], and Zhifu Zhang[3(✉)]

[1] College of Management, Shenzhen University, Shenzhen 518060, China
[2] Greater Bay Area International Institute for Innovation, Shenzhen University, Shenzhen 518060, China
[3] Department of General Practice, Shenzhen Longhua People's Hospital, Shenzhen 518109, China
66252880@qq.com

Abstract. The traditional hierarchical medical system often ignores the linkage among primary medical institutions, and there are still problems such as low patient satisfaction and high hospital operating costs to solve. Therefore, in this study, a new medical alliance model, named the Integrated Patient Care Optimization Model (abbreviated as IPCOM) is proposed, in which a new "parallel referral" mechanism is designed and combined with a "two-way referral" mechanism to enhance the linkage among primary medical institutions and their information communications between large hospitals. Additionally, two objectives (i.e. minimization of the patient costs and hospital costs) are considered in the model, simultaneously. As those two objectives conflict with each other, a well-known evolutionary algorithm named NSGA-II (nondominated sorting genetic algorithm) is employed to obtain the Pareto optimal solutions. Furthermore, to verify the validity of the IPCOM, a simulation model is constructed and compared with the real data provided by a medical alliance in Shenzhen. Numerical experiment results demonstrate that the IPCOM performs better than the traditional model in cost saving, and the simulation results fit well with the real data.

Keywords: Bidirectional referral mechanism · Parallel mechanism · Multi-objective optimization · Medical resource allocation

1 Introduction

The global healthcare sector faces a significant challenge due to an imbalance in the supply and demand of medical resources. This imbalance is particularly evident in the pronounced patient preference for large, well-established hospitals, leading to an overwhelming demand at these high-resource institutions. Consequently, this trend exacerbates congestion and strains resources at these facilities. In contrast, smaller medical institutions with moderate resources often remain underutilized, as indicated by recent studies [1, 2].

Y. Tan and Y. Shi (Eds.): DMBD 2023, CCIS 2018, pp. 244–259, 2024.
https://doi.org/10.1007/978-981-97-0844-4_18

In addressing this disparity, various regions have adopted hierarchical medical systems, showing potential in more evenly distributing medical resource utilization. A prime example is China's "medical alliance" model, a network comprising tertiary hospitals and primary healthcare facilities, anchored by the "two-way referral" system. This system demonstrated significant efficacy during China's response to the COVID-19 pandemic [3]. The United Kingdom's hierarchical structure effectively integrates primary healthcare with hospital systems, utilizing "referral letters" as essential communication links between general practitioners and specialists [4]. In the United States, a hierarchical framework operates wherein patients initially consult community family doctors and receive referrals to specialists as required [5].

While these models highlight essential connections between primary care and higher-level hospitals, they often overlook the benefits of establishing parallel connections among primary medical facilities. Despite improving operational efficiency to some extent, these systems face challenges such as diminished patient satisfaction [6] and the underutilization of medical resources [7]. Consequently, some healthcare consortia are experimenting with a "parallel referral" mechanism, supported by advanced information-sharing platforms, to encourage collaboration among primary medical establishments. However, the universal applicability and benefits of this approach in enhancing patient experience and hospital efficiency have not been thoroughly researched.

Our study aims to bridge these gaps by making two significant contributions. Firstly, we introduce the Integrated Patient Care Optimization Model (IPCOM), a novel model that synergizes the "two-way" and "parallel referral" mechanisms to enhance patient triage processes and medical resource utilization. Secondly, we develop a simulation model with realistic parameters to validate the effectiveness and rationale of IPCOM.

The remainder of the article is organized as follows: Sect. 2 provides a comprehensive review of relevant literature. Section 3 elucidates the IPCOM framework and its accompanying simulation model. Section 4 examines the results and implications of IPCOM, with a focus on model enhancements and simulation accuracy. Finally, the paper concludes by drawing conclusions and suggesting directions for future research.

2 Literature Review

The pursuit of operational efficiency in medical alliances and the equitable distribution of medical resources continues to be a dynamic and multifaceted area of research. This field has attracted a wide range of scholarly approaches, each contributing uniquely to our understanding of healthcare systems.

From a qualitative perspective, the effectiveness of China's urban hierarchical medical system has been a subject of thorough scrutiny, with studies focusing on its construction, efficiency, and broader impacts [8, 9]. On the quantitative side, researchers have addressed pressing challenges like cholera epidemic control and the demands of COVID-19 healthcare. In these contexts, resource allocation strategies utilizing advanced algorithms and simulation techniques have been at the forefront, demonstrating the potential for technology-driven solutions in crisis scenarios [10, 11]. Complementing these approaches, the development of decision-support tools that integrate forecasting, simulation, and optimization has been instrumental in enhancing responses to epidemics and other medical emergencies [12, 13].

Further research has delved into the systematic allocation and utilization of medical resources within hierarchical systems, with a specific focus on optimizing patient experiences. Noteworthy in this area are studies employing temporary color Petri nets for resource allocation [14] and data-driven integer programming models for optimizing resources [6, 15, 16]. Additionally, multidisciplinary co-simulation research on simulation platforms has gained traction as a means to tackle complex resource allocation challenges, demonstrating the value of interdisciplinary approaches [8, 17, 18].

However, a significant portion of existing methodologies predominantly focuses on the two-way referral mechanism, employing quantitative models to efficiently allocate resources across medical alliances and yield systemic benefits [19–21]. These methods typically utilize operations analysis, optimization theory, and data analysis [22–24]. Yet, the integration and potential advantages of linking primary care facilities, especially concerning hospital operating costs and patient satisfaction, have been less explored. Despite a growing recognition of these factors in healthcare management, comprehensive academic research incorporating these aspects is lacking.

Our study seeks to fill this gap by introducing the "parallel referral" mechanism and developing the Integrated Patient Care Optimization Model (IPCOM). IPCOM is designed to consider not only hospital operating costs and patient satisfaction but also to facilitate rational patient triage at a macro level. Additionally, this paper presents a simulation model based on system dynamics theory, validating IPCOM's effectiveness and practicality. This model is critically evaluated for its congruence with actual operational data, highlighting the model's relevance and applicability in real-world healthcare settings.

3 Model Construction

3.1 The Integrated Patient Care Optimization Model

Model Description. The IPCOM, as depicted in Fig. 1, represents an evolution of the traditional healthcare alliance model. IPCOM introduces the innovative "parallel referral" mechanism and seamlessly integrates it with the established "two-way referral" system, creating a comprehensive and dynamic model. This model operates through two distinct but interconnected systems: the two-way referral system and the parallel referral system.

The Two-Way Referral System. This system implements the "two-way referral" mechanism, a widely recognized approach in various medical contexts. It effectively manages the flow of patients between primary healthcare facilities and tertiary hospitals, ensuring an efficient use of medical resources. In practice, patients with severe conditions identified at primary facilities are escalated for specialized care at tertiary hospitals. Conversely, patients with less severe ailments, initially seen at tertiary hospitals, can be redirected to primary facilities for ongoing care. This bidirectional flow facilitates a more balanced distribution of patients, optimizing resource allocation across the healthcare spectrum.

The Parallel Referral System. Grounded in the "parallel referral" mechanism, this system addresses the underutilization of resources in primary healthcare facilities. It operates by logging patients who exceed the capacity of a facility into a Shared Information System, a unified transit platform. These patients are then allocated to other facilities within the network based on resource availability. This strategic distribution of patients enhances the overall utilization of medical resources, benefiting the healthcare system and patients alike. Primary medical institutions can maximize their resource use, while patients experience reduced wait times and timely access to medical care.

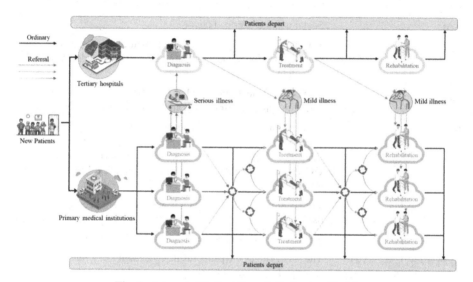

Fig. 1. Integrated Patient Care Optimization Model

Mathematical Model. Medical alliances generate costs during the period of operation, including queuing costs and operational costs. Part of the benefits are mainly obtained by the efficient utilization of medical resources. To optimize the medical alliance system, two objective functions are defined: the first one is to minimize the total cost of the whole system; and the second is to maximize the benefits generated by referrals. The indices for this article are shown in Table 1.

The objective function is determined by the following formula:

$$\min(f_{H\text{cost}}, f_{P\text{cost}}) \tag{1}$$

where $f_{H\text{cost}}$ represents the total cost of consumption of the consortium, and $f_{P\text{cost}}$ represents the total cost of patients. The total cost consumed by the consortium is, in turn, equal to the sum of the hospital operating cost C_O and the referral cost C_R, i.e., $f_{H\text{cost}} = C_O + C_R$; the patient cost is equal to the sum of the operational queuing cost QC_O and the referral queuing cost QC_R, i.e. $f_{P\text{cost}} = QC_O + QC_R$

Table 1. Symbolic description of the improved medical coupling model

Indices	Explain
NH	Number of patients in the nodes of tertiary hospitals
NI	Number of patients at the nodes of community medical facilities
NI^{ori}	Number of patients in the original value community medical facilities
NI^{opt}	Optimized number of patients in community medical facilities
R$_{OH}$	Operational overload factor for tertiary hospitals
R$_{OI}$	Social welfare overload factor
Thr	Threshold for the Number of Patients that can be Carried per unit time for the model node, the parameters of each node are shown in Table 3
F$_{out}^{in}$	Number of Patient Turnover Per Unit Time between model nodes, the specific parameters are shown in Table 4
C	Unit cost of model node, the specific parameters are shown in Table 5 and Table 6, where **C$_O$** is the unit operating cost (Operation Cost), **C$_R$** is the unit referrals cost (Referrals Cost), **QC$_O$** is the unit Operation Queue Cost and **QC$_R$** is the unit Referrals Queue Cost
$N_t = \{t \mid t = 1, 2, \ldots, T\}$	The set of node patients, time t is generally estimated to be 24 h a day
$A_i = \{i \mid i = 1, 2, \ldots, I\}$	Primary Care Organizations/Social Care Collective
$S_j = \{j \mid j = 1, 2, \ldots, J\}$	The set of stages the patient is in, by default $j = 1$ for severe cases and $j = 2$ for mild cases
$P_k = \{k \mid k = 1, 2, \ldots, K\}$	A collection of patient visit periods, default $k = 1$ for diagnosis, $k = 2$ for treatment, $k = 3$ for recovery

$$C_O = \sum_{t=1}^{T} \sum_{k=1}^{K} \left\{ \sum_{j=1}^{j} \left\{ \left[NH_t P_k S_j + \max\left(Thr_{NHP_k S_j} - NH_t P_k S_j, 0\right) * (R_{OH} - 1)\right] * C_{OHPk}^{Sj} \right. \right.$$
$$\left. \left. + C_{OIPk} * \sum_{i=1}^{I} \left[NI_t^{OptP} P_k A_i + \max\left(Thr_{NIP_k A_i} - NI_t^{OptP} P_k A_i, 0\right) * (R_{OI} - 1)\right] \right\} \right\} \quad (2)$$

where **C$_O$** Eq. (2) represents hospital operating costs, takes into account the difference in costs between in-load and out-of-load healthcare organizations, and should also take into account the difference between the period of patient attendance and the stage of the patient, as well as considering the difference in costs between tertiary care hospitals and primary medical alliances

$$C_R = \left(F_{NHP_1}^{NIP_1} * C_{RH}^{S1} + F_{NIP_3}^{NHP_2} * C_{RH}^{S2} \right) * T + \sum_{t=1}^{T} N_t F_{NIP_2}^{NHP_1} * C_{RH}^{S2} + \sum_{t=1}^{T} \sum_{k=1}^{K-1} \sum_{i=1}^{I} N_t F_{HTC}^{NIP_k A_i} * C_{RI} \quad (3)$$

$$QC_O = \sum_{t=1}^{T} \sum_{k=1}^{K} \left(\sum_{j=1}^{J} NH_t P_k S_j * QC_{OPk}^{Sj} + \sum_{i=1}^{I} NI_t^{Opt} P_k A_i * QC_{OPk}^{S2} \right) \quad (4)$$

$$QC_R = \sum_{t=1}^{T} \left[\left(\frac{F_{NHP_1}^{NIP_1}}{2} + NH_1 P_1 S_2 \right) * QC_R^{S1} + \sum_{k=2}^{K} \left(\frac{N_t F_{NIP_k}^{NHP_{k-1}}}{2} + NI_t P_k \right) * QC_{RHPK}^{S2} \right.$$

$$\left. + \sum_{k=2}^{K} \sum_{i=1}^{1} \left(\frac{N_t F_{NIP_k A_i}^{HTC} NIP_t A_1}{2} + NI_1^{optP} P_k A_i \right) * QC_{RIPk}^{S2} \right] \tag{5}$$

where C_R Eq. (3) represents referral cost, QC_O Eq. (4) represents operational queuing cost, and QC_R Eq. (5) represents referral queuing cost, which takes into account the period of the patient's visit, the stage of the patient, the difference in cost between tertiary hospitals and primary healthcare/community care, and the cumulative impact of the time period.

The constraint of the optimization model is presented in the following formula:

$$NH_t P_k = \sum_{j=1}^{J} NH_t P_k S_j \tag{6}$$

where $NH_t P_k$ Eq. (6) represents the number of patients in each period in tertiary hospitals, which is the sum of the number of mild and severe patients in the corresponding period node.

$$N_t F_{NHP_1 S_j}^{IN} = F_{NHP_1 S_j}^{IN} \tag{7}$$

$$N_t F_{NIP_1 A_i}^{IN} = \frac{F_{NIP_1 S_2}^{IN}}{I} \tag{8}$$

where $N_t F_{NHP_1 S_j}^{IN}$ shown in Eq. (7) represents the actual patient admission flow rates for tertiary hospitals and $N_t F_{NIP_1 A_i}^{IN}$ shown in Eq. (8) represent the flow rates for primary care/community care, and the dynamic remittance values consistent with the seasonal week of the year are obtained from the study.

For practical considerations, all patient flows including discharges and up and down referrals, parallel referrals, etc. need to take into account the number of patients in the previous node/period, and should also take into account the limitation of flow thresholds between the corresponding nodes, as shown in Eq. (9)–(14):

$$N_t F_{OUT}^{NHP_k S_j} = \min \left(NH_{t-1} P_k S_j, F_{OUT}^{NHP_k S_j} \right) \tag{9}$$

$$N_t F_{NHP_{k+1} S_j}^{NHP_k S_j} = \min \left(NH_{t-1} P_k S_j - N_t F_{OUT}^{NHP_k S_j}, F_{NHP_{k+1} S_j}^{NHP_k S_j} \right) \tag{10}$$

$$N_t F_{OUT}^{NIP_k A_i} = \min \left(NI_{t-1}^{opt} P_k A_i, \frac{F_{OUT}^{NIP_k}}{I} \right) \tag{11}$$

$$N_t F_{NIP_{k+1} A_i}^{NIP_k A_i} = \min \left(NI_{t-1} P_k - N_t F_{OUT}^{NIP_k A_i}, \frac{F_{NIP_{k+1}}^{NIP_k}}{I} \right) \tag{12}$$

$$NI_t^{opt} P_1 A_i = \begin{cases} \min \left(NI_t^{ori} P_1 A_i, Thr_{NIP_1 A_i} \right), & else \\ NI_t^{ori} P_1 A_i, & \forall i \in A_i, NI_{t-1}^{opt} P_2 A_i \geq Thr_{NIP_2 A_i} \end{cases} \tag{13}$$

$$NI_t^{opt} P_2 A_i = \begin{cases} min\left(NI_t^{ori} P_2 A_i, N_t F_{NIP_2 A_i}^{HTC}, \ Thr_{NIP_2 A_i}\right), & else \\ NI_t^{ori} P_2 A_i + N_t F_{NIP_2 A_i}^{HTC}, & \forall i \in A_i, NI_{t-1}^{opt} P_3 A_i \geq Thr_{NIP_3 A_i} \end{cases}$$
(14)

As shown in Eq. (15), for ease of calculation, the rate of upward referral from primary care/community care is set equal to its critical care inflow:

$$F_{NHP_1}^{NIP_1} = F_{NIP_1 S_1}^{IN}$$
(15)

The number of patients in tertiary hospitals by period and stage is shown in Eq. (16)–(20), which includes three periods: diagnosis period, treatment period, and recovery period, as well as two stages of patients with mild and severe illnesses:

$$NH_t P_1 S_1 = NH_{t-1} P_1 S_1 + N_t F_{NHP_1 S_1}^{IN} + F_{NHP_1}^{NIP_1} - N_t F_{OUT}^{NHPS_1} - N_t F_{NHP_2 S_1}^{NHP_1 S_1}$$
(16)

$$NH_t P_1 S_2 = NH_{t-1} P_1 S_2 + N_t F_{NHP_1 S_2}^{IN} - N_t F_{OUT}^{NHP_1 S_2} - N_t F_{NHP_2 S_2}^{NHP_1 S_2} - N_t F_{NIP_2}^{NHP_1}$$
(17)

$$NH_t P_2 S_1 = NH_{t-1} P_2 S_1 + N_t F_{NHP_2 S_1}^{NHP_1 S_1} - N_t F_{OUT}^{NHP_2 S_1} - N_t F_{NHP_3 S_1}^{NHP_2 S_1}$$
(18)

$$NH_t P_2 S_2 = NH_{t-1} P_2 S_2 + N_t F_{NHP_2 S_2}^{NHP_1 S_2} - N_t F_{OUT}^{NHP_2 S_2} - N_t F_{NHP_3 S_2}^{NHP_2 S_2} - N_t F_{NIP_3}^{NHP_2}$$
(19)

$$NH_t P_3 S_j = NH_{t-1} P_3 S_j + N_t F_{NHP_3 S_j}^{NHP_2 S_j} - N_t F_{OUT}^{NHP_3 S_j}$$
(20)

The number of patients in each period in primary care/community health is shown in Eq. (21), which is the sum of the number of patients in the corresponding period in the sub-community health after optimization of the parallel mechanism:

$$NI_t P_k = \sum_{i=1}^{I} NI_t^{opt} P_k A_i$$
(21)

The number of patients at each stage of the primary care/community health care period is shown in Eq. (22)–(25), which include the diagnostic period, the treatment period, the rehabilitation period, and the stage of optimization of the paralleling mechanism:

$$NI_t^{ori} P_1 A_i = NI_{t-1}^{opt} P_1 A_i + N_t F_{NIP_1 A_i}^{IN} - N_t F_{OUT}^{NIP_1 A_i} - N_t F_{NIP_2 A_i}^{NIP_1 A_i}$$
(22)

$$NI_t^{ori} P_2 A_i = NI_{t-1}^{opt} P_2 A_i + N_t F_{NIP_2 A_i}^{NIP_1 A_i} + N_t F_{NIP_2 A_i}^{NIP_1 A_i} + \frac{N_t F_{NIP_3}^{NHP_2}}{I} - N_t F_{OUT}^{NIP_2 A_i} - N_t F_{NIP_3 A_i}^{NIP_2 A_i}$$
(23)

$$NI_t^{ori} P_3 A_i = NI_{t-1}^{opt} P_3 A_i + \frac{N_t F_{NIP_3}^{NHP_2}}{I} + N_t F_{NIP_3 A_i}^{NIP_2 A_i} - N_t F_{OUT}^{NIP_3 A_i}$$
(24)

$$NI_t^{opt} P_3 A_i = NI_t^{ori} P_3 A_i + N_t F_{NIP_3 A_i}^{HTC}$$
(25)

The parallel mechanism is at the heart of this article, and Eq. (26)–(29) express the principle of parallel referrals among primary medical institutions:

$$N_t F_{HTC}^{NIP_1 A_i} = NI_t^{ori} P_1 A_i - NI_t^{opt} P_1 A_i \tag{26}$$

$$N_t F_{HTC}^{NIP_k} = \sum_{i=1}^{I} N_t F_{HTC}^{NIP_k A_i} \tag{27}$$

$$N_t F_{NIP_k A_i}^{HTC} = N_t F_{HTC}^{NIP_k - 1 *} \left(NI_{t-1}^{opt} P_k A_i \Big/ Thr_{NIP_k A_i} \right) \Big/ \left(\sum_{k=1}^{K} \left(NI_{t-1}^{opt} P_k A_i \Big/ Thr_{NIP_k A_i} \right) \right) \tag{28}$$

$$N_t F_{HTC}^{NIP_2 A_i} = NI_t^{ori} P_2 A_i + N_t F_{NIP_2 A_i}^{HTC} - NI_t^{opt} P_2 A_i \tag{29}$$

The remaining independent variables are restricted as shown in Eq. (30) (31):

$$N_t F_{NIP_2}^{NHP_1}, N_t F_{NIP_3}^{NHP_2} \in [0, 100], N_t = \{t | t = 1, 2, \ldots, T\} \tag{30}$$

$$N_t = 0, \quad if \ t \leq 0 \tag{31}$$

Solution Method: NSGA-II. Since this study is essentially to solve multi-objective optimization problems, NSGA-II [31] which is widely used by scholars, is chosen for model solving in this study, and the pseudocode is shown in Table 2. This study will obtain a series of parameters for the Pareto optimal solution, and then the decision maker will select the optimal parameters according to the actual situation and input them into the simulation system for further verification. This method is worked by MATLAB R2021b.

Table 2. Pseudocode of the improved post-medical associative model

	Algorithm 1: NSGA-II
1	Initialize population P
2	Initialize auxiliary population Q = Ø
3	**While not** termination_condition **do**
4	**for** i = 1 to population_size / 2 **do**
5	Select parents
6	Generate offspring by Mutation and crossover
7	Insert offspring to Q
8	**end for**
9	Q = Q + P
10	Ranking and crowding Q
11	Select the p best individuals to P from Q
12	**end while**

3.2 The IPCOM Validation: Simulation

In this section, we detail the development of a comprehensive simulation model based on system dynamics theory, aimed at validating the IPCOM. As depicted in Fig. 2, the simulation model provides a dynamic representation of a patient's journey through the healthcare system, capturing critical factors and interactions within the medical alliance framework. This model serves as an instrumental tool in analyzing the complex interplay and evolving dynamics inherent in patient care processes.

The simulation model is structured around three fundamental elements: stock variables, flow variables, and visualization techniques, each playing a pivotal role in depicting the patient care continuum.

- **Stock Variables**: These variables represent the patient count at various stages of healthcare, such as diagnosis, treatment, and rehabilitation. The model meticulously monitors changes in these stocks over time, providing a temporal snapshot of patient numbers at different points in the healthcare pathway. This longitudinal tracking is crucial for understanding patient distribution and movement across the healthcare continuum.
- **Flow Variables**: Central to the simulation are the flow variables, which quantify the movement and transitions of patients within the healthcare system. This includes patient transfers between different stages of care, referrals across various medical institutions, and patient exits post-treatment. Incorporating these flow variables is vital for a holistic examination of patient flow patterns and their dynamic fluctuations within the medical alliance. Understanding these flows allows for the identification of bottlenecks and inefficiencies, offering insights into potential areas for system improvement.
- **Visualization**: Building on the above components, the simulation model employs advanced visualization techniques to intuitively represent the patient's medical journey. This graphical depiction ranges from initial diagnosis to eventual rehabilitation, providing an accessible and informative view of the entire process. Such visualization not only enhances the comprehensibility of complex patient flow patterns but also aids researchers and practitioners in identifying operational inefficiencies and areas ripe for optimization within the healthcare system.

Through this simulation model, we aim to offer a detailed and nuanced understanding of the IPCOM's effectiveness in managing patient care. The model's ability to dynamically represent and analyze the patient journey in the healthcare system makes it an invaluable tool for assessing and refining patient care strategies within the medical alliance.

4 Results

4.1 Parameter Settings

In this study, the data for our parameter settings, as presented in Tables 3, 4, 5, 6 and 7, are derived from two key sources. The primary source is the medical clusters within Longhua District, Shenzhen, China. This source offers a focused insight into the local

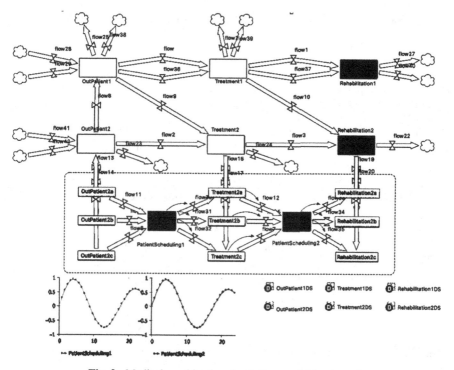

Fig. 2. Medical combination simulation model framework

healthcare system, providing detailed information on patient flow, resource allocation, and medical procedures specific to the region. Complementing this, our second source is the Shenzhen Health Statistics Yearbook. This comprehensive repository offers broader statistical data, encompassing a wide array of health-related metrics and trends across Shenzhen. The combination of these two sources ensures a rich, multi-dimensional dataset, crucial for underpinning the robustness and validity of our simulation model.

Table 3. Key model parameters

Indices	Value	Indices	Value	Indices	Value
R_{OH}	4	R_{OI}	3	T	12/24
I	3	J	2	K	3

4.2 Analysis of Results

The Pareto optimal solutions obtained in this study have been shown in Fig. 3. Figure 3(a) and (b) of the figure show the set of optimal solutions before optimization, while Fig. 3(c) and (d) show the set of optimal solutions after optimization. By comparing the optimal

Table 4. The threshold parameter of the number of patients per unit time

Indices	Value	Indices	Value	Indices	Value
$Thr_{NHP_1S_1}$	104	$Thr_{NHP_2S_1}$	48	$Thr_{NHP_3S_1}$	5
$Thr_{NHP_1S_2}$	113	$Thr_{NHP_2S_2}$	48	$Thr_{NHP_3S_2}$	5.5
$Thr_{NIP_1A_1}$	26	$Thr_{NIP_2A_1}$	3	$Thr_{NIP_3A_1}$	0.17
$Thr_{NIP_1A_2}$	54	$Thr_{NIP_2A_2}$	7	$Thr_{NIP_3A_2}$	0.33
$Thr_{NIP_1A_3}$	80	$Thr_{NIP_2A_3}$	10	$Thr_{NIP_3A_3}$	0.5

Table 5. Parameter of patient mobility per unit time between model nodes

Indices	Value	Indices	Value	Indices	Value
$F_{NHP_1S_1}^{IN}$	94	$F_{NHP_2S_1}^{NHP_1S_1}$	80	$F_{NHP_3S_1}^{NHP_2S_1}$	5
$F_{NHP_1S_2}^{IN}$	100	$F_{NHP_2S_2}^{NHP_1S_2}$	9	$F_{NHP_3S_2}^{NHP_2S_2}$	1
$F_{NIP_1S_1}^{IN}$	6	$F_{NIP_2}^{NIP_1}$	10	$F_{NIP_3}^{NIP_2}$	2
$F_{NIP_1S_2}^{IN}$	100	$F_{NIP_2}^{NHP_1}$	*	$F_{NIP_3}^{NHP_2}$	*
$F_{OUT}^{NHP_1S_1}$	20	$F_{OUT}^{NHP_2S_1}$	75	$F_{OUT}^{NHP_3S_1}$	0.4
$F_{OUT}^{NHP_1S_2}$	81	$F_{OUT}^{NHP_2S_2}$	8	$F_{OUT}^{NHP_3S_2}$	0.8
$F_{OUT}^{NIP_1}$	90	$F_{OUT}^{NIP_2}$	8	$F_{OUT}^{NIP_3}$	1.6

Table 6. Model node unit cost parameters

Indices	Value	Indices	Value	Indices	Value
C_{OHP1}^{S1}	4.8	C_{OHP2}^{S1}	7.2	C_{OHP3}^{S1}	3.4
C_{OHP1}^{S2}	4	C_{OHP2}^{S2}	6	C_{OHP3}^{S2}	3
C_{OIP1}	2	C_{OIP2}	3	C_{OIP3}	1
C_{RH}^{S1}	3	C_{RH}^{S2}	2	C_{RI}	3

objective function values vertically, we can conclude that the optimized model significantly outperforms the pre-optimized model in terms of performance. This result indicates that the IPCOM has achieved significant improvement.

A further specific comparison of the patient cost optimization effect and hospital cost optimization effect is shown in Fig. 4 Comparing the patient cost optimization effect is as follows: within 24 h, the patient cost before improvement is 91000, and the cost after improvement is about 41000, which is optimized by about 55%. within 12 h, the

Table 7. Model node unit queue cost parameters

Indices	Value	Indices	Value	Indices	Value
QC^{S1}_{OP1}	1.2	QC^{S1}_{OP2}	1.8	QC^{S1}_{OP3}	0.6
QC^{S2}_{OP1}	1	QC^{S2}_{OP2}	1.5	QC^{S2}_{OP3}	0.5
QC^{S1}_{R}	1.5	QC^{S2}_{RHP2}	1.5	QC^{S2}_{RHP3}	0.5
QC^{S2}_{RIP2}	1.5	QC^{S2}_{RIP3}	0.5		

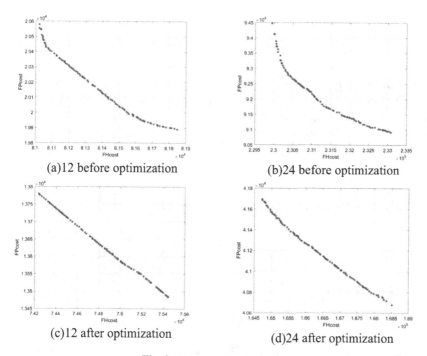

(a)12 before optimization

(b)24 before optimization

(c)12 after optimization

(d)24 after optimization

Fig. 3. Pareto optimal solution set

cost before improvement is about 20000, and the cost after improvement is about 13500, which is optimized by about 32.5%. From the above data, it can be concluded that the IPCOM is significantly better than the pre-improvement model, and the improvement effect is gradually improved with time. The optimization effect of comparing hospital costs is as follows: in 24 h, the hospital cost before improvement is 230,000, and the cost after improvement is about 164,100, which is optimized by about 28.65%. in 12 h, the hospital cost before improvement is about 81,000, and the cost after improvement is about 74,100, which is optimized by about 8.52%. From the above data, it can be concluded that the IPCOM is significantly better than the pre-improvement model, and the improvement effect gradually improves with time.

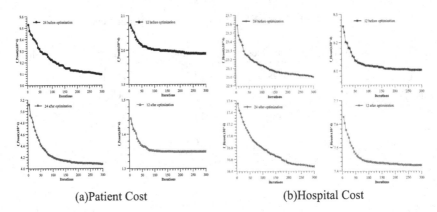

(a)Patient Cost   (b)Hospital Cost

Fig. 4. Optimization effect

In the part of simulation, we fitted actual and modeled data for key nodes. We focused on the diagnosis and treatment phases and chose two time periods, 12 h and 24 h, for observation. The fitting results are shown in Fig. 5: the Cv(RMSE) is 11.55% for 12 h and 6.93% for 24 h in the diagnosis phase, and 20.03% for 12 h and 17.75% for 24 h in the treatment phase.

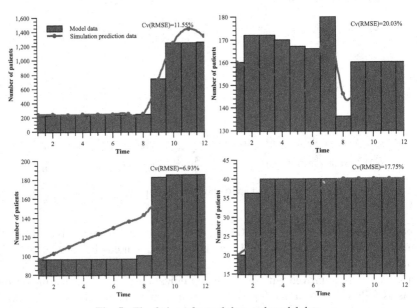

Fig. 5. The fitting of actual data and model data

The results indicates that costs to both patients and hospitals increase slowly over time. Based on a thorough comparison of the pre- and post-improvement scenarios, we found that the IPCOM demonstrated significant benefits in optimizing costs. This high-lights its effectiveness in decreasing both patient and hospital costs by enhancing the con-nection between primary medical institutions. Furthermore, the observed improvements continued to increase over time, requiring further validation of the model.

In order to validate the model, we developed a simulation model. We selected crucial nodes to fit the real and modeled data, with a focus on the 12-h and 24-h time frames. Additionally, we utilized the Cv(RMSE) index to evaluate the match between the model and actual data. The analysis of the current data and model data indicated that the model accurately predicts data during diagnosis and treatment and provides more reliable pre-dictions over a prolonged period of time. Therefore, IPCOM has proven to be effective. The results suggest that the proposed model is a valuable healthcare management tool, contributing to cost-effective patient care and optimized resource allocation in medical alliances.

5 Conclusions

In this study, we have introduced an innovative "parallel referral" mechanism and devel-oped the Integrated Patient Care Optimization Model (IPCOM), a significant step for-ward in the exploration of new medical alliance models. The incorporation of the NSGA-II algorithm, a cornerstone in multi-objective optimization, has enabled us to effec-tively enhance both patient and hospital cost optimization. This represents a notable advancement over existing models, as evidenced by our experimental results.

Moreover, the construction and implementation of a simulation model have been integral to validating IPCOM's accuracy and stability. The alignment of the simulation outcomes with real-world operational data underscores the practical applicability and relevance of our model in the current healthcare landscape.

While the results of our study are promising, they also highlight the potential for further refinement. Future research directions include expanding the dataset to capture a wider array of patient populations and medical scenarios, enhancing the algorithm and parameter settings for improved predictive accuracy, and developing a more comprehen-sive optimization model. These enhancements aim to incorporate a broader spectrum of factors such as medical resource supply and demand, patient preferences, and demand variations. Such efforts are expected to not only bolster the applicability and reliabil-ity of IPCOM but also provide more nuanced and practical solutions for healthcare management and decision-making.

Acknowledgments. This work is supported by the National Natural Science Foundation of China (Grants Nos. 71901152), Guangdong Basic and Applied Basic Research Founda-tion (2023A1515010919), Guangdong Innovation Team Project of Intelligent Management and Cross Innovation (2021WCXTD002), and Shenzhen Stable Support Grant (Grant Nos. 20220810100952001).

References

1. Wang, J.: Patient flow modeling and optimal staffing for emergency departments: a Petri net approach. IEEE Trans. Comput. Soc. Syst. **10**, 2022–2032 (2023)

2. Mason, A.N.: The most essential telemedicine patient satisfaction dimension: patient-centered care. Telemed. e-Health **28**(8), 1206–1214 (2022)
3. Savioli, G., et al.: Emergency department overcrowding: understanding the factors to find corresponding solutions. J. Personalized Med. **12**, 279 (2022)
4. Lechen, Z.L.: Drawing lessons from NHS referral system to strengthen the hierarchical medical service system and grassroots medical informatization in China. Chin. General Pract. **22**, 1904 (2019)
5. Jing, F., Zhang, Q., Ong, J.J., et al.: Optimal resource allocation in HIV self-testing secondary distribution among Chinese MSM, data-driven integer programming models. Phil. Trans. R. Soc. A **380**(2214), 20210128 (2022)
6. Yin, X., Büyüktahtakın, İE., Patel, B.P.: COVID-19, data-driven optimal allocation of ventilator supply under uncertainty and risk. Eur. J. Oper. Res. **304**(1), 255–275 (2023)
7. Ma, Y., et al.: Healthcare utilization and economic burden of myopia in urban China: a nationwide cost-of-illness study. J. Glob. Health **12**, 11003
8. Shi, M., He, H., Li, J., et al.: Multi-objective tradeoff optimization of predictive adaptive cruising control for autonomous electric buses. A cyber-physical-energy system approach. Appl. Energy **300**, 117385 (2021)
9. Wu, Q., Xie, X., Liu, W., Wu, Y.: Implementation efficiency of the hierarchical diagnosis and treatment system in China: a case study of primary medical and health institutions in Fujian province. Int. J. Health Plann. Manag. **37**, 214–227 (2022)
10. Du, M., Sai, A., Kong, N.: A data-driven optimization approach for multi-period resource allocation in cholera outbreak control. Eur. J. Oper. Res. **291**, 1106–1116 (2021)
11. Wang, Y., Zhu, X.: A multi-regional collaborative optimization model of emergency medical materials for responding to COVID-19. Processes **10**, 1488 (2022)
12. Deng, W., Xu, J., Zhao, H., Song, Y.: A novel gate resource allocation method using improved PSO-based QEA. IEEE Trans. Intell. Transp. Syst. **23**, 1737–1745 (2022)
13. Ordu, M., Demir, E., Tofallis, C., Gunal, M.M.: A novel healthcare resource allocation decision support tool: a forecasting-simulation-optimization approach. J. Oper. Res. Soc. **72**, 485–500 (2021)
14. Yu, W., Jia, M., Fang, X., Lu, Y., Xu, J.: Modeling and analysis of medical resource allocation based on Timed Colored Petri net. Futur. Gener. Comput. Syst. **111**, 368–374 (2020)
15. Jing, F., et al.: Optimal resource allocation in HIV self-testing secondary distribution among Chinese MSM: data-driven integer programming models. Philos. Trans. R. Soc. A: Math. Phys. Eng. Sci. **380**, 20210128 (2021)
16. Yin, J., Huang, R., Sun, H.: Anylogic-based multi-subject co-simulation for assembled buildings. Constr. Econ. **42**(S2), 49–52 (2021)
17. Lu, G.W., Tao, X.Q., Duan, D.G., et al.: Research progress of anylogic simulation platform in the field of medical resource optimization. China Med. Equipment **19**(02), 191–194 (2022)
18. Wang, B.B., Mo, X.Q.: Study on waiting area index of outpatient clinic of general hospital based on anylogic simulation. J. Archit. (S2), 42–46 (2021)
19. Xie, J., Zhuang, W., Ang, M., Chou, M.C., Luo, L., Yao, D.D.: Analytics for hospital resource planning—two case studies. Prod. Oper. Manag. **30**, 1863–1885 (2021)
20. Su, Q., Shen, X.J., Hu, Y.Q.: Simulation and optimization of multi-intelligence-based hierarchical diagnosis and treatment. Ind. Eng. Manag. **25**(03), 10–18 (2020)
21. Pan, X., Song, J., Zhang, B.: Dynamic resource allocation in a hierarchical appointment system: optimal structure and heuristics. IEEE Trans. Autom. Sci. Eng. 1–15 (2020)
22. Yan, K., Qiu, H.J., Zeng, Y.H.: Problem discovery of hospital outpatient process based on simulation and field tracing. Chin. J. Hosp. Manag. (02), 131–135 (2020)

23. Dou, Y., Wang, F., Wu, X., Meng, W.: Research on performance evaluation of three level public hospitals based on fuzzy comprehensive evaluation model. In: 2021 IEEE 4th Advanced Information Management, Communicates, Electronic and Automation Control Conference (IMCEC), Chongqing, China, pp. 1380–1385. IEEE (2021)

24. Graham, R.J., et al.: Real-world analysis of healthcare resource utilization by patients with X-linked myotubular myopathy (XLMTM) in the United States. Orphanet J. Rare Dis. **18**, 138 (2023)

25. Singh, M.K., Choudhary, A., Gulia, S., Verma, A.: Multi-objective NSGA-II optimization framework for UAV path planning in an UAV-assisted WSN. J. Supercomput. **79**, 832–866 (2023)

A Two-Stage Approach to Optimize Medical Waste Transportation Problem During Pandemic

Hong Wang[1,2], Xuan Zhang[1], Jinxin Zhang[3], and Ben Niu[1,2(✉)]

[1] College of Management, Shenzhen University, Shenzhen 518060, China
drniuben@gmail.com
[2] Greater Bay Area International Institute for Innovation, Shenzhen University, Shenzhen 518060, China
[3] Faculty of Business, Lingnan University, Tuen Mun, Hong Kong

Abstract. The medical waste transportation plays an important role in controlling pandemic, however, the explosive increase in medical waste (MW) makes it difficult to make optimal decisions. In this study, a two-stage optimization model considering the transshipment strategy is developed to transport MW in pandemic. In the first stage, a transit model is established to determine the transshipment relationship between medical waste generation nodes (MWN). In the second stage, a multi-trip and split-collection vehicle routing problem with collection time (MTSCVRPCT) model is established for MW collection with the objectives of minimizing the maximum total trip duration and minimizing the total transport risk. The transit model is a nonlinear integer problem and MTSCVRPCT model is a mixed integer programming problem, thus, we apply CPLEX solver to solve the transit model and use Non-dominated Sorting Genetic Algorithm-II (NSGA-II) to solve the MTSCVRPCT model. A case study based on the real data in Shenzhen is conducted to demonstrate the workability of the proposed model. Compared with established transportation way, results show that the transshipment strategy can significantly reduce transportation time and risks.

Keywords: Medical Waste · Transportation · Transfer Strategy

1 Introduction

The amount of medical waste (MW) has increased due to population growth and the outbreak of pandemics, which has seriously threatened the health of the population and the development of economic [1, 2]. Especially during a pandemic, for example COVID-19, with a wide transmission range, high infectivity and multiple transmission modes, a large amount of MW was stored in medical institutions, which are medical waste generation nodes (MWN), causing great pressure on the MW transportation.

With the spread of the epidemic and the increase in the number of confirmed cases, the amount of MW has surged dramatically in a short period of time. In this situation, it is vital to collect and transport the MW to Disposal Center (DC) on time to avoid massive

© The Author(s), under exclusive license to Springer Nature Singapore Pte Ltd. 2024
Y. Tan and Y. Shi (Eds.): DMBD 2023, CCIS 2018, pp. 260–273, 2024.
https://doi.org/10.1007/978-981-97-0844-4_19

accumulation of MW. Traditional MW transportation assume that current facilities are capable of handling all waste [3]. However, when a pandemic breaks out, we have to consider many complicated factors. Therefore, some new modes of transportation have been put forward. In cases where existing facilities may not be sufficient, the requisition of temporary facilities can be an effective method [4]. In addition, the risk of infection that MW poses to population during transport is considered [5].

The selection of a proper mode of MW transportation should also be based on the geographical location and distance between MWN and DC. DC are generally located in remote and marginal areas. The transfer strategy enables the MW to be concentrated at the transfer station (TS) before being transported to the DC [6]. At the beginning of the transfer work, the transfer station must be built in the selected location. It is necessary to take this strategy to improve efficiency and save time. However, a fixed-location TS may not be able to accommodate all of the transfer waste due to capacity constraints, and would also incur significant risks because due to construction time. Whether it is a large spread of the pandemic or a sudden small outbreak, a good method must be able to select temporary TS to adapt to each situation. In reality, hospitals, that is, large medical waste generation nodes (LN), have sufficient temporary storage space and disinfection equipment. If these nodes are selected as temporary TS to receive waste from nearby clinics, that is, small medical waste generation nodes (SN), the number of collection points can be significantly reduced. This approach is particularly advantageous when epidemics occur in multiple places and MWN nodes are dispersed.

For this reason, this study is conducted to introduce a two-stage transportation way which considering a new transfer strategy to quickly centralize the dispersed MW. At first, a transit model is constructed to determine which LN act as TS to receive wastes and the transshipment relationship between LN and SN. The objective function of this model is to minimize the total cost. In the second stage, in order to propose collection model, we introduce a multi-trip and split-collection vehicle routing problem with collection time constraints (MTSCVRPCT) to optimize the collection routing. The objectives are defined to minimize the maximum total travel time and the collection risk. The transit model is a nonlinear integer programming model (NIP) that is solved using CPLEX solver. And the transportation model is a multi-objective problem and belong to mixed integer programming problem (MIP), so Non-dominated Sorting Genetic Algorithm-II (NSGA-II) is used to solve it. Finally, a real case in a city in China is implemented to verify the efficiency and practicality of the model and algorithm.

The reminder of the paper is organized as follows: In Sect. 2, we investigate the related literatures. Section 3 gives problem description, model assumptions, mathematical model and solution approach. Section 4 presents a case study in Shenzhen in order to show the application of the proposed model and algorithm. Section 5 concludes the paper.

2 Survey on Related Research

2.1 Traditional Medical Waste Transportation

Due to population growth, the number of medical institutions (such as hospitals, clinics, medical research institute) and the demand for medical services are also increasing [7]. The waste generated by patient in these institutions is known as MW [8]. MW transportation is very important, and many scholars pay attention to it and put forward reasonable solutions. In terms of MW reverse logistics recovery network, Budak and Ustundag built a multi-product, multi-cycle mixed integer linear programming model (MILP), aiming to minimize the cost [9]. Mantzaras and Voudrias considered the optimization model of medical waste in Greece [10]. There is a maximum time limit on the storage of MW in medical institutions. In addition to maximizing profits and minimizing transportation distance, Alizadeh et al. also emphasized the need to minimize the transportation time [11].

MW is a kind of hazardous waste, which will bring negative environmental impact to the environment. Wang et al. designed a multi-objective and multi-cycle two-stage reverse logistics network for urban MW [12]. In the first phase, they predicted the amount of MW, and in the second phase, they minimized the total cost and environmental impact. MW carries viruses, and the transport task must choose the path with the least risk. Homayouni and Pishvaee investigated the design of hazardous MW collection and disposal network by using a multi-objective robust optimization model [13]. The objective functions are to minimize total cost, operational, and transportation risks simultaneously. An enhanced ε-constraint method is embedded to solve this problem. Li et al. also considered transportation risks when investigated the vehicle routing problem of MW transportation [14]. They propose a hybrid integer programming model for vehicle routing problems with time Windows, and use an improved Particle Swarm Algorithm to solve large-scale problems.

2.2 Medical Waste Transportation During Pandemic

Since pandemics can lead to a sustained surge in MW over a very long period of time, many scholars have begun to focus on the inadequacy of collection equipment and DC in emergency situations. Babaee et al. designed an outsourcing strategy to construct a bi-objective MILP model with the objective of minimizing the cost and population exposure risk to solve the transportation planning of MW [15]. Govindan et al. constructed a model for the location-routing problem with the objective of minimizing the cost and risk, aiming to select the number and location of DC and arrange the collection routes [16]. Tirkolaee et al. introduced fuzzy variables to express uncertain MW generation and developed a MILP model to find out the location of new DC and collection routes for vehicles [17].

In addition, the risks posed by MW to the population around the disposal facility and along the transportation path were added to the model. Kargar et al. proposed a model that sets the risk associated with the transportation and treatment of infectious waste as one of the objectives. An improved Goal Programming method was used to solve the model [18]. Polat et al. used time series analysis and waste generation formulas to determine uncertain waste, and addressed the selection of waste treatment centers and the planning of collection routes between waste treatment centers and residential areas [19]. And L-type matrix is used to define risks on waste generation formulation and to provide risk reaction strategies. When there are many MWN, if the waste can be concentrated in the transfer station. Luo et al. built a multi-participant-based collaborative location and a routing optimization model for IMW reverse logistics from an economic, risk perspective [20]. Cao et al. considered multi-period, multi-type medical waste and constructed a mixed-integer model with the objectives of maximizing the total economic benefits, minimizing the total carbon emissions, and minimizing the total potential social risks [21]. Results indicate that constructing TS with flexible capacity is encouraged to handle the sharply increasing MW. In view of the selection of TS and realistic transportation demand, Liu et al. designed an efficiency of transport model which is solved by using an Ant Colony–Tabu hybrid algorithm [22].

2.3 Literature Gaps

In summary, these studies take into account inadequate facilities and incorporate transportation risk into the model. In the case of a large number of MWN, it is a good strategy to choose to establish a temporary TS to concentrate waste. However, the requisition of temporary TS takes time and does not provide a good solution when pandemics are more complicated. Therefore, if LN are selected as TS, this problem can be solved well. LN have enough temporary storage space to accommodate waste from nearby SN. Therefore, the innovations in this paper mainly include: 1) selecting nodes as temporary transfer stations among LN, 2) determining the transshipment relationship between SN and LN, and 3) choosing the final waste collection route.

3 The Model and Solving Method

3.1 Problem Description

Due to pandemic, there are a large number of MWN that are highly dispersed in a region. Therefore, we design a two-stage transportation method that takes into account the transit strategy. The main idea of this method includes the following two aspects:

(1) In the first-stage, to select nodes from all LN as temporary transfer sites and identify SN to be covered by them.
(2) In the second stage, vehicles travel from the DC to LN to collect IMW and then return to the DC to form a closed loop. Figure 1 illustrates the proposed network of the study.

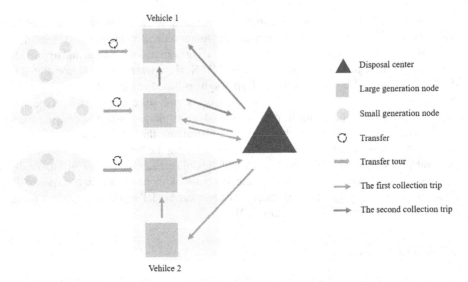

Fig. 1. The proposed transportation network of the study

3.2 Model Assumptions

To facilitate the model formulation, we postulate the following assumptions:

(1) The capacity and average speed of the vehicles are known and remain constant.
(2) The capacity of the DC can meet the amount of MW generated by all nodes and there are enough vehicles to complete the collection.
(3) Each node can be visited multiple times by the vehicles.
(4) The vehicles departing from the DC to complete the transportation tasks and return to the DC.
(5) Vehicles are allowed to have multiple trips.

3.3 Mathematical Model

We herein propose a two-stage model which includes a transit model and a collection model for the MW transportation problem that can be implemented to the situation when a quick system transformation is required. In the first stage, the transit model is used to determine the transshipment relationship between LN and SN. In the second stage, the collection model, i.e. MTSCVRPCT model, is constructed to optimize the collection routing between LN and DC.

Transit Model
Generally, LN have large storage space and have sterilization equipment, therefore, can be used as temporary transit sites. Therefore, we construct the transit model to choose LN that accept all MW from SN and find the SN covered by them. The set, parameters, and decision variables for this transit problem are shown below.

Sets

L Set of large waste generating nodes $l \in L$
S Set of small waste generating nodes $s \in S$

Parameters

MD Maximum transit distance (km)
FCa_l Capacity of large node l, $l \in L$ (kg)
d_{ls} Distance from large node l to small node s, $l \in L$, $s \in S$ (km)
Fq_l Amount of waste generated at large node l, $l \in L$ (kg)
Sq_s Amount of waste generated at small node s, $s \in S$ (kg)
f_l Fixed costs of large node l requisitioned as a temporary transit site ($)
a_l Unit cost of large point l, linearly related to the amount of medical waste transferred, $l \in L$ ($/kg$)
b_s Unit cost of small point s, linearly related to distance of medical waste transferred, $s \in S$ ($/km$)

Decision variables

w_l 1, if the large node l is selected as the transit site, 0, otherwise. $l \in L$
tr_{ls} 1, if that waste from the small node s is transferred to the large node l, 0, otherwise. $l \in L$, $s \in S$

$$\min Z_1 = \sum_{l \in L} f_l w_l + \sum_{l \in L} \sum_{s \in S} a_l q_s tr_{ls} + \sum_{l \in L} \sum_{s \in S} b_s d_{ls} tr_{ls} \qquad (1)$$

$$\sum_{l \in L} tr_{ls} = 1, \ \forall s \in S \qquad (2)$$

$$d_{ls} tr_{ls} \leq MD, \ \forall l \in L, \ s \in S \qquad (3)$$

$$Fq_l + \sum_{s \in S} tr_{ls} Sq_s \leq FCa_l, \ \forall l \in L \qquad (4)$$

$$\sum_{s \in S} tr_{ls} - Mw_l \leq 0, \ \forall l \in L \qquad (5)$$

$$w_l \in \{0, 1\}, \ \forall l \in L \qquad (6)$$

$$tr_{ls} \in \{0, 1\}, \ \forall l \in L, \ s \in S \qquad (7)$$

Objective function (1) minimizes the total cost, including the fixed cost of LN as a temporary TS, the variable cost of receiving waste at LN, and the variable cost of transferring waste at SN. Constraint (2) indicates that waste from a SN must be transferred to a LN. Constraint (3) limits the distance between a LN and a SN. Constraint (4) indicates that the total waste of a large node cannot exceed its capacity. Constraint (5) shows the relationship between tr_{ls} and w_l. Constraint (6) and (7) states the types of the decision variables.

Collection Model

After transfer, all the waste of the SN is concentrated in the adjacent LN, and then vehicles going to the SN to collect the waste. The DC and the waste storage node constitute a set of network nodes $N = \{0\} \cup L$. The vehicle collect waste from each node and transport to the DC. The set, parameters, and decision variables are shown below.

Sets

N Set of nodes $i, j \in N$, where $N = \{0\} \cup L$, 0 denote disposal centers
K Set of vehicles, $k \in K$
R Set of vehicle trips, $r \in R$

Parameters

De_i Cumulative amount of waste at the large node i, which is the sum of own waste and transferred waste, where $De_i = q_i + \sum_{j \in SN} s_{ji} q_j$
ET_i Earliest time to arrive the large node i, the $ET_i = \max_{s \in S}\{d_{is} S_{is}/v\}$
D_{ij} Distance from node i to node j (km)
v Average speed of vehicles (km/h)
h_{ij} Population exposure from node i to node j $(person)$
rp_{ij} Probability of an accident from node i to node j
KCa Capacity of vehicle (kg)
TH Maximum available time for vehicles (h)
CT Time required to sterilize of a vehicle after complete a task (min)

Decision variables

x_{ij}^{kr} 1, if the vehicle k goes from i to j in trip r, otherwise, 0
y_i^{kr} Amount of waste collected and transported by vehicle k at i in trip r
AT_i^{kr} Arrival time of vehicle k at node i in trip r
TD_k^r Total time spent by vehicle k on r trips

$$\min f_1 = \max_{k \in K}\left(\sum_{r \in R} TD_k^r\right) \tag{8}$$

$$\min f_2 = \sum_{i \in N}\sum_{j \in N}\sum_{k \in K}\sum_{r \in R} rp_{ij} h_{ij} x_{ij}^{kr} \tag{9}$$

$$\sum_{i \in N}\sum_{k \in K}\sum_{r \in R} x_{ij}^{kr} \geq 1, \forall j \in N \tag{10}$$

$$\sum_{i \in N} x_{il}^{kr} = \sum_{j \in N} x_{lj}^{kr}, \forall l \in N, k \in K, r \in R \tag{11}$$

$$x_{0i}^{kr} = x_{j0}^{kr}, \forall i, j \in L, k \in K, r \in R \tag{12}$$

$$y_j^{kr} \le De_j \sum_{i \in N} x_{ij}^{kr}, \ \forall j \in L, \ k \in K, \ r \in R \tag{13}$$

$$\sum_{k \in K} \sum_{r \in R} y_i^{kr} = De_i, \ \forall i \in L \tag{14}$$

$$\sum_{i \in L} y_i^{kr} \le KCa, \ \forall k \in K, \ r \in R \tag{15}$$

$$y_i^{kr} \le De_i, \ \forall i \in L, \ k \in K, \ r \in R \tag{16}$$

$$AT_i^{kr} \ge ET_i, \ \forall i \in L, \ k \in K, \ r \in R \tag{17}$$

$$AT_j^{kr} \ge TD_k^{r-1} + AT_i^{kr} + \frac{D_{ij}}{v} x_{ij}^{kr} - M \left(1 - x_{ij}^{kr} \right), \ \forall i, j \in N, \ k \in K, \ 1 < r \le r_m \tag{18}$$

$$AT_j^{k1} \ge AT_i^{k1} + \frac{D_{ij}}{v} x_{ij}^{k1} - M \left(1 - x_{ij}^{k1} \right), \ \forall i, j \in N, \ k \in K \tag{19}$$

$$TD_k^r = TD_k^{r-1} + CT + \sum_{i \in N} \sum_{j \in N} \frac{D_{ij}}{v} x_{ij}^{kr}, \ \forall k \in K, \ 1 < r \le r_m \tag{20}$$

$$TD_k^1 = CT + \sum_{i \in N} \sum_{j \in N} \frac{D_{ij}}{v} x_{ij}^{k1}, \ \forall k \in K \tag{21}$$

$$\sum_{r \in R} TD_k^r \le TH, \ \forall k \in K \tag{22}$$

$$x_{ij}^{kr} \in \{0, 1\}, \ \forall i, j \in N, \ k \in K, \ r \in R \tag{23}$$

$$y_i^{kr} \ge 0, \ \forall i \in L, \ k \in K, \ r \in R \tag{24}$$

$$AT_i^{kr} \ge 0, \ \forall i \in N, \ k \in K, \ r \in R \tag{25}$$

$$TD_k^r \ge 0, \ \forall k \in K, \ r \in R \tag{26}$$

Objective function (8) minimizes the maximum total trip duration. Objective function (9) minimizes the total transportation risk. Constraint (10) denotes that each node is visited at least once. Constraint (11) represents the flow balance equation for each node. Constraint (12) indicates that a vehicle departing from the disposal center must eventually return to it. Constraint (13) shows that the vehicle k must reach the node j in trip r in order to collect the waste at the point j. Constraint (14) indicates that all waste at j has to be collected. Constraint (15) indicates that the total amount of waste collected by the vehicle k on the r trip cannot exceed the vehicle capacity. Constraint (16) guarantees the range of waste to be collected by the vehicle at i. Constraint (17) represents that each node cannot be visited earlier than the arrival time of the transfer waste. Constraints (18) and (19) indicate the time at which the vehicle k arrivals at the j point in trip r, where (19) denotes the time when k reaches the point j in first trip. Constraints (20) and (21) denote the total duration of r trips of the k vehicle, where (21) denotes the duration of the first trip. Constraint (22) indicates that the total duration of each vehicle cannot exceed the maximum duration limit. Constraint (23) to (26) states the types of the decision variables.

3.4 Solution Procedure

The transit model is a NIP model, which can be solved with the CPLEX software package. The transportation model is an extension of the classic vehicle routing problem, which belongs to the NP-hard problem, and can be solved by the exact algorithm and heuristic algorithm. But when the problem scale is large, the exact algorithm is often difficult to solve the problem. Therefore, the multi-objective heuristic algorithm NSGA-II is selected to solve the problem. This algorithm was developed by Deb in 2000, which adopts a better accounting strategy and thus reduces the overall running time of the algorithm [23]. The natural numbers coding method are used, and the length of the chromosome is the same as the number of LN. The decoding takes into account the constraints of: (1) vehicle capacity, (2) vehicle total duration, (3) earliest access time at each node, and (4) the waste at each node needs to be fully collected and transported.

Furthermore, in this paper, the linear affiliation function for identifying compromise solutions from the pareto optimal set is applied to all the obtained pareto optimal solutions. The satisfaction level of the ith pareto optimal solution in the mth objective function is denoted as:

$$u_i^k = \begin{cases} 1, & f_m\left(\overrightarrow{x_i}\right) \leq f_m^{\min} \\ \frac{f_m^{\max}-f_m\left(\overrightarrow{x_i}\right)}{f_m^{\max}-f_m^{\min}}, & f_m^{\min} \leq f_m\left(\overrightarrow{x_i}\right) \leq f_m^{\max} \\ 0, & f_m\left(\overrightarrow{x_i}\right) \geq f_m^{\max} \end{cases} \tag{27}$$

where f_m^{max} and f_m^{min} are the maximum and minimum values of the mth objective function, respectively. In addition, the satisfaction level of each pareto optimal solution is denoted as:

$$u_i = \frac{\sum\limits_{i=1}^{m} u_i^k}{\sum\limits_{k=1}^{N}\sum\limits_{i=1}^{m} u_i^k} \tag{28}$$

N is used to indicate the number of pareto optimal solutions obtained.

4   Case Study

4.1 Relevant Data

This section investigates the validation of the proposed model using a real case study problem in Shenzhen during a major infectious disease epidemic. The collection and transportation network involves 53 nodes of type LN (as shown by the green squares in

Fig. 2), 70 nodes of type SN (as shown by the yellow circles in Fig. 2), and a DC (as shown by the blue triangles in Fig. 2).

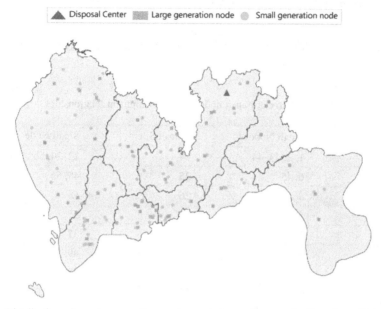

Fig. 2. Distribution of waste generation nodes and disposal center in Shenzhen (Color figure online)

LN are used as transfer stations, and the cost per unit weight of medical waste received is set as 0.1, a cost per unit distance of medical waste transferred for SN is set as 2. Maximum transit distance cannot exceed 10. The maximum amount of waste allowed to be stocked at each LN is based on the number of beds, with a maximum of 3000 and a minimum of 1000. The fixed subsidy cost is a random integer between [1, 5].

During the collection and transportation, it is assumed that the vehicle speed is 40 and the vehicle can load a maximum of 2000 waste at one time. The maximum available time for the vehicle is set to 8 and the vehicle needs to be disinfected for each completed trip.

The distance between each node in this study is the Euclidean distance, and the exposed population on each edge is half of the sum of the population densities of the area where the two endpoints located on this edge, which was obtained from the most recent version of the Statistical Almanac. The probability of an incident on each path is a random number between $[0.1 * 10^{-5}, 0.1 * 10^{-4}]$. The amount of waste at each LN is a random natural number between [500, 1000] and the amount of medical waste at SN are random natural numbers between [100, 500].

4.2 Computational Results

In this subsection, the transit model and the collection model proposed before are solved using the CPLEX solver and the NSGA-II algorithm, respectively, to provide an optimal strategy.

The transit model is solved to obtain the LN as TS and the transit relationships between LN and SN. There are 37 transit sites, and the specific TS and the corresponding transit relationships are shown in Table 1.

Table 1. Matrix of transit nodes and transshipment relationships

Transit Site	Small Node	Transit Site	Small Node
1	1, 2, 43, 44	24	22, 24, 56
2	6, 45	25	48, 55
3	46, 60, 65	26	58
4	5, 12	27	55
5	11, 63, 64	28	37
6	27, 59, 61	29	49, 52
7	13	30	38, 57
9	23, 66	31	51
12	47, 62	36	4, 9
13	14, 17	37	10
14	7, 33	39	3, 8
15	54	40	30, 34
16	26	42	28, 29
17	21	43	31, 32
18	18, 20	45	42, 50
20	68, 70	46	40, 53
21	67, 69	47	39, 41
22	16, 19, 25	53	35, 36
23	15		

All waste stored in LN are collected by vehicles from the DC. The pareto optimal solution set obtained by the NSGA-II method and the compromise solution among all the pareto optimal solutions yielded that the DC needs to send a total of 13 vehicles to collection wastes, with the maximum total trip duration of 6.6478 h and the total infection risk size of 12 people. The optimal route for each vehicle is shown in Table 2. For example, the first row of the table represents all trips of vehicle1. For the first trip, the vehicle departs from the DC to the node 42, and then to node 39. After collecting, the vehicle is fully loaded and needs to return to the DC After unloading the waste, the vehicle starts the 2nd trip and the 3rd trip, the 2nd trip visits the nodes including 39, 38, 41 and 20, and the 3rd trip's visits nodes 20 and 31. Due to the capacity constraints of the vehicle, the wastes from nodes 39 and 20 are split.

Table 2. Collection and transportation routes for each vehicle

Vehicle	Routes
1	0-42-39-0-39-38-41-20-0-20-31-0
2	0-2-51-48-0-48-5-0-5-43-32-0
3	0-30-45-0-45-14-29-0
4	0-29-36-0-36-26-0
5	0-26-6-50-0-50-12-40-0-40-0
6	0-25-34-0-34-9-18-0
7	0-18-27-0-27-15-46-0
8	0-46-35-23-0-23-47-0
9	0-52-3-0-3-13-10-33-0-33-0
10	0-17-19-37-0-37-53-0-53-11-0
11	0-44-22-0-22-24-4-0-4-21-0
12	0-7-8-16-0-16-1-0-1-0
13	0-28-49-0

4.3 Comparisons with Established Type of Transportation

In real life, when a pandemic outbreaks, without a transfer strategy, the DC will need to arrange more vehicle to collect MW from all MSN one by one. In this direct transportation way, the collection vehicle must go to all MWN. We compare the optimization results of the direct transportation method with the transit transportation method. The direct collection way needs 18 vehicles, 5 more than the transit collection. The maximum total trip duration is 6.7154 h, which is 0.0676 h more than transit way, and the total infection risk size is 20 people, which is 8 more than transit way. It can be concluded that in the case of a major infectious outbreak, the use of transshipment measures is significance in order to avoid the risk of infection associated with the accumulation of MW.

5 Conclusions

In order to make full use of existing facilities to timely transport all MW, a new MW transportation network was proposed. At first, we consider the characteristics of waste generation nodes, i.e. there are so many SN, resulting in a scattered distribution of MWN. Secondly, a transit-then-collection approach is proposed, i.e., the waste from SN is first transferred to LN and collection vehicles go to LN to collect all waste. Finally, we use CPLEX solver and NSGA II algorithm to solve these two problems respectively. And the proposed model and solution method are applied to a real case study during a major infectious disease epidemic in a city in China. The results verify the effectiveness of the proposed model and method.

In addition, there are still some limitations that may pave the way for future research. On the one hand, we should improve the algorithm for solving proposed problem in large scales. On the other hand, methods for predicting MW volumes based on epidemiological trends should be incorporated into current models to obtain more accurate solutions.

Acknowledgments. This work is supported by the National Natural Science Foundation of China (Grants Nos. 71901152), Guangdong Basic and Applied Basic Research Foundation (2023A1515010919), Guangdong Innovation Team Project of Intelligent Management and Cross Innovation (2021WCXTD002), Shenzhen Stable Support Grant (Grant Nos. 20220810100952001), and Shenzhen University-Lingnan University Joint Research Programme.

References

1. Haider, N., et al.: COVID-19-zoonosis or emerging infectious disease? Front Public Health **8**, 596944 (2020)
2. Yang, Y., Guo, L., Lu, H.: Emerging infectious diseases never end: the fight continues. Biosci. Trends **17**(3), 245–248 (2023)
3. Suksee, S., Sindhuchao, S.: GRASP with ALNS for solving the location routing problem of infectious waste collection in the Northeast of Thailand. Int. J. Ind. Eng. Comput. **12**, 305–320 (2021)
4. Yu, H., Sun, X., Solvang, W.D., Zhao, X.: Reverse logistics network design for effective management of medical waste in epidemic outbreaks: insights from the coronavirus disease 2019 (COVID-19) outbreak in Wuhan (China). Int. J. Environ. Res. Public Health **17**(5), 1770 (2020)
5. Mei, X., Hao, H., Sun, Y., Wang, X., Zhou, Y.: Optimization of medical waste recycling network considering disposal capacity bottlenecks under a novel coronavirus pneumonia outbreak. Environ. Sci. Pollut. Res. Int. **29**(53), 79669–79687 (2022)
6. Zhao, J., Wu, B., Ke, G.Y.: A bi-objective robust optimization approach for the management of infectious wastes with demand uncertainty during a pandemic. J. Clean. Prod. **314**, 127922 (2021)
7. Ghannadpour, S.F., Zandieh, F., Esmaeili, F.: Optimizing triple bottom-line objectives for sustainable health-care waste collection and routing by a self-adaptive evolutionary algorithm: a case study from Tehran province in Iran. J. Clean. Prod. 287 (2021)
8. Tsai, W.T.: Analysis of medical waste management and impact analysis of COVID-19 on its generation in Taiwan. Waste Manag. Res. 39, 27–33 (2021)
9. Budak, A., Ustundag, A.: Reverse logistics optimisation for waste collection and disposal in health institutions: the case of Turkey. Int. J. Logist.-Res. Appl. **20**, 322–341 (2017)
10. Mantzaras, G., Voudrias, E.A.: An optimization model for collection, haul, transfer, treatment and disposal of infectious medical waste: application to a Greek region. Waste Manag. **69**, 518–534 (2017)
11. Alizadeh, M., Makui, A., Paydar, M.M.: Forward and reverse supply chain network design for consumer medical supplies considering biological risk. Comput. Ind. Eng. **140**, 16 (2020)

12. Wang, Z.G., Huang, L.F., He, C.X.: A multi-objective and multi-period optimization model for urban healthcare waste's reverse logistics network design. J. Comb. Optim. **42**, 785–812 (2021)

13. Homayouni, Z., Pishvaee, M.S.: A bi-objective robust optimization model for hazardous hospital waste collection and disposal network design problem. J. Mater. Cycles Waste Manag. **22**, 1965–1984 (2020)

14. Li, H.L., Hu, Y., Lyu, J.Y., Quan, H., Xu, X., Li, C.X.: Transportation risk control of waste disposal in the healthcare system with two-echelon waste collection network. Math. Probl. Eng. **2021**, 10 (2021)

15. Babaee Tirkolaee, E., Aydın, N.S.: A sustainable medical waste collection and transportation model for pandemics. Waste Manag. Res. **39**(1_suppl), 34–44 (2021)

16. Govindan, K., Nasr, A.K., Mostafazadeh, P., Mina, H.: Medical waste management during coronavirus disease 2019 (COVID-19) outbreak: a mathematical programming model. Comput. Ind. Eng. **162**, 107668 (2021)

17. Tirkolaee, E.B., Abbasian, P., Weber, G.W.: Sustainable fuzzy multi-trip location-routing problem for medical waste management during the COVID-19 outbreak. Sci. Total. Environ. **20**(756), 143607 (2021)

18. Kargar, S., Pourmehdi, M., Paydar, M.M.: Reverse logistics network design for medical waste management in the epidemic outbreak of the novel coronavirus (COVID -19). Sci. Total. Environ. **1**(746), 141183 (2020)

19. Polat, E.G.: Medical waste management during coronavirus disease 2019 pandemic at the city level. Int. J. Environ. Sci. Technol. **19**(5), 3907–3918 (2021). https://doi.org/10.1007/s13 762-021-03748-7

20. Luo, X., Liao, W.: Collaborative reverse logistics network for infectious medical waste management during the COVID-19 outbreak. Int. J. Environ. Res. Public Health **19**(15), 9735 (2022)

21. Cao, C., Li, J., Liu, J., Liu, J., Qiu, H., Zhen, J.: Sustainable development-oriented location-transportation integrated optimization problem regarding multi period multi-type disaster medical waste during COVID-19 pandemic. Ann. Oper. Res. **22**, 1–47 (2022)

22. Liu, Z., Li, Z., Chen, W., Zhao, Y., Yue, H., Wu, Z.: Path optimization of medical waste transport routes in the emergent public health event of COVID-19: a hybrid optimization algorithm based on the immune-ant colony algorithm. Int. J. Environ. Res. Public Health **17**(16), 5831 (2020)

23. Zhao, Z., Liu, B., Zhang, C., et al.: An improved adaptive NSGA-II with multi-population algorithm. Appl. Intell. **49**, 569–580 (2019)

Author Index

Printed in the United States
by Baker & Taylor Publisher Services